Troubling Freedom

Troubling Freedom

ANTIGUA AND THE AFTERMATH

OF BRITISH EMANCIPATION

Natasha Lightfoot

DUKE UNIVERSITY PRESS

Durham and London 2015

Printed in the United States of America on acid-free paper ∞
Typeset in Quadraat by Westchester Publishing Services

....

Library of Congress Cataloging-in-Publication Data
Lightfoot, Natasha, [date] author.
Troubling freedom : Antigua and the aftermath of
British emancipation / Natasha Lightfoot.
pages cm
Includes bibliographical references and index.
ISBN 978-0-8223-5975-3 (hardcover : alk. paper)
ISBN 978-0-8223-6007-0 (pbk. : alk. paper)
ISBN 978-0-8223-7505-0 (e-book)
1. Slaves—Emancipation—Antigua and Barbuda—Antigua.
2. Slaves—Emancipation—Colonies—Great Britain.
3. Antigua—Race relations—History. I. Title.
F2035.L54 2015
305.800972974—dc23   2015020931

....

Cover art: Moravian Church Mission, St. John's Street
(ca. 1830). Aquatint by Johann Stobwasser, Ansichten von
Missions-Niederlassungen der Evangelishen Bruder-Gemeinde
(Basle, n.d.). Courtesy of the John Carter Brown
Library at Brown University.

Duke University Press gratefully acknowledges the
support of the Lenfest Junior Faculty Development
Fund, Columbia University, which provided funds
toward the publication of this book.

TO THE PEOPLE OF ANTIGUA & BARBUDA

& FOR MY SONS

CONTENTS

....

ILLUSTRATIONS

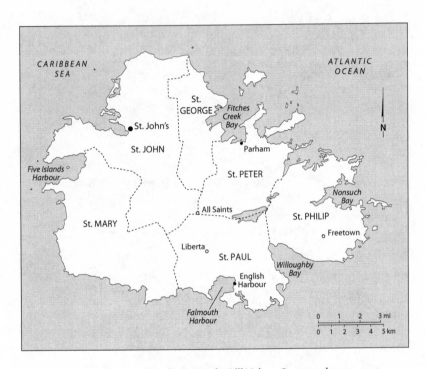

MAP 0.1. Present-day map of Antigua. Map by Bill Nelson Cartography.

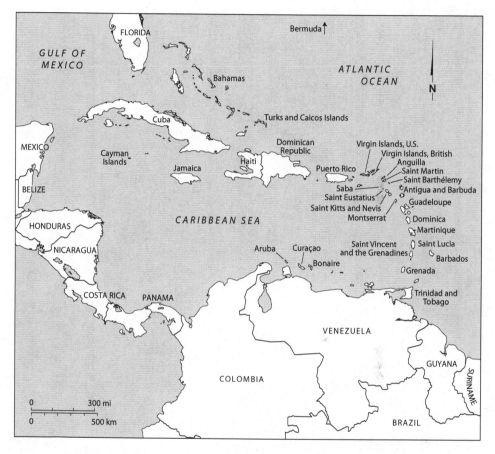

MAP 0.2. Present-day map of the Caribbean region. Map by Bill Nelson Cartography.

ACKNOWLEDGMENTS

....

Many people played integral parts in making this book happen to whom I am eternally grateful. I only have the space to thank some (apologies for not remembering everyone), but know that I treasure all of you who helped me in big and small ways on the journey.

I must first thank those behind the incredible training that I have received as a historian, first as a still-unsure undergraduate at Yale, where Glenda Gilmore saw the scholar in me before I even did, and then at NYU, where I came to intellectual maturity in the hands of so many skillful mentors. The exemplary scholarship and thoughtful insights of my advisor, Ada Ferrer, moved my research along through many stages; her work continues to inspire me. Michael Gomez provided a welcome, eye-opening space for all his students to think critically about the African diaspora as a frame for our work. The incredibly kind Sinclair Thomson made a lasting mark on my thinking with his extensive knowledge of popular resistance. My endless gratitude goes to the brilliant Jennifer Morgan for her pathbreaking scholarship and sage advice. I am indebted to her in too many ways, and still learn from her daily. The anthropologist Constance Sutton reframed how I see the Caribbean. I treasure her teaching and the many life lessons she has shared with me. Also many thanks to past and current NYU faculty whose presence was transformative for my scholarship, including the consummate scholar Martha Hodes; Robin Kelley, with whom a few minutes of conversation changed my approach to everything; and Barbara Krauthamer, who taught me how to teach.

NYU faculty offered me great guidance, but my fellow graduate students made me smarter every day I worked alongside them. Thanks to Tanya Huelett, Aisha Finch, Edwina Ashie-Nikoi, Brian Purnell, Sherie Randolph, Marc Goulding, Maxine Gordon, Peter Hudson, Njoroge

Njoroge, Rich Blint, Erik McDuffie, Derek Musgrove, Harvey Neptune, Melina Pappademos, Yuko Miki, Marcela Echeverri, Laurie Lambert, Mireille Miller-Young, Maggie Clinton, and Sherene Seikaly, among others, for always raising my bar.

My work was undertaken at many different archives, whose incredibly gracious staffs deserve thanks, including the National Archives of Antigua and Barbuda (especially the past archivist Marian Blair and the late Noval Lindsay), the British National Archives at Kew, the School of Oriental and African Studies Archives, the Schomburg Center for Research in Black Culture, the American Antiquarian Society, the Moravian Church Archives (many thanks to Paul Peucker), and the Yale University Divinity School Archives. In addition, thanks to the several institutions that helped to fund my research, including New York University; the Tinker Foundation; the American Antiquarian Society Peterson Fellowship; Yale University's Gilder-Lehrman Center for the Study of Slavery, Resistance, and Abolition; the Ford Foundation; the Schomburg Center's Scholars-in-Residence Program; and numerous centers at Columbia University, including the Department of History, the Institute for Research in African-American Studies, the Institute for Latin American Studies, the Center for the Study of Ethnicity and Race, and the Center for the Study of Social Difference.

I truly appreciate my fellow historians at Columbia University, including Christopher Brown, Mae Ngai, Eric Foner, Celia Naylor, Samuel Roberts, Barbara Fields, Betsy Blackmar, Alice Kessler-Harris, Pablo Piccato, and Karl Jacoby, all of whom have been dedicated mentors to me, as well the endless intellectual energy of many graduate students, including Katherine Johnston, Wes Alcenat, Yesenia Barragan, Nick Juravich, and Megan French-Marcelin. Thanks to my undergraduate research assistants, Gaia Goffe and Brandon Thompson, who helped me move through centuries-old records much more quickly than I would have on my own. Beyond my department I have to thank the Columbia and Barnard faculty with whom I have found intellectual community, including Farah Griffin, Saidiya Hartman, David Scott, Kaiama Glover, Alondra Nelson, Mabel Wilson, Tina Campt, Yvette Christianse, Jean Howard, the incomparable Kim Hall, and my sister-scholar Carla Shedd.

My work is all the better because of the work and insights of many other scholars. I cherish Mark Naison for his unwavering and fierce support of my scholarship since my days at Fordham. Paget Henry introduced me and my research in its earliest iterations to a wonderful community of Antiguan and Barbudan intellectuals. I value his mentorship. Susan Lowes has been a model researcher and true friend. I must also thank Milton Benjamin, Mali Olatunji, Ellorton Jeffers, Ermina Osoba, Marie Elena John-Smith, Edgar Lake, Robert Glen, and Dorbrene O'Marde for their work on Antiguan and Barbudan history and culture. Thanks as well to fellow scholars of the African diaspora whose research continues to inspire me and whose insights have significantly improved my work, including the ever-generous Herman Bennett, as well as Melanie Newton, Diana Paton, Rosanne Adderley, Bridget Brereton, Marisa Fuentes, Lara Putnam, Gad Heuman, Mimi Sheller, Tera Hunter, Martha Jones, Mia Bay, Barbara Savage, Denise Challenger, Ben Talton, Michael Ralph, Vanessa Perez-Rosario, Hlonipha Mokoena, and the lovely Natasha Gordon-Chipembere. Additionally my sincere gratitude goes to Gisela Fosado, Ken Wissoker, and the staff at Duke University Press for bringing this book to fruition. I also have undying praise and awe for Grey Osterud, a magician of the written word, who helped this book make sense. If you enjoy the read it is as much to her credit as it is to mine.

I have too many friends to name who supported my work and sometimes offered welcome distractions from it, but some deserve special mention. My best friend of more than twenty years, Damaris De Los Santos, and her entire family are my surrogate family. No words encapsulate what her friendship means to me. Tanya Huelett makes me laugh while changing how I see the world. She is my kindred spirit. Only for brevity's sake will I list others who I cannot imagine myself without: Victor Villanueva, Risa Rich, Najah Mustafa, Vanessa Fitt, Christine Rocco, Carlos Santiago, Desiree Gordon, Ryan Jean-Baptiste, and my sons' West Coast aunts, Erica Edwards and Deb Vargas.

My family has loved and encouraged me all along the way. My extended family at St. Andrew's Episcopal Church in the Bronx will always hold a special place in my heart. The Swain and Gardenhire families have brought good food and good laughs into my life. The Lightfoot, Carr, and James families and their many branches in Antigua, New York, Canada, and the UK deserve so much more than thanks for their unending love and support. I am honored to be a part of them. I hold dear the memories of my late grandparents, Irene and William Carr and Mildred Bernard; they are my direct connection to the working people who fill the pages of this book. My sister, Michelle Lightfoot, is my greatest champion. My aunts Heather Henry, Donnamae Carr, and especially Gwynneth Carr have always been my second mothers. I miss my late father, William Lightfoot, and his brilliance, his politics, and his sharp fashion sense. I hope the best parts of him live on in me. My mother and first teacher, Jocelyn Lightfoot, is my greatest inspiration. I will always be in her debt. Matthew Swain's love brings me joy. I cherish the life we have built together. This book is for our children, Evan and Avery, who make my heart sing.

···

"ME NO B'LONGS TO DEM"

Emancipation's Possibilities and Limits in Antigua

Antigua's thirty thousand enslaved people, alongside those in all other British colonial territories, were freed on August 1, 1834. Shortly after emancipation, Juncho, an elderly black Antiguan woman previously enslaved on MacKinnon's Estate in the Parish of St. John, described the differences between slavery and freedom.[1] The very moment of freedom rendered Juncho both jobless and homeless. Abolition ended her daily toil in the fields but undermined her material security. Since 1834, she had lived in poverty with her daughter. Juncho declared: "So you see . . . dat make me say me no [love] slabery. Now wen me [young], me hab to work hard, hab dig cane [h]ole, weed cane, pick grass, do ebery ting; but now me ole, and no able to work, dey take away me house, 'cause me no b'longs to dem, but den me [know] me free, and me bless God me am free."[2]

Juncho insisted that, despite the hunger and privation she encountered in freedom, slavery had been worse. She mentioned examples of two harrowing situations that as an enslaved mother she typically faced. She could not nurse a sick child back to health because she was required to toil in the fields all day. When her child transgressed a rule of the plantation, she had to watch, powerless to intervene, as the owner tied Juncho's child to a tree and meted out a violent whipping. In Juncho's account, freedom relieved the sorts of stresses on the mother-child relationship that being the property of another often involved. The impoverishment she endured while living with her daughter and several grandchildren, however, attests to other kinds of stresses black families encountered after 1834.

The striking utterance "me no b'longs to dem" signals that she took solace in the self-mastery that legal freedom brought. As a freedwoman, she had control of her body and her time. Reportedly, Antigua's freedpeople used the phrase "me free, me no b'longs to you!" as a "constant boast" when they ignored or defied whites.[3] The phrase also evokes black women's relief at the freedom to protect their bodies from sexual violation. Juncho and her formerly enslaved compatriots relished their new status and the liberty to express it publicly to all whites within earshot.

Yet Juncho's story, rather than hailing abolition as an unalloyed blessing, also underlines the many difficulties that black working people faced following their legal release from enslavement. She explained: "It true me better off den dan me am now, for since me free, me no get much; sometimes me no eat bread all day, for me daughter hab so many pic'nees (children) she no able to gib me much; but . . . me [know] God gib me free, and slabery is one bad something sometimes."[4] Juncho admitted that some aspects of her circumstances in bondage proved better than those she experienced in freedom. As a slave, she had access to her own house and a private garden, where she grew produce and raised poultry. When emancipation came, her then-former owner expelled her from her home and reclaimed her provision ground as his own. Too old to be employed profitably, she became a liability in this new regime of wage labor.

Her words poignantly convey the paradox of freedom for ex-slaves. Emancipation from chattel status into poverty and continued subjugation meant that freedom, while long awaited and celebrated, entailed material distress and personal uncertainty. Her story also highlights the particular difficulties of freedom for Antigua's black women, who faced an unreliable labor market that favored black men, while the women shouldered responsibility for their children and extended kin, often without assistance from male partners. Essentially, these inadequacies meant that freedpeople similar to Juncho had to imbue freedom with deeper meaning through new social, political, and ontological struggles.

Her testimony reveals that self-ownership marked only the beginning of such struggles. Freedpeople were still poor and bereft of the resources required to improve their material and social circumstances. Their continued efforts were central to the lived experience of emancipation. This book tells the story of how Antigua's black working people struggled to realize freedom in their everyday lives, both before and after slavery's legal end, as well as the transformative nature of their many letdowns and few triumphs along the way.

An Unfinished Freedom

Troubling Freedom explores how newly emancipated women and men defined freedom by tracing its uneasy trajectory in Antigua over nearly three decades. After an overview of the island in the nineteenth century, the book moves to a slave rebellion in 1831 that foreshadowed emancipation's complexities. It continues by chronicling freedpeople's quotidian survival tactics from 1834 through the 1850s, and it closes with an 1858 labor riot that reinforced freedom as an incomplete victory. Studies of freedom in former slave societies throughout the Atlantic World frequently posit emancipation as the start of black people's labor organizing and pursuit of political rights.[5] Framing short-term strategies after slavery within the long-term struggle to obtain political and economic citizenship is vitally important, but it tells only part of freedom's story. The moments just after slavery's end, flooded with chaos and uncertainty for both former slaves and masters, formed a critical juncture that begs closer examination. In this time of flux, both groups made fitful attempts to configure distinct practices of freedom, which bore stark differences that triggered clashes between them for decades afterward.

Impoverished and illiterate freedpeople just emerging from bondage may have held far-reaching goals, but they were in no position to make drastic changes to their new status. Still, they conceived of a freedom that granted them ownership over their bodies and their time, autonomy in their labor, enjoyment of their leisure, and legal and economic inclusion in society—if not as equals with their erstwhile enslavers, then at least as protected subjects. Furthermore, historians have argued that there were greater political and economic constraints among freedpeople in small islands such as Antigua, because freedpeople's universally blocked access to land immediately forced them into underpaid plantation labor.[6] While indeed their landlessness constrained freed Antiguans, this book complicates that sweeping narrative by highlighting their myriad efforts to define and expand their freedom in the face of such constraints. I ask how, despite being mired in poverty, subject to coercion, and denied even the most basic rights at every turn, freedpeople still found spaces in their ordinary lives to feel free.[7]

Freedpeople had to carve out their own forms of liberation. Despite unyielding obstacles, black working people practiced their freedom through struggles to claim space, uphold community, acquire property, and reorganize their time and labor. I have found that ordinary encounters not only between blacks and whites but also among black people evidenced the transformative impact of emancipation in their daily lives. Freedpeople's interactions within and beyond the plantation workplace—such as intermittent strikes, independent provisioning and marketing, the simultaneous practice of obeah and Christianity, efforts to educate themselves and their children, public socializing and amusements, and the founding of all-black villages in Antigua—all show the many contestations over freedom's multiple meanings. Freedpeople's practices of leisure, forms of spirituality, family relationships, and new modes of consumption complemented their struggles against the colony's elites to assert their senses of freedom. Their quotidian survival strategies fed into black working people's rare yet revelatory moments of collective and violent public protest.[8]

Everyday life among black working people manifests the dynamics of British emancipation most profoundly, making plain the disruptions, possibilities, and failures wrought by freedom.[9] Through their daily experiences, freedpeople honed their ideas about freedom, making the exploration of ordinary life critical to our understanding of freedom's complexities. Black working people's quotidian acts reveal that, despite being legally free, constant efforts were still necessary to secure and expand their material resources, their autonomy, and their sense of community. Prior to the genesis of formal, institutionalized modes of political and economic struggle, everyday life in postslavery Antigua was the laboratory for black working people's politics.

Existing histories of the transition to freedom in the Atlantic World do critical intellectual work to define freedom, to expose its inconsistencies when juxtaposed with citizenship as a concept and a practice in former slave societies, and to reflect on existing racial, gender, and class hierarchies that abolition's passage built on and exacerbated. These stories have framed freedpeople's efforts to give freedom meaning within a well-known dialectic of communal unity and consistent opposition to unsympathetic state structures and hostile former owners. I trace black working people's efforts to achieve a more meaningful freedom by reinterpreting a variety of ordinary acts that literate observers often viewed as "resistance" to colonial law and order. The two remarkable moments of civil strife in 1831 and 1858 that bookend this story are also critical to how I rethink this trajectory of resistance. I label these moments as *riots*, in line with colonial parlance of the time. I also name them as *uprisings*, *revolts*, and *rebellions* interchangeably to indicate that they were widespread and prolonged, attracted many participants, targeted the white establishment as well as rival laborers on occasion, and threatened the social hierarchy embodied in property and enforced by law.[10] Ultimately I complicate the concept of resistance, in both mundane and spectacular forms, by pointing out its unintended and restrictive consequences for oppressed communities.[11] The narrative of valiant and unified subaltern struggles against domination by the powerful, while recognizable and seductive, does not account for the range of acts chronicled in this book, which in this chaotic period were as ambiguous as they were courageous.

While freedpeople constantly tried to protect their own interests, their efforts were not always clear-cut acts of opposition to power and did not always advance the broader cause of social justice. Black working people did not consistently subvert the control of colonial elites, as becoming free embedded them even more deeply in the structures of colonial domination. The end of enslavement prompted new forms of accountability to the state, Christian missions, and employers. At the same time, freedpeople tried—often in vain—to force that accountability to flow reciprocally by becoming engaged with colonial law and the public sphere. They acted on an unfulfilled hope that the Crown and local authorities would accept or even facilitate their desire to provide for themselves and their families and to conduct their lives as they wished. Their intermittent collusions, whether intended or not, with the same repressive structures they at other points opposed reveal the broad scope of black working people's immediate practices of freedom. This book explicates the various forms of power that framed freedom, "the shaping quality of the power that comes to reconstruct, or make over, the lives of the ex-slaves."[12]

Freedpeople at times oppressed one another while navigating the multiple forms of oppression that abolition unleashed. The desperation resulting from the subjugation that pervaded their public and private lives prompted them to commit individualistic and competitive acts along with cooperative and communal ones. People of the same race, class, or gender, living in the same plantation or neighborhood or even within the same family, experienced constant pressures to which they periodically responded with violence and confusion, aimed not only at the powerful but also at each other. Release from enslavement did not automatically forge collective bonds of solidarity and struggle; rather, it linked the fates of similarly degraded individuals. Community, when it appeared among formerly enslaved Antiguans, did so in spite of the brutal economic, social, and political constraints of the transition from slavery to freedom. Black working people's efforts to improve their circumstances, whether through collaboration or conflict with their community, still largely resulted in their exclusion and degradation.

Troubling Freedom offers an unromanticized account of aspects of the past that have remained unstudied because of the discomfort that facing them honestly entails. It recounts freedpeople's experiences of freedom as a truly human, complex, and at times contradictory story of lives conducted within the state-imposed limits of emancipation. As Juncho's narrative so powerfully suggests, severe material privation, black working people's compromised volition, the treachery rife within the empty promise of emancipation, and the chronic violence that punctuated life's rhythms within this plantation society all exacted a serious toll on relations between freedpeople and colonial elites, and among freed men and women. However inconsistent their intent or results, such interactions reveal as much about what freedpeople thought freedom meant as do the laws, intellectual currents, and economic practices of the states and empires that institutionally oversaw the dismantling of black bondage.

On Violence

Public disorder and individual and collective violence were crucial elements in freedpeople's troubled pursuit of liberation. In a former slave colony such as Antigua, the power to wield violence was critical to the assertion of freedom. Positing violent acts as a window to freedpeople's politics demands recognition of the centrality of violence to political expression and social organization in societies with a history of slavery. Africans' incorporation into colonial life in the Atlantic World was marked by brutality at the hands of Europeans at every moment, from capture through the process of transport, sale, and seasoning, and culminating in the toil of commodity production under the most terrorizing of circumstances.[13] From the earliest phases of European settlement in the Caribbean, the plantation determined the structure of life for people of all social classes. Each territory's spatial layout, legal procedures, and local economy were shaped by the commercial enterprise of sugar, an industry built on the work of a commodified, racialized, and dehumanized labor force of Africans and their descendants. Notoriously, Caribbean slave owners extracted greater profits from working an enslaved person to death and purchasing a new one than from providing for a slave until old age and creating the conditions for natural reproduction. The mental, physical, and sexual abuse of Africans and their descendants fueled the expansion of Britain's colonial economies.

The advent of an abolitionist movement and legal emancipation did little to change the pervasive yet casual nature of violence in Caribbean life.[14] Black working people understandably resorted to violence to convey their grievances against the colonial state and society, not only seizing the public platform consistently denied them but also reflecting their sense of violence as the language of power that everyone across the class and race spectrum readily understood. I tell a story of the violent undercurrents of everyday living in the context of a freedom so compromised as to mirror slavery in endless ways. Violence punctuated interactions between freedpeople and powerful whites, as shown by the uncanny ease with which ordinary acts of survival were recast as crimes and the swift and excessive punishments meted out to those freedpeople deemed criminals. Brutality also underlined relations among differently placed sets of black people during the postslavery transition, as shown by instances of freedmen's abuse of freedwomen and the collective assault in 1858 by Antiguan working people on working people from Barbuda, Antigua's sister island.

This endemic violence and coercion demonstrates that the official version of freedom in the British Empire was in theory and in practice a strictly bounded condition. Freedom as concocted by the state and executed by colonial authorities did not guarantee stability and autonomy for black people. Rather, it amounted to a test that by design freedpeople would never pass.[15] Elites' discourse about emancipation was rife with assumptions about the cultural deficiencies of Afro-Caribbean people and their inability to function as fully free participants in colonial society.[16] In elites' minds, freedpeople were always already failures at freedom from its very inception. Freedpeople constantly tried to expand freedom, but in many ways, their actions instead shaped how it would fail.

While exploring the pitfalls of freedom as they affected all emancipated people, the book highlights moments in which men's and women's experiences diverged, exploring the gendered inequities that emancipation intensified.[17] In the British Empire, metropolitan elites and Christian missionaries envisioned that abolition would remake male subjects into waged workers, heads of nuclear households, and (eventual) political citizens while turning women into their domesticated dependents. Planters, in contrast, encouraged black women to labor exclusively within the sugar industry, as hard as men and for lesser wages. Freedpeople lived a different reality from elites: women were equally present in the workforce and were substantial or sole contributors to their household livelihoods. They engaged in a multiplicity of occupations within and beyond the sugar industry to make ends meet. Yet in other respects, freedpeople's ways echoed colonial gendered hierarchies, as freedmen often asserted their dominance in freedwomen's lives, especially through physical violence. Ideologies and practices from both inside and outside their communities suppressed black women. Emancipation, while falling short of all black working people's hopes, especially failed to free black women.

The Wider Geography of Freedom

Freedpeople's ways of life, oppositional acts, and protracted subjection in Antigua occurred within the context of groundbreaking changes sweeping the entire Atlantic World in the era of abolition. Antigua's emancipation process remained distinctive while still fitting into the broader trajectory of the postslavery Atlantic World. Significantly, Antigua was the only Caribbean sugar-producing colony to reject the apprenticeship system devised by the British Parliament to give slave owners and their allies continued control over freedpeople's labor and mobility; only Bermuda and the Cayman Islands, which did not depend on sugar plantations, also proceeded to immediate emancipation. The apprenticeship system suspended hundreds of thousands of the empire's African-descended subjects in a liminal space between enslavement and freedom from 1834 to 1838. In theory, it apprenticed former slaves to their former owners to prepare them for free labor; in practice, it extended their bondage, requiring them to work for a stipulated number of hours without pay in exchange for rations and housing. Although African-descended Antiguans avoided the experience of apprenticeship, the freedom bestowed on them remained quite restrictive.

West Indian planters and colonial legislators across the islands shared strategies to contain and regulate freedpeople, and Antigua, the first sugar island to initiate "full" freedom, offered authorities elsewhere a model for methods used to control black working people when apprenticeship ended in 1838.[18] This island's history confirms that immediate emancipation foiled authorities' and freedpeople's divergent objectives as much as gradual abolition did, extending our understanding of black life as well as colonial power in the postslavery Anglophone Caribbean. Historians have heralded Jamaica as the economic and policy-making center of the region and asserted that its history is essential to our understanding of British emancipation.[19] Yet Antigua demonstrates the acutely damaging effects of colonial peripherality on black working people as they transitioned to free status. In a place as small as Antigua, emancipation held different implications for freedpeople's mobility, land acquisition, socialization, and economic advancement compared with Jamaica, where a peasantry emerged and the path to independence from the estates, though equally impeded by poverty, was clearer.

But, despite the distinct conditions and possibilities within various abolition processes, freedpeople in former slave societies throughout the Americas met their emancipation without widespread access to land, citizenship, education, stable wages, or labor rights. *Troubling Freedom* broadens our sense of the strategies for securing freedom in postslavery societies by complicating freedom's definition and the sites of its expression. Indeed, freedom rang hollow in the entire Atlantic World, and Antigua vividly exemplifies freedpeople's attempts to challenge freedom's contradictions. The struggle for freedom from multiple forms of degradation has animated black popular politics throughout the African diaspora, from its beginnings in forced migration through the present.[20] Emancipation constituted a crucial transition in this longer-term process. As nations and empires shifted from slavery and into various kinds of formally free labor with many embedded unfreedoms, freedpeople protected themselves by strategically engaging this changing context. The book's investigation of the politicized intricacies within freedpeople's survival strategies in Antigua allows us to better understand how emancipated women and men approached the many obstacles they encountered in various postslavery societies.

A close look at everyday life after emancipation confirms that self-definition and community formation among Antigua's black residents did occur despite a milieu directly inimical to these developments. The conferral of freedom expanded their cognizance of the racial, gender, and class inequalities impeding their progress. Freedom also enabled their efforts to undo such inequalities, the effects of which both undermined and reinforced their internal hierarchies and external subjugation. White elites anticipated unbroken economic productivity and social deference from blacks in response to the "gift" of emancipation. But freedpeople troubled such visions in the ways they led their daily lives, as they tried to create the conditions for a tangible liberation. That freedpeople expressed their will to be free at all, however inconsistently, remains historically significant given the harrowing circumstances that plagued their progress.

The Hostile Context

Black working people's senses of freedom were framed not only by their everyday survival tactics but also by the conditions elites affixed to emancipation. Understanding freedpeople's struggles requires an exploration of both their self-interested efforts and the hostile context within which they had to act, which was shaped by their fraught interactions with Antigua's other social groups. Local planters and their representatives, who held steadfastly to their socioeconomic dominance, and public officials, who advanced planters' interests, thwarted black working people's exercise of freedom. Protestant missionaries offered freedpeople outlets for self-improvement but also evangelized to prompt submissiveness. Conversations among these groups showed emancipation's deliberate and insuperable limits.

To white elites, the abolition of slavery did not translate into blacks' full political or economic membership in colonial society. Antigua's small but powerful circle of whites believed that abolition meant only that formerly enslaved people would be paid low wages for toiling obediently. They were only to produce sugar, the singular crop on which the island's entire economy hinged. According to local whites, emancipation, instead of conferring automatic rights on blacks, entailed no more than the possibility of earning privileges in the distant future as freedpeople lived up to the state's and colonial society's expectations for their public and private pursuits in their economic livelihoods, spiritual practices, and personal conduct. Emancipation was intended to refashion African-descended slaves with strange habits and "uncivilized" culture into westernized, Christian, and industrious subjects. The standards for achieving this transformation, however, were exacting and undesirable for freedpeople to fulfill. As freedpeople attempted to comprehend and respond to the conditions that local and metropolitan authorities built into abolition, whites altered those conditions to maintain their own power.

In addition to dealing with whites, Antigua's newly freed people had to negotiate with the numerically small but socially visible set of middle-class people of color, who had been born into freedom or were manumitted before 1834. The leading members of this group, who were of mixed European and African heritage, had some property and social standing, as did their counterparts in most other British Caribbean isles.[21] Mixed-race middle-class Antiguans often fluctuated between advocating for the advancement of black working people as they transitioned out of slavery and heaping as much disdain on them as did local white elites. Their ambivalence toward freedpeople stemmed from the uncertainty of their own position in Antigua's social hierarchy. Whites viewed people of color either as a buffer class to manage the "unruly" emancipated masses or as hostile competitors who, despite their ancestry, had the education, resources, and savvy to challenge white dominance in the colony. Newly emancipated people could make only intermittent alliances with this group during their quest to secure a more meaningful freedom. Freedpeople could just as often encounter onerous demands from mixed-race middling Antiguans that they become "civilized" subjects and willing workers, amid the latter's unyielding maintenance of their status distinctions.

The complexities of Antiguan emancipation also stemmed from the structures of and fissures within British imperial control in the Caribbean. At the beginning of the nineteenth century, Atlantic slaveholding states were engaged in an international dialogue about the relative merits of enslaved versus formally free labor.[22] The British, who often led this conversation, chose to experiment with state-regulated emancipation and a wage-labor economy long advocated by many metropolitan thinkers and policy makers. State oversight helped the empire avoid the pitfalls of freedom achieved by force, as exemplified by Haiti's unprecedented slave-led revolution. Metropolitan and colonial authorities agreed that emancipation should produce a tidy social order and a cheap and willing proletariat to continue the sugar enterprise. It should not disrupt the structures of white privilege in the West Indies.[23] In turn, local administrators managing British colonies in Antigua and across the Caribbean crafted a freedom replete with customary and legal inequities that delimited blacks' livelihoods and blocked their progress beyond the lowest rung of the social order.

Emancipation in theory guaranteed black working people's bodily freedom as individuals and freedom of contract as wage laborers. But their extreme disadvantage relative to their employers and their severe disfranchisement through law and social custom, which flowed from the Caribbean's legacy of slavery, severely limited those freedoms. It hindered the formal organizing necessary to surmount these obstacles and secure citizenship for many generations to follow. Antigua's black working people did not gain universal adult suffrage or legalized labor unions until a full century after abolition, which mirrors the prolonged delay in obtaining these rights that the descendants of slaves endured throughout the Atlantic World.[24]

Emancipated people's beleaguered efforts at self-preservation after 1834 were further inhibited by the declining profitability of British Caribbean sugar within the world economy through the rest of the nineteenth century. Cuba and Brazil, as slaveholding territories, brought stiff competition to the English colonies, generating greater quantities of cheaper sugar. Comparatively, British Caribbean sugar plantations were undercapitalized and technologically outdated. Overall, from the 1840s on, the Caribbean region found itself increasingly on the periphery of rapidly shifting global trade networks. The centers of European empire were moving eastward to Africa and Asia. Both increasing challenges within the global market and Antigua's continuous economic decline after 1834 exacerbated internal conflicts over the meaning of freedom.

All social groups had a limited range of options for their advancement in the postslavery era, which rendered freedpeople's struggles even more difficult. Missionaries operated on shoestring budgets; people of color increasingly slipped out of middle-class status and into financial and social insecurity; planters balanced precariously on the brink of ruin—all at the same time that black working people were even more deeply ensnared in poverty. In such desperate times, freedpeople who encountered their supposed social superiors were often met with disdain and suppression, as planters and local authorities criminalized their conduct. The island's legislature blocked freedpeople's search for new occupations and their attempts to modify the routine of estate work through the passage of coercive labor legislation. Missionaries policed freedpeople's personal interactions and frequently condemned their ways of life as unChristian. Continued pursuit of their self-interest as the sugar economy plummeted made freedpeople into adversaries of the state-sponsored emancipation project and disqualified them from citizenship.

Interrogating the Archive and Framing the Narrative

Troubling Freedom assembles many seemingly incongruous documents to construct its detailed portrait of black working people's besieged quest to realize freedom. Most of the sources used in this study—including government correspondence among public officials in Antigua and Britain, planters' records and letters, missionaries' correspondence, and local newspapers—display ambivalence or even outright hostility to black working people's efforts. Such records originate from and represent the power of colonial elites as they impeded freedpeople's progress.[25] These sources mostly obscure the depth and heterogeneity of black thought and action, as black voices appear in the record in brief and secondary fashion. Without reexamining these flawed documents, however, their stories would remain permanently silenced. *Troubling Freedom* explores freedpeople's lives and labors by inverting the perspectives of the literate observers who chronicled Antigua's past to excavate black survival tactics, ways of life, political beliefs, and senses of self.

The archives of the immediate pre- and post-1834 era remain distinct from other periods in their intense focus on black life. The buildup to and passage of emancipation in the British Empire fostered a rare visibility of black working people in the records, as white elites' concerns about public safety and economic productivity after 1834 bred greater scrutiny of black communities' ordinary affairs. Elites' obsessive documentation of black people's labor and public comportment formed a means of control aimed at ensuring that emancipation maintained existent social inequalities, but inadvertently created an abundance of information on otherwise invisible subjects. Yet these records still share with the broader archive of Atlantic slavery and freedom an acute lack of insight into black working people's interiority and their ideological perspectives on freedom.

To examine how Antigua's working people tried to stretch freedom's possibilities and circumvent its limits using such challenging sources, I investigate the plausible politics behind their self-interested acts. The responses such acts elicited among literate observers allow me to parse in detail the significance of mundane black life. Elites knew all too well that freedpeople regularly attempted to contest the status quo as they lived, labored, and socialized in the towns and on rural estates. Elites' disdain at the changes they perceived in freedpeople's labor practices, consumer habits, demeanor, and lifestyles provides rich evidence of these changes as they occurred. On rare occasions, sources feature the lives of specific freedpersons that lend particularity to the broader issues considered in this book. But, more often than not, the study engages the indirect and generalized ways in which freedpeople's daily lives surface in archival documents, retelling elites' anxieties through a different analytical lens, as stories of black working people's survival, aspirations for self-determination, and ultimate frustration.

My interpretation of the sources explores the complex interplay between elite power and subaltern subversion within many aspects of colonial Antiguan public and private life. In this vein, elite laments over freedpeople's expensive new clothing document freedpeople's sartorial expression of their new status and desire for a life beyond fieldwork, but the laments also reveal notions of illegitimacy that haunted black attempts to mimic the fashions of their social superiors. Elites' anxiety over the pervasiveness of "superstition" among freedpeople evinces their continued adherence to obeah despite the vigor of Christian evangelizing, as well as whites' claims of black "savagery" that undercut any efforts to assert their rights in freedom. This book extracts multilayered connotations from the actions and interactions that elites recorded, and it shows that there was far more to black working people's story than has previously been told.[26]

Troubling Freedom engages two interconnected scholarly conversations central to the study of the African diaspora in the Atlantic World: the quotidian lives and cultures of African-descended people and their ideas about freedom. The first has been dominated by scholars of slavery, who have debated the influence of African antecedents as against the effects, both productive and destructive, of forced migration on the identities and cultures of diasporic communities.[27] This book does not focus on that debate, but such scholarship has helped to shape my understanding of African-descended Antiguans' cultural identity from the 1830s onward. At the time of emancipation, the island's largely creolized freedpeople shaped their lives and cultures from a blend of West African and European customs in a Caribbean colonial setting. After the close of the international slave trade in the first decade of the nineteenth century ended the steady stream of African-born slaves arriving on the island, cultural hybridity intensified.[28]

Exploring freedom's meanings sheds equal light on the culture of black working people. Just as knowledge of precolonial African cultures can illuminate community formation in Atlantic slavery, much can be gleaned about diasporic people's social worlds by examining their culture-building practices immediately after emancipation. *Troubling Freedom* reconstructs the material culture of black working people as a means to better comprehend their concepts of freedom, which distinguishes this book from many Atlantic postslavery studies that strictly focus on political and economic activities. Literate elites of postslavery Antigua were not always reliable reporters of black working people's folkways. Yet even with their limited knowledge of and biases against black communities, elite observers recognized that the conferral of freedom was transformative, reverberating in all aspects of freedpeople's lives. Indeed, to assess who black people were becoming and how they lived in the decades after 1834 is to investigate the significance of freedom.

In engaging the second major scholarly conversation on how freedpeople themselves defined freedom, I build on the fitting characterization of freedom as "no fixed condition but a constantly moving target."[29] Over time, black colonial subjects found their ideals of freedom increasingly difficult to attain, since British imperial ideas about freedom contracted markedly rather than continuing to expand. In Britain, the project of freeing the slaves was begun in the late eighteenth century by an assemblage of disparate interests, including lawmakers, evangelists, economists, and the literate public. Abolition served as the strategic means to many political ends, including economic modernization and imperial unity, that were equally if not more important than the goal of liberating Africans.[30] Upon abolition's legal enactment by Parliament in the 1830s, imperial reformers implemented a freedom for Caribbean enslaved people based on liberal, abstract notions of how proletarian workers should labor and live. When freedmen and -women did not respond as expected, colonial elites ascribed the problem to an ever-present sense of blacks' cultural and social "deficiencies."[31] The depressed sugar economy from the mid-1840s onward further impaired freedpeople's ability to challenge freedom's limitations. By the late 1850s, whites in Antigua concluded that emancipation was a failure and that freedpeople were unfit for citizenship. They were destined instead for poverty, crime, and civil exclusion. Given the impossible circumstances freedpeople faced from the moment of abolition, this amounted to a self-fulfilling prophecy.

Despite this predicament, black working people harbored a political awareness bred in the context of their quotidian strategies for survival. Contrary to the opinions of whites, black working people before and after 1834 did not enjoy their freedom primarily through "criminal" acts. They also sought to change the colonial order by claiming rights in accordance with their sense of the law and of themselves as Crown subjects. Freedpeople's assertions of their legal rights were based on their belief in the law as a protector of their interests. They were developing a "legal sensibility," a conception of "how things ought to be and what to do if they are not."[32] Antiguan freedpeople attempted to use colonial law to attain their objectives despite their familiarity with its inequities. At the same time, freedpeople persistently engaged in illicit activities in response to the exclusionary tactics of the state and white-dominated society. Their simultaneous legal and illegal acts took place in the yawning gap between what they believed freedom should mean and what freedom actually allowed. Tactics such as theft, arson, and the serial quitting of estate employment all buttressed their efforts to expand their freedom. The moments of open popular resistance that came in 1831 and 1858 were forceful reiterations of the politicized conflicts and the routine violence that marked black ordinary life in freedom.

Antigua's moments of collective protest that challenged freedom's contradictions reflect a broader trend in British Caribbean history. Between 1800 and 1834, mass uprisings in Barbados in 1816, Guyana (Demerara) in 1823, and Jamaica in 1831 were precipitated by inflammatory ideas that slaves held about freedom and revealed to imperial authorities the problems that would accompany general abolition. Almost every colony in the Anglophone chain was rocked by violent uprisings after 1834, including riots in St. Kitts and mass strikes in Trinidad in response to the inauguration of apprenticeship. The infamous 1865 Morant Bay Rebellion in Jamaica, a bloody struggle with a high death toll, prompted a drastic restructuring of British colonial governance in the Caribbean.[33] Freedpeople consistently used physical aggression to express their anger at emancipation's many inadequacies. The divergent targets of Antiguan black working people's violent acts in the 1831 and 1858 uprisings, the first instance destroying whites' property and the second attacking other black working people, show the stark shift between their hopefulness on the eve of emancipation and their despair after several decades of living with its shortcomings. Violent conflict showcased freedpeople's responses to the conditional nature of colonial abolition, a conditionality that eventually delimited their own visions of freedom and their sense of who could share in its practice.

Charting Freedom's Course

The language I use to tell this story of emancipated people's frustrated efforts before and after 1834 is deliberately chosen to highlight how race and class, as well as gender, played critical roles in shaping Antigua's social hierarchy and delimiting freedom. I refer to Antiguans with any African ancestry as *African-descended people* because skin color was the most salient marker of difference in the colony. Racial categories defined distinct groups subject to white planter control. Those Antiguans who had both African and European ancestry are termed *mixed-race people*, *people of color*, or the *mixed-race middle class*, a status held by the leading members of this stratum. I refer to Antiguans of European ancestry as *whites* or as *white elites*, which indicates the economic and social control over the colony's affairs exercised by prominent planters and officials. I also call white and mixed-race middle-class observers *elites* to denote these two groups' shared demand that slaves-turned-freedpeople adopt "civilized" ways and act in accordance with elite conceptions of law and order.

For the period prior to 1834, I call the historical actors most central to my study *slaves* or *enslaved people*. For the period after 1834, I refer to these women and men as *freedpeople*, *newly freed people*, or *emancipated people* to signify the paramount importance of emancipation in their daily lives. I also call them *black working people* to connote their racial and class status in the colony while still centering their humanity.[34] In contrast, the sources show British colonial officers, planters, missionaries, and other literate white and mixed-race observers calling them *laborers*, *Negroes*, or, later, the *peasantry*. The European term *peasant* especially did not apply to the condition of black working people on this island. Lack of access to land and the dominance of sugar planting prevented Antigua's freedpeople from practicing the independent subsistence and commercial agricultural production that characterizes a peasantry. At best, Antigua had a *semipeasantry*, with a significant proportion of people pursuing multiple occupations, combining small-scale provisioning with employment in the sugar industry or other jobs in the parishes and towns.[35] Elites' use of this misnomer rings ironic in light of their endeavors to prevent black working people's self-sufficiency and independence from the sugar industry. The term also signifies the misfortunes of black working people enduring a freedom that functioned too much like slavery.

Chapter 1 begins with an overview of the social, spatial, and legal contours of colonial Antigua and Barbuda in the late slavery period. This chapter orients readers to the geography, topography, and demography of both places, and the racial and gendered boundaries circumscribing enslaved people's lives and forms of subversion. Chapter 2 examines Antigua's 1831 slave rebellion, in which enslaved people protested the outlawing of their Sunday market with riots in the capital and a series of fires across several rural estates. This uprising shows that metropolitan and colonial conversations about slavery's political future affected slaves' approaches to their daily lives.

The events considered in subsequent chapters illuminate both continuities and changes in black people's everyday practices as they sought to define the terms of their freedom. While their new status bestowed new opportunities, crucial pitfalls of bondage remained well after abolition. Chapter 3 examines the transformations in labor after abolition. Working people contested the official version of freedom through informal and often extralegal negotiations with their employers over issues such as wages, work schedules, workplace duties, the labor of women and children, and the pursuit of livelihoods beyond the plantations. Freedpeople's growing mobility and refashioned work routines prompted planters and lawmakers to respond with severe legal and customary strategies of containment.

Chapter 4 investigates black working people's changing leisure practices as opportunities in the local marketplace expanded, their wages on and off plantations rose (however temporarily), and they asserted their presence in public space in novel ways. Freedpeople's pursuit of improved housing, expanded amusements, and new forms of consumption announced their conviction that freedom should also transform their social lives. But their new religious and secular public engagements opened up further subjection to church and state authority, and were met with sharp criticism from local elites that reiterated discourses of race, class, and gender in operation since slavery.

The next chapter first documents the surge in Christian conversion among freedpeople amid their continued adherence to the African spiritual practice of obeah, and then explores the prevalence of nonmonogamous informal partnerships over Christian wedlock, both of which complicate any assumptions about freedpeople's complete Christianization. Drawing on hitherto unstudied archival records of Moravian Church disciplinary proceedings against what they deemed adulterous relations, the chapter argues that emancipation as a gendered project intensified the inequities of slavery to which black women were especially subject. These proceedings reveal the regularity of surveillance and violence aimed at freedwomen's bodies and their sexuality, as it was differently practiced by Christian missionaries and by the black men with whom they were intimate. Black women's bodies were continually under duress. Legal abolition and the varied efforts to expand freedom afterward particularly generated little in the way of liberation for black working women.

Chapter 6 investigates the successive and severe setbacks to black working people's progress between the late 1840s and mid-1850s. The Sugar Duties Act of 1846 that gradually eliminated protection for British Caribbean sugar in the English market depressed sugar prices and precipitated a financial crisis. Amid such dire circumstances, black working people employed a variety of legal and extralegal strategies to maintain livelihoods both within and outside the sugar industry. Setting cane fires, practicing obeah, and committing petty theft—though deemed criminal by authorities and white elites—appear to have had more economic and political significance than their detractors recognized. These illicit actions represent freedpeople's protest against the retraction of the all-too-brief benefits they had gained during the early 1840s.

Chapter 7 tells the story of the 1858 uprising. Job competition between Antiguan and Barbudan dockworkers sparked the outburst. Over several days, Antiguans progressed from attacking Barbudans to targeting Portuguese immigrant retailers, white planters, and, most prominently, black and mixed-race policemen. Gendered violence also unfolded as Antiguan workingwomen assaulted Barbudan women in ways reflecting the pervasive devaluation of black women's bodily integrity in slavery and in freedom. The rioters' goals and the changing targets of their violence hint at their varied and contradictory conceptions of freedom and who should enjoy its privileges. Ultimately, Antigua's working people launched a futile protest against such a narrowly construed freedom.

Troubling Freedom presents freedpeople's efforts to form an efficient workforce, devout families, and independent communities in response to elite prescriptions for acceptable behavior, all of which failed to convince whites that blacks were worthy of full economic and political inclusion in the colony. Freedpeople's multifaceted conceptions of freedom are revealed in their shifting yet persistent responses to white elites' strategies of domination. As emancipation unfolded in the early 1830s, Antigua's freedpeople appealed to colonial structures of power to try to claim their perceived rights, invoking their perceived legal subjecthood before the Crown. They continued during the late 1830s and early 1840s by asserting their rights as laborers and as participants in public institutions. At later and more repressive junctures, they had to abandon their new strategies altogether and employ familiar practices to maintain their lives and livelihoods. Freedom degenerated to a bare minimum of survival as sugar's profitability declined during the late 1840s. In turn, the legal and public identities black working people cultivated fell away as they continued the extralegal tactics in which they had always engaged. Moreover, some freedpeople's efforts to secure material improvement and social power undercut those of others. As a wide range of efforts proved inadequate to expand local and metropolitan authorities' narrow constructions of freedom, freedpeople struggled against one another, sometimes violently, to seize what little spoils they could. By the 1850s, the idealism that had flourished on the eve of emancipation was all but gone.

Ultimately, this book explores the contentious nature of black community building, asking how it simultaneously supported and derailed the goals that working people pursued in freedom, and how it was repeatedly thwarted by the empire's powerful Others. Though they launched many oppositional efforts that upend a simple narrative of imperial subjugation after slavery, freedpeople still reified the troubled forms of freedom embedded in Britain's emancipation project. This contradictory and dynamic range of activities offers a rare window into black working people's lives and their politics.

....

CHAPTER 1

"A LANDSCAPE THAT CONTINUALLY RECURRED IN PASSING"

The Many Worlds of a Small Place

It is just a little island. The unreal way in which it is beautiful now is the unreal way in which it was always beautiful. The unreal way in which it was beautiful now that they are a free people is the unreal way in which it was beautiful when they were slaves.—JAMAICA KINCAID, A Small Place

As Jamaica Kincaid's famous essay on postcolonial Antigua suggests, there is a haunting connection between the island's beauty and its long history of exploitation, from the beginning of slavery to the present moment.[1] Many elements composing Antigua's beauty—including its fertile soils, its flat and easily traversed landscape, its ease of access to the sea, and its constant, if not searing, stretches of uninterrupted sunshine—laid the groundwork for colonial settlement, an all-consuming staple-crop industry, and African enslavement. This island, tucked in the northeastern corner of the Caribbean Sea, can easily blend into the narrative of Britain's centuries-long imperial ventures around the globe. It is an especially diminutive place among the many "repeating islands" that punctuate modern Caribbean history and culture.[2] But Antigua, while seemingly insignificant to the British Empire, contributed an overwhelming share of its human and natural resources to the making of an Anglo-Atlantic world. Its complex social relations and conflicts shaped many distinct ways of life within its small compass. Like slave societies throughout the Americas, Antigua's history features constant struggles among captive Africans and enterprising Europeans to build divergent social and economic structures from the grist of cane stalks and violence.

Antigua both reinforces and diverges from our understanding of a typical Caribbean slave society. Its small size and economic peripherality distinguish it from better-known places and underline the multiple conflicts that unfolded during the island's transition to freedom. The demographic imbalance that characterized Caribbean slave societies, in which a small number of whites were overwhelmed by a larger number of African slaves and their descendants, was especially severe in Antigua. The social and political power of whites still determined the order of life. But the steadily declining numbers of white residents in Antigua over the late eighteenth and early nineteenth centuries, combined with the lack of financial resources for effective public policing, made the surveillance of slave populations an increasingly scattered and piecemeal effort.

Consequently, Antiguan enslaved people moved around the island under slightly less duress than their counterparts elsewhere. Slaves around the Caribbean traveled frequently between town and country. For huckstering, mingling, or a host of other reasons, Afro-Caribbean slaves regularly sidestepped the legal prohibitions and patrols that policed their mobility.[3] By 1800 Antigua could not even muster similar shows of force, however disregarded they were elsewhere. The large militias and corps of slave catchers that pursued runaways and regulated slave assemblies in such places as Jamaica, Barbados, and Saint-Domingue did not exist in Antigua.[4] These forces, which were cobbled together from poor white, mixed-race, or maroon populations, were impossible to assemble in a place with so few whites, no maroons, and a mixed-race population that whites endeavored to render powerless. The island's local courts and slave owners severely punished the runaways they caught, as they did slaves who committed more flagrant violations against white persons and property. But Antigua's resident whites expressed constant concerns about keeping "order" that colonial officials left unheeded, as slave collectivities in public spaces became raucous and occasionally violent.

In the end, white elites, cognizant of their own inability to regulate slaves' activities beyond work, tacitly accepted the everyday transgressions slaves regularly committed in their socializing about the town and frequent movement between town and countryside. Their tolerance functioned as a safety valve to prevent the disastrous consequences of slave uprisings, which rarely occurred in Antigua, especially from the latter half of the eighteenth century onward. Some instances of slave assaults on whites and a single unsuccessful slave plot to overthrow white rule unfolded in the early 1700s, when sugar was at its most profitable and the white population—and thus the brute force it wielded—was at its height. But by 1790, the ratio of whites to blacks in Antigua was 1:18, versus 1:16 in Saint Domingue, 1:10 in Jamaica, and 1:4 in Barbados.[5] At the turn of the nineteenth century, as the numbers of whites, the revenues from sugar, and the surveillance apparatus all receded, the remaining whites relaxed regulations on slave behavior and mobility. Only in 1831, when whites attempted to forcibly curtail the Sunday market, the greatest of slaves' quotidian "freedoms," did the slaves respond with mass public protests. This moment prompted authorities to swiftly contain the outburst and mete out punitive measures to a few unfortunate suspects.

The issues of slave mobility and lack of white oversight overlapped with another major attribute of early nineteenth-century Antigua: the blurred lines between the principal town, St. John's, and the surrounding countryside. In part this resulted from the physical closeness of the town to most of the sugar estates on an island only fourteen miles long and eleven miles wide (see figure 1.1). Slaves constantly traveled between town and country; rural slaves had many reasons to assume the legitimacy of their presence in many town spaces, and could have easily carried information between the two locales. As Melanie Newton says of Barbados, a somewhat larger island, proximity "brought the socioeconomic dynamics of plantations into towns, and simultaneously, brought the towns to the countryside."[6] This overlap between town and country also resulted from the colony's disinterest in making St. John's an impressive or exclusive metropolitan space. Many contemporary accounts from the late eighteenth and early nineteenth centuries describe the town's best buildings as visibly worn. Observers remarked that slaves moved about and congregated freely in the streets. While St. John's had many features that signified the power of colonialism and white authorities, these were surrounded by shabbiness and punctuated by the constant presence of slaves not only at work but also at play.

Whites in Antigua accommodated the everyday subversions of slaves, but the asymmetrical power relations of a slave society nonetheless meant that clear distinctions existed between trivial and serious transgressions. Slaves who ventured in excess of these quotidian allowances risked

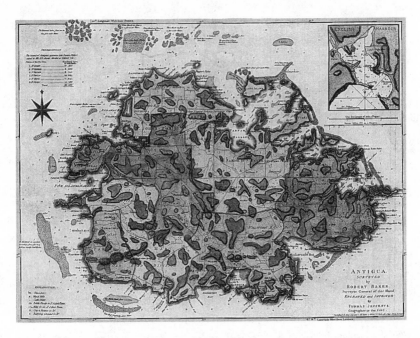

FIGURE 1.1. Map of Antigua (1775). *Antigua Surveyed* by Robert Baker. Reprinted by Thomas Jefferys, London: Barre Publishers.

corporal punishment, imprisonment, or even death. The mundane transactions that provided slaves with small liberties carried with them the constant threat of violence, forcing slaves to maintain a precarious balance between self-interest and deference to the prerogatives of whites. Enslaved people's daily freedoms and the public spaces that formed the setting for those activities to unfold both challenged and reinforced their degraded status as chattel.

Development and Instability in the Making of Colonial Antigua

Violence has marked Antigua's historical trajectory ever since the first clashes between Amerindians and Europeans in the Caribbean. The Spanish claimed Antigua and the nearby island of Barbuda in 1493 but mostly neglected them, given their lack of mineral deposits.[7] Indigenous Caribs from surrounding islands sailed to Antigua and Barbuda to forage and farm, as they had done for centuries, without much interference. But the English sought control of Antigua in 1632, and a group of English colonists from St. Kitts established new plantations there. In response to these new arrivals, who had no intention of abandoning the land as the Spaniards had previously done, the Caribs launched bloody raids that disrupted the nascent English colony. The English eventually defeated and decimated the Caribs, establishing stable settlements in both Antigua and Barbuda by the 1670s.[8] Whites quickly carved Antigua up into plantations, and sugar soon became the king of commercial agriculture on the island and across the region. By 1734, cane planting absorbed about 50,000 of the island's 72,000 acres.[9] Christopher Codrington, one of Antigua's first and most successful planters, took possession of Barbuda, whose soil could not support cane planting, and used the produce from the island's small farming, fishing, and livestock industries to supply his Antiguan estates.

In the 1660s and 1670s, Antigua's sugar output expanded significantly, so that by the early eighteenth century, it exceeded that of most other Leeward Islands.[10] In 1763 Antigua was the fourth-largest producer of sugar in the region, after Jamaica, Barbados, and St. Kitts.[11] Sugar not only turned unprecedented profits but also sparked a drastic transformation. A few hundred white indentured servants from England, Scotland, and Ireland formed the first plantation labor force. By 1700, captive Africans overwhelmingly outnumbered white laborers, as indentured servants increasingly began to survive their contracts and become free, and at the same time the transatlantic slave trade began to reap remarkable profits for European empires.

At first, the overwhelming majority of slaves were African born. Despite planters' preference for Gold Coast "Coromantees" and Dahomean "Papas" and British control of slaving in both regions in the early 1700s, enslaved Antiguans came from various places on the continent. Ship registers show slavers with captives hailing from ports such as Calabar in the Bight of Biafra and from the Kongo Kingdom and Portuguese Angola in the western regions of central Africa, despite their lesser value in the British market and their reputedly higher death rates during the seasoning process in the Caribbean.[12] The rising demand for estate labor stimulated a marked surge in the island's black population, augmented by newly arriving African captives.

Locally born slaves increased in number over the eighteenth century, but the fertility of the enslaved population was exceeded by the high mortality of infants because of the harrowing labor conditions endured by enslaved mothers. Additionally, the wisdom among planters that working a slave to death and buying a new one was more cost effective than keeping a slave through old age reinforced their excessive dependence on new imports. Approximately 138,000 Africans were imported into Antigua between 1670 and 1820. During the peak period of the trade, 1700–60, Antigua received anywhere from 10,000 to 25,000 Africans per decade. Yet its total slave population never exceeded 40,000 persons at any point before 1834, revealing the extreme brutality of slavery and the inability of Africans to reproduce while enduring such harsh labor conditions.[13]

Nonetheless, the demographic imbalance between whites and blacks became even more severe over the long term. In 1678, Antigua had more than 2,300 whites and more than 2,100 enslaved Africans, but a mere thirty years later, in 1707, the island counted only 500 more whites but around 12,800 slaves, with a ratio of more than 5 enslaved Africans to every white resident. The number of slaves climbed rapidly over the course of the eighteenth century, while that of whites did not. In 1805, roughly 3,000 whites controlled the labor of 36,000 slaves. By 1821, the number of slaves had fallen slightly to just over 31,000, in part because of increasing manumissions, but there were more than 15 slaves to every white inhabitant. The 1821 figures also offer a rare view of slaves' gender distribution. Women numbered around 16,500 and men 14,500. Antigua's enslaved population totaled around 30,000 when the 1833 abolition act was passed.[14]

In Antigua, as in other slave societies throughout the Americas, white men often engaged in sexual partnerships with African-descended women, largely through coercion and despite the illegality of interracial unions. Ultimately, the racial and class advantages of wealthy white men within Caribbean slave societies enabled their mastery over women of all ranks. Their sexual conduct and economic power buttressed a gendered and racialized class hierarchy in which they perceived and sought out white women as respectable wives, colored women of mixed ancestry as sexual companions, and black women as objects of sexual fantasies and adventures.[15] These patterns of sexual relations facilitated the emergence of a small but significant mixed-race community in Antigua with a female majority by the 1800s.

Many mixed-race persons remained enslaved through the eighteenth century, but others were manumitted because of familial relationships with propertied whites. Toward the beginning of the nineteenth century, some were even born into freedom, and a rare few owned slaves themselves. This particular stratum in Antigua, often listed in population reports as "free colored," bore a slippery classification indeed, as those counted among this group were not all of mixed ancestry but included black slaves who had been freed during the decades before abolition. Antigua's free people of color, particularly the literate and propertied among them, occupied a political, economic, and social position between powerful whites and degraded slaves. In the 1780s this group numbered around 1,200 adults; by 1821 it included 1,500 men and 2,300 women.[16]

Unlike the African-descended population, men slightly outnumbered women among Antigua's white residents. Figures for their population vary widely and may be unreliable, but most sources point to a decline in their numbers over time. The white presence peaked at around 5,200 in 1724, likely inclusive of men, women, and children, while five years later another report counted only 1,300 white men and 1,100 white women.[17] Their numbers dipped over the late eighteenth and early nineteenth centuries, as sugar estates often failed and the remaining proprietors frequently resorted to absentee ownership. John Luffman, a British traveler to the island in the late 1780s, noted that despite the tax break that planters received for every adult white resident on their properties, an incentive aimed directly at maintaining a "proportionate" balance between whites and slaves, most planters "shamefully evaded" this requirement. Luffman also complained that the planters' tendency to usurp the "ten-acre" lands, which the Crown had designated in 1700 for poor whites to start small farms, also inhibited white settlement.[18] By 1821, the island was home to just 1,140 white men and 840 white women.[19]

Hence, the island's white population was unable to effectively police the activities of slaves with such small numbers and steadily declining profits from sugar. In Antigua, as in most colonial slave societies in the Americas, enslaved men were conscripted into white-led militias, but largely for warfare against competing imperial powers rather than to police their fellow slaves.[20] But in Antigua, even the white men who were supposed to lead the militia often shirked this duty. The island's 1702 militia act admonished wealthy white men who bought their way out of militia service, but the practice continued.[21] In the 1780s, Luffman observed that slaves were unable to hide their amusement at the "unsoldier-like performances" of the local corps, and wondered why "the people in power in the colony should so much neglect that best of institution for public safety, and internal protection, the *Militia*, when the great disproportion of twelve blacks and colored persons to one white is considered as now-existing, and when it is observed that eleven twelfths of the blacks are slaves."[22]

Luffman's fears about security hint at the enduring social tensions between masters and slaves, and whites' difficulties with controlling enslaved people's activities beyond their labors. African-born slaves harbored an understandable desire to recreate a semblance of home in this strange land, despite the diversity of their origins. Maroon bands formed in Antigua during the late 1600s, as slaves collectively fled the ravages of plantation labor. But their presence was short-lived and seldom recorded, as Antigua's rapidly changing landscape doomed them to exposure. Maroons initially took advantage of the island's extensive forested frontier, especially on the hillier southern coast, to create hidden settlements as a base for raiding plantations and establishing independent cultural communities. But unlike islands such as Jamaica, where mountain ranges and rainforests enabled maroon communities to remain impenetrable for decades, Antigua was mostly flat and arid, and white men seeking riches in sugar easily traversed its few hills and many valleys, making slave flight an even riskier venture. White settlers captured many maroons, executing some and returning the rest to enslavement. During the first half of the eighteenth century, some runaways fled Antigua by sea, seizing on the anonymity and de facto freedom to be found in nearby territories. But marronage subsided by the early 1700s as successful proprietors deforested most of the island's interior and absorbed it into estates.[23]

As the sugar industry matured, slavery assumed a more brutal, factory-like character, fostering continued opposition to its injustices among enslaved Antiguans. Open resistance occurred frequently, and some troubling instances let resident whites know that their safety was always precarious. In 1701, a group of slaves at Green Castle Estate murdered their owner, the planter Samuel Martin, beheading and repeatedly stabbing him with their field hoes after he refused to allow them extra days off at Christmastime.[24] The rebel slaves were captured and executed in an equally violent manner. In this episode, the tools of labor had become the tools of struggle, and rare moments of respite for those trapped in an exhausting slave regime became a life-and-death issue.

The next year, likely with Martin's fate in mind, Antiguan authorities established a code for "offences of slaves, and for the better government of free negroes" that sealed the abject social place enslaved people occupied.[25] They could leave the plantation only in the company of a white servant or with a ticket stating the places to which and times within which they were permitted to travel. The penalty for running away was dismemberment of their arms, their legs, or even their nose. They would be killed for striking a white person. The 1702 code was the second such set of regulations passed in Antigua. The third, passed in 1723, was designed to control every aspect of slaves' existence. Slaves could face the death penalty not only for assaulting a white person but also for threatening to harm a white person or attempting to burn whites' property. These regulations solidified the ideology among Europeans that enslaved people were property and aligned with the common wisdom that terrifying brutality was necessary to govern them.[26] Yet this spate of legislation did not deter Antigua's enslaved people from trying to secure their freedom well in advance of the empire's readiness to bestow it.

In 1729, a group of slaves owned by Nathaniel Crump at Coconut Hall Estate in St. Peter plotted to kill their owner and all the other whites in the island; the five ringleaders were executed and a few of their associates transported to neighboring islands. In 1736, an island-wide conspiracy to overthrow white authority led by the trusted slave Court and several of his compatriots, both Antiguan and African born, was thwarted at the last minute. This group organized around a Coromantee cultural identity and its accompanying Akan language and rituals. Some of the conspiracy's principal organizers were practitioners of obeah, an African-based faith and healing system prevalent among slaves in Antigua and throughout the Anglophone Caribbean. Obeah served as a critical tool for plotting this rebellion. As in other instances of slave resistance, the discovery of this conspiracy was followed by public executions—in this case, of nearly ninety convicted participants—as well as numerous transportations. But neighboring islands were just as rife with discontented slaves launching plots against planters, so exiling black rebels was no solution. As David Barry Gaspar has observed, a wave of "general unrest" flooded colonial slave societies in the Caribbean and across the Americas during the first half of the eighteenth century, including Danish St. John, British Jamaica and South Carolina, and French Guadeloupe.[27]

In the late eighteenth century, overt instances of opposition among enslaved people dwindled in Antigua, but everyday struggles against the planter regime continued. As the white population stagnated, slaves took some greater liberties with mobility, spawning less spectacular, more quotidian forms of resistance amid the relentless grind of sugar production. In Britain, public debate over slavery's future intensified.[28] The American Revolution sent shockwaves throughout the Atlantic empires and diminished the financial strength of British Caribbean sugar colonies. Humanitarian campaigners from dissenting Protestant sects led the call for an end to slavery from the 1780s, and enterprising free trade advocates joined the clamor a few decades later. Then the Haitian Revolution (1791–1804) overthrew slavery and birthed the first independent black postcolonial nation, raising serious questions about slavery's future elsewhere. Haiti's violent emergence signaled to other slaveholding empires that emancipation, if attempted at all, was best executed gradually and with the utmost state control.

In an effort to lay the groundwork for an orderly, secure, and protracted process of abolition, Parliament passed a series of measures after 1800 that sought to improve the institution of slavery. The amelioration process began with the abolition of British participation in the international slave trade in 1807. The slave registry bill of 1816, requiring the registration of every slave in the British Caribbean isles, aimed to curtail the clandestine slave trade that flourished after 1807 between the West Indies and the United States.[29] That effort was not entirely successful, as captive Africans continued to be imported into Antigua.[30] The process of reform gained significant momentum in 1823 with the metropolitan government's official recommendations for amelioration of the slave system in the colonies. The dismantling of slavery in 1834 was shaped by significant resistance from the colonies, and its terms were designed to reassure whites that their position would not be fatally jeopardized. All of these measures leading up to legal emancipation eroded West Indian planters' sense of security. They also revealed to enslaved Africans in Antigua and throughout the British Caribbean that they were increasingly gaining protection under British law and slowly but surely moving toward freedom. Uprisings occurred in several Caribbean territories between the 1810s and 1833, as slaves sought their rights and their freedom amid rumors of both being granted by the Crown. In Barbados, slaves misunderstanding that the 1816 slave registry bill promised imminent abolition contributed to a rebellion that broke out on Easter Sunday of that year.[31]

In 1831, Antigua's enslaved community engaged in open and collective opposition to the white authorities for the first time in a century, in response to a legislative ban on their Sunday market. Planters were struggling amid the dangerous combination of demographic imbalance, imperial policy changes, and the threat of insurrection, as thirty thousand slaves hung on the brink of freedom. The island's sugar industry was deteriorating precipitously during this period because of competition from other British islands and from French and Spanish territories in the region. By 1833, Antigua had fallen to seventh place on the list of large-scale sugar producers in the British Caribbean.[32] The halcyon days of sugar and slavery in Antigua had long since vanished, yet planters steadfastly clung to this increasingly unprofitable venture and to their rights in enslaved persons as private property.

Antigua's neglected sister isle, Barbuda, developed radically different forms of enslavement and economic production over the eighteenth and early nineteenth centuries. Yet Barbuda's history, too, demonstrates the disastrous consequences for enslaved Africans and their descendants of planters' unceasing efforts to reduce persons to private property. The links between the two islands meant they faced an equally uncertain future as the empire moved toward abolition.

Private Property and the Unusual Trajectory of Slavery in Barbuda

In 1685, the Crown leased the island of Barbuda, which lies roughly thirty miles north of Antigua, as a private fief to the Codrington family. These famed sugar barons owned some of Antigua's largest and most lucrative plantations in the parishes of St. John and St. Peter. The Antiguan Codringtons were a branch of the prominent planting family that played a central role in the "sugar revolution" in Barbados during the mid-1600s and founded Codrington College, an Anglican seminary, in 1710. At least two Codringtons served as governor of the Leeward Islands in the late 1600s; another served in Parliament from 1797 to 1812; and the family was twice granted a peerage.[33] Barbuda constituted a negligible part of the social, material, and political capital that this family enjoyed throughout the British Atlantic World, but it reveals much about the stark variations in slaves' work experiences on the Caribbean's small islands (see figure 1.2).

Barbuda received a steady stream of African captives beginning in the 1680s, but slave importations ebbed during the mid-1700s, and the population grew naturally thereafter. A century into British settlement, the island could count no more than five resident whites at any given time, usually the Codrington agent and his family. In 1715, its total population

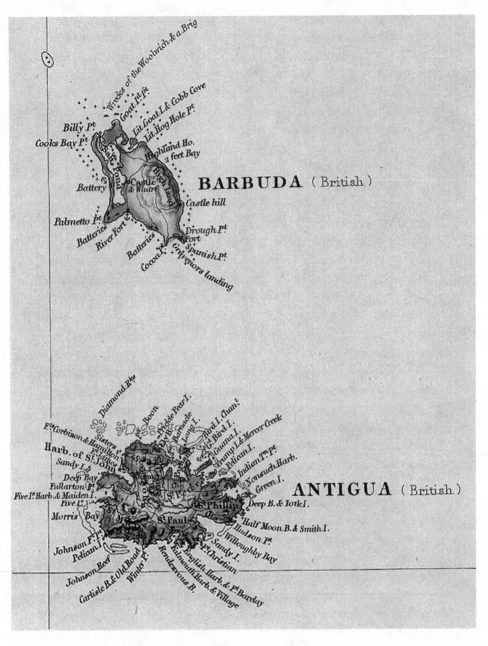

FIGURE 1.2. Map of Barbuda and Antigua (1842). *Map of the Leeward Islands* by John Arrowsmith.

was just ninety-three. Over the next century, this number steadily increased, but not by much, and never exceeded five hundred during the entire period of slavery.[34] The thin and unfertile topsoil of Barbuda, coupled with its exceptionally dry climate, prohibited the development of large-scale plantations, so its economy was developed to complement that of the neighboring sugar islands. Slaves raised livestock and crops, fished, and harvested lumber to supply the Codringtons' plantations and the local markets in Antigua. Slaves who did not pursue pastoral, hunting, or maritime occupations became skilled in crafts such as woodworking and leather tanning. These small-scale operations became Barbuda's primary source of revenue, which peaked at a modest level in the early 1800s and was reduced to a trickle by the mid-1820s.[35] Because of this state of affairs, many elite observers viewed Barbuda as an agrarian idyll. Charles Day, who visited in the 1850s, commented: "Altogether the negro population of Barbuda have nothing like real cares."[36] Some historians have uncritically repeated this claim; for example, Douglas Hall describes Barbuda as "a relatively happy place."[37] But slavery was still slavery, and African-descended Barbudans' bodies were the property of the Codringtons.

The labor required of Barbudan slaves, as on other isles without plantations, like the smaller islets of the Bahamas or the Grenadines, fostered longer life spans than territories with sugar regimes. This allowed for a natural increase of the slave population, a rarity in the history of Caribbean slavery.[38] In Barbuda, this natural increase was especially marked in the three decades prior to 1834, when the island's population almost doubled. During that time, the Codringtons considered supplying their Antiguan plantations with slaves from the increasingly populous Barbuda. The idea of Barbuda as a slave-breeding ground derives from this period of unprecedented demographic growth. Belief that Barbuda was a "stud farm" during slavery has a strong oral tradition among past and current Barbudans, but the historical geographers David Lowenthal and Colin Clarke have declared it a myth.[39] These scholars argue that natural increase was a by-product of Barbuda's female majority and its less strenuous work routine, but that the well-documented difficulty of making enslaved Barbudans leave their home meant that the Codringtons could not generate a profit by selling them. In fact, their managers often complained to the absentee Codringtons about slaves' obstinate refusal to be transferred to Antigua. By 1830, the heir apparent, Christopher Bethell Codrington, privately admitted that he had too little sway among his own slaves to enforce their removal. This would have rendered slave breeding unprofitable.[40] But when the British government offered compensation to slave owners, he tried to convince the Colonial Office that the particular profitability of Barbudan slaves, specifically from breeding and reselling them, should merit his receipt of extra funds. His claim was denied.[41]

Yet since having more enslaved laborers on their Antiguan plantations would have been profitable, it seems likely that the Codringtons used Barbudan slaves' procreation to enrich themselves. According to Lowenthal and Clarke, a total of fifty-two slaves were forcibly removed from Barbuda to Antigua between 1817 and 1832, either to increase the supply of labor there or as a "punishment." For an enslaved Barbudan, simply working on a sugar plantation was a form of punishment. But their separation from kin was no doubt worse. Relative to the island's total population of roughly five hundred, the removal of fifty-two people is significant. This evidence suggests that the Codringtons siphoned off their surplus Barbudans not only to maintain order but also to satisfy their Antiguan estates' voracious appetite for labor. That so many transported Barbudans requested to return home, and that some died while subjected to Antigua's strenuous plantation routine, tells us much about the history of both places.[42] These findings are suggestive, but they do not solve the debate over slave breeding.

The anthropologist Mindie Lazarus-Black attributes Barbudans' continued maintenance of the oral tradition about breeding to their present sense of virility, the legend's usefulness in explaining the prevalence of informal intimate partnerships rather than legal marriages, and the protection of an identity distinct from that of Antiguans.[43] While the "virility" that Lazarus-Black identifies in the legend connotes masculine strength, a connotation that its popular circulation among Antiguans and Barbudans also reinforces, the legend also implicitly attests to Barbudan women's fertility and skilled mothering. Barbudans' insistence on the veracity of the stud-farm narrative should encourage students of history to develop a more critical view of the island's past. That the enslaved were able to survive, form families, and reproduce successfully to create and perpetuate their own culture was a feat. Yet, read another way, the stud-farm narrative suggests that despite the island's reputation for a "milder," less fatal form of slavery, enslavement still involved coercion and the control of women's and men's bodies in the interests of slaveholders.

Correspondence from the late slavery period reveals Barbudan slaves' marked intractability; they often would not submit to any authority and instead acted in their own interest. While the slaves generally maintained a peaceful demeanor, intermittent moments of conflict between them and the agents could not be avoided, and these tended to end in the slaves' favor. This pattern generated increasingly vociferous complaints in the correspondence between Codrington and his agents just prior to 1834. Robert Jarritt, who briefly managed Barbuda before serving as the Codrington representative in Antigua, described Barbudan slaves as "a bad sett [sic], insolent, ungovernable, and almost outlawed" and reported that many refused to work so that they could tend their own provision grounds and shoot game for their own consumption. After recalling an episode in which five slaves who had been jailed for assaulting a slave driver were freed by a gang of their compatriots the next night, Jarritt declared of Barbudan slaves: "They acknowledge no Master and believe the Island belongs to themselves, and any manager living [in Barbuda] & using coercive means to bring them to subjection I have no doubt would lose his life."[44] Two months before emancipation went into effect, Codrington called Barbuda a potential "St. Domingo," declaring "how impracticable it will be to govern a rapidly increasing free population of 500 Negroes among whom two white persons only have hitherto resided."[45]

The hysteria that gripped Caribbean colonialists and the spirit that electrified their slaves after the Haitian Revolution intensified in British territories on the eve of abolition, and was magnified in a place with so few resident whites compared with the number of African-descended laborers. Barbuda was an extreme case, but it offers a historical foil to its relatively more developed neighbor. Antigua's structure and customs were typical of Caribbean slave societies, and more obvious forms of social control over slaves, however compromised by slaves' own self-interested practices, operated in everyday life. A close look at Antigua's spatial layout in the late slavery era reveals that key aspects of the master-slave struggle were deeply embedded in the island's landscape.

The Spatial Dimensions of Antigua's Social Hierarchy

In the early nineteenth century, the deteriorating but still dominant sugar enterprise shaped the island's spatial configuration. Sugar's social relations were embedded in the landscape. The island's precarious

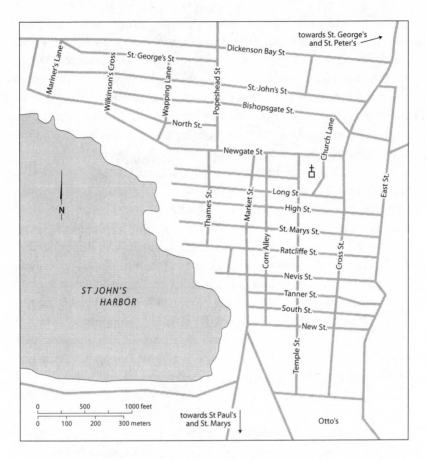

MAP 1.1. Map of St. John's (ca. 1840). Map by Bill Nelson Cartography.

situation as a slave-holding, sugar-producing colony marked the ways
that both planters and enslaved people used, constrained, and continuously redefined space. Like most colonial Caribbean territories, Antigua featured a few small towns and villages surrounded by a sprawling
countryside almost entirely covered with sugar canes. During the final
few decades of slavery, only three towns merited mention in contemporary accounts. Falmouth, which flanked the southeastern naval station
at English Harbour, functioned less as a military garrison and more as a
secondary port through the nineteenth century.[46] Parham, in the north-
east, had decayed by 1800 because its bay was too shallow for oceangoing
ships.[47]

St. John's, the colony's capital, formed the center of social and political life on the island (see map 1.1). Located on the northwest coast, it sat

FIGURE 1.3. Moravian Church Mission, St. John's Street (ca. 1830). Aquatint by Johann Stobwasser, *Ansichten von Missions-Niederlassungen der Evangelishen Bruder-Gemeinde* (Basle, n.d.). Courtesy of the John Carter Brown Library at Brown University.

on 150 acres of land and contained around one thousand mostly wooden structures, a grid of unpaved streets, and the island's principal harbor. The most imposing buildings displayed the white-dominated social hierarchy, through both the race and social class of their patrons and the fact that most had been erected by enslaved labor.

For instance, the main branches of Antigua's three principal Christian churches were clearly ranked. The Moravian church, headquartered on St. John's Street, was a set of simple stone buildings that served an overwhelming majority of enslaved black worshippers (see figure 1.3). The more stately Methodist church, which had humble origins in a wooden chapel on Tanner Street, was erected in stone on St. Mary's Street in 1839. The Methodist congregation attracted enslaved and free worshippers of African and mixed-race descent alongside small numbers of whites. The most majestic church, St. John's Anglican Cathedral, was a towering stone edifice with two steeples built in the 1740s that would acquire more embellishments in the repairs after an 1843 earthquake. The cathedral sat on a northern hill overlooking the town and catered mostly to the white planter and merchant classes.[48]

The stone courthouse at the corner of Long and Market Streets also loomed large among the town's notable structures, for it served not only as the seat of government but also as a site for whites' social events, such as balls, dinners, and bazaars.[49] The strained dynamics of colonial governance regularly unfolded at the courthouse. Antigua's Crown-appointed governor represented metropolitan interests in the island via his communications with the colonial secretary of state, a British civil servant empowered to approve or deny the passage of all legislation devised in the empire's numerous possessions around the globe. The colonial secretary was the ultimate manager of the empire's affairs, but ironically tended to have little experience with life in any colonial setting. As a local resident, the governor was much better qualified to discern the colony's administrative needs, but he still had to answer to the secretary for every decision he made. He also had to balance his obligation to the imperial authorities with the constant pressures to make the laws reflect the will of the local legislature, a body composed overwhelmingly of planters who were selected by a planter-dominated electorate. As the empire moved toward abolition and the Colonial Office expressed a nominal interest in enslaved subjects' welfare, clashes between the governor and the legislature abounded. Governors were increasingly imported from Britain or other colonies rather than chosen from local residents, and planters' ideas about colonial welfare frequently diverged from those held by metropolitan officials.[50]

Many of the other buildings in St. John's, including those housing professional offices and retail shops, were flimsy wooden structures along streets caked with mud and lined with open sewers. Rich and poor town dwellers often lived side by side rather than in segregated districts. While St. John's was bustling, it was visibly shabby. A traveler in the 1850s described it as exhibiting the "anomalous character of all West Indian towns—long, low, unpainted wooden houses, weather stained and dilapidated, interspersed with compact wooden mansions, neatly painted white with green jalousies. The general effect is extremely disagreeable, the good houses not being sufficiently near each other to redeem the other[s]."[51] The worn character of the town's private and public spaces in the mid-nineteenth century evinced the declining prosperity of sugar plantations over the previous decades.

Members of the planter and merchant classes did not have the town to themselves. Although St. John's attracted Antigua's commercial and political elites, it was equally marked by the constant presence of black working people as they strove to eke out a livelihood, conduct their affairs, and seek amusements. The colonial government founded an official market in 1702 at the corner of Long and Market Streets, and after the courthouse's erection on that site in 1747, the market was moved to an adjacent street.[52] Enslaved and free female hucksters dominated the public market. While colonial officials addressed their affairs within, black workingwomen conducted their own business in the street below. Slaves also established their own unofficial weekly Sunday market in a pasture called Otto's just across the town's southern boundary.

The streets, the businesses, the ships docked ships in the harbor, and the homes of whites all bore the unmistakable imprint of enslaved people. William Clark's image of the Long Street courthouse in 1823 (see figure 1.4) depicts the presence of different social groups in this lively public space. The labor of African-descended people is a principal theme. The huckster woman in the lower right corner carries a sack of goods and holds a basket of provisions atop her head while conversing with a black man holding two dead chickens, which could be for consumption, barter, or sale. On the left side, three porters, likely enslaved, struggle to transport a heavy barrel. Clark deliberately highlights the physical exertion and social subservience of black men by avoiding the plausible insertion of draft animals in concert and deliberately juxtaposing them with the privileged white men atop horses and driving a buggy.

Clark's image also shows black people at play, as seen in the pair of black men leaning against the gate and idly observing the passersby. A well-dressed mixed-race woman consorts with a white soldier while shading herself from the sun with a parasol, evoking the prevalence of sexual relations between white men and women of African descent. A black man also can be seen approaching the courthouse gates with his possessions wrapped in a bindle; this lone traveler could be at labor or leisure, or somewhere in between. All of these individuals, though endowed with a lesser social power, occupy the same public spaces as the white women of privilege standing by the courthouse gates under a parasol and the white men riding by or proceeding into the courthouse. The mixed-race woman enjoys the same fineries as the white women in the

FIGURE 1.4. Long Street Courthouse (1823). Aquatint by William Clark, *Ten Views in the Island of Antigua: In Which Are Represented the Process of Sugar Making, and the Employment of the Negroes, in the Field, Boiling-house and Distillery* (London: Thomas Clay, 1823). Courtesy of the Yale Center for British Art, Paul Mellon Collection.

image, including the parasol, but her shoes and stockings, dress, long gloves, and headwear suggest the competition for social status that occurred in public space between these groups. As other sources demonstrate, black working people crowded the rumshops, streets, and homes of St. John's and indulged in drink, dance, loud chatter, and other diversions from work.

Urban slavery differed in certain key ways from its rural counterpart, as enslaved black city dwellers enjoyed greater mobility and a degree of autonomy. Antigua was no exception. Slaves in St. John's were hired out by their owners to fill a range of skilled and nonskilled positions as domestics, porters, tavern keepers, seamen, and apprentices in various trades. Their occupations often fostered more independence than that enjoyed by rural slaves, as the demands of their labor legitimized their mobility in the town streets, whether transporting, selling, or procuring goods or services on their own behalf or for their masters. But the greater autonomy of urban slaves did not mean that they did not work as hard or were not exposed to the same risks of white violence as slaves on sugar estates. And they often navigated such experiences in isolation. Antigua's most infamous enslaved woman, Mary Prince, whose 1831 narrative stirred much controversy throughout the empire, reveals that urban slaves, who lived in white households with a few slaves at most, were deprived of assistance with their labor and networks of social support. She discusses repeated instances of debilitation from overwork and illness and confirms her masters' regular abuse when she came to Antigua from Bermuda, as she initially served as their domestic. In one case, if not for the caring slave of a neighbor, she might have died from rheumatism.[53] Town-based slaves in the Caribbean and throughout the Americas still endured burdensome labor and corporal and sexual abuse, especially since they mainly worked in domestic settings that placed them in proximity to their owners. Enslaved women were at heightened risk, as the town setting also opened up frequent opportunities for owners to hire them out as prostitutes.[54]

The town of St. John's not only bore the signs of slaves' constant labor but also featured sites expressly intended for their punishment and torture. At the height of sugar production, St. John's harbor regularly received slave ships with hundreds of captive Africans bound for estates. An area called "the Parade," where merchants had established shops and gathered to discuss prices and other commercial concerns, also housed the market where the bodies of newly arrived Africans were brutally displayed and sold to the highest bidders.[55] The town jail regularly received enslaved people deemed guilty of criminal acts, but some endured public torture before landing in prison. In 1702, with the second slave code's passage, the public treasury funded the erection of a cage, a pillory, stocks, a whipping post, and a ducking stool on the streets of St. John's.[56] Mary Prince knew this geography of torture well, as her masters banished her to the St. John's cage for a night and had her flogged publicly the next morning for quarreling with another slave woman over their competing claims to a pig.[57] Luffman reported that "the public whipper is a white man, who executes his office by a negroe deputy, and the price for every flogging is two bits."[58] Slaves suspected of flagrant offenses, such as fomenting rebellion, were burned at the stake or stretched on racks or wheels in public. Enslaved people moved about the town with a remarkable degree of freedom, but these punitive landmarks constantly reminded them of their unfree status.

FIGURE 1.5. Mill Yard on Gamble's Estate, St. John Parish (1823). Aquatint by William Clark, *Ten Views in the Island of Antigua: In Which Are Represented the Process of Sugar Making, and the Employment of the Negroes, in the Field, Boiling-house and Distillery* (London: Thomas Clay, 1823). Courtesy of the John Carter Brown Library at Brown University.

While the character of St. John's was distinct from that of the country-side, not much distance separated the town from the surrounding rural estates. People from all social strata regularly traversed the roads leading from the plantations to the capital, whether on horse or by foot. Goods, news, and ideas moved just as freely between the two locales. The countryside remained more sparsely populated than the town, but it was densely packed with cane stalks. The predominance of sugar cane determined who was powerful and powerless in Antigua and shaped the order of life for both groups. The names that designate many places in Antigua today are still English and Scottish surnames, attesting to their possession by the first white men who arrived, hoping to gain riches from sugar (see figure 1.5).[59] The ruins of stone-built sugar mills, hollowed out with time as the staple crop's preeminence dwindled in the twentieth century, still dot the countryside (see figure 1.6).

FIGURE 1.6. Ruin of a sugar mill on Rooms Estate, St. Philip Parish (2009). Photograph by the author.

A few swaths of rural land had other uses, such as cattle grazing or growing other agricultural foodstuffs; slaves' small provision grounds were especially important. But, as a visitor in 1802 noted, "the sugar plantation . . . is the prevailing scenery in the interior of this island. . . . The green fields of cane . . . were intermixed with provision grounds of yams and eddoes, or the dark and regular parterres of holed land prepared for the reception of the succeeding year's plant-canes. A large windmill on each estate; the planter's dwelling house and sugar-works, with the negro huts, in their beautiful groves of oranges, plantains and cocoanut trees, completed a landscape that continually recurred in passing over the island."[60] This description assigns a pleasant and pastoral character to sugar estates. Yet plantation space was founded largely on coercion and violence.

Everywhere black people would have ventured in the countryside carried reminders of their toil and their status as owned, and often as disposable bodies. The small, dilapidated houses in which slaves dwelled on estates stood in the shadow of the more imposing structures in which planters and their families lived, and of the stone and wooden windmills for processing canes. Beyond the social inequities communicated by the spatial layout, plantations also equipped themselves to inflict corporal punishment on slaves who transgressed the rules. Dungeons imprisoned the recalcitrant, irons and chains restricted slave movement, and wooden gallows, wheels, or trees displayed the bodies or body parts of enslaved lawbreakers, dead or alive. Luffman catalogued the disciplinary instruments that slaves knew all too well:

> The thumb-screw, a barbarous invention to fasten the thumbs together, . . . appears to cause excruciating pain. The iron necklace, is a ring, locked or rivetted [sic] about the neck; to these collars are frequently added what are here termed pot-hooks, additions, resembling the hooks or handles of a porridge pot, fixed perpendicularly, the bent or hooked parts turning outwards, which prevents the wearers from laying down their heads with any degree of comfort. The boots are strong iron rings, full four inches in circumference, closed just above the ankles [and] to these some owners prefix a chain, which the miserable sufferers, if able to work, must manage as well they can.[61]

By 1829, more than 140 plantations were operating in Antigua.[62] We can assume that all were replete with the punitive accouterments necessary to maintain chattel slavery in the face of continual resistance by those subjected to it. Whether pronounced guilty by formal trials or by an owner's whim, slaves suspected of wrongdoing in town or country were subjected to bodily torture. The violent tools and rituals that exacted extreme pain and often wrought a slow death were aimed to ensure the obedience of other slaves, who were forced to witness their use. Despite or, perhaps, because of the skewed population ratios and lack of policing that existed in Antigua, whites still peppered the island's landscape with threatening reminders that they wielded absolute power.

The harrowing routine of sugar production clearly manifested the inescapabilty of white power. Since the late seventeenth century, slaves laboring on most of Antigua's sugar plantations could expect a standard six-day workweek from Monday to Saturday, with Sundays off.[63] The workday averaged between twelve and eighteen hours. The labor force was usually divided into three gangs. The first, or "great," gang of able-bodied women and men between sixteen and fifty years of age performed the heaviest tasks, including manuring, hoeing, and weeding fields and planting cane. Lighter tasks in sugar cultivation were done by the second gang, which usually included twelve- to sixteen-year-olds. In addition, the second gang could include new mothers; recent, unseasoned arrivals from Africa; and some aging slaves. These two gangs usually reported to a driver, typically an enslaved but privileged adult male who enjoyed some trust and influence among plantation owners and managers. The driver was responsible for overseeing gang work and, when he or others in authority deemed it necessary, meting out corporal punishment. Children as young as four or five years old and the oldest or most infirm slaves formed the third gang, performing such tasks as collecting grass to feed livestock, carrying water, and cleaning fields of excess leaves, which were used as fuel at the mills, where sugar was processed.

The intricacy of sugar production demanded careful timing. Newly planted cane took anywhere from twelve to eighteen months to mature. Planting was done in the rainy season from September to December, but Antigua was prone to droughts and unpredictable rainfall, so this schedule was always subject to adjustment. Enslaved workers had to weed and manure the fields and dig cane holes and trenches for planting, often with makeshift tools. Like the other small Leeward Islands, Antigua had stiffer, drier soil than other territories in the region, which made digging and planting more strenuous. Here, as throughout the Caribbean, enslaved people's unremitting labor in sugar was debilitating to their health.

During the harvest, which usually fell in the dry period from January to June, fieldworkers were often denied their customary day off and expected to work longer hours each day. Field hands had to be available around the clock to perform the industrial-scale labors that transformed raw cane into the profitable trifecta of sugar, rum, and molasses. The towering plants grew to nearly ten feet tall. In addition to cutting the large and weighty stalks, slaves had to carry them to the mill for crushing right away. If not, the fermentation process would begin quickly in the hot weather, drastically reducing the sugar crystal content of the cane juice. Fieldworkers had to feed the canes into the sugar mills, which used heavy iron or wood rollers to extract the juice. Then the juice was sent through pipes or gutters to the boiling house. After being boiled and cooled several times, the raw sugar was taken to the curing house. Accidents that maimed or killed enslaved workers were especially frequent in the milling and boiling stages, particularly because of their exhaustion from endless days and nights of heavy toil.

Other occupations essential to the functioning of a sugar plantation were just as demanding but enabled slaves to avoid fieldwork. Carpenters, masons, and blacksmiths built and maintained the machinery and buildings used to process sugar canes. Coopers made the barrels used to store and ship sugar. Boilers managed and correctly timed the

processes by which cane juice was transformed into sugar, rum, or molasses. These positions carried some prestige and were filled by those
whom estate owners and managers trusted. Moreover, these jobs were
deemed "skilled" and held exclusively by enslaved men, which fostered
gender inequity within the slave labor force. Field labor and all other
tasks performed by women were always classified as "unskilled," a false
divide that created gender divergences in social privileges under slavery
and differential wages after emancipation.[64] These artificial and skewed
distinctions of gender and skill level were mutually reinforcing and socially influential, since women composed the majority of field hands in
Antigua and throughout the region.

Enslaved women also held positions on plantations that were particular to their sex. Many domestic tasks came under the purview of
women, who toiled as maids, cooks, nannies, wet nurses, seamstresses,
and washerwomen. While both contemporary white observers and many
historians have represented these chores as lighter than those performed
by field hands and embedded with some social privilege, they were labor-
intensive and dangerous in their own way. Enslaved domestics in the
countryside, like their town-based counterparts, were particularly vulnerable to physical and sexual abuse because they labored so closely to
their owners.[65] By the seventeenth century, most domestics in Antigua
and the other Leewards were of mixed ancestry, since African domestic
workers were subject to the sexual advances of white men and enslaved
children often followed the same occupations as their parents. A similar color code existed among male domestic workers and skilled male
workers in sugar production; men of mixed ancestry tended to dominate
those coveted positions. Customary distinctions built on gradations of
skin color bore complicated consequences for how slaves lived, loved,
labored, and occupied space on sugar estates. Lighter-skinned slaves of
both sexes had access to better jobs and housing.[66] Those with visible
European ancestry were more likely to enjoy the few privileges available
within the system, while those of mainly African origin were consistently
relegated to the most undervalued and strenuous work and shabbiest
quarters. The hierarchy of gender, race, and class that distinguished
between African- and European-descended Antiguans all too easily replicated itself in relationships among African-descended people.

Such complicated social hierarchies communicated the extreme subjection that the condition of enslavement entailed. Yet enslaved people's

ways of life also suggested that they tempered their subjection with actions that expressed various forms of quotidian self-interest and resistance. A closer look at the place of Sunday marketing in the slave routine offers some insight not only into the physical and social constraints of enslaved people's existence but also into the subversive possibilities of their everyday acts.

The Market as a Site of Autonomy, Community, and Resistance

Sunday was the holiday for slaves all across the island, providing a welcome respite from their demanding weekday labors. Some owners also allowed half-days on Saturdays. Most slaves enjoyed a few days off around Christmas and Easter.[67] In theory, this schedule allowed for religious observance, but slaves used this time "to amuse themselves or carry on their own affairs as they saw fit."[68] The most important of slaves' business affairs was selling goods on their own behalf, which took place principally in the towns and involved both urban and rural residents. By the early 1690s, this traffic was so significant in Antigua and elsewhere in the Leeward Islands that the joint legislature passed a law to regulate it.[69] Over the next century, an extensive series of laws attempted to curtail the continued expansion of slave huckstering.[70] New regulations were constantly imposed as marketing became firmly entrenched within the slave routine in Antigua. Although colonial elites increasingly associated it with disorderly behavior, the market offered slaves an occasion for socializing, entrepreneurship, and cultural validation within a dehumanizing work regime.

Slaves used their open-air marketplaces, especially in St. John's, to form what Stephanie Camp has termed a *rival geography* that defied the spatial confines of their enslavement. Camp argues that a rival geography comprised "alternative ways of knowing and using plantation . . . space that conflicted with planters' ideals and demands. . . . Where planters' mapping of their farms was defined by fixed places for plantation residents, the rival geography was characterized by motion: the movement of bodies, objects, and information within and around plantation space."[71] The interlinked issues of enslaved people's uncontrollable mobility and their illicit occupation of public space underline their engagement with the market, as well as whites' alarm at its continued existence over the eighteenth and early nineteenth centuries.

Independent marketing was a quintessential feature of slavery in the Americas, as slaves from Charleston to Kingston, Bahia, and beyond took advantage of the economic and social benefits to be had from trading goods among one another and with free people of color and local whites. Marketing was simultaneously subversive and supportive of slave owners' interests.[72] It enabled owners to reduce the rations they provided to their slaves, but the independent socializing it allowed and the pecuniary gains it brought contradicted the submissiveness expected of their human property. Huckstering even enabled some enslaved people to earn enough money to purchase their freedom. Marketing took varied forms around the Americas. In the British Caribbean, local authorities and elites made uneasy compromises that allowed slaves to conduct their markets fairly independently. In contrast, owners in parts of the United States interfered with the marketing activities of enslaved people and in some instances halted them altogether.[73] Marketing was a highly disputed privilege, in no small part because it encouraged activities approximating freedom among the enslaved.

The place of the market in the routine of Antigua's slaves and the social networks that marketing sustained provide a rare view into slaves' material culture and community formation. The market was also a gendered space. Women in particular oversaw the cultivation of provision grounds and the transportation of produce to market, either by themselves or with their children.[74] The organization of these activities in the Americas reflected customs germane to enslaved people's African pasts. Scholars have identified women as the primary producers and distributors of food in precolonial marketplaces in West Africa, and the evidence reveals that this pattern was continued among those in the diaspora.[75] In Antigua, huckstering was likely the sole opportunity for enslaved women to enjoy physical mobility, for they worked principally in the fields and rarely held positions that allowed the sort of movement about the island that enslaved men in skilled occupations enjoyed. Women predominated in the most consistent and significant sites for tasting freedom before formal abolition.

The modest income that enslaved people derived from huckstering gave them a limited degree of economic independence from their owners. Slaves grew the foodstuffs they sold to other slaves as well as to whites.[76] Compared with larger islands in the Caribbean, Antigua had less land available for slave self-provisioning, as proprietors hoarded the majority of arable acreage.[77] Not all plantation slaves enjoyed access to personal provision grounds. Much of the fruits and vegetables that fed Antiguan slaves were imported, because commercial sugar production was more profitable than subsistence-oriented agriculture. Unlike slaves in Jamaica or Trinidad, who farmed on sizable provision grounds that yielded extensive crops for sale as well as consumption, Antiguan slaves, like their counterparts in Barbados, utilized their small grounds and even bartered their rations.[78] When they had no own produce of their own to sell, they obtained it in other ways, including theft from plantation storehouses. Raw materials such as wood made their way to the market, as they were useful for fixing up uninhabitable slave quarters; grass typically used for livestock feed was harvested surreptitiously for sale.[79] Antiguan slaves consistently devised ways to extract free time during their demanding work routine and ensured that their labor and tools were not entirely dedicated to planters' profits. Ultimately, despite the small scale of slaves' own agricultural activities in Antigua, provisioning and marketing mattered considerably to their familial and community livelihoods.

Johnston Browne, who traveled to Antigua in 1832, reported that enslaved people on the estates he visited eagerly spent their breakfast and lunch breaks during the workweek tending provision grounds, in addition to the Saturday half-days that some masters allowed for that purpose. His observations of enslaved women's marketing practices reveal valuable details regarding the gendered nature of marketing in Antigua and the strategies women employed amid their everyday routines to ensure their ability to market:

> As soon as a woman finds that she is pregnant & often before, she tells the manager, to procure an assumption [exemption] from work & punishments. From that day she does little or nothing & although she may be kept in the weeding gang she packs her head up in a blanket or she lies down under a tree all the day long. While under observation & when otherwise she gets away to pick grass for sale, and often leaving the Estate & carrying heavy loads of her own goods into the town. It is by no means uncommon to meet 5 or 10 pregnant women who have been for months refusing to earn a penny for their master carrying large loads of yams or potatoes to town. They carry on a regular trade in marketing on those Estates where they are not sharply looked after. This opens a door for great deception. I have known a woman 20 months absent from her work before she was delivered.[80]

Despite Browne's condemnation of all work outside of sugar as a form of laziness and his scorn for enslaved women's mendacity, he confirms both women's centrality to marketing and the tactics they used to assert control over their time.

Although scholars have suggested that Caribbean planters often ignored amelioration measures, Brown's laments indicate that enslaved women actively claimed its gendered benefits, namely the mandate that removed women from the first field gang during early pregnancy and excused them from work entirely in its later stages.[81] This measure reflected slave owners' anxiety about the low rate of live births among enslaved women. The strenuous labor required of women, which caused frequent miscarriages and stillbirths, undermined their value as breeders.[82] Browne recognized that enslaved women used the respite allowed for pregnancy to siphon off time and goods for their own benefit, challenging the sole use of their bodies for the enrichment of their owners. In investing their time and energy in this rival geography, enslaved women escaped from continued misuse and confinement on the plantation to a space that was culturally familiar and materially central to their livelihoods.

At the markets, enslaved people circulated local currency to a limited extent, but most goods were bartered rather than exchanged directly for cash.[83] This thriving activity had a substantial effect on the internal economy of the island. Slaves' burgeoning market activity dismayed white merchants in St. John's; as early as 1742, they complained about the unwelcome competition, the inflated prices allegedly charged by slave hucksters, and the theft that marketing purportedly entailed.[84] Whites constantly worried that huckstering stimulated stealing from plantations, ranging from covertly taking milk from cows to illicitly collecting fodder in the pastures. Particularly galling was the sale of cane stalks and sugar purloined from their storehouses to confectioners who made and sold sweets. Planters made repeated, albeit futile, attempts to halt slave theft and the bartering of provisions.

Whites also complained about the prevalence of slaves trading the food and supplies given to them twice weekly by their owners, commenting that slaves exchanged their rations "for anything that took their fancy," with "no thoughts of a 'rainy day,'" and then found themselves in a state of "starvation" by the end of the week. In 1814, at the request of local planters, a law was passed to prohibit this practice.[85] Theft was so intertwined with the bartering system that it may explain why marketing was so profitable for enslaved people. In addition to the supplies they were given and the produce they grew, Antiguan slaves probably exchanged goods they had taken from their owners' supplies for those of better quality or greater usefulness. It seems implausible that enslaved families endured weekly "starvation" because they made frivolous bargains. Indeed, the 1814 legislation appears less a paternalistic effort to protect slaves from their own unsound judgment than a measure intended to protect owners from slaves whose interests clashed with their own. Planters and administrators criminalized the practices that slaves found necessary to generate personal wealth and foster beneficial economic and social relationships. Equally important, marketing may have served as a milieu in which slaves imagined a reordering of Antiguan society through their own individual and collective efforts.

Mary Prince openly discussed the subversive possibilities of huckstering in the streets of St. John's, which she clandestinely performed during the gaps in her routine as an urban domestic laborer: "The way in which I made my money was this. When my master and mistress went from home, as they sometimes did, and left me to take care of the house and premises, I had a good deal of time to myself, and made the most of it. I took in washing, and sold coffee and yams and other provisions to the captains of ships. I did not sit still idling during the absence of my owners; for I wanted by all honest means, to earn money to buy my freedom." Prince's endeavors to earn and save the funds to pay her purchase price, though unsuccessful, reveal how garnering money as a vendor supported aspirations to escape enslavement.[86]

Some enslaved and free black hucksters could be found selling various items at the public market near the Long Street courthouse, while others moved about the streets with their goods. Smaller public markets were located at Parham, Falmouth, and English Harbour. But the island's slaves most often marketed their wares in Otto's Pasture, an expansive lot situated just south of the town in the parish of St. John. This market typically was held on Sunday mornings. Otto's Pasture was apparently the exclusive domain of Antigua's African-descended population.[87] Its location near main roads extending to the eastern, central, and southern sections of the island made it more accessible than other markets, and enslaved people on plantations well outside town frequently walked there carrying their wares.[88] Despite the 1702 law mandating that slaves leaving the plantation have a pass or a white chaperone, masses of slaves transported their produce to the town market from quite distant plantations and remained there well after the market ended without either of these legal requirements.[89] Enslaved Antiguans collectively refused to comply with pass laws, and their disobedience was tolerated as long as it did not foment public disorder. When examined more deeply, however, the activities associated with the market reveal it as a primary site of quotidian slave resistance.

"An assemblage of many hundred negroes and mulattoes" arrived at Otto's Pasture from about 6:00 a.m. on a typical Sunday, according to Luffman. He viewed black and brown crowds trading such perishables as fruit, vegetables, fish, and meat, as well as other wares and supplies in a raucous and, to him, unsavory setting:

> The noise occasioned by the jabber of the negroes, and the squalling and cries of the children basking in the sun, exceeds any thing I ever heard in a London market: The smell is also intolerable, proceeding from the strong effluvia, naturally arising from the bodys of these people, and from the stinking salt-fish and other offencibles sent for sale by hucksters, which the negroes will buy, even when in the last stage of rottenness, to season their pots with, and I do not exaggerate when I say that the nostrills will receive the fragrance of this place, when at the distance of a full quarter of a mile from it, to leeward.[90]

Trading at Otto's ended in the afternoon, when marketgoers traversed the streets in search of amusements for the rest of the day. Slaves openly engaged in what Antiguan elites considered indecorous or improper pastimes, including boxing matches and gambling with dice made from seashells.[91] According to Mrs. Lanaghan, an early historian of Antigua, "the Sunday markets were indeed a nuisance most properly got rid of, for they engendered all kinds of dissipation among the lower classes on the Lord's day."[92] A 1740 report to the legislature complained about the proliferation of "dramshops," or barrooms, near the "Negro Market."[93] Apparently, slaves did not feel compelled to maintain sobriety or public order on Sundays, much to the dismay of Antiguan authorities. White contemporaries expressed similar sentiments about the disorder that attended Sunday markets elsewhere around the Caribbean in the eighteenth and nineteenth centuries. A Barbadian catechist in 1725 lamented that "on the Lord's Day, [slaves] work and merchandize for themselves; in the latter of which they are assisted, not only by the Jews, but many of those who call themselves Christians." In 1819 a Jamaican missionary observed: "On a Sunday, . . . several thousands of human beings, of various nations and colours, but principally Negroes, instead of worshipping their Maker on His Holy Days, were busily employed in all kinds of traffick in the open streets." Similarly, Edward Long, who penned A History of Jamaica in 1774, decried the socializing and merriment among Jamaican slaves after the Sunday market:

> It is certain that the sabbath-day, as at present it is passed, is by no means a respite from labour: on the contrary, the Negroes, either employing it on their grounds, or in travelling a great distance to some market, fatigue themselves much more on that day, than on any other in the week. The forenoon of that day, at least might be given to religious duties; but I think it rather desirable than otherwise, that the after-part of it should be spent on their grounds, instead of being uselessly dissipated in idleness and lounging, or (what is worse) in riot, drunkenness, and wickedness.[94]

In Antigua, the language of the numerous and ineffective acts intended to curtail these activities indicates local whites' growing concern over the impropriety of enslaved people's conduct and the potential threat to security that it posed. An act of 1723, for example, required the presence of constables and militia while the market was in progress, because slaves "assemble in great Numbers in and about the Town of St. John's and commit Riots, and sometimes kill one another, to the great Terror and actual endangering of the Inhabitants."[95] This act's invocation of "riots" and insinuation of murder may have overstated the dangers posed by sporting events such as the boxing matches that Luffman observed. On the other hand, slaves' assumption of a threatening public comportment may have been a scare tactic to deter white intrusions into this all-black communal space. In this light, the 1831 uprising in defense of the market was not an unprecedented outburst; rather, it represented an expression of enslaved people's growing resentment against repeated encroachments on an institution central to their community.

Afternoon amusements included less questionable activities such as chatting in the town's streets and attending weekly dances. Dancing, Luffman remarks, was vital to making Sundays "the negroes' holiday." This rare and vivid description of slave socializing is worth quoting at length, as it identifies the dance moves, instruments, and music as distinctly African and acknowledges them as cultural expressions of the slaves' African origins:

> Negroes are very fond of the discordant notes of the banjar [sic], and the hollow sound of the toombah. The banjar is somewhat similar to the guitar, the bottom, or under part, is formed of one half of a large calabash, to which is prefixed a wooden next [neck], and it is strung with cat-gut and wire. This instrument is the invention of, and was brought here by the African negroes, who are most expert in the performances thereon, which are principally their own country tunes, indeed do I not remember ever to have heard anything like European numbers from its touch. The toombah is similar to the tabor, and has gingles of tin or shells, to this music (if it deserves the name) I have seen a hundred or more dancing at a time, their gestures are extravagant . . . but their agility and the surprising command of their limbs, is astonishing; this can be accounted for only by their being habituated to a warm climate, where elasticity is more general than in the colder latitude.[96]

Luffman exhibits an imperialist viewpoint laden with the assumption of European superiority. Moreover, his designation of slaves' folkways as purely "African" might be an overstatement, since European influences had likely crept into enslaved people's cultural practices by the time he recorded these impressions in 1788. But even he, an outsider to Antiguan society, understood that these performances distinguished slaves culturally from their masters. Although slaves may well have engaged in music and dancing in other settings, the market was a principal site where this culturally significant activity took place.

Enslaved people of all ages, from elders to small children, could be found at Otto's. The presence of slave families at the market, where these and other forms of cultural expression were enacted, indicates its importance in enslaved people's rival geography, fostering community building and cultural propagation over generations. Socializing there encouraged identities beyond that of "slave," a status that stripped persons of African descent of their uniqueness, kin and communal ties, cultural heritage, and creativity and reduced them to bare labor power.[97] At the market, plantation slaves came into contact with town slaves in a space that was rarely subject to planters' watchful eyes. If Luffman's reference to "many hundred negroes and mulattoes" is broadly construed, it is likely that free black and mixed-race people also patronized the market at Otto's. The 1831 uprising may well be evidence of the seditious effects of enslaved people's weekly exposure to alternative ways of life.[98]

The places where African and creole slaves and free people of color interacted and enjoyed themselves with little white interference carried a multilayered significance. Time at the market represented a welcome diversion from the physical and psychological burdens of slavery and generated a sense of collectivity. The pastimes that slaves pursued during and after the market were open transgressions of the colonial order. Although these activities were not strictly politicized acts of resistance, some participants understood the subversive nature of their pursuits and deliberately used them as a space to plan for or engage in acts that directly challenged their subordination. Otto's Pasture was deeply tied to the history of slave resistance in Antigua. A century earlier, slaves armed with cutlasses and guns gathered several times at Otto's for rituals and planning sessions before the famed 1736 slave conspiracy.[99] In similar fashion, hundreds of disgruntled slaves acted in unison in 1831, suggesting that enslaved patrons collectively assessed the best methods of protecting the market as a prominent site of slave autonomy, community, and culture on the eve of abolition.

Conclusion

Antigua resembled other colonial Caribbean societies in many respects. White planters built a slave society replete with the restrictions of time and space that made possible the exploitation of all African-descended people; indeed, the exploitation of their bodies was the foundation of daily life. Enslaved people performed grueling labor in town and country under the constant threat of humiliating and sadistic forms of corporal punishment. Barbuda exhibited a distinct form of slavery that was unlike that of Antigua and most other sugar islands, but even this nonplantation regime involved discernible patterns of abuse.

At the same time, African-descended people generated a rival geography and alternative social milieu. Slaves marked the public and private sites they traversed with their own ways of life and pursuit of self-interest. Their Sunday market represents the most spectacular of numerous forms of subversive quotidian practices that stretched their free time and expanded their space, restoring their sense of humanity and community. As the next chapter shows, slaves' collective resort to mass rebellion in 1831 to uphold their right to market appears less anomalous when viewed as an extension of their regular defiance of the boundaries their owners erected around mobility. The mixed results of this rebellion reflect the unresolved tensions between customary allowances and ironclad prohibitions Antiguan whites mobilized that were productive of both slaves' compliance and their transgression.

....

CHAPTER 2

"SO THEM MAKE LAW FOR NEGRO, SO THEM MAKE LAW FOR MASTER"

Antigua's 1831 Sunday Market Rebellion

It is very wrong, I know, to work on Sunday or go to market; but will not God call the Buckra men to answer for this on the great day of judgment—since they will give the slaves no other day?—MARY PRINCE, *The History of Mary Prince, a West Indian Slave*

A measure promoting public piety triggered a widespread conflagration in Antigua in March 1831. The colonial legislature, in part with the encouragement of local clergy and the metropolitan government, abolished the island's Sunday market to keep the Sabbath "holy." In response, enslaved people staged a public protest in the market and, over the subsequent days, set fires on several plantations. The circumstances surrounding this disturbance allow us to explore slaves' grievances that were connected to the institution of the Sunday market but also extended well beyond it. This chapter investigates why slaves regarded their free time to market, which legislators saw as an unofficial courtesy extended by slave owners, as their legally protected right, worth risking serious punishment to defend. Both slave marketing and this uprising, which occurred three years before legal emancipation in the British colonies, show how slaves' everyday lives politicized them and reveal that notions of freedom were circulated and contested in Antigua and the broader English Atlantic world well before 1834.[1]

In Antigua, as in most of the Caribbean, slave marketing was an established custom, but the law did not protect either the time or the space to market. Masters generally maintained this ad hoc system of intermittent free time on weekends and holidays but reserved the right to change it. Antigua's slave owners believed that the market allowed slaves to transgress regulations regarding provisioning and rations, free time and mobility, and public conduct. But for much of the eighteenth and early nineteenth centuries, colonial legislators could not curb slave marketing, despite whites' constant complaints about the "misconduct" that the market engendered among slaves. Enslaved Antiguans regarded the market as a central element in their lives and livelihoods. They treated marketing as an inalienable right and grew incensed by masters' attempts to infringe on it and, by extension, on their free time in general. In the Sunday market, slaves' material pursuits were conjoined with cultural exchange. As their largest and most prominent meeting place, the market created the conditions for slaves to see themselves collectively, as a community with similar origins and common cause. Material needs alone did not drive enslaved people's protests in defense of the Sunday market; they also felt compelled to protect a unique social world in which they realized alternative visions for their lives.

The events following the market ban showed enslaved people's collective and deliberate insistence on defending their interests. Despite their subjugated position, slaves claimed particular rights, including the right to market, and felt that those in power should recognize those rights even though they ran counter to the colonial economic and social hierarchy. Enslaved Antiguans on occasion not only subverted the law but also used the law—or, rather, their perceptions of the law—to secure some autonomy in colonial society. In this way, Antiguan slaves, like their counterparts throughout the Caribbean region, constructed themselves whenever necessary or expedient as colonial subjects with legal standing.[2]

The market's legal undoing linked to broader developments in the British Empire aimed at preparing slaves for emancipation and a system of formally free labor. Changing imperial policy toward the Caribbean colonies and burgeoning abolitionism in Britain underlay the 1831 conflagration. Parliament's 1823 amelioration measures aimed to reverse slavery's catastrophic demographic consequences through regulation of punishments and sustenance, and they also tried to reshape enslaved people's social practices into the mold of Christian convention. Amelioration informed growing local concern for Sabbath observance and lay behind the market ban. The outlawing of Sunday marketing was also connected to the increased missionary presence on the island and the influence of clergy on colonial customs and legislation. Moreover, as abolitionism and the ideology of free trade gained currency, slave owners across the empire faced the possibility of legal emancipation within the foreseeable future. These discussions of abolition on the horizon reached the ears of enslaved women and men, and critical bits of information about their future played a role in slave uprisings not just in Antigua but also around the British Caribbean.

By 1830, after three decades of parliamentary interference in master-slave relations, rising abolitionist sentiment, and some newsworthy slave rebellions in the region, Antiguan elites were gravely concerned. Unsupervised Sunday marketing and its potential to generate further illicit acts symbolized the dangers posed by emancipation to whites' control of an already "depraved" black populace. Their alarm may have prompted local legislators to enforce the law mandating that enslaved people reserve Sundays for Christian observance, after decades of tolerating the illegal assemblies at the market. But this measure backfired.

Maintaining social control in the British Caribbean during the last decades of slavery was an anxiety-ridden enterprise. Vigilant administrators tried to suppress the uncontrollable murmurs about freedom that accompanied every measure regarding slavery decreed by the Crown. Slaves' intermittent attempts to test the truth of these rumors through collective and violent action prompted panic among whites. Renewed white hysteria after slave uprisings caused an unwelcome increase in the surveillance and policing of slaves. But such palpable fear might have also indicated to Afro-Caribbean slaves that they had some power over slave owners that had significant implications for how slaves interacted with one another and with whites.

Ideas about freedom and a sense of abolition's imminence among both slaves and masters had disruptive effects around the Caribbean after 1800. Enslaved Antiguans moved in unison to protect the Sunday market as a precious and time-honored autonomous space in their otherwise oppressive routine. The controversy created an unprecedented occasion for them to voice their grievances regarding their labor and living conditions. Their choice to fight the ban with fires in the cane fields and their continued challenges to the authorities despite the brutal suppression of this rebellion signified their conviction that changes to their status were under way in London but whites on the island were blocking this progress. Ultimately, the 1831 rebellion suggests the contradictory and fluid senses of what freedom would mean among colonial authorities, clergy, and, above all, enslaved people after its official arrival in 1834.[3]

Anxious Missionaries, Reluctant Lawmakers,
and Sabbath Observance in the Amelioration Era

For more than a century prior to the 1831 uprising, administrators, clergy, and merchants in Antigua had raised concerns about the merits of holding a market on the Sabbath. But the law was not used to prohibit these activities until the end of the eighteenth century. How the Sunday market came under attack in Antigua is best understood in tandem with the history of amelioration and the simultaneous rise of abolitionism in Britain. Amelioration itself generated much anxiety among white elites. Caribbean colonialists initially supported amelioration laws, which promoted the natural increase of the enslaved population and made slavery appear more benign, because they seemed more promising ways of preserving the institution and co-opting abolitionism than previous efforts.[4] The first stages of the amelioration process were concurrent with the unfolding of the Haitian Revolution and parliamentary discussions about the abolition of the slave trade.[5] The joint legislature of the Leeward Islands passed its first slave amelioration act in 1798. This act set standard rations of clothing and food, required the provision of medical care, and directed owners to encourage morality among slaves through such practices as monogamous marriage, baptism, and church attendance. Although it did not directly prohibit the Sunday market, that sentiment was clearly implicit in the expectation that slaves would worship weekly.[6]

Sunday observance concerned missionaries in the Leeward Islands much more than it did legislators.[7] Several decades into their proselytizing mission in Antigua, they still found themselves unable to convince the island's African-descended residents to keep the Sabbath. Church attendance was the foremost method to ensure "Christian conduct" on Sundays. But the Methodists and Moravians, the two sects that had been evangelizing among enslaved and free black people since the mid-eighteenth century, could not claim a majority of the black population as adherents.[8] Church leaders and devout members kept an eye on more wayward congregants' Sunday pursuits, but could not ensure that they attended religious services consistently. And enslaved people who belonged to no church at all were free from such influences. Nonbelievers likely preferred attending the various markets around the island to filling church benches. Even white merchants in St. John's, who may have been affiliated with the Anglican Church, kept their retail shops open on Sundays well into the 1820s.[9] Enslaved, free colored, and white people alike regularly "profaned" Sundays by conducting trade. Indeed, there is no indication that the church attendance provision of the 1798 act was enforced among any group in Antigua. Additional legislation to regulate the Sunday activities of enslaved and free Antiguans of all races was deemed necessary because previous laws had been ignored.

In a colony established solely for commodity production and profit, both free and enslaved subjects privileged secular pursuits over religion until forced by the state to do otherwise. Missionaries deplored the widespread flouting of the Sabbath with labor, trade, and socializing. Although in the 1790s they lacked the political power to change Antiguans' conduct, they had enough influence on local customs and whites' opinions that their drive to see Sunday trading abolished required at least the appearance of an official response. Christian churches formed part of a broadening coalition throughout the empire that opposed unholy activities on the Sabbath, especially drinking and trading. Yet Antigua's slave owners and the legislators representing their interests dragged their feet on the issue, likely because the slaves' market had an economic function and served as a safety valve that helped to maintain peace on the island. In 1822, the legislature passed two bills mandating that all Antiguans observe Sundays properly, but they had little effect.[10]

The 1823 parliamentary legislation bore some similarities to the Leeward Islands acts of 1798 and 1822, but sought different ends. The Leeward Islands used amelioration to uphold and defend slavery, while Parliament expressly devised its 1823 amelioration measures so that "the slave populations of the colonies could be prepared for freedom."[11] The parliamentary measures might appear purely humanitarian in intent, but they reflected freedom's implicit conditionality, as British policy makers believed the empire's slaves required significant social improvement before becoming free subjects of the Crown. The program's stipulations included encouragement of marriage and the preservation of family ties, the admission of slaves' testimony in court, and the abolition of corporal punishment for enslaved women. In addition to ending the Sunday market, the recommendations called for the expansion of the Anglican

Church to ensure propriety among slaves on Sundays, implying that other Protestant missions, despite their longer history of evangelizing among enslaved people, had little success in improving their conduct.

Antigua's legislators avoided immediate implementation of Parliament's regulations and maintained the status quo, deeming metropolitan authorities too distant from the colonies and too misinformed by London's abolitionist camp to devise laws that met Caribbean slave owners' needs. As the planter and legislator Bertie Jarvis declared in 1824 in response to recent abolitionist propaganda circulating in the region, "Wilberforce's pamphlet has created a good deal of sensation here, as if he had ever witnessed the care & attention paid to the Negroes in this Island, he would have written very differently."[12] The tools of empire devised in the metropole often clashed with the colonialists' way of life. Legislators in Antigua and elsewhere in the Caribbean, though local agents of the Crown, did not shrink from challenging lawmakers in London in such cases. Slave owners believed that they cared well enough for slaves to refuse to comply with these new rules and reject metropolitan oversight.

Local authorities also waited to enforce amelioration measures in order to preserve "security," a concern directly mentioned in the correspondence between London and Antigua in 1823 and 1824.[13] As enslaved people overwhelmingly outnumbered whites, planters had an interest in maintaining public order by preserving the major features of the existing routine, including Sunday marketing. Additionally, authorities had to quell the rumors circulating in slave quarters around the island that amelioration and abolitionism meant that emancipation was close at hand. A Royal Proclamation was issued in January 1824 to inform Antigua's slaves that the legislature's endorsement of the amelioration program was not a decree of freedom from the Crown.[14] Regional reports of slave unrest following amelioration increased the panic of administrators in Antigua. Whites were horrified at the massive rebellion in Demerara that broke out only a month after amelioration was decreed; there, thirty thousand slaves rose up violently in response to local discussions of slaves' rights and questions about freedom.[15] This sequence mirrored the events of 1816 in Barbados, where twenty thousand slaves rebelled around the time of passage of the slave registry bill, another ameliorative measure that local colonial authorities did not welcome and that slaves suspected was connected with their impending freedom.[16]

Colonial administrators regarded these disturbances as the dangerous effects latent within parliamentary amelioration, while the British government viewed them as evidence of the need for more effective enforcement of the amelioration codes. The imperial officials especially favored the increased presence of Anglican clergy over those from other Protestant faiths in the Caribbean to ensure Christian conversion and morality among slaves. After the 1823 Demerara rebellion, which colonists accused London Missionary Society clergymen of agitating despite their documented disdain for the unrest, authorities in London concluded that missionaries from dissenting sects were less likely to inculcate obedience among slaves. The first two Anglican bishoprics were established in Jamaica and Barbados the next year.[17] The metropolitan government's discourse surrounding amelioration and the prevention of violent uprising was propelled by the belief in the efficacy of slaves' moral instruction, an argument that had been advanced for decades by Atlantic World evangelicals. Legislators in the colonies loathed such religious discourse but could no longer ignore it after 1823. Still, responsibility for the implementation of Parliament's laws lay with these obstinate colonial legislatures, which had little intention of troubling the local social fabric until they absolutely had to do so.

In Antigua, a flurry of legislation appeared to uphold Parliament's mandate to sanctify Sundays but in practice was ignored. In 1824, laws were passed for "more strict observance of the Lord's Day" through the imposition of duties on liquor, the licensing of liquor-serving establishments, and the closing of all retail shops on Sundays. Among the numerous clauses in the New Consolidated Slave Bill of 1827 was a prohibition of all market business past 10:30 on Sunday mornings.[18] These laws were not enforced; appeasing the metropolitan government was important to local officials, but ultimately slave owners' interests took priority. By 1830 Britain's emancipationists were openly advocating immediate abolition of slavery rather than a gradual transition to freedom.[19] Drastic legal action on the part of the colonies seemed necessary to hold on to their dying way of life, and Antigua's legislature complied.

Amelioration sought outright cultural refashioning of slaves through measures especially crafted to "civilize" and groom them for freedom, which did not bode well for the Sunday market. The Crown, influenced by the powerful combination of evangelism and abolitionism, refused to turn a blind eye to those who openly profaned Sundays. Missionaries in the colonies and the supporters of metropolitan abolitionism both played a role in the Crown's vigilance on this issue. Eventually, colonial administrators had to follow London's orders regarding not only Sunday conduct but also the conditions under which slaves were forced to live and labor. They reluctantly enforced legislation that made them uneasy while seeking to keep agitated slaves at bay.

Yet amelioration ultimately fell short of its aims, instead yielding unintended effects, including slave rebellion, which in some ways reinforced English perceptions of Afro-Caribbean people's "savagery." In general, amelioration produced mixed results for England's approach to its Caribbean colonies, because while some authorities responded to the Demerara and Jamaica rebellions with scorn, others expressed limited sympathy with the rebels and especially with missionaries, sometimes even viewing the plantocracy as "savage."[20] At base, this program and the shifts in discourse it prompted provided an opening for slaves around the British Caribbean to claim their perceived rights and to resort to violent measures when they were denied. In Antigua, long-standing tensions between colony and metropole were exacerbated by the debate over enslaved people's treatment. Slaves seized on the opening made by the market ban to raise questions about their rights as Crown subjects and, ultimately, about their freedom.

The Fatal Spark

On February 17, 1831, under direct international pressure, after a decade of weak statutes preceded by more than a century of reluctant enforcement of Sabbath observance, the legislature outlawed Sunday markets as of Sunday, March 20. The rising tensions, along with the circulating rumors about amelioration as a step toward freedom, might have prompted the Antiguan legislature's petition to King William IV, which was sent on the same day that the market ban was finally passed. The petition declared that if emancipation were decreed, compensation should immediately accompany it, not only to ensure that sugar production would continue without a captive labor force but also to fund military protection in the island colonies against the chaos they assumed abolition would trigger among the "Working Classes."[21] Like the slaves, legislators connected abolishing the market to the abolition of slavery itself and pronounced both as threats to public order. By calling slaves *working classes*, legislators inadvertently reinforced the slippage between race and class in colonial society and echoed concurrent anxieties unfolding in England regarding the management of "unruly" working-class whites.[22] Ironically, the clause about compensation foreshadowed events that took place two years later when the emancipation decree was officially passed by Parliament. Antiguan legislators at that time began to consider fully freeing the slaves rather than apprenticing them in order to justify the immediate receipt of compensation funds from the Crown. It seems that Antiguan elites could not conceive of abolition in any way that did not first attend to their rights of private property.

After the enactment of the Sunday market ban, Antigua's governor, Patrick Ross, feared the worst. He immediately called on parish magistrates to employ preemptive tactics and secure a commitment from estate proprietors or their attorneys to establish an alternative marketing day. But planters refused, having come to view the market's abolition as an opportunity to impose further controls over their slaves; the planters preferred that designating another day for marketing be left to their discretion. One planter put it bluntly: "[As] all the proprietors were in the habit of allowing their Negroes a day to sell anything when they wished, they look upon this as an interference on the part of the governor & are determined not to state any day but to allow their indulgences in proportion to their behaviour."[23] In opposing governmental interference in the master-slave relationship, planters in Antigua sought to block any further transgressions against their sovereignty. Given the real possibility of general emancipation in the near future, planters welcomed any new avenues for exercising control over their laborers' mobility and conduct.

While the tug-of-war between the governor and the planters continued, Antigua's enslaved women and men grew increasingly agitated as March 20 drew near. They took all opportunities to register their discontentment with the new measure. Jonathan Cadman, a white Methodist missionary who evangelized among enslaved communities around the region and may have gained Antiguan slaves' trust, witnessed the buildup before the rebellion.[24] In a letter to the Methodist headquarters in London, he revealed that during the days preceding the market's cessation, most slaves were "determined in their minds not to comply with the Law & threatening much evil to all who should interfere."[25] Visiting plantations near St. John's, Cadman observed slaves' angry reactions to the new law, particularly because no other free time in the week was allotted for marketing and other pursuits. While discussing the matter with them, he heard a telling utterance that indicates that slaves conceived of the entire issue quite differently from planters and administrators. Slave voices may be compromised when recorded in the correspondence of local whites. But since few sources present enslaved people's opinions during the events of 1831, the words that Cadman documented deserve close attention.

According to Cadman, "a great number of Slaves, all *without exception*, were willing to give up the Market if they could have another day, I advised them to wait & see what would be done for them, they said 'so them make Law for Negro, so them make Law for Master . . . give us the Day.'"[26] This bold assertion, while born of rage over the loss of their market day, suggests how Antiguan slaves understood the master-slave relationship. Slaves knew full well that the colonial social hierarchy placed them in a position of subservience to the planter class, but the phrase suggests a conception of the law as a social mediator. In this rendering, the law governed powerful local authorities as well as slaves, especially when decreed in Britain rather than devised locally by legislators with sugar estate interests. British law still subjugated people of African descent. But the slaves' statement shows their sense that law could potentially have the opposite effect.

Slaves who declared "so them make law for Negro, so them make law for Master" believed that masters could be compelled by law to accommodate their interests, just as they were compelled by law as well as brute force to accommodate those of masters. Furthermore, the phrase intimates enslaved people's assumptions that the law protected their free time, especially for marketing. The acceptance of such ad hoc customs for so long led slaves to assume the law upheld them.[27] Despite their degraded status, enslaved people staked a claim for their assumed rights, invoking the law as an institution that would enforce them. Or, at the very least, slaves were endeavoring to secure long-desired rights and hoped that such an assertion would usher them into existence. As it did elsewhere in the British Caribbean, parliamentary amelioration influenced Antiguan slaves' thinking on the subject of their rights and the use of law to ensure that masters did not violate them.[28] Over the next few months, Antigua's slaves took advantage of the upheaval of March 1831 to advocate their right to fair treatment by their masters and to raise questions about the possibility of freedom.

Cadman reported, "I have conversed with Hundreds, have gone to the gangs in the Fields, & spoke to them generally, and I have not found one [slave] reluctant to observe the Sabbath if he had another Day for the disposing of his foods. . . . Had a day been given, I am convinced that the Slaves of Antigua would have valued the Boon as highly & accepted it as gratefully, as any Slaves whatever."[29] His declaration raises the question of whether the amusements that followed the market, which were viewed as utterly profane on a Sunday, would be regarded as appropriate if they took place on any other day of the week. The missionary had a vested interest in circulating an image of enslaved people as obedient and potentially religious even in the most fraught moments. But his comments did not consider the fact that the market was also a weekly social event that involved such dubious pursuits such as drinking, gambling, and dancing. Cadman apparently believed that those slaves who previously chose to spend their Sundays at their leisure rather than at worship would immediately flock to the churches when the market day was rescheduled, though that outcome was not guaranteed.

By law, as of Sunday, March 20, the selling of goods on Sunday "in any of the markets, roads, streets, lanes, wharves or any other place within the Towns of this island" was to cease, with the exception of "milk, fresh fish, and horse fodder," which could be sold only during the hours not designated for church services. Anyone found in violation of this law faced a fine of twenty shillings. For all other marketing during the usual working days of the week, the act reiterated old and long-ignored pass laws stipulating that slave vendors had to obtain their owner's written permission.[30] March 20 was exactly two Sundays before Easter, which suggests a push to curtail improper activity during the holy season. Notice of the new regulations was "published by beat of Drum," and parish magistrates were charged with distributing copies of the act to the planters, who were to ensure that they were read publicly to the slaves.

Early on that fateful Sunday morning, a magistrate rode into the "Great Market" in St. John's, presumably at Otto's, announcing to all patrons that as of that moment, no marketing was allowed to take place. The slaves had reportedly prepared themselves to defend their market physically. Hundreds of enslaved men and women were waiting, not with products to vend, but "armed with strong bludgeons secured by twine to the wrists," refusing to be moved. As a group of Methodist missionaries reported to their fellows in England, "their language was frequently violent and menacing and accompanied by furious gesticulations and brandished cudgels. Matters appeared to assume a very threatening aspect. . . . The appearance of a detachment of the 86th regiment which was marched to the entrance of the Great Market, and then wheeled off up the New Street seemed for a few minutes to have struck the fatal spark."[31]

Following many "insolent and menacing" acts among this assemblage of armed slaves against authorities over the next few hours, the 86th Regiment proceeded to disperse the crowd and quell the disturbance, making about a half-dozen arrests.[32] No reports surfaced that any militia member was harmed, but the riotous protests continued throughout the day until "about half past six [when] the last company of 7 or 8 of obstinate women retired to the country."[33] This line hints at the gendered dimensions of this disturbance. Black women were at the forefront of the protest, as befits their dominant presence as vendors and patrons in the slaves' market. Throughout nineteenth-century Caribbean history, women appeared on the front lines of black uprisings.[34] Women's unmistakable presence in the 1831 rebellion and its aftermath broadens our sense of the contours of slave opposition by troubling the traditionally masculine cast of overt resistance.

The sources do not indicate that heated exchanges occurred at any of the island's smaller outlying markets, and the protest at Otto's was quickly controlled. But the slaves' oppositional acts to protect Sunday marketing were not limited to the day of the law's initial enforcement. Many more acts that expressed their anger and asserted their perceived rights occurred that night and during the weeks that followed. Most alarming to whites were the fires lit on six plantations on the night of March 20 and on fourteen more plantations the next night. Another three fires were set between March 22 and 23. On an island with approximately 140 plantations, twenty-three estates attacked by fire in just four nights did substantial damage to property and signified rebellion. Martial law was declared by Governor Ross and remained in effect for the next three weeks.[35]

The actions of both the slaves and the local authorities were marked by restraint, especially in comparison to other, much bloodier rebellions elsewhere in the region at the time. The protest at the market and the arson in its aftermath showed a remarkable level of militancy among slaves. But they took care to hide themselves after their illicit acts. And slaves stopped short of provoking the more effectively armed regiments to shoot at them, both during the initial encounter at the market and on the nights when the militia was dispatched to extinguish the fires. The absence of slave fatalities, coupled with the anxiety that preceded and followed these events, attests to whites' awareness of the precarious nature of their rule and their desire to avert a full-scale uprising. In an attempt to punish possible culprits and deter further incendiarism, eleven enslaved men were charged and tried as leaders of what seems to have been a collective and leaderless action. Of those men, six were acquitted, four were sentenced to a combination of imprisonment and lashings, and the last was publicly hanged.

As the initial restraint on both sides was followed by swift retribution, Antigua offered a cautionary tale to other colonies in the region. News of the fires traveled throughout the British-held territories in the Caribbean, and the actions of Antiguan slaves had reverberations in other islands. On March 28, 1831, the governor of Barbados, James Lyon, dispatched two companies of the 36th regiment and a limited number of Royal Artillery to ward off *suspected* uprisings among the slaves. These suspicions were based on rumors circulating among the slaves "that [their] freedom . . . had been granted by the King, but that [Lyon], the Governor, had withheld the boon" and that "in the event of insurrection [among the slaves], the King's Troops had received positive orders not to fire upon the insurgents."[36] Weeks of inaction by the Barbadian governor and legislative council in response to these rumors quickly gave way to panic as they heard news of plantations ablaze in Antigua and realized that the upcoming Easter holidays might prompt enslaved people to take action. Lyon made personal visits to all the parishes to address slaves and inform them that these rumors were erroneous. Reporting that the slaves appeared cooperative, Lyon admitted to the colonial secretary of state, Viscount Goderich, that the island's administrators were stirred to "greater vigilance than otherwise might have been deemed necessary" by the events in Antigua.[37] The 1831 uprising also affected the actions of local administrators in neighboring territories. In St. Vincent, the abolition of Sunday marketing and the establishment of a replacement day on Saturday was written into that island's Emancipation Act of 1834.[38]

While the Sunday market lay at the center of Antiguan slaves' mass protests in 1831, curiously, the authorities singled out only a few enslaved men for prosecution and did not name the market as the cause of the conflagration. While slaves fought collectively to protect their free time and the place they most often spent it, in court the entire episode was treated as an unrelated violation of private property.

The Scapegoat's Trial

During the course of the fires in Antigua, the 86th Regiment apprehended eleven enslaved male suspects. These men were speedily tried between March 26 and March 29. Six of the men were acquitted, two were sentenced to corporal punishment of fifty lashes, and another two were jailed in solitary confinement for one and three months, respectively, and received fifty lashes before and after their incarceration. The eleventh, John Kirwan, a slave belonging to Dr. Nicholas Nugent, was alleged to be the ringleader of the fires, though the sources suggest that he was more of a scapegoat than a culprit. Kirwan was tried, sentenced to death, and hanged in public on March 30. The records of his trial, which survive in the archive of the 1831 uprising, offer fascinating details about the early moments of the rebellion.[39]

Since slave women frequented the market in large numbers and the very last protesters forced to disperse from the market on the first day of its closure were "7 or 8 obstinate women," the absence of women from the group of suspected incendiaries suggests a gross oversight on the part of local authorities. Enslaved women might well have played a role in the setting of fires on twenty-three plantations over the three nights after the market was outlawed. Colonial authorities in Antigua seem to have conceived of slave resistance as a particularly male phenomenon, leading them to overlook women as agitators in this uprising. Perhaps the amelioration program's encouragement of less brutal treatment of enslaved women also curtailed the local militia's pursuit of possible female participants.[40] If rebellious women escaped detection, the remaining evidence is skewed, allowing us only to speculate that insurgent women might have been involved in the planning, execution, and propagation of the fires.

The proceedings of John Kirwan's trial shed some light on the confusion that surrounded these events. More important, the silences in the court documents suggest that administrators and planters refused to publicly acknowledge the danger posed by angry and organized slaves, as well as the reasons for their collective action. Kirwan's trial by court-martial began on March 26, 1831. The procedures used to try him differed from those used in criminal or civil cases in ordinary Anglo-American courts. The "judge advocate" presiding over the court functioned both as the prosecuting attorney for the state and as the judge, questioning the witnesses and handing down the final verdict. Nineteenth-century English courts-martial did not require judges to be impartial. Their primary role was to defend state power, as "the Judge Advocate prosecute[s] in the King's name." In Kirwan's trial, ten other individuals, called "members of the Court," heard the case. Unlike contemporary jurors, they did not vote to determine the ruling but were allowed to question the witnesses. They were required to have military rank, and direct involvement in the events on behalf of the state was not seen as a disqualifying bias.[41] The ten members of the court that tried Kirwan were all officers in the local regiment that apprehended the defendant and the other suspected arsonists. Three senior officers were also members of His Majesty's Council, which, along with the House of Assembly, formed the legislature that passed the law at the heart of the 1831 controversy.[42] In British colonies, council members were empowered both to make and enforce the laws, and enjoyed respect for their legal expertise.[43] The men who heard Kirwan's case were closely associated with his owner, Dr. Nicholas Nugent, a respected member of Antigua's planter elite, who served as a colonel in the militia and the speaker of the House of Assembly. The solid front created by the elite's control of the legal proceedings, as well as their shared commitment to maintaining order and protecting plantation property, did not bode well for Kirwan's fortunes in court. Although one enslaved man was called as a witness in support of Kirwan, reflecting the recent Crown decision to admit slaves' testimony in court, the majority of witnesses spoke on the state's behalf. The defendant could cross-examine witnesses, but only by communicating his questions to the judge advocate, who would then pose them to the witness.

Court documents are difficult sources from which to reconstruct past events. The inherent biases of trial procedures, the sensational effects of white hysteria, the selective nature of slave testimony given under duress, and the very real confusion surrounding tumultuous events can all compromise the truth of the testimony being recorded. Walter Johnson aptly identifies the problems with similar archives of slave conspiracies in the U.S. South: "The records of the trials that followed the discovery of [slaves'] plans . . . are accounts shaped by slaveholders' fevered projections of their slaves' unfathomed purposes, by the terror of slaves whose lives depended upon the extent to which their confessions matched the expectations of their inquisitors, and by the torture riven so deeply into the archival record of Southern 'justice.'"[44] Moreover, the transcription might be erroneous, incomplete, or heavily edited before reaching the desk of the colonial secretary of state, filtering voices that were heard in the courtroom. Nonetheless, these documents offer a window into what transpired in March 1831 from the locus of a specific plantation and contain testimony from a multiplicity of individuals representing the range of Antiguan society, from slave to planter. The transcripts, however partial, are a crucial resource for reconstructing and understanding what happened at key moments during and right after the fires.

The defendant, Kirwan, lived with his wife and worked as a cooper on Skerrett's, an estate owned by Nugent in the parish of St. Philip. Local missionaries described Kirwan as "a native African," although the court records do not indicate that Kirwan identified himself in terms of birthplace; indeed, this matter seemed not to concern the jurists.[45] As a cooper, Kirwan held a position of some esteem and trust on the estate, but Nugent did not come to his defense or save him from the gallows. According to the missionary Cadman, "before [Kirwan] suffered [hanging], he enquired for his Master, and on being told that he was not there, the poor Fellow exclaimed, 'my Master was a very good man, but I don't know how he come to leave me so.'"[46] Perhaps Nugent was unmoved because he knew that by law Antigua's treasury had to compensate him for Kirwan's full cash value of one hundred pounds.[47] Kirwan insisted on his innocence right up to the moment when he was executed. But the transcripts suggest that the court was intent on holding someone responsible for these crimes against property, whether his guilt had been fully established or not.[48] The court also avoided considering why these crimes took place, concentrating instead on when and how they occurred. It completely ignored the ban on the Sunday market as a key impetus for slaves' incendiarism. Possibly, the court took for granted the fact that the ban had precipitated the conflict, but this omission may also suggest a deliberate stripping of slaves' more calculated motivations from the record.

The first witness was Talbot Jarritt, a private of the 86th Regiment; when first questioned by the judge advocate, he stated that he did not actually see Kirwan himself light a fire in the canes near the slave quarters on Skerrett's Estate on the night of March 21. Rather, Jarritt "saw fire fall from some Individual's hand, [he could not] say whom, the moon being overcast." Then Jarritt said that from where he stood, about thirty yards from the fire, Kirwan appeared within minutes of the fire's ignition, standing "not a yard" away, and his proximity to the blaze served as grounds for Jarritt and other militiamen to apprehend him. During the rest of the judge advocate's examination, Jarritt repeatedly identified Kirwan as the individual he captured that night. Despite Jarritt's admission that he had not seen Kirwan set the fire, he reversed this statement when cross-examined by Kirwan. When Kirwan asked why Jarritt thought he would have wanted to run away, Jarritt responded: "Because he [Kirwan] set fire to the canes. There is no doubt of it."[49] At that point, Jarritt shifted from his direct observation at the time to what he regarded as common knowledge and the indubitable conclusion of the trial.

Insistence on Kirwan's guilt emerged from the testimony of every witness who took the stand on behalf of the state and from the sole witness on Kirwan's behalf, another enslaved cooper by the name of George. Kirwan was initially allowed two witnesses, but the second person he proposed, his wife, was deemed ineligible. English legal convention at the time considered a married woman too closely bound to her husband to have an independent will in all matters, legal or otherwise, so her testimony was disallowed.[50] This ruling effectively deprived Kirwan of his alibi, since she would have testified that he was at home when the fire started. Kirwan posed questions for practically every witness, but his efforts to prove his innocence were futile. The judge advocate usually ended each examination by asking the witness if Kirwan was the person last seen in the burning cane field and taken by authorities. Their affirmative answers condemned Kirwan to death for being in the wrong place at the wrong time.

Beyond the bias that prevailed in the courtroom, details in the testimony provide important clues not just to the trajectory of the fires on the nights in question but also to the experiences of slaves under the full force of colonial law. On the night of March 21, once the governor signaled the beginning of martial law via gunfire and flags, members of the militia reported for duty. Militiamen patrolling St. Philip's had discovered fires on several estates across the parish earlier that evening. For a while all was quiet at Skerrett's, but somewhere between ten o'clock and midnight the section of the estate's cane fields closest to the slave quarters, which most witnesses called "the Negro yard," began to burn. Several militiamen and David, Skerrett's enslaved night watchman, mentioned that the fire began on the neighboring estate, Colbrook's, which was also owned by Nugent, and spread to Skerrett's over the course of the night. That evening, Kirwan's friend George was returning from Gable's, another estate in St. Philip, to Skerrett's, where they both resided. George entered the slave yard, where Kirwan happened upon him and suggested they take a walk. Before leaving, George gave Mrs. Kirwan some yams to boil with some other provisions for supper, which the two men intended to eat after their walk. Kirwan and George left, but not long after they left, according to George's testimony, the two parted ways. George said he returned to the Kirwans' house, took a nap, and woke up a few hours later to hear from Mrs. Kirwan that militiamen had arrested John, but he alleged that Mrs. Kirwan never stated the reason for her husband's arrest. George left the Kirwan house undetected by the militia and reached home safely. He insisted that he never saw fire in the fields that night, but first heard about the blaze when he woke the next morning.

The night watchman, David, testified that he was standing on the roof of a storage house late Sunday night, where he observed the fire spreading at Colbrook's. When he came off the roof, he heard an alarm signaling that Skerrett's was also burning. David reported that he saw Kirwan emerging from the slave yard at Skerrett's at that time. At the same time moment, a handful of militiamen reached the burning cane field at Skerrett's. One of them spotted David and demanded that the black man identify himself. His reply that he was the night watchman must have allayed their suspicions, as they moved on to pursue others. When Jarritt saw and chased Kirwan, he sought David's assistance to subdue him. As Kirwan attempted to run back into the slave yard, Joseph Hancock, a militiaman who followed him, said that he heard "several Negroes exclaiming not to break their houses open."[51] No other slaves were apprehended in the cane field at Skerrett's that night.

These testimonies contain cloudy and conflicting details that shed considerable doubt on Kirwan's guilt as the sole incendiary at Skerrett's. None of the witnesses placed Kirwan at Colbrook's, where the fire supposedly originated, nor did anyone see Kirwan igniting a fire anywhere in the fields on either plantation—not even the watchman who was sitting on a rooftop observing Colbrook's for some time. The testimony of Kirwan's sole witness, George, exhibits serious discrepancies. He explained neither why he and Kirwan parted ways nor why he did not go straight home but ended up at the Kirwans' house. His insistence that he slept through the fire and ensuing commotion is implausible. It seems more likely that he hid that night and then concealed his whereabouts to save his own life. The prospect of capital punishment proved stronger than the bonds of friendship forged under slavery.

A more plausible scenario involves George and Kirwan either playing a part in lighting the fires or being present in the fields when they were ignited. As the slaves rushed to their quarters for cover, Kirwan and George likely became separated; George ran to Kirwan's house, but Kirwan himself failed to reach home. George heard of Kirwan's arrest from Mrs. Kirwan and then saved himself by going home, rather than remaining at the house of the man being held responsible for the fires. If Mrs. Kirwan had been allowed to testify, a different story might have emerged in the court about that fateful night in St. Philip. Instead, Kirwan was found guilty and publicly executed the following day.

The trial proceedings lack any suggestion or even suspicion that the alleged incendiary acted as part of a group. The questions asked of and about Kirwan uniformly configure him as a criminal working alone. Yet at least one line of testimony hints at the existence of collective action. The slaves' exhortations to their compatriots to remain inside and not open their houses to the militia bespeak not only a general fear of the authorities but also the deliberate protection of those who had laid this fiery plot. But the court remained unwilling to recognize that a number of disgruntled slaves perpetrated the fires in St. Philip, much like the demonstrations and rioting at Otto's. The repeated inquiries about whether the slaves at Skerrett's helped to extinguish the fires, which received no clear answers, show officials' reluctance to consider slaves' oppositional sentiments.[52] The court wished to hear that slaves moved to save the plantations on which they toiled. But the only mention of the slaves acting en masse was when they all decided to close their doors and stay inside.

In the process of pinning the arson on Kirwan, a glaring silence surrounds the possible motivations of whoever may have set the many other fires that occurred at that time. The court failed to acknowledge that numerous slaves in Antigua had to have acted in concert to light twenty-three fires in the cane fields of separate estates over a three-day period. The market's abolition was never mentioned, despite the fact that it had triggered enough unrest to require the intervention of the militia. These gaps in the proceedings suggest that the authorities refused to publicly engage the possibility of slaves' underground organizing and the deeper motivation for the fires. That admission might have encouraged further illicit action, or even open rebellion, among the slaves.

In his confidential correspondence with his superiors in London, Governor Ross said that "the root of the Evil" causing the "state of feverish

excitement" among the slaves was their expectation of "early and unconditional emancipation"; they were becoming increasingly "unsettled"
each day, and the banning of the Sunday market was only the immediate occasion for the tumult.[53] The uprising underlined white elites' fears
about the ills that emancipation could bring. In their opinion, Antigua's
slaves showed that they were not ready for freedom when a perceived
infringement on their routine sparked such widespread destruction of
property. The entire colony would be undone if the metropole decreed
emancipation to slaves who vigorously defended their few allowances
and sought to secure more privileges whenever possible. In this light,
the reduction of a wider slave conspiracy to the work of a few individuals
appears to be a tactical move intended to diminish perceptions among
slaves that their actions had any effect. Yet enslaved people knew that the
1831 uprising had heightened planters' anxieties, and they saw this unrest as an opportunity to renew agitation and advance their self-interest.
Enslaved people raised numerous grievances after the uprising that illuminate both the consistency of their subjugation even in the era of
amelioration and their sense that a status change was on the horizon.
Their objections foreshadow the struggles that marked the passage of
legal emancipation in 1834.

Slaves' Grievances and Continued Agitation in the Uprising's Aftermath

Kirwan's fate did not prevent other Antiguan slaves from expressing
their dissatisfaction and seeking redress for their grievances. The Sunday
market had not yet been replaced. The practice of granting free time to
slaves remained an informal arrangement that varied from estate to estate at the arbitrary will of planters rather than being a right recognized
and established by law. As Cadman assessed the slaves' sentiments during the days immediately after the uprising, he noted the inconsistencies. Some slaves at Friars Hill Estate in St. John Parish "admitted that
the Sabbath should be kept holy, but contended that they ought to have
other time to market." Other planters had adopted new schedules. The
Saturday after the fires, the owner of French's Estate in St. Phillip had
agreed to allow the slaves a half-day off for marketing, and the members
of the field gang there said that they expected to get half of the next Saturday off as well.[54] The fact that most of the fires occurred in this parish
may have contributed to the leniency of its proprietors in the aftermath
of the uprising.

Some slaves preferred to take action themselves rather than wait on owners or their representatives to address their needs. On Saturday April 2, 1831, the day after the Good Friday holiday, all of the slaves on Richmond Estate, in the southeastern parish of St. Paul, collectively absented themselves from work and traveled to St. John's for the purpose of marketing without asking or even notifying the estate manager, a Mr. Gilchrist. The next day, Easter Sunday, these slaves did not go to church but returned to town and assembled on the steps of Government House to express their grievances against Gilchrist. The surprised governor described him as an "indulgent master." Yet the Gilchrist whose treatment these slaves were decrying may have been the same Gilchrist who, two years later, was tried and found guilty of violating the ameliorative regulations, including denying slaves food. Gilchrist's 1833 conviction for the criminal abuse of his human property came at a moment when emancipation loomed large and panic had set in among Antiguan planters over the prospect of paying cash wages amid already straitened finances. At that time many planters complained of the hardship that providing stipulated rations for slaves was causing them, but no one else was charged with starving his workers. After his conviction, Gilchrist was released from jail when the judges voted to suspend his sentence.[55] Amelioration laws meant that slaveholders could be held accountable by the authorities for their abuses, but established custom meant that such accountability was not ironclad. Despite slaves' assertions of equality before the law before the uprising, the daily brutalities of this system made them well aware that laws did not guarantee fair behavior on the part of their masters. So, as others had done just a fortnight earlier, the slaves on the Richmond estate took matters into their own hands and launched a public protest against their abuse. The governor was able to disperse this unruly group of disgruntled slaves by promising that the authorities would not punish them. For enslaved people, winning the right to lodge a public protest without reprisals represented a significant achievement.

In another noteworthy instance of collective action, in May 1831 slaves attacked Robert Jarritt, the attorney for the British absentee planter Christopher Codrington, who was heir to his family's centuries-old fortune in Antigua. Moreover, he was the brother of the militiaman Talbot Jarritt, who had helped capture John Kirwan. Talbot died a month after testifying against Kirwan, and the *Weekly Register*, a newspaper edited at the time by two free men of color, Henry Loving and Nathaniel Hill, implied that Talbot's death was a "judgment for the evidence he had given," suggesting that they too believed Kirwan to be a scapegoat rather than a conspirator.[56]

Robert Jarritt made public complaints about the statement and in May 1831 assaulted Henry Loving, one of the two editors, in retribution. A mixed-race Methodist, Loving was born enslaved but was manumitted as a child. He worked vigorously as a representative of the campaign for mixed-race rights in Antigua. Loving and his coeditor, Hill, also a mixed-race Methodist, were both prominent in the local movements for abolition and the granting of rights to Antigua's African-descended population, while Jarritt vehemently supported planters' power and white dominance in Antigua. Although a select few colored men of property had first by custom and in 1822 by law secured the franchise, Loving, Hill, and their contemporaries argued that white elites excluded the greater majority of free colored men from various channels for advancement in the colony; in 1830 they even penned a formal petition in complaint.[57] Free men of color could not serve as plantation managers, officers in the local militia, jurors in local courts, or assemblymen in the government. A year after the Sunday market rebellion, Loving traveled to London to present these issues before Parliament and published his copious correspondence with the colonial secretary.[58] In 1833, this campaign succeeded in securing the legal rights of free colored men; this positioned them to maintain their social privilege and middle-class standing after general emancipation.[59]

Loving's radicalism soon lost him the editorship of the Weekly Register, but he went on to serve in many public capacities in Antigua and the region after 1834, including police chief, private secretary to the governor in Antigua, acting colonial secretary in Montserrat, stipendiary magistrate in Barbados, and registrar and colonial secretary in Montserrat before his death in 1850.[60] He was especially seen as a local upstart and no doubt had offended planters and their representatives before this conflict.

Following Jarritt's assault on Loving, a group of slaves "set out in a mob to murder" Jarritt. He escaped the mob, and the 86th Regiment was deployed to keep the peace.[61] A few days later another unidentified mob, likely composed of enslaved and possibly some free colored Antiguans, attacked two white men in St. John's who had sought to avenge Jarritt. The pair had appeared in town with a horsewhip to assault Loving once more and threaten violence to "any other mulatto fellow who should deserve it."[62] The mob apprehended both men, used the whip to flog its owner, and beat the other man severely, while reportedly cutting a police officer on the head when he tried to disperse the throng. Jarritt avoided another beating by fleeing to the countryside. In the following days, as a magistrate took depositions from several parties involved, the streets outside his office were "crowded, chiefly with idle profligate women."[63] In this instance, as in the Sunday market uprising itself, black women held a prominent place in a public struggle between slaves and planters that yet eludes archival detail beyond a telling mention. The mixed-race members of the throng certainly had an axe to grind, as white men such as Jarritt and his friends had stalled their long campaign for political rights. But enslaved people had their own stakes in this incident, seeking to defend Loving as a friend of their cause and to avenge Kirwan's execution.

Slaves remained particularly aggrieved well after the uprising because their market day had not yet been replaced. In July 1831, another missionary wrote that that "some honorific Planters have given [slaves] a day, but they [the slaves] will not be satisfied unless it passes into Law for they are well aware that this privilege will only [be] continued at the option of Masters."[64] The governor continually pushed the legislature to designate another market day, but to no avail. In his official correspondence, he acknowledged the impossibility of maintaining a uniform policy regarding slaves' free time on an island with so many estates, each with its own proprietor seeking to assert control in distinct ways. Significantly, amid this controversy, slaves bypassed their masters and addressed their grievances directly to the highest colonial authorities. In August 1831, in response to their continued public protests over a wide range of issues, Governor Ross found it necessary to address the enslaved population through two proclamations published on the same day. One condemned and prohibited what he called "Acts of Insubordination," in which "many of the Slaves [were] quitting the Estates in large bodies . . . and [were] presenting themselves at Government-House making, in most instances, causeless Complaints without having previously represented their grievances to their Owners or the Magistrates in their vicinity."[65] The suggestion that slaves take their complaints first to the planters or the magistrates, who were also either planters or aligned with planter interests, effectively dismissed them, as neither of those two groups would take such complaints seriously.

The text of the second proclamation reveals that all Antiguans, slave or free, knew that such public protests, regardless of the reason, amounted to a challenge to their enslavement. It begins by declaring that the island's slaves had been "erroneously led to believe that orders had been sent out . . . for their Emancipation." In order to thwart the insubordinate acts that would "likely" follow the spread of this rumor, the proclamation states that slaves "who may disturb the tranquility and peace of [the] Island" would be subject to punishment by the governor using "all the legal means in his power."[66] As early as 1824, enslaved Antiguans interpreted the local legislature's support for amelioration as a conduit to their own impending freedom. In 1831, they regarded the public struggle over the market and their free time, coupled with the demonstrations over other issues that followed, as decisive developments that could hasten their emancipation. Freedom was always on their minds, and they used both legal and extralegal tactics in pursuit of that goal.

Conclusion

By 1832, though no laws were formally passed to protect slave marketing, the marketing day on most estates was unofficially moved to Saturday, which suggests a victory, however precarious, for the enslaved population.[67] The events of 1831 raise key questions about Antiguan slaves' intent in launching this struggle. The evidence suggests that Antiguan lawmakers publicly denied but privately admitted that the prospect of freedom was the fundamental cause behind the market riot and subsequent fires. Enslaved people who refused to leave the market on the day of the ban and then committed arson in the nights following were clearly conscious of public conversations about the impending passage of emancipation by the Crown, as the language of the governor's August 1831 proclamation reveals.

Ultimately, enslaved people's visions of freedom underlay the acts of arson, as well as their public protests long after the market's abolition. To a certain degree, the Sunday market *was* freedom. The market's dismantling was a serious affront to slaves seeking the physical, material, and communal benefits from this crucial block of free time and space. Sundays served not only as amusement but also as sustenance that helped them endure the trials of their labor during the rest of the week. The market also offered a rare taste of what unconditional freedom could be. The abolition of Sunday marketing at a moment when it appeared to Antigua's slaves that the metropole was moving toward legal emancipation infused their struggle with more zeal. A time fraught with such upheaval presented an opportunity to make their sentiments known. So, despite losing the battle for the Sunday market, slaves continued to contest violations of their bodies and their time in the context of their daily labors and circulated rumors that freedom had already been decreed.

Just how far this rebellion might have gone remains unclear, as the fires were extinguished promptly and later protests were conducted in ways that remained just barely within the law. The historians David Barry Gaspar and Michael Craton have suggested that this and other rebellions in the British Caribbean after 1800 were not attempts to overthrow the plantation system; rather, they were efforts to gain greater advantages within it.[68] The 1831 rebellion tends to support to this argument, as slaves in this case carefully calculated the force and scope of their demonstrations. Presumably, they understood the impossibility of escaping the repression that would have followed more flagrant offenses and more obviously concerted actions. Most immediately, slaves were primarily seeking to protect the space of marketing within their established routine, not to upend that routine altogether. Their sense of possibility was always tempered by the everyday degradations of life in enslavement and the extreme physical danger of collective opposition. In this way, we could view the market itself and slaves' struggle to protect it in 1831 as willing compromises with their enslavement. But this uprising might also signify slaves' move to layer their short-term needs onto their longer-term expectations as imperial subjects. Their efforts may have aimed to shape the freedom they were increasingly anticipating from the Crown on their own terms, which involved the carryover of long-revered social practices in slavery. This prompts us to recognize what Walter Johnson calls the "practical complexity" of slaves' attempted rebellions.[69] Their forethought involved a rational and flexible approach to their desired ends, whether those ends were the market or freedom itself, and to the most feasible means to such ends, whether arson or petitions to the governor.

In the temporary unmaking of the market, black working-class politics in Antigua were renewed. Enslaved people found ways to settle grievances publicly, even without access to formal rights in the public sphere. In particular, their claiming what they defined as legal rights to market, to fair treatment by their owners, and to metropolitan mandates for freedom suggest Antiguan slaves' sustained engagement with colonial law, however imperfectly they comprehended it, and a construction of themselves as legally protected subjects. Their invocation of law and their claims to rights formed another avenue for slaves seeking to dismantle their oppression by using the very system that supported it, which produced mixed results for their cause. Alejandro de la Fuente observes that slaves' claims on colonial states "encouraged reliance on colonial institutions while discouraging other forms of resistance, thus contributing to social stability and peace. In both cases some degree of state intervention could serve well the larger concerns of the empire."[70] In British colonial Antigua, however, and likely in other empires as well, slaves asserted their claims on the state simultaneously with their use of subversive tactics that rejected the very terms of governance, such as public violence and arson. This multifaceted approach alarmed white elites not only in 1831 but also after freedom's conferral. The 1831 uprising was not an isolated instance in this vein; on this occasion, Antiguan slaves' rebellion resembled those of their counterparts elsewhere in the British Caribbean after 1800, though Antiguans usually acted in a more restrained, less violent fashion. All of these struggles added urgency to the antislavery movement in the British Empire and had some influence on the passage of legal emancipation in 1834.[71]

Most important, the 1831 conflict and its aftermath expose an irony embedded within the history of slavery and freedom in the Atlantic World. The importance of marketing in Antigua and beyond demonstrates slaves' limited degree of autonomy within the institution of slavery, built from unceasing efforts to carve out and protect temporal and physical space for self-provisioning and trading. But as the years that followed legal emancipation in 1834 show, many restrictions on the freedom of black working people continued, born of the forces of international commodity production and manifested locally in the harshness of labor regimes. Antigua's whites used the law and religion to simultaneously erode the market and regulate slaves' use of their autonomous time. The measure rendered slaves' enjoyment of their Sunday holiday, that part of their routine most closely approximating freedom, dependent on their performance of their leisure in "proper" and holy fashion. Attaching such conditions to their small slice of freedom in an attempt to mold slaves into more obedient, civilized, and Christian subjects was a failed strategy that local and metropolitan authorities would employ consistently after formal abolition.

As many historians have argued, emancipation represents an extension of, rather than a decisive break with, many forms of domination that African-descended people endured during slavery. Emancipation did not radically transform the terrain of struggle for freedpeople, as the politics of race and the global labor market blocked their escape from the abject position they occupied. Black people would resort to the same combination of legal and extralegal maneuvers during the next few decades as they struggled, however idealistically or desperately, not just to survive but also to thrive.

CHAPTER 3

....

"BUT FREEDOM TILL BETTER"

Labor Struggles after 1834

Heigh! me massa . . . me neber slave no more. A good massa a very good ting, *but freedom till better.*—Anonymous sugar worker from Harvey's Estate, 1837, quoted in James Thome and Joseph Horace Kimball, *Emancipation in the West Indies*

In 1837, a few black workingmen from Harvey's Estate in St. Mary Parish spoke with two American abolitionists, James Thome and Joseph Horace Kimball, as they toured the countryside. The pair was in the British Caribbean to collect stories of the region's progress as evidence of abolition's feasibility in the United States. Their carefully crafted account highlights freedpeople's industriousness and deference, presenting Antigua's transition to wage labor as trouble-free. Intermittently, however, freedpeople's oppositional sentiments emerge within the text and present an alternative version of emancipation's consequences.

The men declared that freedpeople worked harder because they got paid for their work and that flogging would never function as an incentive to labor. Harvey's had four hundred slaves before 1834, but "a great number had since left because of ill-usage during slavery."[1] In these men's eyes, the main benefit of freedom was choice of employment: "They said that it was far better to be free, because they could work with the massa that they liked best. 'If manager no treat a me good, me can give him a month's warnin and go away from him.'"[2] The men from Harvey's Estate presumed that conflicts between workers and supervisors were commonplace after abolition, a situation that Thome and Kimball chose not to consider because it was inconsistent with their political agenda. Significantly, these quotations were omitted from the second edition of their *Emancipation in the West Indies*, suggesting that the more widely the narrative circulated, the further the text was edited to create the appearance of harmony in postslavery Antigua. But the men's frank response about negotiating the terms of their labor demonstrates that freedom had emboldened black working people to pursue better wages and working conditions. They often chose to quit one plantation for another that they deemed preferable or to seek different forms of employment altogether. Black working people and white planters clashed over the terms of labor in this way for the century following abolition.

One of the men who spoke with Thome and Kimball divulged another sentiment about freedom that reveals its implications for freedpeople's sense of identity and purpose. In the United States, as in Antigua before abolition, planters often argued that blacks preferred the security of slavery to the uncertainties of freedom, provided that they were "treated well." The pair deliberately questioned the workingmen to refute that contention. When presented with the choice between being enslaved under a good master and being free, this man exclaimed, in the authors' version of local dialect: "Heigh! me massa,' said he, 'me neber slave no more. A good massa a very good ting, *but freedom till better.'*"[3] This man conceived of a freedom in which his needs and wants, rather than those of his employer, structured his life and livelihood.

What did freedom mean to the thousands of Antiguans emancipated by this act of the Crown? How did they launch new economic pursuits and carve out new ways of life? How did they connect their freedom as laborers to their freedom as persons? This chapter explores formerly enslaved people's endeavors to secure better labor and living conditions, which functioned for them as foremost ways of feeling free after 1834, and the tactics used by local colonial administrators and planters to block those efforts. In fact, some of Antigua's most prominent planters doubled as the legislators who devised inflexible labor laws or as the magistrates who ruled against freedpeople who challenged those laws. Black working people's determined but often unavailing attempts to control their time and movements indicate how elusive freedom was when planters continued to dominate the economy and the law.

The chapter first examines the public debate prior to 1834 over the apprenticeship program devised by British policy makers to maintain order during the colonies' transition to wage labor. Antigua, unlike most of the other Caribbean colonies, decided to forego the four-year scheme and proceed directly to abolition. The choice against apprenticeship stemmed from a vision of master-servant relations in freedom that looked much like slavery, as well as policy makers' anticipation of speedy financial compensation for lost property in slaves. The racialized discourse that pervaded this debate as it unfolded in administrative correspondence and the local press presumed black people's innate inability to function as free individuals. Their perception of blackness as a "problem," along with their economic self-interest in extracting labor from and exerting control over black workers, motivated whites' very circumscribed definition of freedom and ensured that freedpeople's efforts to advance materially and socially would be met with hostility.

The rest of the chapter explores black working people's strategies following the conferral of freedom, heeding historian Woodville Marshall's call for scholars of the British Caribbean to pay more attention to "the nature and range of blacks' hopes and expectations" from freedom and to explore how those were frustrated by the colonial social order.[4] The approximately thirty thousand Antiguans emancipated on August 1, 1834, not only embodied the sugar colony's labor power but also held their own longstanding, wide-ranging desires for freer lives. The material presented in this chapter has, of necessity, been reconstructed from a colonial archive that routinely deemed the activities of emancipated people illegitimate and largely rendered them illegible. Emancipated Antiguans' expectations and the strategies they used to realize them compose what scholars of subaltern subjects in various parts of the globe have identified as a *moral economy*, which includes the informal institutions, conventions, ethical beliefs, and customs that underlie subaltern economic practices.[5] In postslavery Antigua, the moral economy of freedpeople assumed a range of forms, such as strikes, serial quitting, and claiming a greater share of personal time. The failure of these practices to ensure freedpeople's economic security and social inclusion indicates the extent to which the "full" freedom conferred on enslaved Antiguans was in fact limited and contingent. Yet the chapter's brief look at the colossal failures that marked Barbuda's post-1834 transition throws the possibilities for freedom in Antigua into sharp relief.

Only months after emancipation, Antiguan planters tried to codify the conditions under which black working people would labor by devising restrictive legislation known as the Contract Act that firmly tethered emancipated people to estates. It was prompted by the disputes regarding time and work discipline that arose as newly emancipated people sought to expand their provisioning and marketing activities or engage in other pursuits of their own choosing. A related and equally charged issue concerned freedom of movement, as black working people sought to live where they wanted and move about the island as they pleased in search of work and leisure. Eventually, some freedpeople attempted to leave Antigua altogether. Their mobility within and beyond the island greatly alarmed planters, for it signaled their waning control over what had been a captive workforce. The Contract Act had damaging effects on black working people's bargaining power, but it did not entirely block their self-interested economic and social practices. Emancipated people's multilayered challenges to the Contract Act were similar to the tactics they had previously employed as slaves, simultaneously evoking their standing as subjects of the British Crown to prevent the encroachments of powerful local whites and engaging in extralegal tactics to uphold their material interests.

Whites' responses also exhibited continuities from the era of enslavement. Elite discourses prior to 1834 regarding black working people's "irrational" habits and "unnatural" character shaped the legal statutes designed to decrease freedpeople's options for labor, residence, and mobility. White planters and officials strove to control Antiguans of African descent in the immediate post-1834 moment with a vigor that had diminished during the last decades of slavery. Public and private conversations among white elites indicate their sense that the only acceptable version of black freedom was a gradual transition under constant white oversight. Though often spontaneous and ultimately unsuccessful, working people's quest for expanded lives and livelihoods prompted their repeated contestations of power across the island. Their consistent challenges to the inequities imposed by the authorities and their employers indicate their evolving senses of the meaning and the practice of freedom.

To Apprentice or Not to Apprentice:
Antigua's Uneasy Transition to Immediate Freedom

The trajectory toward the abolition of slavery in Antigua paralleled that of the other sugar territories in the British Caribbean with one marked departure: the rejection of apprenticeship. The apprenticeship program was crafted when the abolition bill was being constructed in Parliament in 1833. Originally, this scheme mandated that all freedpeople over the age of six would remain apprenticed to their former owners for six years after August 1, 1834. Apprentices were compelled to work for a set number of hours and were not paid wages but compensated with food, clothing, and housing.[6] Afro-Caribbean working people's resistance and other problems in the system led the British government to end the program two years earlier than planned. As the historian Thomas Holt points out, Britain devised the apprenticeship to prepare the empire's supposedly childlike slaves for their intended roles in the free-labor market as well-behaved proletarians.[7] Essentially, apprenticeship functioned less as a crash course in free-market economics for ex-slaves and more as a temporary relief to white elites anxious about both the financial loss of unpaid, controllable labor and the social dangers posed by freedpeople who outnumbered them. Antiguan whites displayed similar concerns, but their views on apprenticeship, slavery, and the free-labor market steered them toward a different course of action.

In October 1833 the *Antigua Herald & Gazette* printed the parliamentary abolition bill in its entirety and reported on the debate conducted by the island's legislators regarding the question of apprenticeship. The article declared that the "inherent evils" in the apprenticeship plan were "confessedly numerous, manifest and almost appalling" and stated that "aversion from the apprentice scheme is so universal in the upper classes and so prevalent in the lower ones" that the proposal was likely to be rejected.[8] Local planters vehemently opposed apprenticeship because of the economic burdens it entailed. Early in 1834, the legislature devised a formal plan for the island's enslaved people to proceed to full freedom instead. This plan was geared toward securing planters' material interests at the metropole's expense, as the planters thought that immediate emancipation would guarantee immediate receipt of parliamentary compensation funds. Antiguan authorities hoped that other British islands, especially Jamaica and Barbados, as the largest and most lucrative sugar producers, would follow suit to further legitimate this scheme, but only two small non-sugar-exporting territories, Bermuda and the Cayman Islands, went this route.

Antigua received Bermuda's decision to forego apprenticeship with great enthusiasm.[9] However, other islands loudly voiced their disapproval of Antigua's plan. As the *Antigua Herald & Gazette* remarked: "We have not occupied our paper with any of the proceedings of the other islands on the subject of the emancipation bill, because it would be little else than the same Cuckoo-note from Barbadoes to Jamaica. Each and all have adopted the apprentice-scheme without as far as we can see any important alteration." Just below this declaration appeared a quote from the Grenada Free Press that decried Antigua's decision, lamenting how difficult it would be to manage their apprentices in the wake of full freedom in Antigua. The Grenada Free Press expressed hope "that his Majesty's Government, under the pressing emergency, and the responsibility thus thrown upon them, of preserving the peace of the Colonies, will, in the face of popular clamour, disallow the Antigua Act."[10]

Antiguan planters, already struggling to make their estates turn a profit, were principally concerned about the higher costs that they feared apprenticeship would entail. A February 1833 petition to the legislature from three prominent estate proprietors outlined the reasons that made apprenticeship undesirable.[11] A particular source of "anxious irritation" was the obligation to employ apprentices without either the sanction of corporal punishment or the inducement of wages to compel them to work. In addition, petitioners decried the limitation of the workweek to forty-five hours, a sharp decrease from the average of sixty to seventy hours per week expected of adult slaves.[12] The historian William Green argues that these concerns were magnified in Antigua. Much of the provisions that fed Antiguan slaves were imported, and the cost of maintaining apprentices would remain high during apprenticeship while the amount of labor they performed—and thus planters' sales and profits—would be considerably reduced. "Having the dual advantages of a dense population and a comparatively large body of resident proprietors," Green concludes, "the Antigua planters were disposed to gamble in favour of full freedom."[13] Green's assessment misses the mark, as whites' presence in Antigua had dwindled considerably by the 1830s, and the prospect of government funds also underlined the decision. But his mention of Antigua's "dense population" implies another factor that, while unstated in the apprenticeship debate, likely influenced planters' thinking: the minimal availability of land relative to the population. Apprenticeship was not as necessary in Antigua as it might have been elsewhere to keep freedpeople from forming peasantries independent of the sugar industry, as propertied elites controlled the majority of arable land.

In October 1833, the joint committee on emancipation formed by Antigua's legislature reiterated the drawbacks outlined in the planters' petition and objected to another key feature of the apprenticeship program: the hiring of stipendiary magistrates to oversee the emancipation process and mediate labor disputes. The committee feared that these magistrates would be "unacquainted . . . with the peculiar habits, customs, and character of the people, and ignorant of the municipal institutions by which they have hitherto been governed."[14] As they had done during slavery, planters continued to subvert metropolitan authority in the era of freedom. Eventually, to appease London, Antiguan officials established stipendiary magistrates but appointed prominent planters and their cronies to the posts, ensuring that the magistracy upheld local power relations rather than adhering to metropolitan dictates.

In foregoing apprenticeship, Antiguan planters sought greater as well as more rapid financial compensation. As the historian Kathleen Butler shows, planters throughout the West Indies were quite anxious about the potential pecuniary losses from what they deemed an inadequate system for compensating slaveholders.[15] The British government promised each colony a portion of the total monetary worth of the empire's slaves equal to the percentage that the colony's slave population represented of the total number of slaves in the empire. This scheme fell short of most proprietors' expectations for claiming a fixed value for each slave, as would have been done in a slave market, based on that slave's age, sex, health, and skills.[16] Claims would be processed and paid in London rather than in the colonies, allowing the London-based creditors of heavily indebted West Indian planters to extract their due before the proprietors received any funds. Antiguan planters worried that the inadequacy of the payout for their forfeited slave property would intensify their economic distress in an increasingly competitive international sugar market.

To circumvent these difficulties, Antigua's planter-dominated legislature devised an emancipation plan with substantial benefits to estate owners, foremost among them being the instant receipt of compensation from the metropolitan government at a rate of thirty pounds per slave.[17] The Antiguan legislature also pressed for full emancipation to secure a repeal of duties that the colony had paid on all export commodities since the 1600s. Lord Stanley, the colonial secretary, approved Antigua's choice to proceed to full freedom, but well in advance of 1834, he rejected all of the perks the local legislature tried to attach to emancipation.[18] According to the historian Douglas Hall, this rejection provoked planters to retract their support for immediacy, but the legislature had to proceed because the plan to fully free the slaves had been widely publicized. Reversal would have carried a "risk of riot." Antiguan planters had to wait for two years to receive compensation, as did all other colonial proprietors, and received on average fourteen pounds per slave.[19]

While Antiguan planters and legislators portrayed their decision as a humanitarian initiative designed solely for freedpeople's benefit, they presented their rationale in a virulent racial discourse that repeated the beliefs underlying the institution of slavery. During debates over whether planters or working people themselves should finance medical care when they grew ill or old and frail, legislators frequently referred to the "improvident character of the Negro race," which was known for "confinement of their plans and ideas to the present moment and . . . utter disregard of what to-morrow might require."[20] The repetition of this point throughout the conversation on emancipation suggests that Antiguan whites had naturalized black improvidence.

Yet other sentiments reveal whites' disturbing sense that a prolonged state of slavery had helped breed such character among black working people. This belief in slavery's ills did not stem from whites' acknowledgment of their own culpability in arresting black progress; rather, they thought that blacks had grown so accustomed to having their basic needs provided for by their masters that they would be unable to support themselves in freedom, save for white intervention. The earliest justifications for the December 1834 Contract Act, which tied the right of residence on an estate to continuous employment, turn on this assumption. The speaker of the house, Nicholas Nugent, warned: "If [the planters] lose the opportunity of securing to [freedpeople] the advantages of fixing themselves to permanent locations, . . . they will become an erratic, wretched, wandering people, a downright Gypsey population without home, house or tie."[21] In his conception, freedpeople were by nature unable to become stable, productive citizens; instead, they would become wandering paupers dependent on relief, draining the treasury and threatening public order.[22] White supervision was the only antidote to this self-fulfilling prophecy of black failure.

At times this discourse assumed a scientific posture. In debates over responsibility for health care, for example, legislators spoke of the "cachectic constitution of the Negro race, and how exceedingly subject they are, over and above the ordinary catalogues of human infirmities, to elephantiasis and leprosy in various forms, inveterate ulcers, ruptures, and so forth."[23] The ill health of enslaved Antiguans actually stemmed from the rigors of the plantation labor regime. But white colonialists ascribed biological inferiority to the island's African-descended population in ways that implied their subhumanity. These assumptions about blacks' mental and physical deficiencies undermined the possibility that white elites would ever regard them as fully functioning free citizens.

A related but contradictory discourse that emerged during the apprenticeship debate posited freedpeople as becoming *eventual* citizens in the unspecified but distant future. Elites regarded themselves as tolerant and progressive for even entertaining this notion. As the *Antigua Herald & Gazette* remarked: "But we should do well to remember that the boon to the slave proceeded from his master, and that the thrall has been emancipated from the intermediate state of apprenticeship by the spontaneous act of his owner. That he may prove worthy of it, and from an obedient drudge become an orderly and decorous citizen, is our sincere wish and fervent prayer."[24] Planters and legislators expressed incongruous sentiments about the willing submission of these obedient drudges to white control and their potential for waywardness and disorder when left to their own devices. Before emancipation, the press sporadically flirted with the idea of grateful freedpeople eventually becoming worthy of citizenship. But the competing narrative of blacks' natural inferiority suggests that white elites never viewed freedpeople as deserving of those rights.

Surprisingly, the authorities did acknowledge enslaved people's opposition to apprenticeship and likely took it into account in their decision. The *Antigua Herald & Gazette* stated: "So deeply rooted is the prejudice against the system, in the minds of the laboring population[,] . . . that it would appear at present absurd to urge the trial of a measure, which is deficient in almost every element likely to produce a chance of success."[25] The reactions of their counterparts on other British islands who actually were apprenticed attest to the potential of freed Antiguans' outrage at a condition that, in its inadequate housing, paltry rations, and unpaid labor, too closely resembled slavery.[26]

Antigua's white elites felt secure enough in their monopoly over land and in freedpeople's limited options for livelihood beyond sugar plantations that they could skip apprenticeship. Construing freedom as a greater benefit than apprenticeship, they failed to anticipate the repeated and sustained challenges black working people brought to the new system of labor. The grievances of Afro-Caribbean apprentices elsewhere paralleled the grievances that Antiguan freedpeople voiced, despite their immediate emancipation and access to wages. August 1, 1834, marked not the end but rather the beginning of a decades-long struggle to truly feel free.

Contesting the New Labor Regime in Antigua and Suffering from Neglect in Barbuda

The official day of emancipation reportedly passed with solemn observance within the newly freed community. Henry Loving, the mixed-race newspaper editor–turned–police chief, reported to Governor Evan MacGregor: "The eventful First of August arrived, proceeded, and ended, without one circumstance of a public or private nature to agitate the frame of Society, or to mark the transition from a state of Slavery to that of Freedom. There never was an occasion in this Island, not excepting the Sabbath, where a day was kept with such universal reverence and unbiased holiness."[27] Formerly enslaved Antiguans greeted emancipation with thanksgiving, while those in nearby St. Kitts rioted upon the announcement of the apprenticeship program.[28] Yet, if their Sunday markets are any indication, freedpeople may have celebrated their freedom in livelier and more subversive ways that eluded elite observers. More important, contrary to Loving's optimistic assertion, Antigua's transition from slavery to freedom did in fact "agitate the frame of society."

Loving wrote to the governor about the aftermath of abolition in his new capacity as chief of the Antiguan police force. In 1834, in response to security concerns among whites at the prospect of freeing several thousands of enslaved people, a standing police force was established, and by 1838 it had replaced the volunteer militia as the main source of security on the island.[29] Loving's letters to the governor document Antigua's troubled transition to freedom and the many tactics freedpeople employed to refashion the emancipation process to suit their interests. His writings also suggest the ambivalent relationship between the black working class and the mixed-race middle class. Despite his advocacy of immediate emancipation for slaves, his observations as police superintendent reflect a disdain for freedpeople's social and economic practices similar to that expressed by whites.

Loving's reports attest to black working people's refusal to comply with their former masters' expectations. Tension between white employers and African-descended workers in the sugar economy manifested itself as soon as the workweek commenced. Gangs on "a few plantations" reported to work "cheerfully," but other plantations with two or three hundred laborers reported that only ten or twelve appeared. According to Loving, it "appeared that the great majority of the Peasantry was either bent on a whole week's relaxation, or were calculating how far they might benefit themselves by striking."[30] By collectively absenting themselves from work, freedpeople were signaling to planters that the terms of their labor had to change. As free wage laborers, they expected some say in their wages and conditions of work. If their demands went unmet, they would either purposely decrease productivity or withdraw from sugar plantations altogether. As Loving's erstwhile nemesis, the estate attorney Robert Jarritt, declared a month after emancipation, "I do not suppose more than one third of the Negroes in the island are at work. Some estates have a gang of 7 or 8, others a few more, I have only 22 on this estate, but we cannot reckon on them for a day—sometimes they leave at breakfast time, sometimes at noon."[31]

A primary grievance of black working people concerned their labor time. They contested the length of the workday and wanted to perform some tasks, such as feeding cattle and horses, when they saw fit. In the same vein, many chose to work through their breakfast and lunch breaks so their workday would end sooner.[32] Similar struggles over time occurred elsewhere in the British Caribbean. Jamaican apprentices sought to work longer hours from Monday through Thursday so that Fridays could be shorter, allowing them more free time to work provision grounds.[33] Planters objected to any adjustments in the work schedule in both locales.

Antiguan freedpeople took serious issue with the requirement of labor on weekends. In May 1836, Richard Wickham, Loving's successor as police chief, remarked that "the labourers on most properties are exceedingly reluctant to work on Saturday, many not working on that day for the whole year, a fact which must greatly diminish their industry, as well as their wages, and in many instances, lead to habits of idleness and immorality."[34] But Saturday had become the ad hoc market day in the wake of the 1831 conflict; rather than forfeiting wages, freedpeople might have earned extra money at the market. Jarritt also lamented the free time black working people claimed on the weekends, telling his employer, Christopher Codrington: "Saturdays and Mondays we get very little work done, it being generally Tuesday morning before they think of going to work."[35] While his claim may have been exaggerated, working people in Antigua might have adopted the habits of their contemporaries in the English working class, who often took "Saint Monday" off to recover from their weekend activities.[36] Black working people's collective withdrawal of labor and assertion of control over their time were acts of defiance that openly challenged planters' authority. Equally serious, the irregularity of the workforce prevented planters from maintaining pre-abolition levels of production and profit. The decrease in Antigua's total exports of sugar, rum, and molasses between 1834 and 1838 reinforces the conclusion that freedpeople performed estate work inconsistently.[37]

At the same time, Barbudan working people were agitating for freedom and the payment of wages for their labor in a regime entirely governed by the dictates of a single proprietor. Since this island was private property, historically, Antigua's laws had no jurisdiction in Barbuda, though the two islands were connected through proximity and the Codringtons' business affairs. Laws passed in Britain did not even govern Barbuda, except for one line in the Codringtons' 1685 lease that reserved the Crown's right to occupy Barbuda's shores for military purposes, if necessary. Barbuda was such an afterthought for British colonial officials that it was omitted from the 1833 abolition bill. At the time of emancipation, Barbuda and its five hundred slaves presented a legal dilemma for the Antiguan legislature.[38] Even after Codrington and the Antiguan legislature determined that general emancipation applied to Barbuda, the position of its freedpeople remained unresolved. Although Barbudans were entitled to wages for their work, up to early 1835, they had received none. They petitioned the resident manager, John Winter, for access to more provision lands, and instead of wages they were offered full ownership of the produce they raised.[39] And they did not own the property on which they worked, since the Codringtons leased every square foot of Barbudan land. As Hall points out, the lines were blurred between Barbuda as private property and as British colony, and between Barbudans as free colonial subjects and as servants of the Codringtons.[40]

In May 1835, Loving met with freed Barbudans who were demanding clarity about their status. Loving mediated an agreement between them and Winter specifying their wages and hours and the housing, food rations, and medical care they would be provided. This agreement allowed the use of allotted provision grounds and certain sections of the coastline for fishing, although it restricted freedpeople's access to both land and sea and warned that all trespassers would be prosecuted.[41] Moreover, these rights were extended only to a select group of Barbudans. With Barbuda's dwindling revenues, many freedpeople could not obtain sufficient employment on the small island. This loophole allowed the manager to reject the more "unruly" members of the black community. Winter chose to employ only the "industrious & moral heads of Families," which led to the emigration of more than one hundred Barbudans to Antigua from 1835 to 1837.[42]

The transportation they had so dreaded during slavery became for many emancipated Barbudans the only hope for survival during freedom. Barbudan exiles, already marked as unruly by their dismissal, alarmed whites by their breaches of "order" after arriving in Antigua. In April 1835, controversy erupted over Thomas Beager, who had been forced to emigrate following a labor dispute with Winter and was sent to work on a Codrington plantation. Instead, he settled with some Barbudan friends living in St. John's. His case aroused much concern in the press about how easily Barbudan orders were ignored in Antigua, the inapplicability of Antiguan law on Barbudan shores, and the legal ambiguity created when Barbudans committed offenses in Antigua.[43]

Meanwhile, back in Barbuda, the Codringtons and their agents ignored the 1835 agreement. In 1840, Barbudan freedpeople complained to two visiting magistrates from Antigua about the nonpayment of wages, refused requests for medical care, and the unavailability of warehouses to store provisions and regular transportation to Antigua to sell them. Five years into freedom, the island had no courts, schools, or resident clergy. As difficult as the postslavery adjustment was for emancipated Antiguans, freed Barbudans fared worse because they were unable even to negotiate with those in authority.[44] In contrast, Antigua's freedpeople carved out a few spaces in their routine that facilitated their pursuit of opportunities they had been denied when enslaved. Considerable numbers of black working people pursued entrepreneurship, education, and other advancements right after abolition. But the passage of the Contract Act in December 1834 complicated the notion of free labor and limited their right to negotiate wages. This act and its ancillary legislation remained the bane of Antiguan working people's existence for decades after emancipation.[45]

Freedpeople's Challenges to the Contract Act and Search for Alternative Livelihoods

The Contract Act sought to speedily push emancipated people back into plantation work by contracting them to a certain employer, most likely their previous owner, for a fixed period of time, up to one year.

One-year contracts became standard around the island. Black working people, largely semiliterate if not entirely illiterate, usually entered into these contracts verbally, in the presence of two witnesses.[46] Although the governor described the Contract Act as intended to "protect laborers against being overworked by designing persons," its true purpose was revealed in the numerous clauses specifying the punishments that would be meted out to laborers for various offenses. In fact, the only provision that regulated planters in the act's original version was a clause preventing employers from hiring labor on any other terms than the yearly contract at a fixed wage, ruling out day work. This measure aimed to create uniformity across the island so that working people could not negotiate or break their contract to obtain work on better terms elsewhere.[47]

The act's provisions reveal the severity of the work regime that planters sought to maintain. Any absence for even part of a day resulted in the loss of the entire day's wages; no absence was treated as excusable. The punishment for "negligent or improper" performance at work that might jeopardize the employer's property, including drunkenness, was imprisonment with hard labor for up to three months. Neglect of a child not yet of laboring age was also punishable.[48] This clause implicitly targeted freedwomen, who were responsible for raising the sugar industry's future workers, showing that their gendered function as child bearers shaped the plantation regime in freedom as it had during slavery.[49]

The Contract Act's provisions obstructed freedpeople's rights to negotiate wages and other terms of their labor, or to cast their lot with whichever employer or occupation they chose. In February 1835 the secretary of state for the colonies, Thomas Spring-Rice, rejected the act approved by the Antiguan legislature because of its severity. Spring-Rice recommended modification of some of the harshest penalties, clarification of the act's language, and fairer regulation of contracted laborers vis-à-vis employers, who were governed by much milder rules.[50] But there was always a one- to three-month lag between the passage of acts by the Antiguan legislature and their review by the British colonial secretary.[51] In the interim, the authorities proceeded as though their acts were already laws.[52] Just before Spring-Rice rejected the first version of the act, Loving stated: "The crop, I am of the opinion, would have never been proceeded with, so far as it has but for the enactment of the Labourer's Contract Act."[53] In other words, the December 1834 version of the act was in effect locally well before the Colonial Office rejected it;

indeed, it alone ensured the resumption of sugar production after the disruption occasioned by the labor force's emancipation.

The Antiguan legislature modified the Contract Act in August 1835, and this new version gained approval from London before the year's end. Despite a few modifications of the punishments for major offenses, the basic intention to reduce the bargaining power and mobility of waged laborers remained. In the new version, "misdemeanour, miscarriage, or ill behaviour on the part of servants in husbandry, &c" was punishable by a month's imprisonment, the retraction of wages, or firing. Misdemeanors included "absenting without reasonable cause," "willfully neglecting to work," or "willfully damaging employer's property." Wages could also be docked for absences due to sickness, although employers were made responsible for covering the cost of medical care to ailing employees.[54] In sum, the new legislation still reinforced planters' control over formally free labor.

A particularly restrictive feature of the Contract Act in its final rendering was the attachment of housing to contracted labor, which reinforced the power of the plantation regime. Laborers' occupation of plantation housing served as an automatic entrance into a yearlong contract, but employers had the right to fire, and thus evict, a laborer with only a month's notice. Secretary of State Spring-Rice argued for the injustice of this arrangement, noting "the imposition of such a Restraint upon the free exchange of a man's labour for the best Wages which that Labour can command, is alike at variance with justice to individuals, and with the best Interests of Society at large"; yet this clause remained unchanged.[55] Freedpeople had nowhere else to live immediately after emancipation. Most remained in plantation housing for at least two years, which placed them under the authority of the proprietor or estate manager.

In theory, the amendments to the Contract Act were not solely constructed for the benefit of the planter class. The revised law allowed workers to register a complaint against employers who had unfairly withheld wages, and employers found guilty were fined.[56] Immediately after emancipation, the Colonial Office created the position of stipendiary magistrate for the Caribbean colonies, and at least one magistrate was appointed for each of the six parishes in Antigua. Although their primary functions included the mediation of disputes between black working people and their employers, magistrates were largely appointed locally, and were either members or cronies of the planter class, so they were hardly unbiased. A Methodist missionary remarked that "this almost ruinous defect might be partially supplied by your Excellency's *Specially* appointing to the Magisterial office men who are unconnected with the landed interest of the Colony and who are not professionally or Commercially dependent on Estates."[57] At the time of the Contract Act's passage, Governor MacGregor acknowledged that the current magistrates' inability to be neutral regarding labor disputes was due to a "disposition" deriving from "long established habit during the system of slavery" and petitioned the colonial secretary to send two magistrates who might be more balanced mediators.[58] His request was denied. The revised Contract Act allowed any worker judged guilty of an offense by a stipendiary magistrate to appeal to the higher-level Court of King's Bench and Grand Sessions, which convened intermittently during the year to hear criminal cases.[59] But the justices presiding over this court would surely uphold planters' interests, since these prominent positions were also usually reserved for those with close connections to the planter-dominated legislature. Therefore, while laborers were free to file suit under the Contract Act, the likelihood of having their cases assessed by impartial judges, never mind securing a favorable verdict, was quite slim.

Other laws strictly regulated freedpeople's pursuits off the sugar plantations. The Vagrancy Act, passed within days of emancipation, required all persons to have some semblance of a "proper" livelihood; unemployment was a criminal offense punishable by imprisonment and hard labor.[60] Loving, months later, complained to the governor about increasing numbers of porters in St. John's, whom he suspected were idle but who avoided vagrancy arrests by displaying the requisite badges. Soon after, at Loving's suggestion, enterprising individuals seeking to escape the plantations and move into other occupations open to black people, such as porters and hucksters, faced steep licensing fees.[61] Planters and the officials who supported planter prerogatives blocked formerly enslaved Antiguans' search for work off the plantation. Antigua's harsh system of governance for freedpeople served as a model for administrators and planters elsewhere in the British Caribbean, who instituted similar policies at the end of apprenticeship in 1838.[62]

Despite strict laws and formidable punishments, freedpeople often refused to comply with planters' directives. Well after the Contract Act's passage and approval, plantation laborers remained unpredictable and unproductive. A planter remarked in March 1835: "People are most fickle and uncertain in their labour. Today they are satisfied with wages which tomorrow they spurn at. But should we get in though slowly, one hogshead of sugar per day is the average through the island although three & four used to be."[63] The police chief commented in May 1836: "The labourers continue to act occasionally in a capricious manner, under a transient impression of receiving a larger hire or from some momentary impulse of dissatisfaction."[64] Ultimately, despite the colony's intent to control labor through the Contract Act, it was not clear that planters and magistrates managed to uphold these regulations. Examining the activities of black working people on the ground illuminates the strategies they deployed to avoid or at least reduce their exploitation. After the passage of the Contract Act, black working people continued some of the oppositional strategies they had practiced as slaves that freedom offered slightly greater room to attempt. For example, they were determined to preserve and extend their free time. They also sought new forms of livelihood. Even while engaged in the same sugar work they had performed under slavery, they found or created new occupations so that the estates were not their only source of income.

Though the initial, stricter version of the Contract Act was in place, planters could not count on a stable labor force. Loving reported in February 1835: "On many estates, they [working people] have hardly made a contract before they attempted to abrogate it, while on others, they have lingered at the work for a short time, till an open rupture has been the result. In several instances . . . they flatly deny before the magistrates the existence of any contract."[65] Defying the terms of the law, working people claimed the right to seek better wages on other plantations and to explore employment options outside the sugar industry. Black workingmen and -women regularly took advantage of planters' inability to settle on a standard wage across the island, a discrepancy that persisted for several years after emancipation. The difference of a few pence in daily wages among neighboring plantations was sufficient inducement to move.[66]

Some working people broke their contracts for compelling personal reasons. In August 1837, John James, a freedman employed on New Division Estate in St. Mary Parish, decided to go elsewhere after a broken engagement to a woman on the estate. He arranged to begin work at the Hill House plantation in St. John Parish soon thereafter but was promptly brought by his old employer before the magistrate Darius Davey because he had failed to give the required month's notice. James was sentenced to two weeks in jail and fined four shillings and sixpence sterling. Upon his release, he went to work at Hill House but was again summoned before Davey. The magistrate convicted James again for the same offense, this time sentencing him to a month's imprisonment. After the solicitor general, Robert Horsford, appealed to Antigua's governor, James was released from jail.[67]

Working people believed that they had the right to abrogate their contracts as they saw fit, since they owned their bodies and their time. As shown in James's case, planters, in response, attempted to enforce the Contract Act as harshly as possible, but the inconsistencies of their hiring practices offered freedpeople enough room to maneuver around the law. James's ordeal implied a lack of planter-class unity, as he was immediately able to find a second job, despite his new employer presumably knowing that he would have been under contract elsewhere. Indeed, the Contract Act, though it primarily regulated freedpeople's work discipline, also inadvertently restricted estate owners in ways that reveal existing tensions within the planter class during the immediate postslavery transition. Planters scrambled to quickly tie black working people down in annual contracts, not just because of their fickleness but because all other estates presented competition in the race to assemble a workforce from a limited pool of freedpeople. When Colonial Secretary Lord Glenelg heard about James's case, he warned the governor that in "the present state of the West Indies, with high wages and a great demand for labor in particular colonies, any severe code for regulating the relation of master can scarcely fail to defeat itself."[68] Local planters and metropolitan administrators had to acknowledge that colonial success depended on the energy and willingness of black labor, which, in some respects, still had to be courted in the 1830s.

Contract disputes almost always resulted in verdicts in favor of employers, but that did not deter freedpeople from asserting their self-ownership. Between late 1837 and 1838, 352 people were convicted of breaking their contracts, 51 were convicted of jobbing without a license, and 87 were convicted of vagrancy.[69] Many labor disputes might not have resulted in court proceedings and so escaped the historical record. Correspondence between planters and legislators brimmed with reports of partial workdays, work stoppages, and feigned sickness, as significant numbers of men, women, and children absented themselves from required labor. In the coastal towns—St. John's in the north, English Harbour in the south, and Parham in the east—workingmen easily assumed alternative occupations. Many became fishermen, fish pot makers, bargemen, and porters, though a large portion were suspected by observers to be "idlers" or "hangers-on."[70] The threat of imprisonment for vagrancy did not stop black men from entering the towns in search of new livelihoods.

The range of trades represented among black people in St. John's troubled elite observers well into the 1840s. Some may have been inhabitants of the town before 1834, but emancipation brought an influx of laboring men seeking escape from estate work, which renewed upper-class disdain for their presumed idleness. A contemporary description of a row of businesses in early 1840s St. John's exemplifies this derisive attitude:

> In different parts of the town are numbers of small shops, of about six or eight feet square, in which varieties of trades are carried on. In one may be seen a cobbler—no! I beg their pardon—a *cordwainer*; himself shoeless, busily employed in forming; from his not very fragrant materials, a pair of creaking high-heeled boots, for the use of some black exquisite. A bunch of human hair attached to the end of a long stick, and moving with every breeze, bespeaks the abode of a barber and hair-dresser; while a multiplicity of shreds of cloth, half-finished vests, a goose, and other *et ceteras*, with a group of mortals seated *à la Turque*, proves beyond doubt that the inmates were of that particular class of beings, nine individuals of which are required to form one ordinary man.[71]

To elite observers, black entrepreneurial activities were by definition illegitimate and were carried out by people with subhuman qualities. But to freedpeople, these occupations evinced a new kind of freedom unfolding in the towns.

Immediately after emancipation, black women began to work less regularly on the sugar estates, alternating their labor in the fields with tending to their homes and children, cultivating provision grounds, huckstering from plantation to plantation, or vending their produce at markets in town.[72] Fewer black women than men moved permanently off rural estates to pursue alternative livelihoods, showing the gendered limits of spatial mobility in plantation societies. But they too sought to maintain some independence from the staple industry. Freedwomen used the same tactics employed under slavery, when family obligations shielded them from accountability to the plantation. Their inconsistent presence in the fields after 1834 was especially crippling to sugar production, given women's numerical predominance in the first and second field gangs.

Scholars of the British Caribbean have long debated whether or not there was a flight from estates among freedpeople, and recently more attention has been paid to this phenomenon among freedwomen. The scholarship has established that the practice varied between islands, hinging to a large extent on topography, the availability of land for independent cultivation, and the extent to which colonial law and planters' customs prevented freedpeople from gaining access to land. On larger islands, such as Jamaica, freedpeople were forced to leave plantations to secure land for self-provisioning. Smaller islands tended to maintain a larger plantation labor force, as little surplus land was available.[73] Bridget Brereton has established that freedwomen on Antigua and St. Kitts did not enjoy the luxury of withdrawing their labor; in the early 1840s they worked in field gangs in similar numbers as they had done while enslaved.[74]

It is clear from the sources that Antigua's black women still toiled in the fields after emancipation. But they also made resolute efforts to protect their time and, with it, the right to pursue their own material interests despite the increasing constraints of the sugar economy. Even when forced back into the fields, they continued provisioning and huckstering on the side and on occasion joined together to assert control over their labor time. Between June and August 1838, for example, at least seven black women and three men employed on Cook's Estate entered a prolonged dispute with their manager regarding Saturday labor. The women testified to the magistrate that "they had not been ordinarily required to work on Saturday; that it is inconvenient for them to do so . . . and that they have required [Saturday] for marketing and for washing their clothes to enable them to attend church on Sunday."[75] They presented their claim strategically, aware that their right to take Saturdays off would more likely be upheld if they suggested that their labors on their own behalf enabled them to behave as devout Christians on Sundays.

Not coincidentally, at least three of the women and one of the men in this group did not work on the third anniversary of Emancipation Day, a political act that drew the ire of the plantation manager. August 1, 1838, was designated by the Antiguan legislature as a day of public thanksgiving to commemorate abolition, which may have signaled to these freedwomen they were allowed to abstain from work. The manager of Cook's Estate, George Brand, called on the parish magistrate to extract a replacement day from those who had been absent on August 1, which that year fell on Wednesday, and requested that the designated day be a Saturday. This dispute set off wider inquiries into work patterns at Cook's, and in the end all nine men and women faced fines of nine shillings and a week in jail with hard labor for violating the Contract Act. The governor released them after four days in consideration of the women who were "withdrawn from the care of their children," indicating either the state's proactive support of women's family obligations or, more likely, a necessary reaction to their unending complaints.[76] Planters and magistrates used the force of the law to push freedpeople to surrender control of their labor power; doing so would fulfill local and metropolitan expectations that emancipation would produce willing and rational proletarians. Yet these measures could not get working people to relinquish their long-established customs or give up their search for other paths to material and social advancement.

While adults often found ways to alternate between the field and more independent ways of earning a livelihood, parents seemed particularly intent on permanently removing children from plantation labor in order to gain an education. Many freed families sent their children to live in the towns, either with their kin or as house servants. In October 1834, Loving described black youths as "embracing all that artificial consequence, that love of dress, that hatred of laborious occupation," which had caused the "real want and misery" he witnessed among many free people of color in Antigua's towns prior to abolition.[77] Loving saw the newly freed as destined to make the same mistakes as their manumitted predecessors. His scorn aside, the comment hints at black working people' goals for themselves and future generations. They encouraged education and improvement in their children's appearance in order to avoid long-term associations with slavery and to facilitate their advancement in life. Even when children remained on the plantations, parents put the younger ones in school all day and stopped older children's field labor early so they could also go to school. The Methodist educator and catechist Charles Thwaites reported being "presently surrounded by the Infants who attend the Day schools. These after being catechised and sang and prayed, go away to make way for the elder Scholars, who attend when they come from the field."[78] The long-standing Methodist and Moravian missions, as well as the Anglican Church, which began proselytizing the populace after amelioration, managed schools for freedpeople. An estimated 8,000 children were enrolled in church-run schools across the island in 1836, with at least 3,500 of that number enrolled in day schools.[79] Adult freedpeople also used their free time to pursue literacy and further education, either at missionary night schools or by receiving instruction from their children.[80]

The number of children who actually attended school, however, fluctuated with the rhythm of the sugar crop. When the crop was in season, usually December through June, or when drought-prone Antigua experienced a prolonged rainfall, opportunities to make money drew black working people's children into the fields. Thwaites noted that Methodist night schools had fewer numbers in July 1838, after heavy rains had fallen.[81] Planters were alarmed by the withdrawal of youth from plantations. Legislators feared that young people's orientation toward education rather than field labor was "destroying the germ of the future prosperity of the island as a sugar colony."[82] The colony's financial prospects now lay in the hands of black working people who were intent on advancing beyond fieldwork.

Some freedpeople quit their former plantations entirely in order to reunite with relatives from whom they had been separated under slavery. As Samuel Smith recalled in his memoirs, his great-great-grandmother Rachael and two of her daughters immediately set out from Old Road Plantation to find a third daughter who had been sold away years earlier to Sandersons Plantation in St. Peter Parish. Overjoyed upon their reunion, the family decided to stay there rather than return to the harsh regime at Old Road.[83]

The American abolitionists Thome and Kimball, on their 1837 visit to Antigua, observed the expansion of familial bonds after the end of slavery. They were informed that the rise in marriages after emancipation reflected freedpeople's desire to formalize relationships with intimate partners living on different plantations after 1834. According to the pair, missionaries and planters alike were pleased, for legal matrimony seemed part of a trend toward domesticity and Christian propriety. Members of both groups told the visiting abolitionists that "every year and month [freedpeople] are becoming more constant, as husband and wife, more faithful as parents, and more dutiful as children."[84] Given Thome and Kimball's interest in painting a positive picture of West Indian emancipation, they likely overstated both local whites' support for familial bonds among their workers and blacks' support of monogamous marriage. As the Cook's Estate dispute hints, some planters were concerned about the familial responsibilities working people claimed after 1834, because greater mobility and fuller lives meant less labor power to cut canes.

Individualized strategies of selective labor via unpredictable absences and the exercise of mobility were black working people's first resort in the context of the Contract Act's restrictions. But collective expressions of black working people's dissatisfaction with the plantation workplace also occurred on occasion. The 1835 Emancipation Day strike publicly manifested the critical divergences between the benefits freedpeople expected and what little they actually received.

The 1835 Emancipation Day Strike

The first anniversary of emancipation—August 1, 1835—stirred the island's working people to mass action: a one-day strike by roughly 1,800 working people contracted to estates around the island.[85] Richard Nanton, an estate owner in St. Mary Parish, reported on Monday, August 3: "In all my neighbourhood, all the labourers on various estates refused to perform any work whatever, manifesting an insolence of conduct and behaviour extremely improper, and subversive of all regularity and order."[86] According to the governor, these women and men struck in response to "expectations of some important amelioration in their condition[,] . . . conceiving that they were to obtain houses and grants of land, and, in many instances too, that a sum of money for distribution amongst them had been remitted to [the governor] by his Majesty."[87] William Byam, a councilman and proprietor of estates in St. Peter, explained that he overheard his workers saying that "after the 1st of August . . . their houses were to become their own and that they would no longer work for 1 s[hilling] a day."[88] Freedpeople protested their continued degradation and asserted claims to compensation for their enslavement.

That day, black working people congregated in large numbers around several plantations and proclaimed their intent to strike until their anticipated benefits were received. The authorities responded swiftly, as rumors of this impending action had reached the planter class in advance. The police chief, Loving, informed the governor that the day before he had "received information . . . of the intention of the labourers in the southern district of the island to strike work this morning for increased wages." He continued: "This . . . has been carried into effect; and I am also sorry to say that those of Popeshead Division [in St. John Parish] have adopted the same course."[89] Loving and a small detachment of militiamen appeared at two neighboring estates, Jarvis's and Blizard's, in

St. George Parish, in an attempt to prevent laborers from striking. Loving identified the workers on these plantations as notorious for their "obstinate bearing" on previous occasions. This coercive measure was effective; all the workers present reported to the fields by mid-morning.[90] While there were no reports of actual violence, the dispatching of militia shows that whites considered public gatherings of aggrieved black workers a threat to security.

The reasoning behind this mass demonstration suggests that freedpeople continued to regard British law as a protector of their interests in freedom, just as they had done during the final years of slavery. This expectation of state protection heightened as the conferral of freedom seemed to turn black people into subjects of the Crown. Although they remained excluded from formal politics, they acted as political beings possessed of some rights. The 1835 strike stemmed from their daily struggles to turn their liberation into more than a legal formality. The strikers reportedly believed that a change in the law had entitled them to homes, land, and monetary compensation from "His Majesty."[91] The amendments to the Contract Act that had been made that week actually said that merely living on an estate automatically meant entrance into a yearlong labor contract. But freedpeople circulated rumors of reparative measures and claimed rights to their putative benefits. In doing so, black working people again petitioned royal authorities in the metropole to defend their interests against their oppressors on the island.

Black working people had access to enough information concerning the colony's governance, whether through the press or by eavesdropping on elite conversations, to discover that the law most critical to their lives and livelihoods would be modified around August 1, 1835. Some may have even learned that British officials had demanded that Antiguan legislators moderate some of its harsher provisions. The strikers may have genuinely mistaken the act's modifications as redounding purely to their benefit; more likely, they deliberately misinterpreted the provision tying housing to compulsory labor in order to stake out a negotiating position. Their insistent efforts at socioeconomic advancement prompted their attempt to alter the Contract Act's terms and their demand that the state grant them the kind of material benefits that would foster a more meaningful freedom.

A stipendiary magistrate in St. John's concluded that the striking workers from Richard Newton's estate who were brought into his court that day did not state precisely what was their motive for refusing to work, but that they had thought there had been some alteration in the law as regarded them and were waiting to see what it was. Whereupon the magistrates represented to them the folly of their proceeding, and explained to them what the alteration in the law really was; they told them at the same time that they could not compel them to go back to work and that they were free to go where they pleased, but that their houses and ground belonged to their employers. . . . This mode of reasoning appeared to have had its due effect upon the parties, for they immediately promised to return to their usual labour.[92]

Authorities' best interests lay in billing this episode as black working people's "folly." But freedpeople had clear economic and political interests at stake, as their demands concerned the tools for social and political advancement. Material means secured social power. By law, the right to the franchise hinged on the possession of a certain amount of money, land, or the lease or ownership of a house judged to be of a certain value. Since land, homes, and money, the three main expectations or demands articulated by the strikers, were what qualified the island's residents for electoral participation, their goals could have extended beyond basic material gains.[93]

The authorities quickly thwarted this small-scale but widespread and significant collective action. Yet the nature of freedpeople's demands and the timing of the strike to coincide with the anniversary of emancipation reveals their perception that their freedom was incomplete. The surviving documentation says too little about individual participants' demands to allow us to conclude that all shared the same goals. But black laborers all over the island knew that improvements in their economic and social standing could be won only through mass struggle.

Participants in this strike suffered threats to their livelihood, and they were forced to return to work. The case of Daniel Carty, who absented himself from plantation labor on August 3, not only shows the consequences suffered by individual strikers and their families but also underlines the larger contest between workers and their employers over the uses of time. Carty lived and labored on Old Cotton Work Estate in St. Peter, owned by the Codrington family and managed by Jarritt. Carty received his week's wages on Sunday, and early the next morning, he proceeded to Parham, the nearest town, ostensibly to procure his weekly provisions. When he returned around ten in the morning,

Carty found that the house he occupied on the estate had been emptied and all of his furnishings and other belongings placed alongside the closest main road. Jarritt evicted him because he was absent at the beginning of the workday—the very day when laborers around the island had launched a mass strike. Pleading his case to Loving, Carty reported that as many as ten other laborers had been evicted, including his wife and two of his brothers, and that another brother, George, and a sister, Damsel, who both reported to work at nine, had found the windows of their homes taken out, but the rest of their belongings remained untouched when they were discovered to be at work. Jarritt met Carty in town later that same day and informed him that he would be arrested if he ever returned to Old Cotton Work.[94]

Antigua's legislative council, which held a series of emergency meetings on August 3 in response to the strike, recommended that the payday on plantations be immediately moved from Sunday to Monday.[95] This measure continued the legal attack on Sunday commerce and amusements that began prior to the 1831 uprising, and undermined the conduct of business at markets now generally held on Saturdays. The authorities offered no redress to Carty, in spite of his denial of sympathy with the strike when he was interrogated; he lost his job and his housing, and his relatives labored under threat of dismissal. This story illuminates the coercive character of sugar plantations in postemancipation Antigua. Whether Carty had planned on shopping or on striking, he had defied his employer's claim to his time. Planters' punitive measures struck fear in individual workers and their loved ones and undid community solidarity. Vocal opposition to the status quo endangered freedpeople's ability to secure a livelihood and protect their families after 1834. Yet planters' tactics could not stamp out working people's determination to act on their grievances. Tensions between employers and working people continued, and similar struggles surfaced in later periods.

Indeed, freedpeople continued to regard Emancipation Day as an annual day of reckoning. Disputes over the control of time and assertions of other labor rights escalated around August 1. The freedwomen and -men on Cook's Estate in 1838 used August 1 to negotiate better terms of employment. Black working people's acts suggest their awareness of the power that stemmed from planters' dependence on their labor, yet the poverty and disfranchisement that they sought to combat thwarted their efforts to sustain successful protests. The countless prosecutions under the Contract Act and the rapid repression of the 1835 strike indicate planters' effective containment of working people's aspirations. The attachment of housing to labor contracts completely blocked freedpeople's movement, bargaining power, and employment options, forcing some to employ even more drastic measures to secure mobility.

Freedpeople's Struggle to Vote with Their Feet

During the late 1830s, a number of black working people launched risky ventures to migrate to other British Caribbean territories. Unable to attain economic independence and political voice in Antigua, they tried to vote with their feet by going to places that offered more opportunities, particularly Trinidad and Guyana. This move was fraught with contradiction, because migrating obligated them to be indentured for several years until their labor had repaid the cost of their passage.[96] It is possible that those who left were unaware of the indenture that awaited them. But freedpeople's choice to emigrate and planters' reaction to the possibility of their leaving speak to the shortcomings of "full" freedom as rendered in Antigua. However hard they worked to improve their circumstances, black working people faced financial hardship and myriad constraints in a small society where their employer was also their landlord and often their local magistrate or assemblyman as well. The desire to break out of semicaptive labor was widespread, but achieving it proved quite difficult, as there were only two means of escape: leaving the estates for another place to live on the island or leaving Antigua altogether.[97] The possibility of freedpeople's departure for other Caribbean territories deeply alarmed planters and legislators, and they erected serious obstacles to thwart it in 1836 and 1837.

Shortly after emancipation, workers in the Leeward Islands learned of better wages for sugar plantation work in Trinidad and Guyana, which both had a marked labor scarcity relative to their abundance of land. Their local governments aggressively recruited workers from other islands. Emigration agents and the plantations receiving transplanted workers stood to profit considerably, for both colonies' governments paid a bounty averaging fourteen pounds per laborer.[98] Strikingly, between five and ten times the number of black working people from St. Kitts, Nevis, and Montserrat migrated in search of work than did their counterparts in the more populous Antigua during the first decade after 1834. Douglas Hall concludes that the relatively low numbers of Antiguan emigrants resulted from the strength of working people's local ties, which were fostered by friendly societies, churches, and especially independent villages, institutions that were more often absent in the other Leewards.[99] It is true that Antiguan freedpeople enjoyed more social outlets than their counterparts on smaller islands. But a close examination of the sources suggests that the authorities' concerted efforts to thwart emigration caused clandestine, and therefore unrecorded, emigration from Antigua rather than shutting it off entirely. Freedpeople were legally stripped of the option to migrate to other territories, and the authorities portrayed those who attempted to do so as being "enticed" into leaving by others rather than as individuals seeking a better future for themselves and their families.

As early as 1836, plantation proprietors and managers enlisted the aid of police in finding missing workers bound to labor for them under the Contract Act. The widespread knowledge of employment opportunities elsewhere, coupled with the severe drought that precipitated layoffs and wage decreases on Antiguan estates, impelled some to leave the island altogether.[100] Local police regularly raided ships in the harbors in search of fleeing freedpeople. Although the authorities acknowledged that "the fact of emigration is too evident to admit of the slightest doubt," the lack of information about passengers' identities enabled those escaping labor contracts with local plantations to depart.[101]

As authorities sharpened their antiemigration tactics, requiring prohibitively expensive passports for travel off the island, black working people had to devise craftier ways to leave. Unable to board ships in local harbors bound for Trinidad or Guyana, some fled in small boats to the nearby island of Montserrat, from which they could gain passage to the larger territories.[102] Many clandestine Antiguan emigrants went unrecorded, while many others were caught and forcibly returned. The historian Neville Hall's concept of "maritime marronage," which describes Caribbean slaves' flight from small isles to freedom in larger territories, aptly fits Antiguan freedpeople's maneuvers as well.[103]

In September 1836, the legislature passed An Act for Preventing a Clandestine Deportation of Labourers, Artificers, Handicraftsmen, and Domestic Servants, which devised a protracted process for obtaining a required "certificate of leave" for any departing freedpeople. The island's secretary had to publish in the newspapers the name, last known address, and previous employer of any potential travelers for thirty days before a certificate could be granted. Also, an extremely harsh set of penalties, including exorbitant fines of five pounds and/or imprison-ment, would be levied on those found leaving illegally, the shipmasters transporting them, the employment agents who recruited them, and even the secretary or local magistrates who helped them obtain the required documentation without the proper steps being taken first.[104] Yet subsequent reports show freedpeople still attempting to leave the island. For instance, the British abolitionists Joseph Sturge and Thomas Harvey reported that in November 1836, while en route to Antigua, they met a Guyanese emigration agent seeking laborers from Antigua and elsewhere for temporary stints in Guyana. He "complained bitterly" that Antiguan workers "were in a wretched condition; and yet those who wished to emigrate, were impeded by fictitious charges of breach of contract, and other obstacles thrown in their way by the planters." Despite these difficulties, he managed to recruit "thirty-two negros of both sexes, carpenters, sailors, house-servants, and a few field-laborers, to indent themselves for various periods of one to four years, at a rate of wages of three to seven dollars per month, and generally on higher terms after the first year."[105]

In January 1837, twenty-three Antiguan black workingmen were de-tained while on board a schooner off the coast of Montserrat bound for Guyana. Their stories provide insight into local authorities' alarm over emigration. Four of the men were field laborers at Willock Frye's Estate in St. Mary in the southwestern corner of Antigua, an optimal starting point to set sail for Montserrat. Two others were also plantation labor-ers. The remaining seventeen lived and worked in St. John's; all had skilled occupations, such as cook, artisan, seaman, and carpenter. Only the six plantation laborers and one of the town laborers were said to have been "enticed" into leaving for Montserrat by an Antiguan mixed-race shipmaster, Captain John Ord, who was known to recruit labor for Guya-nese plantations. The others made the trip on their own, in two different groups.[106] Montserrat's authorities and Antigua's lieutenant governor collaborated to return all the men after receiving planters' complaints. Evidently, the local authorities only recorded testimonies from the individuals Ord brought to Montserrat. The summaries of the men's statements, which are quite similar, attest to Ord "enticing" them on board with offers of clothes and money and preventing them from going ashore at Montserrat. At that point, or so their stories go, they asked Ord whether they were being "stolen" to another country—pretending their ignorance of the agent's intention to contract them in Guyana as

indentured wage laborers. Each statement ends with an apologetic desire to return to Antigua. The statements of the seventeen men who left
of their own accord were not sent to the authorities in Antigua, because,
the officials in Montserrat explained, their testimonies "embraced, generally, no facts of importance, from the caution and reluctance observed
by them."[107] The telling silence of the majority of these emigrants in-
vites us to imagine the myriad reasons that prompted their flight and the
maritime networks freedpeople built between Antigua and Montserrat
to foster their escape.

Enticement functions as the overarching framework through which
Antiguan authorities interpreted labor migration. They suppressed any
narratives of voluntary flight that could raise suspicions among other
colonies and the Colonial Office that they had mismanaged emancipation. The authorities believed that Ord, whom they regarded as a mixed-
race "rabble rouser," seduced unsuspecting black working people into
leaving Antigua against their will and without any knowledge of the situation that awaited them.[108] Although they may have been urged by recruiters to leave their untenable present for an unknown future in a new
territory, this interpretive spin allowed the authorities to blame others
for their own neglect and to cast the desperate actions of impoverished
working people as illegal behavior that required greater state control.
Indeed, the language of the October 1836 anti-immigration legislation
displays a paternalistic bent. The stated reasons for preventing emigration included ensuring that working people were not "kidnapped" and
that they could not shirk their obligations to their young, elderly, or infirm dependents.[109] Although many of those who left Antigua were adult
black men, details from the lieutenant governor's correspondence with
London suggest that black workingwomen, as well as entire families,
also migrated. In a trial set to resume in Montserrat the day after the
twenty-three men aboard Ord's ship were apprehended, for example,
William Count, his wife, and their children faced charges of illegal emigration from Antigua to Guyana via Montserrat.

Antiguan authorities' acknowledgment of the attractiveness of reloca-
tion might tacitly confirm a major weakness of the local planter class:
that their profits hinged on the willingness of recalcitrant freedpeople to
devote their labor power to sugar production. The admission that freedpeople were voluntarily leaving the island would have had social and political ramifications as well. Why would supposedly fully free Antiguans
opt to start over as indentured servants on foreign terrain? In material

terms, the greater size of Guyana and Trinidad offered the prospect of better wages, independent production, and possibly even land ownership. Freedpeople might have perceived that movement to a new and larger territory would have enabled not only their economic advancement but also their escape from the constant surveillance and repression they faced at home. In such a small place, eluding authority was nearly impossible. Antigua had a single set of powerful people in control, and an antagonistic exchange with them in one instance meant difficulties for black working people in all other contexts. Antiguans of African descent might have regarded emigration as a route to a material and social freedom they had yet to experience. Yet, in reality, Trinidad and Guyana were characterized by similarly inflexible racial and class hierarchies buttressed by the same regular intrusions into black laboring people's lives, prompting them to approach these regimes via the same sorts of survival strategies that Antiguans were also engaging. Emigration represented for freedpeople a lateral move at best.[110]

Emigration reflected badly on Antigua's public image, because it made the island's social order appear unstable, a reputation that authorities expressly sought to refute or at least contain. Antiguan officials often worried about how their emancipation process was perceived by the sugar colonies that had instituted apprenticeship. In 1837, in discussing the reluctance of authorities on neighboring islands to abolish the apprenticeship, Governor Colebrooke acknowledged that "the principal obstacles . . . proceed from an erroneous impression of the effects of the arrangements in Antigua."[111] The emigration controversy did not improve regional impressions about how well Antigua was handling full freedom. But authorities' vigilance against illegal emigration and the stringent requirements imposed on legal passage effectively thwarted freedpeople's efforts to leave, allowing whites' alarm over emigration to subside by the close of the 1830s.

Conclusion

Freedpeople in Antigua left an indelible record of their challenges to the colony's entrenched labor regime and social order. The oppositional practices they adopted immediately after freedom mark the ways that 1834 transformed labor relations. The range of their actions—including modifying their work routines on sugar estates, pursuing alternative livelihoods, launching intermittent strikes, and attempting to leave Antigua altogether—display a keen understanding of the hindrances to their economic and political progress. These actions also show the complexity of what freedom meant to black people in Antigua, and likely the rest of the Atlantic World as well.

Emancipated people's interpretations of freedom differed sharply from the narrow definitions imposed by local and metropolitan elites. Freedom not only meant that ex-slaves were paid for their labor but also introduced a host of possibilities for them to gain control over and improve their lives. Black working people displayed deeply rooted desires for autonomy and citizenship, especially as they broached questions regarding material reparations from the state in 1835. Their efforts were influenced by their conception of Crown law as the best vehicle to secure the equality that too often eluded them at the local level. As Woodville Marshall observes of apprentices elsewhere in the region, "They recognized that access to justice was an attribute of citizenship . . . and that law was the foundation of free society."[112] The law continued to disappoint them, however, prompting extralegal acts at critical moments in their quest for self-protection and advancement. But Barbudan freedpeople's predicament revealed the extreme vulnerability that resulted from the absence of laws to govern the transition to freedom. Barbudans' status remained questionable in light of the Codringtons' perpetual and unchecked rights over the entire island.

Black working people's subversions in Antigua undermined, but could not entirely dismantle, the unfreedoms embedded in the contract labor system that state-sponsored emancipation built. The exigencies of emancipation in the Atlantic World meant that elites struggled to maintain the profitability and productivity of sugar plantations amid marked price fluctuations in world markets. The severity with which the planter class handled the transition to wage labor in Antigua, along with the island's small size, limited the extent to which freedpeople could become independent of the sugar plantations. These constraints also shaped the contradictory choices that freedpeople made as they engaged in this struggle, such as indenturing themselves elsewhere in the Caribbean despite being formally free in Antigua.

While the conflicts between planters and black working people may appear to be solely or primarily class struggles, they were profoundly shaped by whites' conceptions about race and had broad political ramifications. For white elites, Antigua's reputation in the British Empire was at stake, along with its economy, when freedpeople did not respond to the new labor regime as they had predicted. Anxiety about controlling the labor of freedpeople spilled over into anxieties about controlling black aspirations for social advancement, as the conferral of freedom threatened the maintenance of oligarchic rule. Racial difference underscored the intensity of the struggle. Presumptions of African "peculiarities" overshadowed Antiguan whites' understandings of freedpeople's actions, and freedpeople demonstrated their acute awareness that differential access to resources and power fell along racial lines. Freedpeople's claims to their rights and insistence on independence were remarkable in the hostile context that prevailed right after 1834. Efforts to destabilize the stringent colonial social order continued through the next decade. Black working people engaged the public sphere with new vigor, demanding better wages, expanded forms of leisure, and greater participation in civic and religious institutions. They devised innovative ways to articulate a more meaningful freedom.

···

CHAPTER 4

"AN EQUALITY WITH THE HIGHEST IN THE LAND"?

The Expansion of Black Private and Public Life

Another peculiarity among this tribe is the freedom with which they address their employers. This has even increased, if anything, since emancipation; for now they are free, they appear to think themselves upon an equality with the highest in the land.—MRS. LANAGHAN, *Antigua and the Antiguans*

Though freedpeople understood the rigidity of colonial Antigua's social hierarchy, they challenged the superiority of their former masters by publicly asserting their new status. Local elites construed freedpeople's changing demeanor and actions as an unwarranted subversion of public order. To white observers, their efforts at self-improvement revealed the insolence with which this "tribe" was already endowed and threatened elites' sense of control.[1] The conflict between former slaves and former masters that was brewing after 1834 intensified in the 1840s, as freedpeople's labor struggles were compounded by their zealous pursuit of well-being and social mobility.

In the early 1840s, black working people sought the tangible improvements they expected from emancipation, and, in turn, tried to purge the traces of slavery from their existence. The expansion of their social obligations and material desires, which was initially encouraged by the British project of molding ex-slaves into willing wage earners, enabled freedpeople to construct private spheres and alternative public spaces, both of which undermined the empire's singular use of them as expendable proletarian labor. They vigorously extended their previous efforts to secure social and economic improvements through their claims to rights as workers and colonial subjects. But the new opportunities of the early 1840s carried clear limitations, for they were regulated by the dictates of both the state and the Protestant churches. Though they unfolded mainly beyond the workplace, freedpeople's struggles for self-improvement drew sharp criticism from planters and other white elites, whose obsession with managing every aspect of black life and replicating the dynamics of the planation throughout colonial society rendered freedpeople's self-interested actions illegitimate.

Black working people's endeavors included the construction of new homes and the formation of free villages, further modifications in the plantation labor routine, and new consumption patterns and leisurely amusements. Their new possessions and their diversified activities redefined the private and public practices of freedom. Their efforts to fashion new ways of life carry special significance, as many aspects of everyday life and culture among Afro-Caribbean people in the wake of emancipation were mostly conducted outside white surveillance and have not been adequately understood. Their forms of consumption and claims to private space, as well as their engagements in public life and amusements, formed part of a burgeoning Afro-Creole culture that scholars have traced within many nineteenth-century Atlantic communities. Freedpeople's new ways of life exemplified not only the social transformations that swept the British Empire after slavery's end but also the oppositional cultures long existent in the African diaspora.[2] These Afro-Creole manifestations, which encompassed popular protests, labor organizing, spirituality, and festivals, "involved at the same time cultural loss, cultural retention and reinterpretation, cultural imitation and borrowing, and cultural creation."[3] Afro-Creole culture featured a hybrid set of practices and values arising from freedpeople's simultaneous emulation of European elite customs as a route to respectability and class advancement, and their continued embrace of black folk culture, which was based on both African antecedents and innovations amid enslavement.[4] Freedpeople's material culture and institutions signaled their negotiations with and their progress within this unequal postslavery society. Their cultural expansion unfolded individually and communally, as freedpeople exhibited more confident self-presentation in their daily social practices. They protected their private spaces more vigorously, while gathering in and moving about public spaces more boldly. Freedom set these new social dynamics in motion, fostering new possibilities for the use of space and time among black communities.

Freedpeople's new forms of material culture shifted the linkage between freedom and commodity exchange in the nineteenth-century Atlantic World. During enslavement, freedom meant the exclusive right of propertied individuals to reduce both people and things to their "ownable," commodifiable characteristics.[5] This process transformed African captives into chattel slaves in the Atlantic marketplace. The expanded claims to space, leisure, and material goods made by formerly commodified African-descended people altered prevailing patterns of consumption. Through these acts, black working people reaffirmed their humanity and sought to be reincorporated into the life of the empire as whole beings with material preferences, rather than as possessions embodying the prerogatives of others.

White elites in Antigua were determined to contain this encroaching throng of social inferiors. They jealously guarded the racial and class privileges to which they knew freedpeople aspired, despite the fact that black working people were unlikely to succeed in upending the island's social and economic hierarchy. Ultimately, black working people's daily drudgery, not only on sugar estates but also in homes, shops, and other public spaces, helped to maintain the social power of whiteness in the colony. Any act on the part of black people that defied their degraded existence appeared bothersome or even threatening to whites. Yet many of freedpeople's new practices were born of the same social remaking that British emancipation was intended to achieve.

Freedpeople's mimicry of British elite customs both troubled and reaffirmed the conditional freedom they had endured since 1834. White elites reaped the material benefits of westernizing impulses among the freed community, but simultaneously derided freedpeople's lack of respectability. Whites' responses to these actions reveal how mimicry preserves power over colonial subjects. As Homi Bhabha explains, mimicry among colonial subjects births "a reformed, recognizable Other. . . . In order to be effective mimicry must continually produce . . . its difference."[6] Whites regarded freedpeople's unorthodox self-presentation and amusements as proof of their enduring and insurmountable cultural difference and racial inferiority, increasingly heaping scorn upon them during the early 1840s.

Black deference to white superiority faded quickly after emancipation. In the postslavery Anglophone Caribbean, "the poor were highly visible, and the elites expressed contradictory attitudes in their detailed observations and discussions of [their] dress, demeanor and entertainment."[7] White elites' conversations often focused on respectability as a mark of white privilege. White male colonial officials, travelers, and missionaries registered their disapproval of black amusements and consumption. But white female observers concerned themselves more intensely with demarcating the boundaries of social status and noting the divergences in private and public conduct among black, mixed-race, and white Antiguans. White women in colonial settings, who were "custodians" of the moral and cultural values of white communities, sought to limit the public presence of all African-descended people, not only to protect their own respectability but also to inhibit sexual relations between white men and women of color.[8]

Unlike many other colonial spaces, where female missionaries penned valuable sources for tracing social life, none to my knowledge have survived for Antigua. Many of this chapter's details about freedpeople's new modes of public life and consumption come from the observations of Mrs. Lanaghan, whom scattered sources also cite as "Flannigan" or "Lenaghan"; her first name sometimes appears as either Frances or Amelia. Details about her life are elusive, but she was likely the wife of a local merchant or planter, and part of the local elite.[9] While some debate exists over its authorship, this two-volume account of Antigua, titled *Antigua and the Antiguans* (1844), melds cultural, historical, anthropological, sociological, and environmental details about the island and its people, framed within nineteenth-century West Indian white women's social privilege and its accompanying contempt for black folkways, which suggests the pen of someone from this social stratum. Mrs. Lanaghan displayed class and race anxieties about freed black subjects and their pursuits in the disdainful tone of her writing. But her writings contain particular details about issues concerning households and social relations missing from accounts written by white West Indian men, which makes her treatise an invaluable source that documents freedpeople's lives beyond their labor.

During the early 1840s, elite Antiguan whites of both sexes felt that black working people were attempting to climb above their designated station in life. That perception was accurate: people of African descent sought fuller and more complex forms of freedom that allowed them not only autonomy but also integration into colonial life. Ultimately, freedpeople aspired to attain a healthy balance between independence and inclusion, but they endured exclusion even in the moments of greatest possibility after 1834.

The Free Village Movement: Housing and the Struggle for Autonomy

Antigua's freedpeople desired as much independence as possible from the sugar industry. Yet little arable land was available for them to cultivate, given the small size of the island, the extent of its engulfment by plantations, the severe soil erosion that resulted from sugar planting, and planters' determination to hoard even the infertile lands they owned. These factors, coupled with low wages, prevented freedpeople from leaving the plantations and settling on individual plots of land immediately after 1834. The formation of a peasantry was impossible in Antigua, in sharp contrast to larger British Caribbean territories, such as Jamaica, Trinidad, and Guyana, where many African-descended people became independent cultivators after apprenticeship ended in 1838.[10] Despite the obstacles, Antiguan freedpeople continued to desire autonomy through property ownership. But during the first few years after abolition, the majority of black working people still resided on plantations in the housing they had occupied as slaves. Slave barracks were poorly constructed and featured stone or wood walls, dirt floors, and roofs of cane or palm leaves.[11] These shabby structures were highly susceptible to fire and natural disasters endemic to the Caribbean, especially earthquakes and hurricanes. Densely clustered houses permitted little or no privacy. Samuel Smith, an Antiguan laborer born into a family that lived in former slave barracks more than fifty years after emancipation, vividly described the ills of estate housing: "Nothing to separate one family from the other. We use to live together like a flock of cattle, like goats or sheep in a pen. The truth is there was no difference to speak of between the life of the animals and ours."[12] Plantation houses were both uncomfortable and degrading to their inhabitants.

Living in slave barracks did more than carry the stigma of slavery for black working people; it also kept them under the watchful eyes of estate owners or managers, a gross social inconvenience that had legal repercussions. Proprietors arbitrarily deemed black people from other estates who were visiting friends and relatives on their estates to be trespassers on private property. Between June and August 1839, trespass charges were brought against Emanuel, George Nugent, and London, three black men married to women residents on different estates from the ones on which they lived and labored. When each man attempted to visit his wife, plantation managers hauled him before a local magistrate to face fines or jail time if he could not pay. Governor William Colebrooke and Solicitor General Robert Horsford's correspondence suggests that the charges against these men were eventually dismissed.[13] But the threat of a trespass charge reinforced constraints on black working people's movements and undermined family ties. As black working people sought to expand the limits placed on their occupation of space on or off the plantation, planters and legislators endeavored to contract them. As planters enforced the provisions of the 1834 Contract Act that tied housing to estate labor and local authorities forcefully blocked emigration to other territories, proprietary rights to local homes and land offered freedpeople the only real opportunity to enjoy independent private space and a better quality of life. Land ownership also yielded economic benefits and carried the potential for enfranchisement.

Despite extensive hoarding, planters had not been able to usurp all the land on the island. At the time of emancipation, a sizable amount of unoccupied land remained in the parish of St. Paul, set aside by the Crown in 1700 to encourage and subsidize settlement by white colonists, ex-soldiers, and servants who had been released from their indentures. A few small farms were established, but when the settlement scheme failed, most of the land reverted to the Crown.[14] In 1835, a few progressive public figures, including Henry Loving, the police chief, and James Scotland, a barrister, called for this unused land to be parceled out to freedpeople to foster their social advancement through industrious labor. Planters' vehement objections blocked the adoption of this proposal.[15]

Missionaries were instrumental in the process by which freedpeople finally gained access to land and the first free villages were formed. Resident clergy consistently appealed to the authorities to set up a land-distribution program, but to no avail. In January 1835, the Methodist missionary Matthew Banks wrote to Governor MacGregor:

But I should humbly suggest to Your Excellency the expediency of encouraging the establishment of *independent villages*. The *Huts* which the Negroes occupy on estates are not considered as their own any more than a *Stable is allowed* to be the *property of a horse*, otherwise, all those who *without legal process* have been unhanging the doors and windows of the Negroe houses, would have exposed themselves, to all the legal pains and penalties of *Housebreaking*. Free ingress and egress to the Friends of the occupants may be forbidden at pleasure by the director of an Estate. A person going to an estate to visit an afflicted relation is liable to be arrested by a rural constable and sentenced by a rural Magistrate to imprisonment as a trespasser and a vagrant. Besides, by their being herded together on Estates . . . they are not merely deprived of some of their most valuable civil rights as free subjects of the British Crown; but it endangers their *religious liberty*; for they may be, and in some instances they *are* prevented, by the bigotry, prejudice, superstition or caprice of a director, from availing themselves of that mode of Divine Worship in their own neighbourhood which best accords, with their religious views and from receiving those religious teachers by whom they wish to be instructed in the things of God.[16]

Banks recognized the political dimension of the violations of freedpeople's rights that living on sugar estates entailed. But his letter also reveals the most important goal that fueled missionaries' vigorous support for the establishment of independent villages: villagers would be free to attend the churches of their own choosing, which would promote their adoption of the Christian faith and the morality it inculcated. Resident missionaries who sought to strengthen their fledging parishes led the crusade and achieved remarkable results, finding ways to usher villages into existence without direct support from lawmakers.

Through missionary advocacy, individual planters breaking with their peers to profit from the burgeoning demand, and, most important, black working people's efforts to garner resources toward this end, land was finally leased or, more rarely, purchased, in the late 1830s. The drought of 1836–37, which plunged many planters into debt and prompted worker layoffs, contributed to freedpeople's move away from plantations. Beginning in 1836, the Moravian mission offered small plots of land for rent on the property surrounding their chapels in the east and south of the island, Newfield and Grace Hill.[17] That same year, a proprietor in the southeastern parish of St. Paul offered parts of her estate for sale, ushering into existence the first independent village in Antigua's history, which was appropriately named Liberta.[18] By 1842, approximately 3,600 black working people, or roughly one in ten Antiguans, lived in 1,037 homes in twenty-seven free villages.[19]

In 1839, the island's governor, Colebrooke, surveyed the stipendiary magistrates, the police chief, Methodist and Moravian clergy, and the public figures whom villagers most frequently encountered in their daily lives to obtain information about "the condition and habits of the laborers and settlers of the free villages."[20] The police chief, Martin Nanton, described the residents of free villages as "generally tradesmen," a designation encompassing a wide range of occupations held by men, such as estate work, carpentry, domestic service, and fishing. Many others also engaged in woodcutting and limestone burning to generate salable commodities. According to Nanton, these tradesmen labored on nearby plantations or in the towns and harbors, while their wives and children were based at home and maintained family provision grounds for both subsistence and profit. Tradesmen would also engage in provisioning when employment opportunities were scarce.[21]

The construction of village homes often replicated that of estate housing, with dirt floors, walls of stone or wood, and roofs of leaves, given their residents' limited means and the difficulty of acquiring better construction materials. But black working people were eager to move. Even in the early twentieth century, when insolvent planters who left Antigua to return to England or elsewhere tore down their houses, estate residents seeking to settle in villages would clamor for the remains. Samuel Smith recalled: "Now that stuff was far from being enough to provide for the great need of the people that wish to leave the estates, so there was always a serious rush by the people to get the torn down materials. Sometimes the planters would stop the public sale and sell privately to the chosen ones. People that did not have the fortunate position to buy the second-hand wood, but were determined to move away from the estates, would build the houses from wood, from the caps [the bushes] and from trash [dried cane leaves] and mud."[22]

Wattle-and-daub construction, with light wooden walls covered by mud, remained typical of most rural black working people's homes into the early twentieth century.[23] These houses could not withstand manmade or natural disasters. The wooden houses in or near the town were equally flimsy. They were often placed on piles of bricks or stones so they could easily be moved to another site, which, according to Mrs. Lanaghan, happened quite often among this careworn population.[24] A rare 1914 image of Hyndman's Village (figure 4.1) just outside St. John's reveals the precarious state of housing amid the poverty that marked village life. The British commissioners who took this photograph described Hyndman's as a "slum." But on closer look, the children are well dressed despite their lack of shoes, which suggests black people's efforts

FIGURE 4.1. Hyndman's Village, St. John Parish (1914). Photograph of housing and people in a "slum" (Hyndman's Village), Antigua. Crown Copyright. Source: PRO, CO 152/340/23, folio 145.

to maintain dignity even in dire circumstances. Three-quarters of a century earlier, black working people settled such village "slums" only by overcoming incredible odds and, unsurprisingly, struggled to survive financially thereafter.

Residents of rural free villages suffered from a lack of basic services. No observers mentioned the presence of stores in these villages. Access to medical care was limited. The police chief reported that food, shelter, and health care were available to villagers through the Daily Meal Asylum, a charity that served severely impoverished Antiguans. Village life did not shield residents from having to resort to alms.[25] Yet, while lacking in services, free villages offered a modicum of privacy that plantation huts did not. Some houses sat on plots of considerable size, especially in the less developed southern parishes.[26] Nanton estimated that families there held from half an acre to as many as five acres of land.[27] Even in more crowded villages in other parts of the island, residents' property was their own and their occupancy was not subject to the prerogatives of hostile employers.

Methodist and Moravian missionaries pointed to crucial advantages of village life over estate life. They concurred that freedpeople had autonomy over their homes and unrestricted access to provision grounds, guaranteeing that they could reap the fruits of their labor. Methodist clergyman John Cameron reported that sugar estates continued to provide housing and allot provision grounds to working people, but their tenure was "precarious." Any disagreement with management meant sure eviction, and thus automatic forfeiture of any produce growing on their provision grounds as well.[28] As a result of their greater housing security, the clergymen emphasized, free villagers tended provision grounds more industriously than estate residents.[29]

Black working people increasingly tried to avoid living on sugar estates because firing was coupled with homelessness. This arrangement figured largely in the rash of aforementioned trespass cases in the late 1830s and early 1840s. Cameron observed that laboring men evicted after disputes with their employers usually left their families behind on the plantation, and estate managers would charge them with trespass when they returned to visit. The practice of eviction formed a cornerstone of Cameron's argument: it "destroys the domestic order," "does violence to . . . feelings of humanity," "interferes . . . with religious duties," and "opens a wide door for licentiousness and crime."[30] In short, the terms of estate contracts trampled on the values that missionaries were attempting to instill in their congregants.

The clergy argued that free villages made freedpeople more industrious, decent, religious, and stable. Their enthusiastic accounts portrayed villages as the centerpiece of respectable black life. The Moravian clergyman C. Henry Warner connected village settlement, enthusiasm for education, and the strengthening of Christian devotion as he declared that school attendance among the children of villagers was rising. Church-sponsored education had a "pleasing effect" on children, making them "decent" and "orderly," and spilled over to parents, who bought Bibles and hymnbooks as their children became literate. Villagers were also choosing Christian marriage rather than cohabiting in common-law arrangements. In Warner's eyes, village residents exhibited a praiseworthy desire for "civilized life."[31]

Antiguan missionaries' claims about local free villages aligned with the discourse of Protestant missionaries elsewhere in the British Caribbean. In Jamaica, Protestant missionaries were heavily involved in the creation of free villages and encouraged black working people to form "respectable homes" centered on European-style families based in Christian marriage. These aspirations were upended, however, by the persistence of Afro-Jamaican cultural practices and economic strategies that hampered Christianization, Europeanization, and proletarianization.[32] Antiguan freedpeople had markedly similar responses to missionaries' attempts to refashion their ways. The Atlantic World's slaveholding states gendered the freed figure as male and posited him as the head of household. Missionaries, in line with the state's social vision for emancipation, encouraged monogamous marriage and female domesticity as part of the "civilizing" mission, while planters, upholding the state's economic interests, expected free women to engage in wage labor on sugar estates.[33] This contradictory mission yielded mixed results in Antigua, given both the demands of the labor market and freedpeople's consistent challenges to the cultural confines of Christianity.

Contemporary observers of Antiguan free villages consistently characterized the typical village household as male-headed and assumed that women were at home performing unwaged labor. Yet both the details and the silences in these surveys suggest the equal involvement of black workingwomen in building homes and maintaining livelihoods in the free villages. Women's work in tending provision grounds was essential to families that purchased or rented village plots. Daughters also contributed to household subsistence, even though the surveys, like contemporary censuses in the metropole, only specified sons' occupations.[34] As the Moravian clergyman Warner noted, black working people were "not unwilling" to engage male children in rural occupations provided they were not prevented from attending school, but parents were decidedly averse to putting female children to work in the cane fields.[35] To the extent that they could afford to do so, newly freed Antiguan families attempted to keep girls and women out of plantation gangs. As Bridget Brereton explains, Afro-Caribbean families removed women and girls from field labor to protect them from sexual violation by coworkers and overseers. This pattern was based on more urgent concerns than reverence for the Christian concept of family.[36]

Yet the sources detailing black women's newfound domesticity in the villages confirm that they still performed waged work both indoors and out. Moreover, many women were on record as heads of household, as landowners or leaseholders in villages. Of twenty-two homes surveyed in Bolans, a Valley District village, the washerwoman Lucy Barnard, the huckster Polly Morris, and the plantation laborer Patience

Smith were reported as renting an acre of land each. Four out of fifteen families surveyed at a village known as The River also had women listed as proprietors; Jane Charles and a woman called Sarah each rented half an acre, while Caroline Freeman and Rebecca Adams each rented a full acre. Similarly, at Fisher's, Susannah Finch and Elizabeth rented a half-acre and an acre of land, respectively.[37] Black working people met their urgent need for income in whatever ways they could. Women's employment continued after emancipation, and these surveys prove that women were able to garner enough resources to become independent small farmers.

Freedwomen and -men who settled in independent villages enjoyed a host of new economic and social opportunities. Though they did so to further their own agendas, missionaries helped to make these opportunities available. Importantly, village residence offered working people a chance to restructure the terms of their labor on sugar plantations, which rankled planters. The existence of free villages threatened the profits and power that planters derived from their dual position as employers and landlords of black working people.

Free Villagers and the Restructuring of Estate Labor

While missionaries lauded the villages as bastions of industry and Christian propriety, planters vilified them for fostering breaches of law and order among unruly freedpeople. Theft was a recurring source of concern among planters. As in the past, where slaves illicitly obtained provisions from estate storehouses to supplement their allotted rations, black working people still adhered to a moral economy in which they were entitled to use any plantation's resources to meet their material needs, whether or not they were employed on that estate. An 1839 letter to the editor of a weekly newspaper signed "An Agriculturist" expressed indignation that free villagers, whom he called "squatters" to brand their access to land illegitimate, were allegedly pilfering from nearby estates:

> At this moment the mountain districts in St. Mary's Parish swarm with squatters who, renting from half an acre to an acre of land find it wholly inadequate to the support of their families, they have therefore recourse to the woods of the neighbouring plantations, where they can steal with impunity, because the remote locality forbids detection. In this way they supply the town with large quantities of Wood

and Charcoal, and when a contiguous woody tract of land is wanting, the deficiency is readily made up from the nearest field of canes, this also is a profitable article in the market. Persons thus employing themselves can treble the amount of a day laborer's wages, and as might be expected . . . a great many plantation laborers have abandoned their comfortable domiciles to augment the number of hands thus so lamentably employed.[38]

Similarly in 1844, the estate manager W. H. Martin declared: "Many smuggling villages had been built all round our coast, which has added very much to the withdrawal of labour from plantation work." This estate manager regarded all independent labor as a criminal enterprise.[39] By offering alternatives to employment on sugar estates, villages threatened planters' control of the large, low-paid labor force on which their profits depended. Theft functioned as shorthand for a number of anxieties that villages engendered among local elites. Ultimately, planters presumed that the labor power of African-descended Antiguans should remain under their control, so any threat to that control constituted a form of theft. In addition to jeopardizing the supply of labor from without, free villages also undermined plantation work regimes from within.

The free village movement disrupted many tactics that planters used to control their employees, especially through the restrictions of the Contract Act. Black working people who resided in villages rather than on estates averaged a higher rate of wages by avoiding the deduction taken for housing. However, the costs of maintaining independent housing would absorb that wage increase. The outlay of cash for purchasing land or continuously paying rent, as well as the high prices for even the shoddiest of building materials to erect or secure the structure of a home, meant that free villagers would likely feel this "raise" only minimally. But their strategies to obtain higher wages were still historically remarkable. Free villagers often established independent gangs: a group of people would hire themselves to a nearby plantation to do task work at a rate negotiated between the employer and either the group's designated foreman or each individual. These rates were usually higher than the wages offered to contracted workers. As much as they could, independent gangs also determined the conditions of their labor, including the start and end of the workday and the timing of breaks. A magistrate for St. Paul Parish reported that the independent gangs there were composed of more women than men.[40] The fact that black women were willing to join gangs that workers themselves organized and controlled demonstrates that their reluctance to enter labor contracts stemmed less from an aversion to toiling in the fields and more from their desire to avoid the financial, physical, and sexual vulnerability that the terms of contract labor engendered.

Plantation workers elsewhere in the Caribbean, including Cuba and Guyana, also formed itinerant labor gangs to secure better work conditions within stringent labor regimes. The gangs' negotiations signaled an early form of collective bargaining.[41] The flexibility of gangs benefited working people who were also engaged in alternative moneymaking pursuits and provided women an easier way to balance wage earning with domestic responsibilities. The existence of independent gangs, like that of free villages, offended planters who were still convinced years after freedom that the best labor force was a captive one. As Douglas Hall points out, "job-workers . . . came and went not at the planters' convenience but their own, and thus undermined the basic routine of work essential to estate cultivation." Even planters able to afford the higher wages that jobbing gangs demanded complained of their "hastily, and so improperly performed," work.[42] The system represented the slow but sure decline of planters' control over freedpeople.

Planters could do little to change the labor market in the early 1840s, when freedpeople had apparently managed to tip the supply-demand balance in their favor. Planters attempted to standardize wage rates for specific tasks through the formation of "agricultural associations,"[43] but these clubs failed to achieve the desired effect. As independent gangs became a major source of manpower on estates, black working people increasingly labored on plantations at wages they set and came and went at their own discretion, which meant that the labor force was never as stable as planters would have liked.

Interestingly, according to local magistrates, gang labor bred hostilities among black working people as well. The contracted laborers who worked longer and earned less resented the shorter working hours and higher wages of independent gangs.[44] Estate residents sometimes found themselves having to redo the shoddy work of independent laborers; as the stipendiary magistrate William Walker remarked, this situation was "productive of jealousy, and led to bickerings."[45] At the same time, magistrates observed that many black working people contracted to plantations frequently absented themselves, violating their contracts in order to enlist in jobbing gangs on other estates.[46] Ultimately, contracted workers figured that it was more profitable to join independent gangs than compete with them.[47] Joining a jobbing gang with higher pay and a more flexible schedule might have been the first step that black workingwomen and -men living on estates took toward independent village residence.

Wages for jobbing gangs and contract workers rose considerably after an earthquake in February 1843 destroyed thousands of homes across Antigua and the sugar works on most of the island's plantations.[48] Rebuilding allowed significant numbers of freedmen to become tradesmen or tradesmen's assistants. Much to planters' dismay, the availability of alternative employment exacerbated the scarcity of labor for sugar production. As wages soared after the earthquake, some workers made enough money to shorten their workweek to three days.[49] In 1844, the estate manager W. H. Martin decried the "enormous price of labour" and the concessions made to black working people in order to guarantee their consistent presence on estates. In his opinion, Antigua's sugar industry suffered from "the want of a little firmness" among proprietors and managers, who were "too readily induced to give something extra, such as rum &c. when the [laborers] are troublesome, rather than lose them for a few days."[50] The earthquake left estate residences in shambles, prompting many more freedpeople to move to villages. A new village sprang into existence on the outskirts of St. John's only months following the earthquake, as a proprietor sold off undeveloped lots.[51]

Independent villages were an attractive alternative to estates throughout the 1840s, providing black working people with opportunities to improve the quality of their labor and leisure. Thousands of families flooded the villages; by 1846, sixty-eight villages had a total of more than nine thousand residents.[52] The transition to free villages formed a central part of an entire spectrum of changes in black working-class life. A more independent home life and better wages also ushered in new kinds of material desires and amusements among freedpeople, which underlined their more visible public practice of freedom. In the early 1840s, elite observers were dismayed by black working people's new tastes, in part because these displays signaled their broader social and political aspirations.

"Citizens of the World": Freedpeople's Consumption and Sunday Socializing

The standard of living among freedpeople people rose as wages peaked and working hours grew more flexible, allowing for greater independence and the time to pursue enjoyment. Local authorities were quite aware that freedom had wrought changes in working people's personal tastes and aspirations. In 1844 a magistrate expressed alarm at "the manners, the Habits, the Tastes of the Slave, [having] been converted into those of the independent Peasant," who "assumed now of the character of a Citizen of the World, carries his labor to the best Markets, [and] furnishes his table and surrounds his cottage, with what may be termed luxuries."[53] Reaping the fruits of their labor and capitalizing on the widening opportunities of the early 1840s, black people improved their material circumstances and sought pleasure in their everyday lives. Yet freedpeople recognized the negative impressions their pursuits made on white elite women and men, as the concerted efforts of missionaries, magistrates, and planters to root out these practices made clear. An oppositional politics that intentionally provoked or, at the very least, relished the disdainful reactions of whites informed their new patterns of consumption and leisure.

Once they received cash wages for their labor, freedpeople purchased items that provided everyday comforts. Mrs. Lanaghan observed that freedpeople in town had clean and well-cared-for "culinary articles" and "smart-colored cups" in their kitchens.[54] She declared that the best worker housing on estates, typically belonging to "head negroes" or skilled artisans, boasted sofas, mahogany tables, "decanters, tumblers, wineglasses[,] . . . plates and dishes, tea-cups, and various other kinds of gaudy crockeryware." Some of the grander items may have been castoffs from the "big house," but the families of black men of rank were spending money on housewares that displayed their status. Even the homes of field workers contained basic articles of furniture, such as locally made chairs and wooden boxes.[55] Mrs. Lanaghan could have exaggerated the sumptuousness of freedpeople's living quarters because of her anxieties about their penchant for consumption. But her observations support the conclusion that black working people furnished their homes as well as they could.

During slavery, African-descended Antiguans had dressed as elegantly as possible, whether at the market or on special occasions. The sight of enslaved men and women wearing fancy clothing and adornments at Christmastime captivated the late eighteenth-century traveler Janet Schaw. Those who were proceeding to the town market to enjoy the festivities were "universally clad in white muslin"; the men wore black caps, while the women sported turbans made from gauze or silk handkerchiefs.[56] Their self-adornment and social gatherings reinforced enslaved people's claims to their own bodies and their rights to pleasure, defying the everyday use and abuse of their bodies for the profit and power of their masters.[57] The passage to freedom and the receipt of wages intensified the use of pleasure and adornment as oppositional practices. Antiguan freedpeople's dress grew quite ornate in the 1840s, showing their appreciation for refined Victorian fashions despite their modest stations in life. Sunday unquestioningly remained the "Negroes' holiday," and black working people looked their best while socializing in public. Mrs. Lanaghan vividly described black women cutting cane and feeding horses "in a state approximating to nudity" during the week, but they sported white muslin dresses adorned with colorful ribbons, silk stockings, and netted "Victoria" cloaks strung with flowers on Sundays. Instead of the madras cloth that enslaved women had tied on their heads, freedwomen wore bonnets with colored trim and floral accents and carried decorated parasols for shade.[58] Not to be outdone, men who were bricklayers, carpenters, or domestic servants by day donned colored waistcoats with velvet collars, leather boots, broad-brimmed hats, and kerchiefs. "So great [were] their metamorphoses" on the Sabbath, Mrs. Lanaghan exclaimed, that it was "impossible" to recognize them.[59]

The mention of these people's rugged labors during the week discursively renders them undeserving of such finery on the weekends. Mrs. Lanaghan's inclusion of the detail regarding black laboring women's so-called nudity invokes a familiar Anglo-Atlantic trope that buttressed racial and gender constructions of women of color. The "unfeminine" nature of naked black and brown women toiling in the colonies was a commonplace assumption made by whites writing about life in the British Empire for at least two centuries.[60] Mrs. Lanaghan's concentration on black women's nudity offers an undesirable yet sexualized image of black women, reinforcing the conviction that refined clothing could not nullify their inherent savagery. The text betrays her own fears during this time of social flux as much as it tells us about black people's garb while at work or at play.

The popular amusements enjoyed by black people in the 1840s created quite a stir among Antiguan elites. Because clothing remained a principal feature of black working people's socializing, whites' anxieties over freedpeople's amusements were inextricably tied to their alarm over freedpeople's "extravagant" sartorial styles. The public entertainments that black working people pursued exhibit Afro-Creole culture's "duality of conformity and rejection of European norms."[61] For example, black communities in town and country regularly planned "subscription balls," which required entry fees or prior contributions. They were attended by a "*glittering throng*" of fashion "votaries" in brightly colored formal clothing; the women wore elaborate jewels and adornments in their hair.[62] Those who paid extra could obtain the coveted privilege of performing the first dance. Music played and freedpeople danced well into the night at these affairs, as participants knew how to "trip the light fantastic toe," in European styles such as the quadrille, as well as "native" forms of "African" dance accompanied by banjos and tom-toms. Mrs. Lanaghan unsurprisingly framed these noisy, all-night events with her usual scorn, portraying them as disruptive, inimical to law and order, and frequented by the "worst characters."[63] Christmas holidays featured the grandest balls. Invitations on fine stationery employed polite language, addressing invitees as "Miss" or "Mr." These "quadrille parties" were filled with black men and women sporting the most colorful and elaborate clothing and jewelry they could obtain. The hall was ornately decorated, with branches, flowers, and fruits of all kind, and the hosts offered an extensive array of delicacies of local and imported origin. Echoing the planters' anger at the free villagers' moral economy, Mrs. Lanaghan suspected that theft or trickery sourced the fine decor and food at these balls, as black working people pilfered regularly from their employers.[64]

Similarly elaborate displays accompanied the celebrations that followed christenings and weddings, where cake, fruit, and wine were served. The stipendiary magistrate L. Graeme lamented to the governor: "Wages are lavished in so unprofitable and expensive a manner. At weddings, christenings and at Divine service, I have seen field labourers dressed in superfine cloth coats, trousers, and vests of the latest patterns and highest cost, which in England would expose persons in the same station and rank of life to the derision of their associates."[65] Babies were "smartly dressed" at their christenings, in white robes and bonnets, and were occasionally shaded with parasols. Mrs. Lanaghan bemoaned as well that before emancipation, black babies were typically given names with West African origins, such as "Quasheba" and "Sambo," but following freedom and "the march of intellect" through the West Indies, parents favored European names such as "Arabella Christiana" and "Augustus Henry."[66] Freedpeople's naming choices rejected their previous subjugation and indicated their aspiration to attain a more elevated station in life. Her choice of the names Sambo and Quasheba as examples of increasingly abandoned names among the freed community is telling, since both circulated in the Anglophone Atlantic World as the respective signifiers of "docile" and "defiant" slaves.[67] Even more telling is that laziness was associated with each trope; she unsubtly suggests here that despite their new trappings and practices of freedom, freedpeople were the same troublesome subjects they had always been during slavery.

The pomp and circumstance of black weddings especially discomforted white observers. Mrs. Lanaghan observed that black weddings involved processions in horse-drawn wagons and feasts featuring lavishly decorated cakes.[68] The Quaker minister Joseph John Gurney, who observed a wedding of "common laborers" on a sugar estate while visiting Antigua in 1840, registered his surprise at the couple's fashionable dress. The groom wore a "handsome waistcoat, with a brooch, white pantaloons, and Wellington boots." He also remarked that wedding cakes and dinners were "extravagant" and that champagne was served.[69] Missionaries on the island had reason to rejoice in the popularity of weddings and christenings among freedpeople. But even those who did not share Gurney's Quaker standards of plainness in dress and moderation in food and drink were alarmed by the seeming excesses. These reports of black weddings emphasize that their accouterments did not align with the social rank of the participants, hinting at white elites' contempt for freedpeople's bourgeois veneer. Mrs. Lanaghan disdainfully remarked that "the greater part of these 'blushing brides'" who dressed in silk and satin "have been living several years in a state of concubinage with different persons, and are perhaps the mothers of several children."[70] To whites, the prevalence of nonmarital family formation in freed communities prevented black women from claiming respectability even at the moment of wedlock, rendering brides' finery ill-suited and the nuptials themselves illegitimate. Revealingly, Mrs. Lanaghan called wedding guests "black buckras," a play on the term buckra used by Afro-Caribbean people in slavery and freedom to designate white people. This phrase was gaining currency among whites at the time, in response to the penchant exhibited by black social strivers to "imitate in everything their *fairer bretheren.*"[71] The phrase *black buckra* connotes whites' vehemence in upholding the racialized colonial order that freedpeople's leisure and consumption sought to trouble.

Black working people pursued new pastimes and sartorial styles to assert their simultaneous distinctions from and similarities to elites. They signified their change in status from slave to free by changing how they lived and how they looked. As Robin Kelley suggests of twentieth-century black working people at leisure in the United States: "Seeing oneself and others 'dressed up' was enormously important in terms of constructing a collective identity based on something other than wage work, presenting a public challenge to the dominant stereotypes of the black body, and reinforcing a sense of dignity that was perpetually being assaulted."[72] Their search for autonomy and advancement bred new consumption patterns that built on their long-standing cultural practices of African and creole origin, such as dance and Sunday social-izing. Their increasing exposure to Anglo-Protestant ideas about "re-spectability" that circulated in religious, legal, and social discourse also prompted freedpeople's changing self-presentation. But respectability, a racially bounded privilege in this colonial setting, would always remain beyond freedpeople's reach, regardless of how much they looked and acted the part. Black working people's expressions of self-determination through clothing had, at best, mixed consequences. Their assumption of bourgeois styles of dress reinforced the impossibly high bar erected by colonial respectability and provoked ridicule by white elites.[73] Their improvements in their outward appearance drew the contempt and mockery of white observers and officials, who constantly tried to con-tain blacks' intent to advance beyond their proscribed social roles as de-graded laborers.

The Christian church particularly tried in earnest to stamp out the conspicuous consumption that accompanied black working people's leisure activities. Missionaries knew all too well that freedpeople were diverging from the path of austerity and industriousness preached by the Protestant churches to all congregants, whether black or white. In fact, freedpeople's consumption at times directly conflicted with their Chris-tian duty. In rainy weather, Gurney observed, freedpeople "are less will-ing to come out to their places of worship. . . . They now have *shoes and stockings* which they are unwilling to expose to the mud."[74] The Wesleyan Methodist Sunday school regulations specifically prohibited students from wearing jewelry and attending balls, horse races, and theaters.[75] The privilege of religious education required abstention from material goods and secular amusements. Similarly, the Moravian church ejected members from its congregations for participation in activities deemed illicit by the clergy. For instance, Henry Edward and Thomas, members of the Grace Hill Moravian Church, were excluded in October 1845 for attempting to throw a dance at Johnson's Estate in St. Paul Parish, where they worked as field laborers.[76] Attempts to curtail consumption and worldly amusements among freedpeople aligned with prevailing Protestant sentiments concerning the ungodliness of luxuries for all believers, and these attempts were compounded by the English colonial urge to keep luxuries beyond former slaves' reach. But instilling Christian modesty in people who were eager to relish their freedom was an ill-fated undertaking.

Black working people also regularly participated in more common socializing, including such English holidays as Guy Fawkes Day, which commemorated the foiling of a 1605 plot to blow up the Parliament building. In Antigua, the holiday was marked by what the traveler Charles William Day sneeringly called "miserable" displays of fireworks in St. John's and black hucksters' noisy cries to hawk their wares.[77] This homemade celebration showed black working people's appropriation of metropolitan tradition, molding a version of this holiday that involved craftsmanship and economic gain. The grogshops that proliferated in the town of St. John's during the early 1840s attracted a motley, inter-racial collection of patrons, not just from the black working class but also from Antigua's minuscule white working class, along with a few disreputable white men from the upper class. "Soldiers, sailors, dingy-looking blacks and unfortunate females[,] . . . and men of better rank of life, who ought to blush to be found in such places," reportedly gathered in these rum shops. Mrs. Lanaghan and other members of the white elite regarded these places as "store-houses for crime," although white men who might belong to the elite by day were attracted to the bawdy excitements and the sexual access to black and white women's bodies to be had there by night. To passersby, the grogshops emitted "the various sounds of cursing and quarreling, idiotic laughter, discordant singing, and incoherent talking, as the miserable frequenters arrive at different stages of intoxication."[78] The local market also continued to serve as a site for less refined pastimes among black patrons. During the era of slavery, dances, boxing matches, and gambling took place during and after market hours.[79] Mrs. Lanaghan's descriptions of the market in the 1840s do not mention the amusements that may have taken place there, but she condemned the entire enterprise as a "complete Babel," where aggressive and noisy transactions between buyers and sellers continued well into the night.[80]

Estate laborers in the countryside also pursued enjoyments that elite observers deemed inappropriate. Dances in particular aroused alarm. In St. Paul Parish in 1841, the magistrate William Walker witnessed weekly Sunday dances on several sugar estates "where the refuse of society . . . are freely admitted." He reported that these dances generated "riots and disturbances amongst the labourers" that involved "struggling, blows and wounds, necessitating the interference of the rural constables."[81] While black workingwomen and -men socialized to relieve the stresses of their labor, the authorities construed their drinking and dancing as the cause of criminal acts and licentious behavior.[82] The unharmonious nature of black social gatherings gravely concerned white elites. The violence that peppers descriptions of freedpeople's dances in this period uncannily parallels that found in accounts of the slaves' Sunday market a century earlier. Both events were accompanied by assaults by black people on one another and, more worrisomely to whites, on private property.

These amusements evoked the "irreverence, transcendence, social realism, self-empowerment, and collective individualism" that Tera Hunter identifies in black working people's dancehall culture in the southern United States after the Civil War.[83] In Antigua, the tradition of Sunday socializing despite religious indoctrination about Sabbath observance remained central to black working people's sense of community and autonomy. Although the archive only hints at the complexity of black people's interior identities during this transitional period, the documents convey whites' persistent tendency to connect black socializing with crime, reflecting sentiments well entrenched since slavery regarding black people's "natural" penchant for extralegal behavior.

Any activity that failed to meet white expectations of black obedience was deemed illicit in colonial Antigua. But slavery's end made freedpeople's social pursuits appear much more threatening to elite dominance than when black bodies were still property. Day, the traveler, revealed just how repulsive colonial whites found freedpeople's new confidence as they cavorted in public spaces: "I consider the black population of Antigua the most inhuman of all the islands. Their impudent familiarity is something astounding. 'Me good as Queen Victoria,' said a huge ugly negress in my hearing. 'Me good as Prince Albert,' was the remark of a fiendish-looking negro. All this would be simply laughable, but for the mischief which such doctrines produce."[84] Day's objections to freedpeople's speech are compounded by his revulsion at their physical appearance. He deliberately rendered this man and this woman subhuman, yet lying beneath his disdain was his anxiety that two ordinary working people would dare to equate themselves, even in jest, with the empire's monarchs. Ultimately, the "mischief" of which Day spoke encapsulates the manifold acts through which emancipated Antiguans built not only a material culture but also a sense of self-worth. These two black people may have simply sought to irritate a visibly scornful white observer with the boldness of their speech, but their words could also signify their new and ever-expanding practices of personal freedom.

Conclusion

Though colonial Antigua's racial and class hierarchy essentially remained intact during the early 1840s, changes in their material circumstances shifted freedpeople's attitude toward local elites. The transformation of black working people from being commodities to consuming them set whites on edge. They decried the expanded range of public space that freedpeople occupied, the new amusements in which they engaged, and the modified labor routine that created time to enjoy them. Whites' own social positions grew more precarious, as black labor was better recompensed and black working people became more assertive. The solicitor general and magistrate Robert Horsford complained in 1845 about "the marked diminution of the deference which [freedpeople] have hitherto been accustomed to pay those in authority over them. . . . There seems to exist amongst many of them . . . a false impression that the temporary independence which they have latterly been able to obtain has placed them much more upon a footing of equality with their employers."[85] Horsford's use of *temporary* to describe freedpeople's independence suggests his expectation—or hope—that their insolent demeanor would soon have to revert to the obedience of old times. A Methodist missionary also lamented in 1845 that "ten years ago, I believe there was more piety in our town members than there is now. . . . Emancipation, good crops, money, the large outlay after the earthquake, & consequently prosperity to the working population, the enlargement of the elective population, together with other minor things all combine to produce a reaction in the colony, anything but friendly to saving religion."[86] Access to cash, consumer goods, and property also created new avenues for access to political processes. The institutions serving the material, social, and political interests of freedpeople, such as churches and free villages, facilitated black working people's assertion of new public roles. These institutions did not overturn the social hierarchy, as many of them operated in accordance with elite objectives, but the sense of empowerment derived from participation potentially poised freedpeople for a different sort of struggle against the colonial order.

A critical aspect of the colonial state's vision for emancipation involved the creation of material desires among freedpeople that would require regular wages rather than subsistence living, in effect binding freedpeople to the estates. According to Frederick Cooper, Thomas Holt, and Rebecca Scott, this expectation served as the test that would distinguish the universal "economic man" that freedpeople of the empire might potentially become from the "peculiar Africans" that they were as slaves.[87] In the 1840s, Antigua's colonial officials, missionaries, and planters concluded that freedpeople had not become reliable and productive laborers, as evinced by their move to the villages, their spotty presence in the cane fields, and their shrinkage of the workweek. The new tastes and desires reflected by their participation in the consumer economy did not satisfy white observers either, but instead unleashed a more intensely racialized discourse about their unwarranted class pretensions, their allegedly natural criminal tendencies, and the repulsiveness of their bodies. Indeed, the empire's test of freedom, as it was rendered in postslavery Antigua, was construed to result in freedpeople's failure.

Yet black working people at this time experienced a modicum of success in achieving a sense of freedom in their everyday lives. They were gaining greater economic independence, treating themselves to finery previously reserved for whites, and seeking enjoyment on their own terms. Their activities did not merely serve to insinuate them within the mainstream: they were creating a culture that was all their own, born of their constant struggles and their intermittent breakthroughs. Their pursuits attested to their partial transformation into proletarians, but they also reminded whites of their collective opposition to absolute domination. The oppositional practices of freedom, however mitigated by the strictures of the colonial enterprise, seemed to expand consistently during the early 1840s. A closer look at intimate relations among black working people during this time reveals that, even as black lives evidenced improvement on the surface, the pressures of freedom precipitated a more insidious private struggle to survive that bore especially violent consequences for freedwomen.

CHAPTER 5

"SINFUL CONEXIONS"

Christianity, Social Surveillance,

and Black Women's Bodies in Distress

The increased attendance and attention at the public means of grace are very gratifying; nor is it less pleasing, to observe the earnest desire on the part of many who have been excluded, to return to the fold, and to be restored to their former privileges. I was visited lately by a young woman, who had been excluded about two years ago for immorality. . . . She then told me, that her heart was too full to speak about her case now, but, "ever since my exclusion," she said, "I have felt as if I had no friend; I have enjoyed neither health of body nor peace of mind, and my daily and nightly prayer is, that my sins may be forgiven, and that I may be taken back to my church."—BROTHER C. B. ELLIS of Gracehill Moravian Church, 1852

The story in the epigraph of this unidentified woman can easily be read as the strengthening of her once-wavering religious faith, but her difficulties after her exclusion from the church prompt reflection on black women's multidimensional experiences with the pitfalls of emancipation. Amid the attention-getting outward signs of material improvement in the freed community, impoverishment disproportionately affected women. Antigua's sugar production and profits had waned since 1834. The exceptional wage increases in the early 1840s resulted from black working people's bargaining strategies rather than any reversal in the sugar industry's fortunes, and proved short-lived. Moreover, black workingwomen consistently received lower wages than men. Christian churches, which offered material benefits, such as illness insurance, and social services, such as meals and education, became increasingly important as freedpeople navigated the uncertainties of economic life. This woman's loss of membership in the Moravian Church could have had material, as well as spiritual and emotional, consequences. She may have endured physical and social discomfort while struggling in the grip of poverty without the safety net of the church.[1]

The story's most critical element, the reason for her exclusion from the church, is unspecified in the missionary's account of her restoration to membership. But the "immorality" for which most black women were expelled, church records indicate, was nonmarital sexual relations. Christian churches in the nineteenth-century British Caribbean encouraged cultural conformity and spiritual devotion as a way to engineer a black freedom steeped in order and obedience. Missionaries, who largely endorsed the imperatives of the colonial state, had a vested interest in refashioning ex-slaves into willing sugar laborers and law-abiding subjects. To that end, churches and the state focused on black congregants' sexual relations and marriages—or sexual relations outside of marriage. They sought to restructure black families by promoting wedlock, nuclear households, and patriarchal authority, as opposed to the female-headed, extended family structure that formed the basis of enslaved people's social worlds.[2]

Black women and men throughout the Atlantic World had formed family through multiple intimate partnerships and extended kin networks since they arrived in the colonies in chains. These practices stemmed from African cultural antecedents and were compounded by the frequency of death and the constant threat of sale in slave societies, which regularly disrupted family ties among Africans and their descendants. Informal unions and extended rather than patrilineal kinship patterns persisted well into the era of freedom.[3] As Christianity spread throughout the Americas, European missionaries roundly condemned what were common and culturally acceptable practices in black communities. In British Caribbean colonies, freedpeople's increased church membership brought forth new forms of interference with their informal sexual relations. Clergymen tried but failed to fully dismantle the flexibility in family formation prevalent among Africans and their descendants. Yet to a considerable degree, and often with unhappy consequences, the churches succeeded in modifying the structures and lived experiences of family and sexuality. Freedpeople in Antigua experienced the pressures of dismal material prospects and church-enforced monogamy in deeply gendered ways. Men and women still jointly provided for their households. But women lost some of the independence that non-monogamy had afforded them, as the church sought to tether men and women together in more-official and often repressive ways.

Emancipation failed to bring material and social advancement to all African-descended Antiguans. Freedpeople's social and sexual relations also demonstrate that slavery's end particularly disadvantaged black women more than black men. Black women, though nominally free, were not fully liberated. They faced physical subjugation and socioeconomic distress, as their bodies, their relationships, and their livelihoods were subject to scrutiny and violence in many settings. Black women's plight in freedom extended the bodily devaluation and physical brutality they endured from both white and black men during slavery, which only intensified amid Antigua's precipitous socioeconomic decline over the decades after abolition. The literature's reluctance to acknowledge the violation of black women's bodily integrity by black men under slavery stems from a long-standing impulse to portray black families as a refuge from white domination and to prove the resilience of their social ties despite the extremity of their oppression.[4] The silence about gendered fissures within black families in freedom stems from similar sources. But failing to acknowledge the sometimes-troubled relations between freedmen and freedwomen distorts our understanding of their historically divergent positions. Hilary Beckles concludes that white slave-owning men were not the sole perpetrators of gendered violence against enslaved women in the Caribbean. They "contended daily with physical and social abuse from the subordinate masculinity of male slaves who shared their degradation and psychological terrorisation. Male slaves not only whipped, chained, and imprisoned female slaves under managerial instruction, but in their domestic relations some brutalised them as a normal expression of their compromised patriarchy."[5] Black men's physical assaults on black women continued well after abolition. This routine violence is connected to the larger structures of power that all freedpeople encountered in the context of the Christian church, the sugar market, and the colonial state.

This chapter first examines evangelism among black communities by the Methodist and Moravian Churches and the hybrid nature of black religiosity, which combined the African-based spiritual practice of obeah with Christianity. Freedpeople generally supported the churches, but did so in part to secure the material benefits of membership. Missionaries worked to improve freedpeople's socioeconomic prospects, for their outreach programs brought them more congregants. Church membership offered black working people many options for social advancement in Antigua, but the benefits of church affiliation came with strict social limits. Churches also functioned as a regulatory force, mandating particular kinds of behavior in the name of piety.

The chapter surveys the Moravian Church's records, which chronicle hundreds of exclusions and potential exclusions of members between the 1830s and 1840s, to explore gendered social relations within the freed populace and the particular disadvantages that black women suffered in the context of the family. In its push to promote Christian marriage, the Moravian Church regularly attempted to police freedpeople's nonmonogamous intimate relationships. Black women and men both consented to nonmonogamous relations, but women experienced the greatest social and material dangers from multiple-partner arrangements. The frequency with which women found themselves charged with transgressions meriting exclusion reveals the gendered inequalities that structured black women's lives in freedom. Moravian records show that black male communicants were also regularly chastised by and expelled from the church for their sexual and social practices. The records documenting men's acts of wrongdoing often indicate the abusive or controlling behavior that marked their relationships with women. Even as men were punished for running afoul of church mores, their control over women and women's corresponding powerlessness are apparent in the archive. Women's disempowerment was exacerbated by waning economic opportunities and expanding hostility to black progress among white elites. Considering the Moravian church's exclusions along with other documents exposes the perils facing black women in Antigua, not just from the state, the marketplace, and the church but also from the men in their own homes.

Obeah's Continuity amid the Spread of Christianity

Freedpeople flocked to Christian churches and joined them in considerable numbers. This upswing may have signified the spiritual conversion of people of African descent. But obeah, a system of West African spiritual beliefs and practices, did not disappear in the face of Christian evan-

gelism, a fact that casts doubt on the completeness of missionary proselytizing. Obeah flourished in black communities throughout the British
West Indian colonies, in spite of the fact that it was illegal and was often
decried as witchcraft. The persistence of obeah today in the English-
speaking Caribbean illuminates the multilayered power relations underlying the last five centuries of the region's history. Obeah informed
criminalization and punishment, cultural production and representation,
and community formation and stratification.[6] Scholars have defined
the practice in a variety of interconnected ways: as a system of health
care and scientific practices, a means of social control and mediation of
status in black communities, an alternative system of governance and
meting out of justice, and a central form of creole religious expression.[7]
It was also a tool for organizing rebellion; in 1736, enslaved Antiguan
conspirators used obeah rituals to lay careful plans to overthrow white
rule. After emancipation, black people in Antigua increasingly used colonial courts to address perceived injustices, but they still believed in and
practiced obeah as a traditional method of conflict resolution tailored to
their community's needs.[8] It played a key role in the expansion of black
working people's practices of freedom and their survival strategies in the
early 1840s.

Since the era of slavery, elites' efforts to encourage law, order, and
Christian devotion among people of African descent were undermined
by the widespread influence of obeah on their spiritual and social practices. The mixed-race Methodist lay leader Anne Hart Gilbert declared
in 1804 that Antigua's slaves lived "in a state of inconceivable darkness
and diabolical superstition," and she worried that local preachers' unfamiliarity with blacks' culture made them "pass too lightly over the sin of
witchcraft."[9] The earliest law against obeah in Antigua, passed in 1809,
penalized "persons pretending to exercise Witchcraft, Fortune-telling,
or by Crafty Science to discover Stolen Goods" with a year's imprisonment and a stint in the town pillory.[10] Mrs. Lanaghan mentions that the
legislature passed this law in response to a rash of mysterious poisonings of planters and their relatives. Echoing Gilbert, she deemed obeah
"one of those dark and fearful practices which [the slaves] brought with
them from Africa, where the devil is still openly worshipped and temples
built to his honor."[11]

Mrs. Lanaghan cobbled together her account of obeah's presence after
1834 from a number of stories overheard among black working people.
Her narrative exhibits explicit dismissal and fearful undertones, a duality

that marks elite attitudes toward this belief system. She mulled over the latent potency of the practice while condemning what she considered the superstitious ways of black working people. After remarking that poisonings declined after emancipation, she lamented the deaths of the daughter and son of an Englishman within days of each other that were widely suspected to be the result of poisoning by an obeah adherent who lived and labored on the Englishman's estate. She followed with the tale of a black groom to a St. John's magistrate hoodwinked out of his best clothing by a charlatan promising to cure his ulcerated leg with obeah rituals. Unhealed, the groom apparently went to the local courts to seek redress and recover his garments.

Multiple accounts confirm black communities' use of obeah to protect their persons and possessions or harm those of others. The British abolitionists Joseph Sturge and Thomas Harvey, on their 1837 visit to Antigua, encountered a single working mother living in the Moravian free village, Newfield, who armed her child with an "obi" horsehair necklace to protect against her child's "limber" neck. The minister Brother Morrish, who was guiding the pair through the village, promptly chastised her for the sinfulness of her "superstition."[12] Mrs. Lanaghan reported the widespread belief within black communities that obeah men and women could insert glass, teeth, stones, rags, and the like into human flesh. Ordinary black men and women consulted obeah practitioners regularly to either inflict injury on an enemy or undo a suspected injury to themselves. Belief in obeah also prompted black working people to hang glass bottles around their homes and provision grounds to protect against theft, a practice found in many black communities around the Atlantic World.[13] These vignettes inadvertently confirm obeah's role as an alternative system of justice for black communities, where rights were protected and transgressions corrected without the interference of the white authorities. At the same time, the groom's story also suggests that patrons dissatisfied with the results of obeah might seek redress in colonial courts.[14]

Obeah gravely concerned Antigua's elites, who sought to control the social and economic activities of freedpeople. Obeah men and women made their spiritual leadership a means of independent livelihood, as they typically required cash from devotees seeking their services. Alongside the concerns about witchcraft that had dominated elites' approach to obeah during slavery, they worried that obeah practitioners exemplified and promoted idleness rather than industriousness. A stipendiary magistrate told the lieutenant governor in 1841 that "the detected 'obeah doctor' [has made] his appearance amongst the other classes of 'rogues and vagabonds' who prey on the community, instead of earning their livelihood by honest means. . . . [It] is not easy to effect the detection of any of these parties under the present state of the law for the terror which they inspire prevents others from bearing testimony to their arts."[15] While the magistrate thought that education could stamp out obeah, the continuance of the practice among communities exposed to decades of missionary teachings suggests otherwise. As Sturge and Harvey deduced during their visit, "a belief in the Obeah, and other superstitions, is not quite worn out, even among the members of churches."[16] Freedpeople in Antigua adhered to Christianity and African cosmology simultaneously, as did their enslaved and free counterparts throughout the Atlantic World.[17] Signifying both black economic autonomy and African cultural innovation, obeah threatened the authorities' attempts to shape black working people into a dependent and orderly, as well as Christianized, proletariat. The churches, however, worked feverishly to pressure black working people into compliance, via both spiritual messaging and material means.

Social Regulation and the Material Benefits of Christian Churches

Christian churches in Antigua offered significant material benefits to converts, but deliberately did so in ways that promoted the transformation of black church members. There were personal, social, and cultural costs to using the services that churches provided adherents. The Moravian Church boasted by far the greatest number of converts from freed communities, while Methodism and Anglicanism, Antigua's two other principal denominations, held much less sway among them. The popularity of Moravianism stemmed not from its particular doctrines or practices but, ironically, from the preferences of planters in the West Indies and proslavery advocates in London. The Methodist and Moravian churches held similar views on the equality of all men, however subdued those views were among missionaries trying to secure a foothold in slave societies. But Moravian missionaries were perceived as encouraging submissiveness among slaves, while Methodists offered avenues to lay leadership for educated mixed-race and free black believers, which made them appear more dangerous and fostered greater support for the Moravian presence. Methodism boasted a mixed cohort in Antigua, even attracting some white congregants, given its association with respected planter families, such as the Gilberts, who helped to found the faith on the island around 1760. Anglicans only began a vigorous campaign to proselytize among slaves in the 1820s, coincident with parliamentary amelioration. The state church's long association with the white establishment bred curiosity among once-excluded worshippers of African descent, and their outreach in the form of schools and soup kitchens attracted many new black congregants. Yet Anglicanism was still overwhelmingly white in postslavery Antigua. After 1834, Moravian congregations continued to attract the greatest number of black working-class worshippers and, unlike the other two sects on the island, counted its missionaries and their families as the only white believers in Antigua.[18] The Moravian church thus functioned similarly to a plantation or the colonial state itself, in that a small number of whites wielded excessive control over the lives of thousands of black working people.

Antiguan colonial authorities, eager to demonstrate the progress of conversion as a sign of emancipation's stability, tracked the number of Christian congregants. In 1839, the Moravian church claimed twelve thousand congregants.[19] By 1845, 46 percent of the island's population had joined either Moravian or Methodist congregations, but just 14 percent was Anglican.[20] The material benefits to be had from church membership, particularly the clergy-brokered free villages, were a powerful incentive. The churches legitimized black families and offered freedpeople a new form of access to public life. As Mindie Lazarus-Black observes, "these institutions symbolized progress and provided avenues for social mobility" among Antigua's former slaves.[21] These benefits accelerated their transition to more independent living and promised a pathway to the fulfillment of their expectations in freedom. The specific obligations that accompanied church membership, however, circumscribed black working people's social lives and placed subtle constraints on their material advancement.

The church-run educational system in Antigua exemplifies the ways in which religious programs for freedpeople functioned simultaneously to their advantage and to their detriment. The obvious benefits of even a rudimentary education for semiliterate laboring people made them flock to schools in remarkable numbers. But the schools did not offer them a path beyond their degraded position within plantation society.

The woefully inadequate resources of church schools meant that they did not teach the skills necessary for advancement, but relied on rote learning from religious texts that encouraged compliance with authority.[22]

Missionaries and free laypeople of color operated the earliest schools for black children in Antigua. Much to the chagrin of local planters, they were open to enslaved children and those who were free, although free children predominated.[23] Immediately after emancipation, black working people eagerly sought out education for themselves and their children. The provision of schools for black children peaked during the next decade, especially because the Emancipation Act included British government funding through 1845. However, for more than two decades after 1834, the planter-run legislature appropriated no funds for education.[24] Funding came from the churches and a few charities, such as the Ladies Negro Education Society and the Mico bequest.[25] By 1838, ninety-seven schools were operating in Antigua, providing day, night, or Sunday instruction to 6,854 children and adults. The fifty-five schools controlled by the Methodist mission, the Moravian mission, and the Anglican bishopric had a total of 4,595 students.[26] A number of schools on plantations depended on support from proprietors or parents.[27] Day schools catered to children of all ages, while adults sought instruction at Sunday schools or at noon and night schools during the workweek. Despite these high enrollment figures, freedpeople's poverty meant that schoolchildren often had to go to the fields instead.

Missionaries encouraged freedpeople to view education as part of their Christian duty and used schooling to foster regular attendance at church on Sundays. In 1838, the Methodist missionary James Cameron, believing that "the Negro is such a peculiar creature of circumstances, or habit, and so little accustomed to examine the consequences," encouraged clergymen to take attendance at service to ensure that only regular churchgoers would receive the privilege of education.[28] Prevailing biases about blackness informed missionaries' special efforts to root out not simply the universal sinfulness they ascribed to humanity but also what they regarded as the particularly wayward tendencies inherent in people of African descent.

Missionaries did their best to persuade skeptical planters that schooling was worth the time away from the fields it required since it would help to produce a willing proletariat. James Thome and Joseph Horace Kimball observed that, during Bible instruction, "those passages which inculcate *obedience to law* are strongly enforced; and the prohibitions against stealing, lying, cheating, idleness. &c., are reiterated day and night."[29] The sincerity of missionaries' conviction that the schooling they provided served the best interests of planters is evident in their comments about occasions when freedpeople prioritized work over education. In 1838, the Methodist clergyman James Cox happily reported that "the decrease of scholars in Antigua is a matter of congratulation with us; (with the exception of those drawn away by the Moravians) as so many *have gone to work* and in most cases to *agricultural labour*."[30] In the early 1840s, Charles Thwaites, the Methodist school superintendent, proudly reported to Mrs. Lanaghan that almost all of his pupils pursued "agricultural employments" after leaving school, seeking to allay the anxiety that freedpeople's education fostered among whites: "To a country whose . . . entire dependence, is placed upon the cultivation of the sugar-cane, this conduct upon the part of its rising generation must be very important. . . . [The] lower classes . . . [should] not, because they are free, despise the hoe."[31] Mission schools operated on the premise that their own evangelical work would advance the long-term success of Antigua's sugar industry.

Church-sponsored friendly societies, just like mission schools, operated as instruments of control over the black working people they served. Most of the island's mutual-benefit organizations were affiliated with the Moravians, Methodists, or Anglicans, and chapters were usually based in particular congregations.[32] Friendly societies were similar to insurance; subscribers regularly paid a small fee and drew benefits in case of emergency, including medical aid, poor relief, shelter, and education. These benefits, though small, were crucial to survival. In Antigua, the friendly societies that were established before emancipation served both enslaved and free people of African descent. Clergymen and progressive members of the mixed-race middle class managed the societies' funds and daily activities.[33]

Friendly societies proliferated after emancipation. Most provided health care and death benefits to free villagers who worked independently, either on or off plantations; contracted workers on estates may also have joined, given the many advantages of membership. Members were entitled to receive funds if they were ill and unable to work, and female members received compensation after childbirth. Burial payments were doled out to survivors on the occasion of a member's death and after the death of a member's spouse or children. Each society had an elected executive committee to manage its business. Certain officers were designated to collect dues, and the membership made policy decisions by voting at regular general meetings.[34] A total of 12,500 people, who represented a sizable portion of the island's black working-class population, had joined a friendly society by 1845.[35] The societies on the island amassed a remarkable amount of funds within the first few years after freedom. In 1842, they were described as financially "flourishing." The public services they performed met with an appreciative response from local authorities. Following the 1843 earthquake, the churches' affiliated friendly societies offered a £150 loan to help rebuild the Methodist chapel and a £50 grant for the rebuilding of the Anglican cathedral.[36] Black working people had become charitable donors rather than the objects of charity, placing them in a new position in the public realm. These societies were a source of collective strength, enabling black working people to oversee community affairs with a degree of autonomy and introducing them to modes of leadership and activism that might also have subtly politicized them.[37]

At the same time, Antigua's friendly societies enforced deference to religious dictates regarding moral conduct. Friendly societies operated under strict rules set by the clergy, and members had to meet the church's standards of respectability. In practice, friendly societies functioned as a form of church policing. Their regulations clearly indicate that churches had particular investment in regulating black people's intimate relations. For example, women members of Moravian societies could only receive childbirth benefits if they were married.[38] Children were often born to unmarried couples, after emancipation as well as under slavery, so this stipulation must have denied benefits to many members at a time when they were most needed. Equally seriously, it also fostered the ostracism of workingwomen by their nominal friends.[39]

Moravian societies had especially explicit and stringent rules regarding members' moral conduct, which meant that claimants for benefits might face special scrutiny. The regulations specified that members could not receive benefits for illnesses resulting from "drunkenness, debauchery or disorderly living." Conviction of and imprisonment for a crime meant not only expulsion but also the forfeiture of all fees previously paid.[40] Given the frequent encounters freedpeople had with the wrong side of the law, this condition no doubt caused numerous expulsions. The contradiction between the lives black working people led and the lives missionaries and clergymen wanted them to lead limited the material benefits they could anticipate from society membership. If Antiguan freedpeople wished to flout colonial conventions, or merely live by their own terms, friendly societies were inhospitable.

Missionaries advocated for and facilitated the socioeconomic advancement of freed communities within the structural limits inherent in the colonial racial hierarchy, which distinguished their agenda from that of planters. But they harbored no belief that education, mutual-benefit societies, or any other church-based organizations should undermine the social system that rested on the exploitation of black labor and was legitimated by the dominant class's notions of orderly behavior. At best, membership in the churches and their ancillary institutions gave black working people access to new forms of social organization that were, in practice, quite restrictive. Even more seriously, the archives reveal that church membership engendered unsavory intrusions into the private lives of freedpeople, adding another layer to the gendered imbalances at work in black families and intimate relationships.

Church Surveillance and Gendered Imbalances in Freedpeople's "Sinful Conexions"

In Antigua, as in other societies, freedpeople rushed to legitimize their intimate relationships through Christian marriage. During the six years following 1834, Anglican clergy performed a total of 2,591 weddings, compared with 251 marriage ceremonies in the six years before abolition.[41] In Antigua, as elsewhere in the Atlantic World, enslavement itself was an insuperable obstacle to marriage, since marriage was a contract, and slaves—who were themselves property owned by others—could not enter into private contracts with one another. Slaves' marriages were legally unrecognized. Moreover, from 1834 to 1843 only Anglican clergy could perform legally valid marriages under colonial law. After abolition, some ex-slaves apparently took advantage of the nullification of their previous marriages in dissenting churches and entered new marriages in the Anglican Church with other partners, sometimes without the consent or knowledge of their existing partners, creating legal and social problems.[42] Many others openly flouted the rules of life-long, monogamous marriage while remaining within the social sphere of their dissenting churches. Yet the temporary invalidation of marriages contracted in the Methodist and Moravian churches did not stop the clergy in those denominations from trying to strictly enforce marital obligations among their members.

The Moravian Church fought against nonmarital sexual relations among congregants through its system of church discipline. Despite the system's mixed results, the church persisted determinedly in this practice. The review process, which the Moravians termed *conferences*, largely unfolded from adulterous offenses, which by Moravian definition involved cohabitation or nonmarital coupling and the inevitable pregnancies that resulted. Clergy often called these relations between men and women *sinful conexions*. Exclusion could result from other "unsavory" forms of public comportment, such as drunkenness, foul language, or attending parties deemed illicit because lewd conduct was assumed to have occurred there. The entire process shamed black men and women and placed them in a suppliant position before church authority. The procedure required freedpeople not only to expose intimate details of their private lives for clerical consumption but also to beg for readmission to the community, extending the relations of power already at work between freedpeople and the church. The process of exclusion was prolonged: an offender would first be warned; then prevented from enjoying various privileges within the church, such as receiving communion; and finally excluded, kept from all church activities and removed from the community.[43] Exclusion from the church carried material consequences: the denial of opportunities for schooling, the loss of the benefits and services provided by friendly societies, and even expulsion from a Moravian free village.[44] A congregant who repented and reformed could be readmitted after spending weeks, months, or even years outside the church community, and in some cases exclusion resulted in a permanent severing of all ties.

The sinful conexions the clergy found in the multiple-partner structure of black families shows that freedpeople balanced the performance of Christianity with the maintenance of heterodox social formations. As they did in practicing obeah alongside Christianity, black working people sought access to the benefits of church membership while continuing to engage in intimacies that were validated only within their own cultural milieu. According to an 1840 instruction book for Moravian missionaries, "married persons are also the objects of great solicitude to the missionaries; that holy state being awfully profaned among the heathen."[45] Moravian exclusion records are full of attempts to track the myriad informal intimacies between the sexes in Antigua's freed community and convert them into formal wedlock. Often, missionaries pressured the men in these relationships, asking when they would marry their partners, while the women involved were listed as sinfully cohabiting but given no responsibility for transforming their sinful conexion into a marriage. For instance, in March 1841, John Nicholas, a worker at Byam's Estate in St. John Parish, came under Moravian scrutiny for extramarital cohabitation with a laboring woman named Phebe. John admitted that Phebe "did wash & cook for him," an arrangement that the archives indicate many freedmen and -women established whether living together or not. This response formed a largely unsuccessful denial of full cohabitation when faced with potential exclusion. Upon first interrogation, John confirmed his intent to marry Phebe, yet upon second inquiry he answered negatively and "in a surly manner." By April 1841 he was excluded.[46]

Given their intention to establish patriarchal families, it is logical that the clergy treated marriage as the man's prerogative. But women sometimes expressed a desire to avoid marriage, showing their determination to make their own choices. These cases demonstrate the critical importance of extended kin in freedwomen's lives, despite the church's insistence on the primacy of the nuclear unit, as relatives often collaborated in a woman's decision to marry or not. For instance, a pregnant woman, Dianna, was betrothed to Cornelius of Galley Bay Estate in January 1845, but many of her relatives, including George and Charles Denbow, objected to the impending nuptials, citing Cornelius's inability to support a wife and child after his recent stint in an insane asylum. Similarly, in March 1846, Charles, a laborer at Hawksbill Estate, impregnated Susanna Joseph and offered to marry her, but she and her parents refused his offer because he was sickly and had a swollen leg. When men's prospects for providing for a family were clearly limited by ill health, women under the guidance of family would express hesitation to marry. Susanna and Dianna may have preferred to keep their options open for future partners who may have been able to provide them and their children greater material security. But unmarried pregnant women were the objects of special concern for the clergy, and were often at the center of many exclusion conferences. In all but the most extraordinary cases, those women were swiftly excluded, as were Susanna and Dianna.[47] But neither Cornelius nor Charles was excluded. For the Moravians, pregnancy and motherhood formed a gendered burden of proof, allowing the men involved to escape the scrutiny that women had to endure. By denying benefits after the birth of an illegitimate child, the friendly society reinforced the church's strictures on women.

The overwhelming majority of investigations of and exclusions for sinful conexions, as well as a range of other transgressions, resulted from information provided to the clergy by "helpers," female or male lay leaders whom Moravian missionaries appointed to assist them in their outreach to local congregations in their foreign missions, likely for their credibility in their communities.[48] The records are not consistent, but they seem to indicate that female helpers often advocated for women when they faced exclusions or accused others of exclusion-worthy offenses. Helpers conducted surveillance, giving the missionaries extensive knowledge of their congregants' social worlds. The Moravians thus functioned not only like the plantation but also like the colonial state, both by using locals to implement their will and by intricately documenting their subjects' ways in order to condemn and potentially transform them. In Antigua and throughout the Moravian missions in the Caribbean, helpers were well positioned to identify freedpeople who committed the acts that qualified as church misconduct. Their position may have elicited respect, but helpers also drew the ire of freedpeople.[49] The sinful conexion between Phebe and John Nicholas was detected by the helper Zecharias, to whom John was reportedly "quite insolent."

The establishment of the office of helper and the constant threat of exclusions within the Moravian Church structure fostered an atmosphere of suspicion within the congregation. The records show that congregants often used the church to retaliate against their personal enemies and to regulate community relations more broadly.[50] More important, the exclusion process exposes the extent of black women's vulnerability. Proceedings regulating sinful conexions often found black women caught between the impossibility of upholding church standards for sex and marriage in their community and the difficulty of preserving their self-interest and, quite often, their physical safety in the context of non-monogamous relationships with men.

Marriage and Nonmonogamy: Twin Perils in the Lives of Antiguan Freedwomen

In May 1841, Frances, an assistant helper from Otto's Estate in St. John's, was accused of having a sinful conexion with a married man, Jacob, who lived in nearby Gamble's Estate, by his wife, who is unnamed in the record. Jacob's wife reported that Frances regularly visited Jacob while she was out. Their relationship also had an economic dimension; Frances tended Jacob's provision grounds, while Jacob worked on Frances's boat. Jacob's wife also discovered that Jacob visited Frances late at night. After she followed Jacob en route to a visit with Frances, Jacob's wife got into a fistfight with Frances upon discovering that the other woman was wearing an open nightgown. This altercation later prompted Jacob to beat his wife "on Frances's account." The entry ends with Frances and Jacob having admitted engaging in all these actions but denying "that there was anything more between them." A month later, Frances appeared in the records for continuing her affair with Jacob and having a "dreadful" fight with both Jacob and his wife that landed the trio in police custody and left a "shocking" cut on Jacob's wife's forehead. Frances was expelled from the church by July, but, curiously, Jacob was not.[51]

The details in this case reveal fissures of gender and class within the freed community, as well as the ongoing tensions between church dictates and freedpeople's everyday practices. Jacob's attraction to his mistress may have involved material benefit as well as desire. Frances also held some power in the community of Moravian congregants, having achieved a position as an assistant helper. Jacob's wife reported Frances to the church as a woman who publicly enjoyed esteem within the church while privately carrying on the same sort of affair that the church prohibited. The triangular relationship between Jacob, his wife, and Frances were punctuated by violence, in particular against Jacob's wife. Frances fought and injured Jacob's wife not only because her relationship with Jacob was summarily interrupted but also because her antagonist caused her humiliating exposure and subsequent demotion in the church social hierarchy. Jacob beat his wife because he believed that he had a right to continue his affair. Moreover, though his wife's exposure of their private tensions to the church may have prompted his violence at that time, it may not have been the first time that he beat her. The record also suggests that Jacob may have assaulted Frances during the fistfight that resulted in police intervention. The subtext of abuse in Frances and Jacob's relationship may have regulated her behavior with him as well.

Jacob's wife remained degraded throughout the recorded proceedings. She used the church's disciplinary proceedings to shame her husband and demote his mistress from her place of privilege in the church, but that was her only measure of power. Did she believe in monogamous marriage? Was she motivated by love lost? Or did she seek revenge against an abusive husband, and against his mistress, who enjoyed a slightly better material and social standing than she did? Her motivation for involving the Moravians remains concealed. Yet, even by appealing to church authority, she could not shield herself from the abuse and the abandonment that could have resulted. It is not clear that the church provided any meaningful assistance in the wake of this melee, since the public nature of the investigation and exclusion process served to destabilize the marriage as much as the affair itself. Another kind of epistemic violence is inherent in this problematic archive. Following the nineteenth-century norm governing marriage, the accusing woman's identity was subsumed by that of her husband; despite their estrangement, she is recorded only as "Jacob's wife." The document contains neither her name nor any other distinguishing personal characteristics; she appears only as a victim of the choices made by the more powerful others in her intimate circle.

In June 1841, Lucy, a workingwoman on Otto's Estate in St. John Parish, brought her husband, Ambrose, before the church to report that since their marriage that March, Ambrose had continually abused her. The Moravian clergy "several times cautioned [him] not to do so, but to no purpose." His violence had apparently escalated a few days before the proceeding, when he beat Lucy severely and inflicted a cut on her breast with a stick. As in the case of Jacob and his wife, adultery lay at the center of this conflict, as Ambrose had a sexual relationship with Barbara, another Moravian church member on Otto's Estate. Ambrose and Barbara were both excluded in July 1841. In this instance, too, church membership added new pressures to what might have been an acceptable arrangement in the absence of Moravian affiliation. Routine violence and encroaching paramours may have greatly distressed married women like Lucy and Jacob's wife, but devotion to the faith meant upholding a monogamy that blocked their search for other partners to fill the material and emotional gaps left by their husbands' extramarital relations.

Nearly five years later, in late January 1846, Ambrose and his wife, Lucy, reappear in the record for exclusion proceedings that Lucy likely initiated with the assistance of the parish helper, Elizabeth, who was present for the inquiry. At this point, the pair had separated. Lucy applied to the driver at Otto's for her own housing after Ambrose had beaten her and compelled her to leave their house. This record reveals that their marital discord stemmed from Lucy's continued suspicion of his affairs and new information regarding their age difference. Lucy's dim eyes and her being "so old, that she could well be [Ambrose's] mother," the record said, rendered her less able to perform her wifely "duties," which remain unspecified. Yet despite Lucy's supposedly failing eyesight, she readily identified a "girl" who had "taken up" with Ambrose among the crowd at a recent gathering of estate residents held at their home.[52] According to Ambrose, Lucy "began to annoy him with her jealousy" of the girl, a jealousy that the clergyman who composed this record agreed was "without sufficient cause."

In retaliation, Lucy left the house to alert a man with whom the girl had formerly lived, and when she returned home, she found herself locked out. Lucy also reported that Ambrose beat her, to which he replied that he only slapped her, causing a "swollen cheek." That same week, Ambrose was excluded again. Two weeks later, in mid-February 1846, Lucy reappears in the record; she had been beaten so badly by Ambrose with his apparent weapon of choice, a stick, that she was now too lame to work on the estate and needed friendly society benefits for two weeks. This last and most severe instance of violence coincided with the exclusion conference over Ambrose's connection to the girl at the gathering; Lucy certainly endured more than a swollen cheek in the aftermath. The record notes that Ambrose beat Lucy before he was even informed of his exclusion, which suggests that freedmen flew into rages at freedwomen over their attempts to make them answer to church authority regarding their private affairs, regardless of the outcome.[53]

Married women in Antigua endured considerable anxiety because of the church's constant condemnations of adultery, their heightened competition with other women, and relentless abuse from their partners. Exposing philandering husbands and their lovers to the Moravian church discipline process offered women a space to voice their grievances against both parties. Yet the church failed to rescue women petitioners from the extreme violence and abandonment by men that often resulted from trying to enforce the rules of marriage in a context where nonmonogamous sexual relations prevailed. Jacob's wife received multiple beatings from both her husband and Frances for attempting to expose their illicit relationship. Although Ambrose was excluded from the church both times that Lucy brought him to answer for his sins, his exclusion brought her no protection; Lucy faced repeated beatings after Ambrose's first exclusion, and she was beaten and ejected from her home the second time she brought charges. Lucy's injuries from Ambrose's repeated assaults disrupted her remunerative labor. In these interactions, black women's bodies were ultimately disposable, subject to coercion by black men, other black women, and even the church.

In fact, women appear intermittently in church discipline proceedings for perpetrating the same sorts of brutalities against other women as men did, which offers potent evidence of how commonplace violence against women was in Antigua. An exclusion conference was held in March 1841 for Leah and Cecelia, two workingwomen on Galley Bay Estate who fought during their labors at the sugar mill over a man who was seeing them both simultaneously. The cleric reviewing their case was especially distressed, not by their assaulting each other but by their "use of the most disgraceful language." In the end, Leah escaped without punishment because she could "govern her temper & tongue better" than the "vile" Cecelia, who was excluded the next month.[54] The church assumed the duty of ensuring proper behavior among women members, and women who cursed and fought in public could be excluded. The Moravians regarded it as their special mission to address the "peculiar difficulties thrown in the way of unmarried females," since "those who have been born in a state of slavery, have been accustomed to see and to hear so much evil, that the moral sense is, in the majority of instances, grievously enfeebled."[55] The Moravians focused their makeover of Antigua's black community on marriage and public comportment, but they accepted abuse in the private relations among freedpeople as routine. These cases suggest that the church was less concerned with ensuring black women's safety than with enforcing black members' adherence to the unequal conventions of gender embedded in the rules of their faith.

It bears repeating that in Antigua women as well as men sought multiple sexual partners, yet they found themselves on the losing end of these situations once the church became involved. In December 1838, Thomas Henry reported his wife, Elizabeth Roses, to the clergy. Elizabeth was brought up before an exclusion conference for her "continued adulterous conexion" with John Anthony, a fellow congregant in the Spring Gardens Moravian Church in the town of St. John's. Apparently, the affair had gone on long enough to throw doubts on the paternity of Elizabeth's baby, named Thomas after her husband; so the elder Thomas left her. When Elizabeth attempted to baptize the child, the church's helper informed the church of the alleged affair and insisted that baby Thomas might be illegitimate. The clergy then refused to conduct the ceremony. The record also discloses that Elizabeth had previously been found to be adulterous, casting doubt on her innocence in this case. The record of this proceeding closes with instructions to the clergy that, if proven that someone other than Thomas fathered the baby, Elizabeth should be excluded for attempting to deceive both her husband and the church. (How paternity might be established if Elizabeth failed to confess her adultery in this case is never explained.) John Anthony was to be excluded, however, only if the pair was found guilty of adultery in this instance.[56]

The entire archive of Moravian exclusions displays the church's obsession with cataloguing freedpeople's sinful behavior by forcing them to give public accounts of their private sexual activity. This pressure fell particularly heavily on women. Ultimately, this attempt to discover the father of Elizabeth's son was performed to shame her, the same intent that underlay the exclusion of unwed mothers. When Elizabeth and Thomas appeared a second time for exclusion proceedings a few weeks later, in January 1839, the record notes simply that "nothing further could be elicited as to the guilt of the parties accused." Yet by April 1839, Elizabeth was excluded, while John Anthony was not.

Many exclusion cases feature men and women who decided to leave their spouses for various reasons. In an era when legal divorce was not available to people outside the ruling elite, no matter how severe their spouse's offenses, many couples who separated acted as if they were free to contract new relationships. This custom tended to catch men and women in the crosshairs of Moravian regulations, as those who had separated from or been deserted by their spouses and found new partners could be excluded from the church for conducting an extramarital affair. A particularly remarkable instance appears in the records just before emancipation. In January 1834, Daniel James, the former husband of the enslaved woman Mary Prince, whose 1831 narrative made her a cause célèbre in the Anglo Atlantic World, was excluded for having "lived in concubinage with Mary Ann Williams, during the absence of his wife (Mary Prince) in England."[57] In her narrative, Prince reports her marriage to the freedman Daniel James during Christmastime 1826 at the Spring Gardens Moravian Church in St. John's. At the time of his exclusion conference in 1834, Daniel James might not have seen or heard from Prince for six years, as she left Antigua with her owners in 1828. Prince's choice to pursue freedom meant that she had to remain in England, rather than return to her husband in Antigua. The archives do not confirm her whereabouts after she testified in 1833 at the trial for a libel suit brought by her owners against her abolitionist editor, Thomas Pringle, in London, but it is widely assumed that she remained there as an impoverished servant until she died.[58] In 1834 the Moravian missionaries in Antigua must have believed that Prince was still alive, given the flurry

in the press about Prince's narrative and the ensuing court cases. Therefore, James was pronounced an adulterer. Men as well as women were
caught in the snares of Moravian Church regulations that undermined
personal freedom in the push to maintain marital sanctity.

The end of legal enslavement in Antigua catapulted black men and
women into new forms of familial and social relations that sometimes
involved violence. In response, whites created structures and laws that
severely circumscribed their access to support from their social and
spiritual communities. We should refrain from reducing such violence
to a matter of individual pathology. It is critical to understand it as a consequence of the mutually reinforcing gendered structures of inequality
within Britain's colonial enterprise that devalued black women physically
and ideologically, including slavery, "free" labor, the Christian church,
and the institution of marriage.

The Gendered Consequences of Material Privation

Freedom created new opportunities for acquiring wages but also placed
new strains on working people. Their incomes had to stretch much
further than whatever money they had garnered through independent
enterprises during slavery, when they were issued rations of food and
clothing. Even in the rare moments when the wages paid on sugar estates rose, freedpeople struggled to make ends meet.[59] Snippets of information noted in passing in the records of the Moravian Church and
magistrate's courts suggest that these material difficulties had gendered
consequences. The fragmentary but loaded details reveal an unstable
combination of freedwomen's adoption of problematic, even damaging,
expedients and the material costs of attempting to be monogamous. In
the collision between the flexibility of intimate relations that characterized the black community and the church's dictates regarding marriage, women got the short end of the stick. Multiple partnerships and
extended family structures enabled freedpeople to amass and preserve
resources just as much as did male-dominated nuclear families, a fact
that missionaries failed to recognize. But women who continued to act
on the assumption of flexible domesticity were subject to censure from
their husbands and the church.

In one revealing case, a working woman who acquired new possessions without her lawful husband's knowledge had abuse heaped on
her because of suspicion that her purchases were financed via immoral

means. Christian George of Galley Bay Estate, a Moravian Sunday school teacher, left church one Sunday in December 1842 and went to visit his wife, Mary Magdalen, who lived on Otto's Estate. It is unclear from the record whether they were separated due to previous marital conflicts or whether this arrangement mirrored the arrangements of "abroad" marriages prevalent under slavery. Upon his arrival at Mary's home, he found two new chairs that she had bought from a carpenter at Galley Bay. When he did not receive "a satisfactory answer" regarding how his wife came by the chairs, he "got into a violent passion and said she had w__d [whored] for them, broke the chairs to pieces; & gave his wife . . . a beating." The record suggests that, although Christian was not excluded, he was likely demoted from his position as Sunday school teacher.[60] Their names add irony to the case, as the verbally and physically abusive husband is named Christian, while the wife accused of "whoring" for chairs carried the name of the prostitute who followed Jesus. Mary could have purchased the new furniture with money she had saved from her wages, but Christian assumed that Mary procured the chairs by having sexual relations with another man. Furthermore, Christian might have been anxious about Mary's economic independence from him, which the chairs made visible. His inability to control his wife while they were living and working separately precipitated his accusations and violence against her. The beating and charge of whoring undermined her progress both physically and ideologically. When the expectation that both spouses would contribute to a joint household economy was overlaid with Christian dogma about patriarchal authority, freedwomen's independent quest for economic security was often met with competitiveness, jealously, and violence from the men with whom they were intimate.[61]

In October 1844, Job, a laboring man on Galley Bay Estate in St. John Parish, was excluded for throwing a large stone at Benjamin, an "old relation" of his wife, Amelia, after discovering that she visited Benjamin regularly to give him some victuals. Benjamin reported Job to the local magistrate, which led to Job being fined five pounds. In the wake of this conflict, Amelia fled their household for "fear of further outrages" and went to stay with her family. Amelia was apparently helping to care for Benjamin, who was part of her extended kin network. Her husband, however, interpreted Amelia's continued connection to and sharing of household resources with a male relative as a threat to his position. Job's conflict with Amelia reflects his concern that she had dispersed their resources in violation of his patriarchal authority. That Job faced state and church intrusion as well as a hefty fine did not ameliorate Amelia's distress. A few weeks later, when Job sought readmission to the church, his request was supported by the testimony of the helpers, as well as of Amelia, that the couple had been living "for some time in peace, though not in one house, she not consenting to live with him."[62] Amelia apparently refused to resume living with Job out of concern for her safety. This suggests that in rare cases the churches allowed separation; in this case, Amelia's reasons for not returning to Job's house were judged not to constitute willful desertion, just as her providing assistance to her kin was not treated as a violation of her wifely duties.

Anthony Floyd and his wife, Patience, were both considered for exclusion in December 1845 because of their "repeated quarreling & fighting" in front of their seven children. One spat erupted over Patience's decision to purchase a half-bottle of rum instead of the whole bottle that Anthony instructed her to procure. As a result, Anthony beat Patience. According to the record, "He could not deny to have beaten her, but declared that she had also collared and beaten him and thrown stones at him. His swollen finger bearing witness, she at least admitted to have beaten him." The record notes their suspension from communion until they improved their behavior. The unnamed helper in this case testified that "the greater faults are with the husband" but, after speaking with them both, concluded that they "seemed to have made up their mind to live in peace and love together."[63] Patience offers a rare recorded example of a freedwoman who exerted physical force in a conflict with her husband, although in many unrecorded cases they may well have done so in self-defense. Moreover, the record hints at the efforts that she and other women made to preserve their scanty material resources and protect their physical safety. Patience might have bought a half-bottle not only to save cash but also to reduce her husband's alcohol intake, as alcohol was understood to increase men's propensity for violence. Unfortunately, her decision backfired. In the end, however, Patience and Anthony determined that the benefits of church membership were valuable enough to induce a promise to keep the peace.

Many of the records of the Moravians offer details about the interpersonal conflicts that led congregants to face exclusion proceedings. An equal number of cases contain only a line or two, but they indicate women's unspoken but ever-present struggles regarding material resources. The advent of freedom prompted some men to cease providing for the women in their lives. On August 20, 1834, less than three weeks after emancipation, Paul of Willock's Folly Estate turned his sister Dolly out of the house "without cause." He also reportedly told the clergy and the helper who attended his conference that he "did not care a damn whether he was excluded or not."[64] Preexisting tensions may have led Paul to expel Dolly in such a callous manner, but his expectation that August 1 freed him of his obligations to his sister and required her to find her own waged work and lodgings certainly figured into his action.

Amelia, about whom the archive reveals next to nothing, faced similarly troubling circumstances. Her story occupies merely half a line. She was formerly of Gamble's Estate, but, as of April 1840, she relocated to the town of St. John's to be a "street girl."[65] This euphemism implies that Amelia may have become a prostitute, joining the vast numbers of black women who performed sexual labor in the Caribbean's urban centers.[66] The record contains no indication that Amelia had connections of any sort, whether familial or intimate, and the use of the term girl could form part of the euphemism or indicate her actual youth, which would add another layer of tragedy to her story. Despite the hazards facing women in intimate relationships, family and partners were the primary sources of freedwomen's social and material support beyond their own labor. Amelia's move from estate work to prostitution could signify her devastating loss of such a network, which forced her to survive by selling sexual access to her body.

Conclusion

Christian churches carried contradictory significance, offering freedpeople civic and material support but imposing intense scrutiny and regulation of black community formation. Church archives, though disturbing for their hostile perspective and their inability to capture the fullness of ordinary people's lives, still bear rich evidence of the quotidian interactions that shaped the experience of freedom. In particular, the records of Moravian exclusions provide a rare lens into the social worlds of freedpeople and reveal how white people in positions of authority intruded into freedpeople's private lives. In turn, both collective and competing notions of family are visible within black communities, as men used violence to assert their authority over women and women sought to protect themselves physically and materially. The repeated failure of women's efforts reinforced the subordinate and disposable status of their bodies. We also witness the ways in which black women and men simultaneously reinforced and destabilized the order of Christianity, offering important clues to the ways in which colonial Antigua's social order as a whole was troubled by the passage of freedom.

The Moravian exclusion records force us to engage the problematic nature of the archive itself, especially as it pertains to the historical experiences of black women. Lists of sexual and social "perversions" proffered titillating details of freedpeople's private lives for clerical consumption and reflected the church's peculiar fixation on controlling freedwomen's bodies. The church's use of local helpers and the construction of lists of transgressions fostered a sense of power over the black working-class population, but these repeated offenses actually demonstrate the opposite conclusion: church members remained disobedient and unruly. How many freedwomen espoused the idea of monogamous marriage remains doubtful, given that many sought multiple partners, but when they did marry, they had social as well as religious reasons to hold husbands accountable. Moravian exclusion conferences offered a space, however unreliable, for freedwomen to voice their grievances in the context of relationships that often rendered them powerless.

Black women who relied on the church to regulate their intimate relationships still faced abuse and abandonment, not only by men but also by the church itself, which shamed and excluded them for noncompliance. These archives offer us only glimpses into black women's lives. Yet these fragmentary and biased records of their troubling interactions with black men and with the church help us comprehend the myriad stresses under which they operated in a freedom constrained by their racial disadvantage, their poverty, and their gendered vulnerability.

....

CHAPTER 6

"MASHING ANTS"

Surviving the Economic Crisis after 1846

All our population are awake to the coming evil.—JAMES COX, a Methodist missionary, letter to the Methodist Missionary Society, 1847

A string of unfortunate developments in the late 1840s within and beyond Antigua multiplied the adversities facing freedpeople. Metropolitan policy changes, international market competition, planters' self-serving tactics, and natural disaster sent the island's economy spiraling into decline. All Antiguans, the missionary James Cox declared, became "awake to the coming evil,"[1] but it fell most heavily on freedpeople. In these desperate times, black working people found new ways to "mash ants."[2] In Antiguan parlance, *mashing ants* meant being resourceful in the face of challenging circumstances and tackling hard work; people who were too dainty to even step on ants would be unable to survive hard times. As black working people mashed ants through legal and extralegal channels during the late 1840s and early 1850s, elites complained even more vehemently about freedpeople's disregard for law and order.

White elites dispensed with the emancipation project's "humanitarian" approach toward black working people, which had prescribed deference to authority and conformity to Anglo-Protestant cultural standards as the key to freedpeople's material improvement and social integration, not as equals, but as industrious and law-abiding subjects. According to Douglas Hall, Parliament's Sugar Duties Act of 1846, which ended the favorable tariffs on imported West Indian sugar, heralded the end of "the great social revolution." As the West Indies went into a financial free fall, colonial authorities showed little concern for freedpeople's welfare and social inclusion, concentrating instead on "efficient and economical administration." Black working people were expected to contribute "constant and productive labour."[3] White elites expressed even more negative opinions about black working people in the wake of 1846, regarding them as destined for lives of lawlessness, and growing convinced that, although blacks' low-paid labor would always be needed, people of African descent could not function as full members of society and were unready for citizenship.

Concurrent iterations of racialized discourse circulating in Britain regarding freedpeople's degeneracy—such as Thomas Carlyle's "Occasional Discourse on the Negro Question" (1849), reprinted as a pamphlet with a more vitriolic title, "Occasional Discourse on the Nigger Question" (1853)—influenced white elites in Antigua.[4] This diatribe on the failures of British emancipation featured the familiar imperial caricature of Afro-Caribbean people in slavery and freedom, "Quashee," who wallowed in idleness while eating pumpkins rather than working in the fields. Quashee's defiance and indolence portended the sugar industry's undoing and signaled his inherent inability to become a productive member of society.[5] Interpreted through the lens of such a damning ideology, black working people's acts of self-preservation only intensified the harshness of whites' views. Freedpeople endeavored to protect their rights and obtain new ones through legitimate channels, such as petitions to legislators and campaigns for political participation, but these efforts were futile. All the while, they continued to use a broad range of informal survival tactics, which local elites criminalized as violations of public order. Panic about perceived surges in criminal behavior among black working people in both the town and the countryside gripped white elites. The local authorities attempted to contain these practices with limited success, which exacerbated whites' association of blackness with criminality during this period of economic and social instability.

A substantial body of scholarship on the criminalization of working-class people suggests that, in writing the history of everyday illegalities, we must recognize the blurred lines between acts that signify social protest and acts that are simply unlawful. The archives that document illegal activities rarely include the voices of the accused or pay full attention to the conflicts, ideologies, and allegiances that underlay their actions. Yet, historians agree, the constancy of oppressed people's illicit acts and the anxiety rife within authorities' responses can illuminate multilayered discourses and relations of power in society.[6] Although not all crime is political, subversive politics exist within a wide range of working-class actions that go beyond the narrow designation of *criminal*.

In Antigua, freedpeople's myriad ways of obtaining a livelihood, from independent provisioning to theft, were officially classified as crimes or viewed by elites as potentially inciting criminal behavior. Upon closer examination, these activities appear to have a more politicized signifi-cance than white observers acknowledged. Between the late 1840s and the mid-1850s, whites' increasing concerns about security and produc-tivity amid the economic downturn generated an atmosphere of sedi-tion, in which black working people were seen as constantly flouting law and order. In fact, both their legitimate and illicit actions represented a protest against the retraction of the small gains freedpeople had briefly enjoyed during the early 1840s. As the possibility that freedpeople might secure basic protections under the law faded, freedpeople resorted to whatever means were necessary to obtain a bare subsistence and endure the dire times in which they lived.

Economic Decline and the Abrupt Reversal of Black Social Progress

The economic downturn that accelerated during this period was precipi-tated by a metropolitan measure that crippled the sugar industry in the British Caribbean, the Sugar Duties Act of 1846. The new law gradually re-duced the tariffs on sugar produced outside the British Empire until 1851, when the duty on sugar from the West Indies would be equalized with that from all other ports, including Cuba and Brazil, where slave labor still prevailed. The 1846 act ushered in a crisis of unprecedented proportions, bankrupting several major West Indian mercantile firms, making credit unavailable to Caribbean planters, and cutting sugar prices in half over the ensuing decade. As the historian William Green observes, this calamitous situation meant that colonies such as Antigua, which remained heavily de-pendent on sugar as their main export, had to double their output to aver-age the same profits. Freedpeople employed on plantations would have had to work twice as hard to obtain the same pay. As the price of sugar fell, so did wages.[7]

Antiguans understood that all other forms of labor and trade de-pended on the profitability of the sugar industry. The Sugar Duties Act was met with protests from all ranks of society. In October 1847, the Methodist missionary James Cox pleaded with the staff of the Methodist

Society headquarters in London to "use [their] influence with the members of Government, or with certain persons in the legislature to prevent the accumulation of human suffering which must inevitably result from this measure."[8] In December 1847, the Antiguan legislature conveyed their "alarm and apprehension" at the impending "ruin" of Antigua's staple industry to James Higginson, the governor, and composed a petition to Parliament.[9] In February 1849, the legislature entreated the metropole again to continue Britain's efforts to suppress the slave trade from Africa to Cuba and Brazil and protested that planters in these locales profited unfairly because their workforce was enslaved.[10] The local press echoed these opinions. A November 1847 issue of the *Antigua Observer* contained this assertion: "We would call upon the British Parliament . . . to . . . [make] it *guilty* to purchase Sugar *knowing* it to be the product of Slaves who have been stolen. We are trading honestly and fairly; we ask the British Government to *protect* our honest trade, and if they cannot compel others to be just and honest too; in the name of common justice and humanity, to deliver themselves from a participation in guilt."[11] This argument, which implied that British trade policy favored slaveholders and invoked abolitionists' rationale for boycotting slave-produced goods, underscored how falsely the planters represented themselves as they pursued their economic interests. Such pleas for justice were simultaneous with their more intense exploitation of black workers.

In an attempt to maintain their profits as sugar prices plummeted, planters rapidly reduced wages.[12] In 1845, daily wages averaged from one shilling to one shilling and sixpence.[13] By 1847, the average had slumped to sixpence, a decline of 67 percent in just three years.[14] Hall concludes that sugar workers' wages remained at this abysmal level for the next two decades. The rising cost of living, coupled with falling wages, created substantial economic hardship for working people.[15] In 1847, a magistrate declared: "The Laborers have submitted to this reduction without a murmur."[16] But this pronouncement was premature. Black working people's rare, yet significant, public protests and their myriad everyday strategies for getting by reveal deep dissatisfaction with their predicament after 1846.

Concurrently with the Sugar Duties Act, policy changes for which Antiguan planters were responsible decreased black working people's bargaining power. Claiming that their enterprises were suffering from a "labor shortage" in light of the flexibility that workers had carved into the plantation routine, planters devised two immigration schemes.[17]

There was no scarcity of local labor; these schemes aimed to secure more compliant workers than the thousands of freedpeople on the island. The importation of white contract laborers had the double benefit of reinforcing the extent of planters' control over the labor force and augmenting the number of white people on the island, which had fallen still further, as the economic collapse forced many bankrupt planters and their families to leave Antigua.[18]

The first scheme, which involved the importation of fewer than one hundred English and Irish farm laborers in 1845, had completely failed within a year. Most of them were entirely unable or unwilling to perform the strenuous and unremitting labor that toiling on sugar plantations entailed. According to the stipendiary magistrate Robert Horsford, the plan was fatally marred by the "want of care in the selection of none but persons of sober, steady and industrious habits."[19] White working people could be condemned for the same "deficiencies" as their black counterparts if they disappointed planters' expectations of productivity.[20] Those English and Irish immigrants who did not die from the harsh labor regime and tropical environment either became paupers on the public dole, as many were likely too ill to work, or sought employment off the plantations. Some left to seek opportunities in the United States.[21]

In 1847, more laborers arrived from the famine-stricken island of Madeira, a Portuguese colony off the West African coast whose economy was controlled by the British.[22] Portuguese Madeirans migrated to British Caribbean territories in remarkable numbers, with more than 33,000 coming to the region between the 1830s and the 1860s; the overwhelming majority settled in Guyana.[23] Lesser numbers went to Trinidad, Jamaica, and Antigua, and minuscule groups were scattered throughout the other Leeward and Windward Islands. Antigua received about 2,500 Madeirans over this period, a small but not inconsiderable number on an island with a population of 36,000.[24] The Madeirans, unlike many nineteenth-century immigrant laborers, may not have had to cover the cost of their passage to Antigua.[25]

Madeiran laboring people, whose ancestry was predominantly white, were indentured for the first year of their contracts at one shilling per day, twice the wages being offered to blacks; the white immigrants' wages were slated to return to the prevailing level of a sixpence per day the next year.[26] The legislature deliberately raised prices on the imported items most frequently consumed by freedpeople, including flour, cornmeal, and salted pork and fish, so that the extra revenue could be used for the importation of laborers.[27] In 1846 Governor Cunningham himself realized that freedpeople had good reason to object to this policy: "If the importation of manual laborers is paid for out of the Public Funds, it would appear that the Colonial Laborer is taxed to bring into the Country those who are to lessen the value of his labor."[28] Lower wages and higher living costs strained relations between freedpeople and the Madeirans, whose markedly higher pay would have been a badly kept secret at best, although a year later the new governor, Higginson, claimed that the tension stemmed from a lack of "humility" among the "emancipated race."[29]

Madeirans came as families, but men typically served as the main breadwinners. These white men were paid a "family wage"—that is, an income regarded as sufficient to support a dependent wife and children—while wages for workers of African descent were set at a level that required all family members to earn money. Unencumbered by debts for their passage and enjoying the privileges of whiteness, Madeirans could look forward to concluding their estate contracts quickly and prospering independently afterward. Yet the largely Catholic Madeirans were met with suspicion in this Protestant stronghold, so their integration into Antiguan life was not entirely smooth. One newspaper observed: "The State is doubtless bound to provide for the Christian instruction of the [Madeiran] people, but in these days of ultra-liberalism when truth and falsehood are bandied together as if there were no difference between them, we should prefer the enlightened efforts of a few sound hearted Protestants on the voluntary principle, to any state endowment in aid of a Church which while bearing the Christian name is an apostate to the truth."[30] Public expressions of religious prejudice did not prevent the Portuguese, along with other small pockets of Catholics, from practicing their faith in their homes and other informal spaces. A Catholic schoolroom in St. John's, which appeared in the record in 1847, probably also housed weekly worship.[31] By 1859, a Catholic priest, J. Ryan, was officially stationed in the island, in response to Antiguan Catholics' request for a clergyman from the nearby formerly French and staunchly Catholic island of Dominica. A decade later, Antigua's first Catholic church was erected in the center of St. John's, at the corner of East and Church Streets, suggesting that the Madeirans enjoyed some social and economic influence.[32]

More than 1,100 Madeirans arrived during the first year, roughly three hundred men, three hundred women, and five hundred children. From this total, eighty-nine men, sixty-five women, and ninety-three children died, and an estimated one hundred clandestinely fled the island to try their luck elsewhere. As with their English and Irish predecessors and the thousands of captive Africans before them, the conditions of labor and life in Antigua proved difficult for the newly arrived Madeirans. Governor Higginson considered the experiment a "success," because it produced "a favorable effect upon the available native supply" of labor.[33] The presence of Madeiran workers indeed forced more freedpeople to submit to the declining wages and stringent terms of contractual estate labor. Those Portuguese who stayed on the island quickly surpassed black working people socioeconomically. Within a decade, significant numbers of Madeiran indentured servants had left the plantations to become traders in St. John's. The historian Sister Mary Menezes argues that the similarly rapid transition from estate labor to petty retail made by Madeiran immigrants in Guyana resulted from the flexibility of their contracts and their familiarity with commercial enterprises in Madeira.[34] In addition, as white people, Madeirans were able to secure lines of credit from merchants and banks that were routinely denied to people of color. In Antigua, many Madeirans became proprietors of bakeries and rum shops by the late 1850s. By 1870, one Portuguese merchant, Antonio Camacho, owned and operated a five-hundred-acre plantation, and in the late 1880s he purchased another seventeen hundred acres, valued at ten thousand pounds.[35] While some Madeirans intermixed over subsequent generations with black working people, another segment of this group remained a class apart, retaining economic and phenotypic forms of privilege through the 1900s.[36] Madeirans' progress offers a potent indication of the advantages enjoyed by nonblack communities in colonial Antigua, showing the deeply intertwined character of race and class.

At the same time that their wages fell, black parents had to pay school fees for their children. After the parliamentary grant for the education of freedpeople in the colonies ended in 1845, the island's officials failed to subsidize the schools.[37] The local government only moved to introduce agricultural training in order to secure the sugar workforce and ensure that freedpeople did not seek to escape their assigned station in life. Antigua's governor and a stipendiary magistrate recommended to local missionary educators and the Colonial Office that the schools "combin[e] industrial training with the other objects of education. [The clergy] may be assured that the moral well being of the Negroes, not less than the prosperity of all classes, will depend upon their being trained up to the exercise of industry in the arts and labours which are their natural portion."[38] While religious educators publicly supported the idea of industrial education, a Methodist missionary privately wondered whether a "feasible" plan of action would ever be devised, and noted that at "present the Negroes (as Lord Stanley calls them) will send their children where they please and bring them up as they please."[39]

Lack of funding remained the main problem facing the schools. Governor Higginson, in light of enrollment figures in 1847 that were much lower than those for 1838, remarked on parents' struggles to contribute to their children's schooling.[40] Although the missionaries publicly professed that black working people were faring well despite wage reductions, in their correspondence they were less sanguine about their congregants' circumstances. By April 1848, one clergyman was lamenting the financial condition of the Methodist schools despite an increase in members: "The reduction of wages of our laboring population has of course diminished their pecuniary resources: and now we begin to feel it most keenly! . . . They had to shut the day school! They ran in[to] the city—as children can be instructed in Mico Charity schools. The teachers therefore have received notice to quit on the 1st May, and *The school will be shut!*"[41]

While school closings were rare, school attendance across the island had waned. A magistrate reported that during the second half of 1848, Sunday school attendance had risen and day school attendance had declined because of "poverty, which withdraws the children from the day schools to earn what they can during the week."[42] Higginson again observed lower numbers in schools in 1849, which he connected to the cessation of metropolitan education funds, the lack of local government assistance, and the "straitened pecuniary means of parents consequent on the diminished value of their labor." Despite acknowledging these structural constraints, the governor still espoused racist reasoning for diminished attendance, citing not poverty but blacks' incomprehension of the benefits of education that made them "reluctant to curtail their own comforts . . . to secure for their children prospective advantages . . . which are by them unappreciated."[43] Black working people persevered in the effort to educate their children, but their material circumstances meant that sometimes their children went to school with unpaid fees, and other times children had to forego attendance at school in order to contribute whatever pittance they could earn to the family's livelihood.

Natural disaster compounded the chronic misery of the late 1840s, when a severe hurricane in August 1848 laid waste to a significant portion of the island. The damage was estimated at approximately ninety thousand pounds. A missionary commented, "This will greatly add to the previous embarrassment and destitution of the people."[44] Stipendiary magistrates had already reported that some impoverished workers were moving back onto estates and entering into contracted labor. In the wake of the hurricane, even more villagers resorted to resettling on sugar plantations when they could not afford to rebuild their houses.[45] Friendly societies, too, were declining during this period.[46]

The local, regional, and imperial events of the late 1840s brought profound instability to the Antiguan economy. Black working people were acutely aware of the renewed pressures on their lives and labors that these developments precipitated. Small groups of black workingmen seized rare opportunities to publicly decry the untoward effects of such changes through legitimate channels. But freedmen's attempts to claim political rights and protection from material distress ultimately reveal the insuperable barriers they faced.

Freedmen's Political Claims and the Vulnerability of Colonial Subjecthood

Former slaves and former masters agreed that the Sugar Duties Act signaled not merely the expansion of free trade but also the empire's abandonment of its Caribbean colonies and its backpedaling on antislavery principles, marking a rare moment when the two groups' interests aligned. Their concurrence quickly vanished after 1846. As black working people bore a disproportionate share of the suffering that ensued, men from Antigua's black working-class community collectively registered their dissent by composing petitions to the government. By inserting their voices into public debates, Antiguan freedmen were asserting an "active masculine citizenship," as did their counterparts in Jamaica and Grenada, who sent similar petitions to Parliament.[47] Freedmen based their appeals on their contributions as laborers and Christian family men to colonial Caribbean economy and society. The petitions illuminate the linkage freedmen that posited between their state-granted freedom and the British government's duty to uphold their material interests. Black men's inability to shield their people from extreme hardship, however, revealed that their so-called citizenship was, at best, performative and easily dissolved when powerful whites faced economic pressure. Ultimately, the denial of these public claims reinforced the fact that Britain's conferral of freedom spawned a subjecthood devoid of economic or political rights.

In December 1847, freedmen publicly disparaged the Sugar Duties Act and Britain's apparent choice to patronize slave produce of other empires. Groups of black workingmen from St. George Parish, St. John Parish, and the free village of All Saints, in which the corners of four of the island's parishes met, penned three petitions to the governor and the legislature. These petitions, with 286 signatories in total, represented men with various occupations on sugar estates, including "Laborers, Ploughmen, Cartmen, Boilers, Coopers, Masons, Carpenters, and other Handicraftsmen." Similar petitions were submitted by workingmen in St. John's and St. Peter and St. Phillip Parishes.[48] Freed communities in every corner of the island worried about the effects of the 1846 legislation.

These appeals declared that the petitioners were "once Slaves, but now emancipated by the gratuitous act of the British nation, as free laborers, dependent for the maintenance and support of themselves and families upon their labors alone." They proceeded to argue that the implementation of the Sugar Duties Act would make that difficult or even impossible: "Many of the Proprietors have expressed their determination to abandon the cultivation of their estates; whilst others . . . have declared that they will be compelled either to do the same, or to reduce the rate of wages so low, that they will cease to be remunerating to your Petitioners."[49] These freedmen advanced a multilayered argument, connecting British abolitionism, freedpeople's humility, Christianity, industriousness, and the principles of free and, especially, *fair* trade in products made by waged rather than enslaved laborers:

> That your Petitioners, in looking a little further, can point out other and greater evils likely to accrue from this introduction of slave made Sugars into the British Markets, in the way of the increase of Slavery itself, which, it is evident, must follow in the course of things, to the complete and hopeless ruin of your Petitioners. Your Petitioners would deprecate the injustice, the horrors, the cruelties that must take place in transporting an additional number of Slaves from Africa, since the traffic will be carried on, not as in the time of your petitioners' forefathers, under proper regulations imposed by authority;

but under all those aggravated circumstances attendant upon illicit trade and smuggling. . . . That your petitioners regret, from philanthropic motives, that the course pursued by the British Government is calculated to render nugatory all hopes of free labor being at any future time established throughout Sugar making countries generally, inasmuch as the Governments of Slave countries, seeing that Slave labor is now more advantageous and profitable than free, will take no steps eventually to abolish the state of Slavery; but on the contrary, will leave no effort untried to perpetuate it, to the great detriment of your petitioners in a moral and religious point of view, since [without] cultivation, this island, in common with the British West Indies, must fall back into a state of ignorance and barbarism.[50]

The careful wording excuses Britain's previous slave trading and exploitation of slave labor while condemning their continuation by competing empires. The petition advances the same argument concurrently made by the Free Soil Party in the United States: that the cheaper price of slave-made goods, compared with goods produced by free labor, would expand slavery at free workers' expense and ultimately destroy the entire economic system.[51] The petition remains silent about the importation of Madeiran laborers, which depressed free workers' wages. It mobilizes the favorite trope of the postslavery era, emphasized by Carlyle and other critics of emancipation, that the lack of productive—or, rather, proletarian—labor on sugar estates could encourage black depravity in order to reinforce the moral importance of their current employment. In short, black working people petitioned to advance their own agendas, but did so using language palatable to the empire.

Such savvy use of language suggests that literate and aspiring members of the freed community spearheaded the petition. It also indicates heavy missionary influence. Missionaries had grown quite worried about the negative effects of the Sugar Duties Act on their parish revenues. They vigorously promoted the gender and class structure of freed communities that these petitions presumed. The image of bread-winning emancipated men heading families and the threat of "ignorance and barbarism" in the absence of estate labor signal the presence of Christian ideology in the text.[52] The petitioners intended this notion of patriarchal, civilized, Christian families to appeal to Parliament, but it also reinforced visions of domestic dominance that they likely harbored themselves. Their entreaty resolutely ignores the fact that black women had labored alongside men in sugar fields and headed their own households in slavery and in freedom. Despite the multiple motives underlying these petitions, they indicate freedpeople's awareness of the metropolitan policy's damaging effects on their daily lives.

Even the few legal rights that a small number of better-off freedpeople had managed to secure since abolition were jeopardized by white elites' desperate grip on power in this time of economic flux. Black working people launched two public struggles over the politics of parish vestries—in 1847 and 1848. Vestries were locally elected bodies within each parish that managed the affairs of the Anglican Church, which as the state church received public funding, and administered such civil matters as poor relief, schools, and road construction. To raise the necessary funds, vestries set and collected taxes. In the late 1830s, the traveling abolitionists Joseph Sturge and Thomas Harvey described the class structure of these bodies: "The vestry are chosen by the freeholders" and "do not appear to extend relief to worn-out field laborers."[53] Obtaining the franchise for vestry elections did not carry as much significance as did the franchise for elections to the island's legislature, but it did provide access to crucial aspects of public life and formed a stepping-stone to further political participation.

The scant records regarding the vestry conflicts of 1847–48 indicate that a small number of African-descended men who had become freeholders by virtue of owning or renting a certain amount of real property managed to secure this franchise, and a few had even been elected to seats on their local vestries. Most electors emerged from the ranks of former free people of color, who met the requisite property qualification for enfranchisement in both vestry and assembly elections well before 1834.[54] Freedpeople's access to waged labor and private homes in villages enabled some men to qualify as freeholders and vote in vestry elections, although the women who acquired freeholds from their labors were automatically excluded. The vestry's functions tended to uphold gender, racial, and class distinctions.

As freeholders, black people were subject to parish taxation. Whites who controlled the island's vestries did not guarantee all black freeholders a right to the parish franchise, but they targeted all freeholders for taxation. To freedpeople with extremely low wages and pecuniary obligations as members of Moravian and Methodist Churches and friendly societies, paying high taxes to maintain the Anglican Church seemed unfair.[55] Taxation disproportionately burdened black working people and benefited planters and other powerful whites socially; paying higher taxes tied freedpeople to wages and thus to field labor and made poor people even poorer, preserving the separation of classes so revered by white elites.[56] Black working people openly expressed their dissatisfaction with the attack on their resources that taxation signified.

Parish taxes were collected from free villagers for the first time in the 1840s. In April 1847, a group of free villagers in the parish of St. John displayed "riotous conduct" at the courthouse when ordered to appear for nonpayment of parish taxes. A local newspaper declared that "the peace of the City and of the Island was jeopardized," an exaggeration revealing whites' fears as this public protest unfolded. Reportedly, despite the disturbance, "a great number" of the angry villagers were persuaded to pay their taxes.[57] The newspaper advised anyone who might attempt a similar demonstration in town the next week to report to their local churchwarden's office instead, indicating awareness of black freeholders' continued disgruntlement. Saying that white and colored freeholders had been paying their taxes "cheerfully" for "hundreds of years," the newspaper argued that these villagers should feel "pleased at the circumstance of their being thus put on a footing with their fellow-Parishioners in being afforded an opportunity to contribute to the support of the Parish in which they are the proprietors of Land."[58]

The events of the next year, however, suggest that the equal footing supposedly fostered by the obligation to pay vestry taxes did not exist, for the legislature changed vestry election guidelines to seal the exclusion of most potential voters and candidates of color. The requirement for the franchise in vestry elections for the previous century, ten acres or twenty pounds worth of owned or leased property, was drastically increased to fifty acres or seventy-five pounds' worth of property. Governor Higginson reported to Colonial Secretary of State Earl Grey the justification for these new vestry regulations, stating that although he personally "preferred a lower standard especially for voters, it was contended by the advocates of the Bill that the extensive and, it may be said, irresponsible powers confided to the vestries, justified the higher qualification." Offering an even more questionable defense of the decision, Higginson declared: "[I] unhesitatingly den[y] that there is any intention or desire, either on my own part, or on that of the Legislative Council and Assembly, to curtail the privileges of the emancipated Race, or to exclude them from that share in the management of Public Affairs, to which they may, either by property or intelligence, be considered entitled."[59]

Higginson, like many of his predecessors, grossly misrepresented this and other affairs in the colony to maintain the appearance of social harmony and administrative control in his correspondence with his superiors in London. But a letter from the attorney general to the governor's private secretary confirms that the measure sought to block what white elite men saw as an encroaching, unqualified throng of new black freeholders who, in turn, supposedly prevented rightful electors from voting: "Persons were admitted to sit in vestries without any property whatever, while the largest Freeholders and taxpayers, as in the case more especially in the Parish of Saint Mary, were by means of this loose pretence of suffrage, excluded."[60] Although freeholders of African descent had not grown so numerous as to block the election of white vestrymen, the fact that they took the places of some wealthy white men who regarded these offices as rightfully their own meant that the very existence of nonwhite vestrymen concerned white elite men seeking exclusivity in all forms of local governance. St. Mary Parish contained a number of free villages, so the attorney general's mention of that particular parish as a site for alarm carried clear racial and class implications. The governor apparently supported the ruling, as the attorney general reported that a number of "gentlemen of the colony," including "His Excellency himself," raised the matter to him, prompting him to compose the new law mandating the higher property requirements.[61]

Black and mixed-race freeholders recognized the restructured franchise requirements as a deliberate obstruction of their participation and moved in unison to protest this exclusion. In protest, a group of 128 black and mixed-race men composed a petition to Grey. The petitioners complained that property owners with a direct stake in a parish were being expressly blocked from the vote, but that plantation attorneys who owned not one square foot of land in a parish could vote on behalf of absentee proprietors, and those who represented multiple properties could vote multiple times. They pointed out the number of men who had formerly participated in vestry elections as voters and as candidates, as well as many new electors, who were now excluded: "Your Memorialists do therefore most humbly affirm that this Act, which professes it to be for 'the better regulation of Vestries' is subversive of their rights and privileges, that it is unjust, unwise, impolitic and unconstitutional. *That its direct tendency is to depress one class, in order to elevate the other.* That it virtually excludes the emancipated Freeholder whilst it admits the Absent proprietors to vote by proxy, through an unqualified representative, in imitation of the privileges exercised by Peers of the Realm when in Parliament assembled."[62]

The language of this petition is less humble and more direct than that of the earlier appeals, since in this case the petitioners were not joining their voices to a broader imperial cause. As slaves had done in their Sunday market protests in 1831 and freedmen had done in the 1835 Emancipation Day strike, black and mixed freeholders in 1848 exhorted the metropole to uphold their political rights at home in the face of local white elites' obstruction. They decried the class and race biases underlining the new policy, and the reference to the "emancipated Freeholder" reminded the Colonial Office that this act thwarted the progress that emancipation was theoretically intended to generate. The allusion to local attorneys exercising the political rights of English nobles aimed to arouse metropolitan authorities' suspicions of colonial whites' legal and social impropriety, capitalizing on familiar discourses circulating in the empire about West Indian white society as a "lesser" version of Englishness.[63] Their assertion of the act's unconstitutionality communicated the petitioners' familiarity with their rights under colonial law. Not only did the Colonial Office reject this petition, but Grey's response suggested that the Colonial Office could not be called on to defend black people's interests in Antigua, remarking that such petitions should be directed to the island's legislature instead.[64]

As they did in Antigua, black workingmen in other British Caribbean territories, such as Jamaica and Barbados, built temporary coalitions with middle-class men of color to publicly contest the racial and class biases in political procedures.[65] Across the region, this search for economic autonomy and political inclusion became increasingly futile. Politically powerful whites in the West Indies blocked the ability of dissenting electorates of color to challenge their rule, even at the parish level. In Antigua, as small groups of freedpeople launched intermittent attempts to force progress through legitimate channels, the majority also struggled to protect their interests thought extralegal means. Those activities earned them only further policing, surveillance, and criminalization by white elites.

Survival and Subversion in the 1850s

In the 1850s, black working people coped with their dismal circumstances by utilizing the same oppositional tactics employed since enslavement. Colonial elites responded to them as they had always done, with disdain and swift containment. Freedpeople's strategies during such desperate times reveal the most critical and most politicized aspects of their everyday lives. Black working people relied heavily on provisioning to escape complete domination by the sugar industry. Many freed families performed irregular labor on or fully withdrew from sugar plantations and engaged in family-based provisioning on privately held land. By the early 1850s, as some indebted sugar estates folded, freedpeople had gained greater access to land, and remarkable numbers had taken up residence in free villages again.

In 1852, the legislature surveyed 111 of the roughly 140 operational estates on the island to assess the state of labor. From a total of fifteen thousand people identified as agricultural laborers in Antigua, only six thousand reported employment with sugar estates, meaning that the remaining nine thousand were independent agriculturists growing crops for personal and familial benefit and profit.[66] This autonomous labor took place mainly within the eighty-seven free villages, which were expanding at that time. Although the figures for estate laborers and independent cultivators are approximations, the survey indicates that independent cultivation had edged out employment in the sugar industry. The land available to black farmers was generally not as fertile as that on the remaining sugar estates, and most families had only small plots.[67] But provisioning yielded foodstuffs and some income, so those who could manage avoided fieldwork that profited the planter rather than themselves and entailed supervision by overseers.

Contemporary descriptions featured the "thousands [of] proprietors or renters of small tracts of well and diligently cultivated land" and the "immense quantities of produce, sugar, molasses, arrow-root, fruits, and provisions and vegetables of all kinds" for sale at the market. A "semipeasantry" of sorts had emerged as a by-product of the downward spiral of sugar production.[68] Douglas Hall argues that Antigua's planter class should have recognized that the diversification of commercial agriculture would have revived the lagging economy and, at the same time, harnessed the energy of rural working people. Antiguan planters, however, continued to invest their slight resources in the colony's centuries-old economic triumvirate: sugar, molasses, and rum. The island's economy slid into a prolonged decline.[69] Conflicts continued to brew between planters and black working people, who moved back and forth between estate labor and independent cultivation, depending on their personal circumstances and local economic fluctuations.

Although this conflict between planters and freedpeople might appear to be exclusively about class, racialized dimensions subtly underscored it. Planters and administrators explained black working people's limited engagement with the sugar industry primarily in essentialist terms, in keeping with long-standing assumptions about the inadequacy and fickleness of black people. Lieutenant Governor Mackintosh declared in 1851 that "the establishment of numerous free villages . . . rendered the labourer here more than ordinarily intractable and capricious."[70] Racist discourse naturalizing the negative attributes of black working people permeates the sources from this time. In his scathing narrative about Antigua, the British traveler Charles Day remarked: "Some estates are cultivated on shares with the negroes, but it does not answer; for when the negro gets a few pounds, he becomes insolent, will not work, and is altogether too independent."[71] Taken together, these statements do more than evidence planters' usual anxiety over the loosening of their controls over the black working populace; they also presume that black working people were unfit for independent labor. The conferral of concessions to black working people, such as homes or land of their own, only served to "worsen" their situation, given their indolent "nature." In 1834 whites in colonial Antigua had believed themselves to be reforming black people by launching the project of full freedom. By the 1850s, they had come to see black working people as beyond help and configured themselves as guardians of order against what they now felt was an inherently criminal black character. White elites had always seen crime as a favored tactic of black working people, but their sentiment shifted from a critique of freedpeople's practices to a critique of their *nature*, as the unbridled black aspirations and "insolent" behavior of the early 1840s was followed by oppositional actions born of desperation in the 1850s.

Arson in the cane fields signaled popular unrest, as it had done in 1831. Over the month of April 1850, the press reported deliberate burnings on ten sugar estates located in all but one of the island's six parishes; five of the fires took place in the eastern parish of St. Peter's. The incidents ranged from the torching of a few heaps of megass on the Vernon and

Betty's Hope estates, to the igniting of laborers' homes, a chapel, and the boiling house storing several hogsheads of sugar and casks of molasses on Gilbert's Estate, to the destruction of a cane field on Crabb's Estate that was expected to produce thirty hogsheads of sugar at crop time.[72] Two important details help to frame the story of the 1850 fires: the recent decrease of one shilling in the price of Antiguan sugar that was due to oversupply in the world market and a spell of unfavorable weather on this characteristically dry island. In a momentary display of wishful thinking, a local newspaper expressed the hope that "none of these misfortunes might be traced to incendiarism—and that our peasantry will strive to maintain their good character and not be induced to resort to acts of dishonesty or insubordination, notwithstanding privations now being endured in consequence of the distress and trying condition in which the island is placed from the want of rain."[73] Multiple fires around the island within a two-week period clearly indicated the work of purposeful individuals expressing the sentiments of many discontented subjects. However, the sources do not indicate that anyone was apprehended or deemed responsible for these fires.

The geographer Bonham Richardson has examined a series of fires in Antigua during the 1890s, which occurred in an uncannily similar context of depression in the sugar markets and a long stretch of drought. He asserts that the setting of cane fires by impoverished black working people carried dual significance as an act of destructive resistance that also brought material opportunities. Fires sent a clear message to planters from disgruntled working people, but they also forced emergency harvesting that required extra labor and generated much-needed wages.[74] Richardson's analysis of the fraught atmosphere generated by acts of arson applies to the 1850 fires as well: "The windswept blazes themselves reinforced and publicized Antigua's socioeconomic malaise because of the fires' contagious social effects. . . . Local newspapers condemned the fires. Planters fumed in anger and frustration. Government officials dutifully sent memos to London detailing property losses and explaining how the economy was threatened." Among black working people, too, the fire would have dominated their conversations; some "doubtless expressed sympathy with the incendiaries and must have suggested more burning."[75] Cane fires epitomized both the dangers of relying on a single crop and the social instability bred by this unsound economic regime. Time and again throughout the nineteenth century, black working people resorted to arson to express their frustration with colonial society.

The continuing practice of obeah also antagonized Antiguan administrators. This African spiritual practice had troubled white authorities and elites since the earliest days of slavery. But in the early 1850s, officials' alarm soared, suggesting that the practice itself may have expanded as working-class life grew harsher and freedpeople sought alternative ways to overcome their tribulations. Yet the increase in obeah-related "offenses" might not correspond to an actual rise in obeah's practice but rather to white observers' nascent belief that Antigua's black laboring communities were beyond reform and redemption of any kind, whether economic, social, or spiritual. The practice of obeah was a familiar offense in this vehemently Protestant colony. While the standards that authorities used to identify obeah are never specified in the sources, white elites were confident that they knew obeah when they saw it or heard of it. In 1851 the House of Assembly introduced a bill to amend the 1834 Vagrancy Act by adding a prohibition against obeah that doled out harsher punishments to its practitioners, including up to a year's jail time with hard labor and public whipping.[76] Diana Paton argues that in Jamaica the revival of flogging as a central form of criminal punishment in the 1850s emerged from the rising conviction that the "rehabilitation" of prisoners had failed, which was clearly linked to whites' belief in the futility of the entire emancipation project.[77] Without giving any figures regarding the number of obeah-related incidents, lawmakers justified the legislation as a response to obeah's "lamentable increase . . . (the evil effects of which on the credulous minds of the peasantry can scarcely be overestimated)."[78]

Whites' panic over obeah is evident in incidents that were covered extensively by the press. For example, William Burnett was charged in January 1850 for attempting to heal Maria Winter—whose racial identity was unidentified, but whose regular access to medical care suggests some middle-class stability—from her "rheumatic affliction in the head and shoulders." According to Winter's testimony before the police, when her doctor failed to cure her after more than a year under his care, her husband recommended that she seek Burnett's services. At their meeting, Burnett performed several ritualistic actions, such as submerging castor leaves in vinegar and water, making the sign of the cross, and eventually extracting several pieces of glass from various parts of her body and from the mattress on which she slept. Winter ended her testimony by saying that her health improved significantly because of Burnett's efforts. Burnett reportedly faced the court "very boldly" to accept his sentence of three months' imprisonment at hard labor. In fact, many practitioners who were punished continued their obeah work afterward. In 1856 John Horsford, a mixed-race missionary who visited Antigua, declared that the punishment of whipping attached to obeah, though a lamentable "relic of slavery," did not stop "the very same persons who have been tried, condemned, and scourged . . . [from the] commission of the identical offence, and have a second time been whipped." Despite this punishment, Horsford reported, "the crime has been thrice committed."[79]

In response to the Burnett incident, the *Antigua Weekly Register* remarked: "It shows, that notwithstanding all the efforts used to enlighten the population, a deplorable degree of superstition still prevails. We have heard of many instances of a similar kind, wherein the credulity of the ignorant has been imposed upon by designing knaves who managed to get well paid for their impositions; and we deeply regret that a more exemplary punishment was not inflicted on the Obeah man in this case."[80] Elites who were uneasy at obeah's persistence believed that freedpeople were socially and mentally deficient, having resisted the dogged efforts of church and state to "enlighten" and control them. Freedpeople expressed an unwavering belief in obeah's efficacy and a strong respect for its practitioners. The prosecution of obeah practitioners as vagrants and the insertion of public whipping into the anti-obeah legislation was intended not only to root out the incidence of obeah but also to bring shame and embarrassment to its leading figures, who wielded an authority within the black working community that subverted medical authority, missionary influence, and, ultimately, colonial power.

Antiguan black working people sought out obeah women and men to mediate relationships and settle problems both within and beyond their community, which fostered a fear of obeah among some whites. The traveler Charles Day mentioned a local magistrate and attorney for Cade's Bay Estate in St. Mary Parish, Mr. Lipscombe, who lived "in constant dread of poison from obea, and scarcely dared to drink a glass of water." That the working people on his estate flaunted their dislike for him and that his home mysteriously burned to the ground two months prior to Day's visit probably heightened Lipscombe's suspicions.[81] Indeed, locals of all ranks saw this system as carrying significant power to help or harm, and no acts of legislature could do much to change how Antiguans perceived it.

The following year, an angry letter to a local newspaper decried the law's ineffectiveness in stopping obeah, calling the flogging of guilty adherents a "farce," as they were "sturdy negroes," and lamenting that the number of practitioners was still increasing.[82] The writer, "Oedipus, Jr.," observed that the new law had served to break up the "three or four establishments" in the town of St. John's, where "the Sabbath and the Bible [were] desecrated in the catching of Jumbies or sprits, and open boasts [were] made of the power of the professors and the number of lives they had taken." But the dissolution of these obeah houses only led some to flee the island, while others who merely "removed their practice to the country, [had] been repeatedly detected and undergone the farce of punishment."

Oedipus, Jr., lamented that "the Barrack in St. John's became the focus of the Black Art and was resorted to by vast numbers of persons, some as students working for their degree—others as go betweens or messengers and the majority for the purchase of Fetishes or Charms to save them from the vengeance of the Law, to give them Luck, the hope of cure or the means of doing evil." Since the early 1800s, small numbers of liberated Africans had entered Antigua through Britain's naval policing of the transatlantic slave trade.[83] This letter suggests that some were incorporated into the island's standing police force. Increased security came at a price, however, as the African soldiers housed at the St. John's barrack helped to expand obeah's practice. Oedipus, Jr., reported, "The African troops who were last quartered here[,] . . . full of the superstitions of their country, perambulated the island throughout its length and breadth, imposing on the credulity of the laboring population, and with more success than the missionaries, undermined all the good they had been doing."[84] This renewal of African cultural knowledge buttressed obeah during an era of prohibition. In seeking to militarize the colony and police the freed communities, the authorities resorted to a low-cost measure that inadvertently supported freedpeople's exercise of personal and spiritual autonomy. Obeah offered a refuge to freedpeople seeking order and protection in a time of financial distress and governmental abandonment.

Antiguan colonial administrators also perceived a loss of control over the freed populace in the numbers of so-called vagrants roving about the streets of St. John's. The 1834 Vagrancy Act had attached a criminal charge to idleness among freedpeople, and local elites deemed any black person engaged in independent labor in town a vagrant. But economic opportunities in St. John's dwindled with the sugar economy, swelling the number of idlers in the town. While vagrancy among black working people likely stemmed from unemployment, authorities drew only one conclusion from its prevalence: degeneracy brought about by the conferral of freedom. In the mid-1850s the public discourse increasingly assigned a threatening demeanor to these degenerate idlers. In 1856, both local newspapers highlighted the "rabble-rousing" nature of the town's black inhabitants, one more fervently than the other.[85] Governor Hamilton said that ever since he had arrived in 1855, the island had been plagued by the "existence, in the heart of the chief town, of a numerous rabble, physically strong, ready at any time for any act of violence, and habitually using threats of violence."[86] Local officials and the press linked this behavior to certain social ills, especially drinking, but policing them exhausted public coffers and created further unease.

Black working people's liquor consumption caused whites particular distress. In June 1847, a stipendiary magistrate reported to the governor that "the Spirit Shops established in the Rural Districts exercise a demoralizing influence over the laborers," and he noted that, although the practice had declined, it was still customary for "many estates" to give rum to their workers as "the means of securing a preference in procuring labor."[87] Furthermore, between July and December 1850, Portuguese Madeiran immigrants established five rum shops in the town of St. John's, which deepened the magistrates' "fear [that] the habits of tipling and drunkenness are on the increase" in town.[88] Drinking alcohol and frequenting bars were a normal part of many freedpeople's leisure pursuits. But local elites and authorities interpreted drinking as a sign of this population's increasingly corrupt character.

Complaints about the numbers of people seeking poor relief rose over the decade. The Daily Meal Society, one of the few institutions assisting paupers in the parish of St. John's, stated in its 1851 annual report that its finances were exhausted, which was due not only to the decline in funding from the other parishes and private benefactors but also to "the increase in the number of applicants for the benefits afforded by the institution."[89] The Poor Law guardians, who administered the distribution of public poor relief, served several hundred individuals during the year 1852–53.[90] Following this report, white elites criticized black working people for resorting to public assistance rather than seeking to subsist through their own hard work. Indeed, the blacker the paupers' rolls became, the more intense grew the discourse about black idleness.

Many officials responded by trying to devise schemes to encourage industry among working people. Assemblyman William Ledeatt sought to diversify the island's export crops and hone the agricultural skills of local black working people through the Antigua Association for the Encouragement of Industry, which would pay workers from the profits of new crops and operate as a limited liability company with shares purchased by private investors. In an 1853 letter from the colony's treasurer, Thomas Price, to Ledeatt, Price expressed hope that the scheme would "take on fresh hands from the same indigent class, so as to spread as widely as possible the advantages to be derived from honest industry, and still further to relieve the Poor Law Guardians."[91] This plan, like several others proposed during the 1850s, seems never to have been implemented despite enjoying some support. Calls for the diversification of agriculture and new terms of employment did nothing to remedy the distressed state of labor, the supposed prevalence of crime, and the planters' myopic focus on sugar despite its plummeting profits.

"Honest industry" seemed especially on the wane to white observers, as black working people not only sought state relief but also committed a growing number of petty crimes and crowded in the jails. Records of arrests and imprisonments document their marked increase, generating rather than allaying whites' unease. For instance, in the second half of 1850, people convicted of summary offenses totaled 1,286. A large fraction of these charges were for indecent and abusive language, "an offense to which negroes [were] chiefly addicted," as well as for disorderly conduct on estates requiring the assistance of constables to quell. Yet the reporting magistrate concluded that these crimes were "mostly trifling."[92] In the second half of 1855, the number of summary offenses had jumped to 1,815. The attorney general, Robert Horsford, used this statistic to highlight Antigua's current "state of depravity in which honesty is the exception rather than the rule of life." Horsford declared, "There is scarcely an individual . . . who has not had experience, in his own person, of the many acts of petty theft and depredation daily committed upon our properties."[93] By the mid-1850s white elites found nothing trifling about working-class crime; theft, rather than foul language, aroused the most concern. The nature of the crimes that freedpeople committed may not have changed. Rather, whites' concerns about black working people's comportment shifted from anxiety over lack of deference to fearing for the safety of their persons and property as the economic situation worsened.

Antiguan elite observers interpreted theft as evidence of the laziness and innate corruption of black working people, but as many scholars have demonstrated, in the context of a harsh labor regime, theft forms a key part of a larger body of practies expressive of a dissenting moral economy among working people.[94] Tera Hunter elucidates the politics of "pan-toting" among emancipated workingwomen in the U.S. South: "African-American women claimed rights and privileges as waged workers in part on the basis of their former status as slaves who had produced the wealth of their masters without compensation." Surreptitiously taking leftover food home to their own families "helped to alleviate some of the onerous consequences of low-wage labor for black women."[95] The same can also be said of Antiguan working people who, while earning substandard wages in a tightening economy, claimed the available goods of their better-off employers to ease the strain on their incomes.

Long before the onset of this crisis, Barbuda's black working people had regularly resorted to extralegal tactics to subsist, and the aftermath of 1846 aggravated their desperate straits. Given the island's marked absence of binding laws, authority, or infrastructure, self-interested acts by black Barbudans were inevitably perceived by Antiguan whites as violations of order. Who had the right to take goods and materials from wrecked ships was hotly contested between ordinary Barbudans and the Codringtons. Whites in authority in Antigua suspected Barbudan workingmen, many of whom had maritime experience, of luring ships to crash on the island's coral reefs and rocky coasts so they could salvage them, returning only some of the cargo to the Codringtons.[96] Barbudan freedpeople lived and labored under such tenuous arrangements that they garnered resources by any means necessary. Two suspicious shipwrecks on Barbuda involving French ships occurred in 1847 and 1852, generating interimperial tension and raising alarm about the island's lawlessness. In the 1847 case, the shipmaster reported that when he opposed the salvage begun by the Barbudans he met, he was nearly "mugged with a knife and almost knocked out by a piece of wood that one of them threw at [him]."[97] In 1850, three Barbudans, led by a man named Lovelock, shot a man in the leg while aboard a boat coming onto Barbuda's shore; he insisted he was attempting to get water, while the Barbudan men believed that he was trying to steal sheep. The case was thrown out because Antiguan authorities determined that the incident occurred while the ship was docked in Barbuda, where they had no jurisdiction.[98] That Barbudans had escaped prosecution for a life-threatening act confirmed to elites that the disorder perceived among Antiguan freedpeople could be far exceeded in Barbuda, where the law was apparently meaningless. As in the 1830s, Barbuda served as a more extreme foil for the conflicts unfolding in post-1846 Antigua.

In Antigua, white elites ignored the hardships suffered by black working people and sought only to decrease the delinquency that they regarded as a sign of blacks' inherent criminality. The search for a remedy led them to the familiar conclusion that proletarian labor on sugar estates could best cure blacks' social deficiencies. In 1856, just three years after Ledeatt's abandoned plan, another enterprising assemblyman, Thomas Foote, proposed the employment of the jail's inmates on one of the island's many insolvent sugar estates. His plan, in contrast to Ledeatt's, said nothing about wages, reflecting the prisoners' unfreedom. In this gendered scheme, male prisoners would perform fieldwork, female prisoners would do domestic labor, and young offenders would be schooled until midday and then work as a weeding gang in the field. At the workday's end, all would return to jail. This plan assumed that the profits from the sugar would go to the local government, which would also cover the duty on the produce raised from the estate, "so that 150 Hhds. [hogsheads of sugar] from this estate [would] be equal to 300 on any other."[99] The proposal was modeled on ideas then circulating in Britain and other parts of the empire about the efficacy of labor in rehabilitating criminals. The "ticket of leave" system in Britain that allowed convicts to labor for wages instead of remaining imprisoned was highly controversial and, according to the attorney general, Robert Horsford, had been "virtually abandoned" by the time of Foote's proposal.[100] But Jamaica had begun a penal labor system only two years earlier, suggesting that such initiatives were in vogue regionally.[101]

Foote's program, though deemed flawed by other assemblymen because of its cost to the government, was commended by a local newspaper, which argued that inculcating "industriousness" would be an effective means for "the reclamation of the hundreds of little and dissolute young vagabonds of both sexes, in and about the city, who live by systematic plunder and pilfering, [and] the saving of hundreds of others from entering on a similar career."[102] While praising Foote's program, Horsford suggested that legislators wait to see whether similar convict labor schemes proved successful elsewhere before adopting it. He then posed a telling question: "What is left us but to endeavor to make the *present* system more punitive, and coercive?" He dedicated the remainder of his speech to the merits of harsher and longer sentences for convicts.[103] Horsford reverted to the recurring racialized narrative of a criminality so entrenched that only coercion would be effective. The record is unclear regarding whether Foote's convict labor scheme was actually attempted, but even its contemplation at this moment is particularly revealing of a changing attitude around emancipation's efficacy. Whites in Antigua and elsewhere in the English Caribbean, as Paton argues for Jamaica, labeled the entire black working class "irreformable" at the very same time that they sought to implement penal labor.[104]

Ultimately, freedpeople's legal and extralegal pursuit of their self-interest undermined whites' commitment to the "nobler" goals of emancipation. In 1853, a local newspaper declared that "the abuse" of slavery "having past away, the moral error which was in part the consequence of it ought also to disappear." It continued: "Twenty years of equal rights and privileges to all classes is an ample time for coming to a juster conclusion on this subject. We ought to be now discerning that sloth and indolence are not the accomplishment and final polish and top-dressing of humanity. . . . It is a miserable thing to be wallowing in error on any subject. But it is a specially miserable thing to be wallowing in error where the consequences are so fatal as in the present instance."[105] Black working people, while navigating their unstable social worlds and opposing domination however they could, flouted elites' sense of law and order. In turn, by the mid-1850s, white elites concluded that the project of emancipation had caused more degeneration than uplift.

Conclusion

From the late 1840s through the mid-1850s, freedpeople's fortunes declined precipitously. Colonial and metropolitan policy failed to protect the few rights they endeavored to claim. At the same time, whites' harsh reactions to blacks' struggles intensified the criminalization of everyone of African descent. In response to the economic damage that would be caused by the Sugar Duties Act, freedpeople addressed appeals to Parliament; locally, they sought redress from the taxes imposed by parish vestries. These efforts to protect their economic and political interests were disregarded by the white-dominated public sphere, and freedpeople increasingly found themselves excluded from legitimate forms of politics. But black working people's multilayered struggles had always combined legal and illicit tactics, and they relied more heavily on the latter as the former proved unsuccessful. Freedpeople confronted the inequities of labor and life in Antigua through responses that ranged from the destructive spectacle of arson through their faith in obeah to their customary forms of moral economy, which showed their commitment to the most basic freedoms held dear since 1834. Though the material and social gains of the early 1840s were obliterated by the 1850s, black working people still vigorously pursued living wages, flexible working conditions, mobility, spiritual fulfillment, and some semblance of leisure.

Antigua's whites viewed black working people's determined attempts to secure and advance their self-interest in the face of impossible structural constraints as subverting law and order, a tendency they regarded as natural to the black race. By the mid-1850s, most Antiguan whites concurred that the great experiment of emancipation had failed and that only the vigilant policing of black working-class communities could contain the problems they posed. Local whites' discourse on the subject altered quite quickly, replacing the cautious optimism they had previously expressed. In her 1844 text, Mrs. Lanaghan routinely employed racialized descriptions of freedpeople's character, calling them "difficult and tiresome," "strange and harassing," and "far from perfect" in a single paragraph. But she simultaneously explored the benefits of abolition, noting the decreased incidence of severe criminal offenses and planters' opinion "that negroes are more easily managed as free men." She expressed "hope to see the negroes improved in their mental, as they already are in their temporal[,] affairs," and a wish that they would fulfill their expected "duties" so as to "finally meet their reward." She even praised freedpeople's "solemn" spiritual observance of August 1, 1834.[106] As they had done in the debates just before emancipation, in the early 1840s white elites believed that black people's prospects for inclusion and, perhaps, equality lay in the unspecified future—provided that their behavior remained within prescribed limits. Whites' underlying racial assumptions indicated that at best such possibilities were entirely conditional or, indeed, fated to end in failure. By the 1850s, however, common discourses among white elites explicitly confirmed their self-fulfilling prophecy: freedpeople would *never* act in ways meriting even a qualified offer of eventual advancement. White colonial power solidified as the economy contracted and the polity grew more hostile to blacks' inclusion and progress.

Whites posited freedpeople's deplorable position not as the result of colonialism's handiwork but as a sign of their intractable nature.

In these increasingly dismal times, black working people's endeavors to cobble together a livelihood took more extreme forms, which not only shadowed their interactions with powerful whites but also affected their interactions with one another. Freedpeople's unending socioeconomic depression bred individual and collective rage that they occasionally expressed through violence. In 1858, labor competition between native Antiguans and migrant Barbudans fueled a four-day riot in which freedpeople of Antiguan origin launched brutal attacks on their similarly disadvantaged Barbudan counterparts in St. John's. The contours of this disturbance show the complex identities and self-contradictory worldviews that black working people developed in the context of a meaningless freedom.

CHAPTER 7

···

"OUR SIDE"

Antiguans' 1858 Uprising and

the Contingent Nature of Freedom

Much disaffection still exists among the lower classes and I see . . . many another rebellion "looming in the future." The *air militaire* is rampant and should
the niggers attempt another[,] . . . the future historian of Antigua will have
abundant material for his pen to descant about.—ADAM NICHOLSON, a
sugar estate manager, 1858

Black working people in Antigua unleashed a violent uprising in
March 1858. Another rebellion did not unfold in its immediate aftermath,
despite the deep discontent that worried the estate manager Adam Nicholson months later. The hardening of whites' racial attitudes, apparent in
his ready use of the epithet *nigger* to refer to freedpeople, intensified in the
wake of the riots.[1] This revolt expressed black working people's increasing
sense that freedom, despite their earnest attempts to make it meaningful,
was being deliberately withheld from them by colonial elites as a matter
of policy.

The events of 1858 also indicate that the historical alignments and
divergences in Antiguan and Barbudan black working people's experiences bred hostility between them. Their proximity only exacerbated the
antagonism, as the members of the two groups lived in the same vicinity
in St. John's and competed for employment during the lean times of the
1850s. On March 22, 1858, an altercation occurred in St. John's, reportedly
in a rum shop, between two black stevedores, the Antiguan-born Henry

Jarvis and the Barbudan-born Thomas Barnard. Their personal confrontation grew into a four-day rebellion among hundreds of black working-women and -men that prompted a newspaper on the neighboring island of Dominica to declare Antigua in a "state of siege."[2] The conflict arose because Barnard procured a job in the St. John's harbor that eluded Jarvis. Barnard emerged victorious from the row, but later that evening, Jarvis, accompanied by other Antiguans, assaulted Barnard and many other known Barbudans in the Point, a working-class neighborhood near the harbor. The Point covered only a few streets, and its compactness made it likely that residents were familiar with one another's faces and possibly their names and birthplaces as well.

The following day, Tuesday, March 23, the local police were called to intervene after a large crowd of men and women stormed Barnard's house and smashed it to pieces. The police superintendent and a local justice of the peace quelled the riot, and the group temporarily disbanded. That evening, however, another crowd assembled where Barnard's house had stood, its numbers apparently swelling to several hundred. This group broke into the homes of other suspected Barbudans, damaging property and inflicting bodily harm on whomever they found. Antiguan women attacked Barbudan women with as much force as Antiguan men used against Barbudan men.[3] The superintendent armed six policemen and ordered them to fire into the crowd. Their musket balls and bayonets wounded three or four rioters, and the rest dispersed after showering the policemen with stones.[4]

An infuriated throng of black working-class Antiguans assaulted their Barbudan counterparts again on Wednesday. They also attacked the homes of some policemen and special constables commissioned to contain the uprising.[5] On Thursday night, the rebels assembled in front of the St. John's police station on Newgate Street seeking to force their way inside, after they learned that Barnard, the Barbudan dockworker at the center of the controversy, had taken refuge there. They pitched stones at the building, breaking all the windows, and while the group cheered, the policemen shot into the crowd, killing five and wounding several others. Rioting continued in front of the police station and on the surrounding streets in St. John's throughout the night. By four o'clock in the morning on Friday, March 26, the group had found a way to break into the station. As the rioters clearly understood, it housed the colony's arsenal, and capturing these weapons would have shifted the balance of power and enabled the rioters to pursue their violent agenda more effectively. The constables and policemen responded by firing their guns and wielding their bayonets, killing three participants and wounding more.

The governor, Ker Baillie Hamilton, reportedly learned of the riot earlier in the week but remained at his country home. On Friday, he appeared in town to proclaim martial law, enact an island-wide curfew, and call in mounted constables from all parishes to suppress the rioters. As a small police force had replaced Antigua's standing militia after 1834, Hamilton pleaded for help from the neighboring French island of Guadeloupe, whose authorities sent over 150 soldiers and twenty-four artillerymen. Volunteers from the planter, merchant, and white working classes in the town and countryside helped to detain some of the rioters.[6] In total, eight rioters were killed and fourteen were wounded, 115 men and fifty-seven women were arrested, and three other women and two other men were released on bail. Almost all of the 140 people who were tried were convicted. Their sentences ranged from two months to three years imprisonment, and many punishments featured some combination of cash fines, solitary confinement, and hard labor.[7]

Local elites and government officials tended to frame the riot as lawlessness stemming from the depravity of the crowd. The press linked the outburst to rioters' frequent visits to rum shops over the course of the four days. The newspapers criticized Antigua's authorities for their slow response to the life-threatening emergency and for underestimating the danger posed by the rebellious throng, especially if they had been able to seize the arsenal. The possibility of armed black rioters taking possession of the capital stirred up long-standing fears among local elites in Antigua, that hearkened back to the Haitian Revolution. Elites wondered aloud whether this uprising was purely spontaneous, or whether the "boatsmen's row" had triggered a premeditated attack against authority.[8] A group composed mainly of white planters and merchants and some mixed-race men of means exploited the riot to create a political frenzy and press for Hamilton's removal as governor.[9] Ultimately, elite observers and the authorities realized that this series of events may have begun as a common street brawl but had burgeoned into a rebellion against white rule. Whites had long feared that black people would wreak vengeance on the "superior" class and seek their violent overthrow. Beyond white elites' immediate and predictable reaction that fused scorn with hysteria, the 1858 uprising illuminates enduring, multilayered tensions within postemancipation Antigua.

The insurgents themselves, as the central actors in this upheaval, deserve particularly close examination. The two scholarly works that mention the 1858 uprising, although only in passing, interpret it as a by-product of the failing economy and the fragility of law and order on the island. These histories avoid engaging any more deeply seated motivations for the disturbance than the personal competition between two dockworkers.[10] I regard 1858 as a critical turning point in freedom's tortured course and treat it as a key site for tracing the complexities of identity formation among black working people. The rebellion was the explosive consequence of freedpeople's broad visions for better lives being frustrated by restrictions that narrowed their freedom over time.

The hundreds of rioters who took to the streets in March 1858 envisioned a variety of ends from their participation in such unprecedented violence. All of the rioters likely had multiple personal, economic, or political motivations for rebelling that the archive does not fully reveal. But the context of freedom denied underlaid this spectacular event. Significantly, the riot had unmistakable gendered dimensions. Court testimony, newspapers, and administrative correspondence vividly describe black women leading angry crowds through the streets, brandishing weapons, attacking their chosen antagonists, and appearing in their comportment and dress to be "like men," a telling phrase that fits with the historical tendency of colonial elites to masculinize black workingwomen. The intriguing words and actions of female rioters highlight both their ideological links with their male cohorts and some subtle distinctions that indicate the gendered inequities of emancipation.

This explication of the 1858 uprising's many dimensions begins with a closer examination of the four-day progression of events, investigating the demographic composition of the crowds in the Point and exploring the multilayered tensions that fueled Antiguans' aggressive pursuit of Barbudans. Then I look specifically at Antiguan women's involvement in the riot and suggest the gendered grievances that may have propelled their actions on the front lines of the rebellion. The chapter goes on to examine how and why rioters shifted their violence from Barbudans to other social groups, including Madeirans, planters, and policemen. I view Antiguans' resort to public violence as a rare assertion of power, however contradictory, by a disempowered people.

The events of 1858 confirm that freedom for British imperial subjects of African descent was conferred as a conditional privilege rather than as a universal right. Freedpeople's vehement words and violent actions stood as futile claims for rights and critiques of the gender, race, and class inequities that pervaded colonial society. The adversities they endured through the mid-1850s vividly demonstrate the lived effects of the bounded nature of freedom as crafted by the British state. Antiguan white elites had long maintained their political and economic dominance at the expense of black working people's welfare and advancement. In response, Antigua's freedpeople reified the exclusion they suffered and turned it against others, aggressively trying to oust a similarly distressed community of Barbudan freedpeople. As Antiguan working people seized control of the streets of St. John's over those four days, they tried to assert the kind of power that freedom had failed to give them over others who, they felt, contributed to the obstruction of their progress. But subjecting their perceived antagonists to physical pain, humiliation, and material loss in those brief moments only magnified their own enduring economic and political damage from a freedom unfulfilled.

The Social Dynamics of Revolt

Many sources narrate the events that unfolded in March 1858 from the panicked perspectives of elites. In order to reconstruct the experiences and viewpoints of participants in the uprising, however, the transcripts from the trials in May 1858 are essential. As documents central to the colonial state's criminalization of black working people's activities, trial transcripts can be compromised sources. Errors in transcription, the difficulty of recounting precisely what occurred in the midst of mass chaos, and the selective or distorted nature of testimony given under the duress of possible imprisonment and torture all make the record imperfect. Nevertheless, the trial transcripts are filled with fruitful material for reconstructing this historical moment. They provide a critical window onto what the disturbance looked like on the ground, who was involved, and why Antiguan rebels committed such violent acts.

Notably, the transcripts are the most complete record of rioters' explicit utterances in the course of action, revealing a discourse of this insurgency. Rioters themselves rarely spoke on their own behalf in the court to describe their actions; rather, witnesses and victims, both Antiguan and Barbudan, testified to what they allegedly heard rioters say or saw rioters do in the course of the uprising. When these rebels did testify, they reported the actions of others more frequently than they claimed responsibility for their own deeds, showing that loyalties often broke down in the courtroom as people strove to deflect culpability and punishment from themselves. But rioters' reported words and actions, though filtered through others' perceptions, remain the best indicators of the ideologies informing their violence.

Estimates of how many people were involved in the rioting vary considerably. Some witnesses reported seeing crowds of three or four hundred, while others said that one or two thousand people collected on the streets at given moments during the course of the rioting. Remarkably large numbers of black working people participated, and the crowds swelled from one day to the next.[11] Many of the offenses the rioters committed were described in graphic detail in court. The transcripts provide limited background information about those who testified, such as their age, occupation, and racial background, but they assume that the overwhelming majority of the rioters were of African descent. The occasional details in the transcripts, along with other sources about black townspeople, allow us to ascertain who most of these participants were and how they conducted their everyday lives.

The riot was mainly confined to the Point, a neighborhood on the northwestern end of the town of St. John's. It encompassed the streets bounded by Dickenson Bay Street to the north, Newgate Street to the south, Cross Street to the east, and the water's edge on the west (see map 1.1). The Point was home to black laboring people, especially dockworkers, given its proximity to the harbor. It was peppered with small, flimsy wooden houses, resembling those in free villages. Few businesses besides rum shops were found in its streets. In a densely populated neighborhood such as the Point, rumors would have traveled swiftly, and the noise produced by any disturbance would quickly attract attention and even draw a crowd. In the early twentieth century, the Point was reputed to be a "law unto itself."[12] The women and men who lived there held a range of manual and service occupations, such as maids, porters, coopers, and laundresses. Some rioters during the trial reported employment on sugar plantations that bordered the edge of town.[13] Others may have cultivated small plots or independently produced other goods that they sold. Given the contracting economy, some may have been unemployed and therefore categorized as vagrants. Members of the town-based rabble associated with the recent increase in crime might have participated in the outbreak, but so did many who had previously been law-abiding or had merely partaken in the town's harmless pleasures. Some participants attended the Moravian, Methodist, or Anglican churches, which we know because of the intermittent references to weekday services in the transcripts.[14] Others may have shunned organized religion altogether. Some may have practiced or believed in obeah, considering the pervasiveness of this spiritual system among black working people; some witnesses identified the tools of obeah among some of the uprising's women participants.

Those rioters detained by authorities were generally illiterate; of the 172 arrested, only 4 were able to read and write, and just 31 others were able to read but not write. Very few of those arrested would have qualified as middle class.[15] But a lack of formal instruction did not mean that people were unaware of current events. Information regarding affairs in Antigua, other Caribbean islands, the metropole, and the wider British Empire circulated constantly in the local press. The literate and semiliterate individuals involved in the rebellion could easily have read newspapers aloud to others or passed on the news in conversation. Illiterate people participated in discussing the issues of the day in such places such as the market, the harbor, and even the rum shops in town.

Barbudan men and women in the Point during the 1850s suffered the same dismal socioeconomic circumstances as did the Antiguans, and competition for the few jobs that were available fueled Antiguans' animosity toward Barbudans. Witnesses testified that, during the first two days of the uprising, groups of Antiguans specifically sought out Barbudans to inflict harm on their persons and their homes. William Wills, who was convicted for his actions in the riot, recalled: "I met a great mob looking for the Barbudian houses. I met a great quantity of my countrymen Antiguans."[16] Nativist feelings toward newcomers whom they regarded as foreign lay at the heart of their rage. But the violent acts that Antiguans perpetrated against Barbudans expressed a number of critical issues beyond their xenophobia that beg further exploration.

Antiguan Rioters and Their Barbudan Targets

Antiguans constructed a relationship of power between themselves and their Barbudan victims, not just through physical acts of violence but also through forcing them to engage in ritualized displays of deference. Antiguan women rioters in particular demanded acts of submission by employing brutal and sexualized violence against Barbudan women. For example, a Barbudan woman, Mary Ann Punter, reported that on the morning of Thursday, March 25, a large crowd, led by Grace George and Rebecca Hazlewood, entered her home in the Point. They dragged her out into the yard, collaring her and beating her with a stick. A witness to this encounter, Charles Stephens, reported: "They made Mary Ann Punter kneel down and beg their pardon. They brought her out of [the] yard to the gate and made her kneel down. Some said we will get Mary Ann to honor us."[17] Another Barbudan, Jane Beckwith, recounted a similar sequence of events: she was dragged from her home, collared, and forced to "beg pardon" of the Antiguans who were beating her. An Antiguan-born woman, Frances Donowa, testified that a gang of women rioters invaded her home, called her a "bitch," and stripped her naked while beating her in the same manner as the others. She met this unfortunate fate because she was suspected of harboring Thomas Barnard, the Barbudan dockworker at the origin of the controversy. Donowa testified to knowing the rioters' "features" but not their names, an unfamiliarity that, combined with her alleged alliance with Barnard, may have led rioters to assume she was Barbudan.[18] Although Donowa was Antiguan, her sympathies for a Barbudan rendered her a traitor to the rebels' cause.

These acts of humiliation and forced submission were gendered. Women aggressors led these assaults on women victims and demanded their self-abasement. Men participated in these exchanges infrequently. Sarah Frank, the Barbudan sister-in-law of Thomas Barnard, reported that a group of about six women and one man by the name of Henry Lewis came into her home and stripped her, beat her, and dragged her into the street in much the same fashion.[19] Antiguan men usually perpetrated violence against Barbudan men, although in a few instances mixed crowds of Antiguan men and women attacked Barbudan men. Testimonies recalling the physical exchanges between Antiguan rioters and male Barbudan victims never mention their being stripped or having to beg pardon of their assailants.

The assaults Antiguan women inflicted on Barbudan women mimicked the violence perpetrated against black women under slavery and in freedom, a disturbing and revelatory parallel indeed. By stripping their victims and making them beg pardon, Antiguan women asserted power over their Barbudan counterparts in ways that were often used by men, both black and white, to subjugate black women. Black women on both islands had suffered acts of rape and other sexualized punishments.

The words *beg pardon* evoke the suppliant position into which white men forced many black men and women, as well as the subservience that black men demanded of black women in the context of sexual relationships. This gendered trauma was then reenacted by women themselves in the context of rivalry and conflict between two groups of black people. The deliberate staging of these assaults suggests the normalization of black women's abuse to the extent that Antiguan women themselves could reproduce and deploy it against other women, unconscious of the ways in which it reinforced their own oppression. Antiguan women's domination of Barbudan women shows that, amid the collective struggle waged by Antiguan men and women to reclaim Antigua for its "countrymen," the women used the gendered forms of violence they knew best.

Barbudan male victims often fled their assailants more quickly than their female counterparts were able to do and escaped prolonged thrashings. For example, the Barbudans Reese Thomas and Thomas Roberts received blows but boarded ships docked in the harbor to avoid further violence from the crowd.[20] Barbudan men were hit by stones, sticks, and Antiguans' fists even while attempting to flee. Thomas Roberts testified that his arms were so badly injured that it was difficult to swim to the ship on which he sought refuge.[21] More unfortunate Barbudan men could not avoid severe and potentially life-threatening encounters with Antiguans. Israel Junior tussled with the Antiguan Anthony Davis in the course of a larger brawl that unfolded at a rum shop in the Point. After punching Junior in the eye, Davis dragged him outside and through a pile of mud in the gutter, leaving him in a heap on the street.[22] The Barbudan stevedore at the center of this conflict, Thomas Barnard and his son, Thomas Jr., were repeatedly sought out and stoned every day of the riot, and the homes of both the elder and the younger Barnard were destroyed by the throng.[23] Yet amid such extensive violence, no Barbudans were killed at the hands of Antiguan rioters; the only deaths suffered by Antiguans or Barbudans were during encounters with local police. Antiguans knew how to beat Barbudans severely without inflicting fatal blows. Such carefully calibrated violence suggests a discipline born of experience with a historically violent labor regime, as well as a self-restraint aimed at avoiding arrest and indictment by the authorities.[24]

Another noteworthy phrase besides *beg pardon* that the rioters repeated is *our side*. Many of those injured in the riots recalled that when a single rioter faced off with a potential target, the rioter would shout "our side," and, within moments, an angry crowd would assemble to join in the confrontation. The words *our side* functioned as a call to collective action, expanding smaller standoffs with a few assailants into a mass attack, or directing the crowd to a particular location to target the next victims. For example, one witness reported: "[Frederick Armstrong] saw Barnard under [the] house. . . . Frederick Armstrong being the leader singing out 'our side.' They said 'we will have him out tonight.' . . . Armstrong sang out 'our side follow me' and they went to Miss Robins'. They divided and part went to Lawyer Adlam."[25] This degree of coordination suggests a systematic and concerted effort. Although the uprising began spontaneously, the crowds became more organized and deliberate as the unrest continued.

The trial transcripts do not discuss any hostility between Antiguans and Barbudans before the fight between the two stevedores. Yet Barbudan working people might have seemed threatening to their Antiguan counterparts well before March 1858. The phrase *our side* suggests that territorialism informed Antiguans' approach to the increasing numbers of Barbudans in the Point. In addition to seeing them as competitors, Antiguans may have regarded Barbudans as interlopers from a foreign place associated with lawlessness. Black working-class Antiguans aggressively protected the insecure niche they occupied on their native island.

Barbudans' reputation stemmed from their island's history as a private estate owned by the Codringtons, who imposed neither the discipline of sugar plantation labor nor any system of law and order. The small community of African-descended people, who were the island's only permanent residents, enjoyed an unusual degree of independence under slavery, but they endured a protracted and difficult transition to freedom because their labor was no longer profitable to the white proprietors. Emancipation brought widespread impoverishment, as the Codringtons and the succession of managers failed to provide freedpeople with either steady wages or access to land. Some Barbudans migrated to Antigua in search of a livelihood, but others were sent there as a punitive measure after labor disputes. The problem of administering the island remained unresolved because the renewal of the Codringtons' lease in 1855 failed to establish any legal jurisdiction over Barbuda. Only in 1860 did the Colonial Office formally annex Barbuda to Antigua and, through a Crown Order in Council, finally make the laws of Antigua applicable there. The historians Douglas Hall and Brian Dyde both argue that the 1858 uprising helped bring about this decision.[26] At the time of the unrest in 1858, Barbudans' unsavory reputation for disorder remained prevalent among Antiguan whites, and the Barbudans living in Antigua conjured a history of forced expulsions and unregulated migration. Contrary to what we might expect, however, Barbudans' history of unruly and subversive behavior did not serve them well among black Antiguans. Closer examination of the violence Antiguans directed against Barbudans in St. John's suggests that the newcomers' foreignness and ill repute contributed to hostility against them.

During the course of the rioting, many Antiguans loudly proclaimed themselves to be *countrymen*, because of their native birth, and expressed the sense that Barbudans were not entitled to anything. During the assault on Thomas Barnard at his home, Eliza Joshua was said to have shouted that "the whole of the Barbudans should be beaten out of the law." This suggests that by reason of her and her compatriots' Antiguan identity, the assaults that they committed against Barbudans fell under the cloak of legality, while Barbudans in and of themselves did not.[27] The police constable Hezekiah Cuff overheard Rebecca Gordon, whom he described as a "very violent" rioter, tell another officer "that he had shot one of his countrymen which he had no right to do."[28] The Madeiran Antonio de Freitas recalled that when he saw Thomas Brown grab a stick to arm himself for the ongoing standoff at the police station on Friday morning, he told de Freitas that "he must fight for his own country."[29] Masses of rioters were alleged to have been roaming the streets exclaiming: "Foreigners had come to take bread out of the mouths of 'the people.'"[30] "The people" thus sought to oust the foreigners who threatened their daily bread. A conflict triggered by a personal rivalry exploded into a decidedly politicized battle. Barbudans, who struggled just like Antiguans to subsist, were redefined as encroaching on what little Antiguans had to show for themselves after twenty-four years of freedom.

Black insurgents deployed an uncannily similar language of material deprivation while perpetrating similarly violent acts against foreigners in Guyana's 1856 Angel Gabriel Riots. In that case, black working people attacked Portuguese Madeiran immigrants and demolished their shops in the capital city, Georgetown, to protest their economic distress and increasing exclusion from huckstering amid the rising prosperity of Madeiran merchants. The conflict even spread from its origins in Georgetown and the surrounding county of Demerara to Guyana's outlying Essequibo and Berbice Counties. A major catalyst for the unrest came from the musings of a black street preacher, John Sayers Orr, nicknamed "the Angel Gabriel," who was said to have proclaimed that the "Portuguese took the bread out the mouths of poor people who lived formerly by huckstering."[31] As did Antiguans, the distress of the 1850s prompted black laboring Guyanese to blame foreign competition for their unyielding impoverishment, but unlike Barbudans, the Madeiran targets in Guyana benefited from both racial and class distinctions from their attackers.

The testimonies of the Barbudans targeted by Antiguans do not say that they attempted to fight off their attackers with all the force they could muster. Their general reputation for unruliness might have made them especially careful to render themselves in court as nonviolent. Sarah Frank, for example, reported that her assailants had dared her to fight them, but she refused.[32] Instead, she and other Barbudans presented themselves as scrambling to make as quick an escape as possible from their attackers. Only the Barbudan Edward Williams admitted taking measures to defend himself, and he did so only after he had been assaulted and his cousin had been killed. He testified: "I was attacked at Point on Monday night as a Barbudian and I took out [a] sword for my protection on Thursday evening." Even Williams's testimony regarding how he acquired the sword portrayed himself as a victim. On the way home from service at the St. Mary's Street Methodist chapel on Thursday evening, he happened upon the dead body of his cousin, who had been shot in the street. His cousin had a sword in his hand, although Williams took care to point out that his cousin had been "doing nothing with" the weapon. Williams decided to take the sword from his cousin's hand to use for his own protection.[33]

Rather than galvanizing their own "side" to retaliate, Barbudans sought safety among their network of kin and friends or, eventually, with the authorities. As the Barbudan William Harris recalled: "[William Wills] came into my yard with a stone in his hand. I ran as quick as I can and received a blow with a stone which knocked me down speechless. After I recovered from the blow and got up one Robins saved my life." Harris went on to declare: "I saw [Wills] throw the stone which knocked me down. . . . I told Mr. Davey the magistrate it was [Wills] who cut me."[34] Barbudans were angry about the acts of violence perpetrated against them, but their testimonies created a sense of undeserved victimization rather than infuriated vengeance. Barbudan men and women who fought back carefully excluded those acts from their testimonies.

They relied on local authorities to suppress the violence and punish the Antiguan aggressors. William Harris reported his stoning to a magistrate, and the stevedore Thomas Barnard turned to the police station for refuge after his house was destroyed. Barbudans' historically tenuous relationship to the law and its representatives was completely reversed in the 1858 uprising.

Repeated incidents of larceny and the destruction of several Barbudan homes indicate that economic competition underscored Antiguans' political intent to humiliate and eject all Barbudans from the island. John Blucher, an Antiguan rioter, was reported to have declared: "If we can't catch the Barbuda people to mob them, then we will break their houses."[35] The Barbudan brothers Edward and Richard Ned testified that on Tuesday the twenty-fourth, the Antiguan Job Caddy stole two shillings and a knife from their home as they hid at a neighbor's house to escape what would have been a sure beating if discovered.[36] Antiguans who subjected their minds and bodies to the debilitating and degrading labor available to them in the place of their birth felt themselves more deserving of work than Barbudans. Antiguans were emancipated into poverty and disfranchisement. By the 1850s, instead of enjoying exclusive access to promising opportunities, they were competing in an unstable economy for the bare minimum of livelihoods. Barbudans lived in the same neighborhoods, had attained the same material standing, and were obtaining jobs sought by Antiguans—a situation likely to incite the ire of many Antiguans, especially those who already harbored the idea that Barbudans were undeserving and believed that any available jobs in Antigua belonged to them by right of birth.

Antiguans' brutal actions expressed a virulent nativism against Barbudans. The uneven effects of colonialism produced a palpable divide between similarly degraded subjects facing the same unjust circumstances. Antiguan black working people understood their progress in freedom contingently, perhaps taking cues from the ways that their own degradation had historically formed a main source of white privilege on the island. Through acts of cruelty and declarations of birthright, they distanced themselves from another black population to articulate their own grievances and claims. Mimi Sheller analyzes a parallel ideology in Jamaica, where constructions of otherness underlined black workingmen's claims for state protection amid the economic crisis of the late 1840s. There, free black men sought to establish their right to better-paid labor by distinguishing themselves from black women and indentured immigrant Indian and African laborers. In that context, "new indentured communities offered an 'other other' against which native black Jamaican virtue could be measured."[37] Antiguan rioters expressed a similar sense of entitlement in asserting their rights as countrymen and configuring Barbudans as "other others" in their midst. But in Antigua, black working people expressed their demands not through formal written appeals but in concerted street violence. Both women and men characterized their hard-won gains as a birthright worth defending with violence and worth denying to Barbudans, whom they treated as unwanted economic competitors from a different island.

Women Rioters as "Countrymen" on the Front Lines of Revolt

Black workingwomen appear prominently on the front lines in many descriptions of the 1858 conflict. As evidenced by the transcripts, Antiguan women acted as "countrymen," indicating that they, like their male counterparts, envisioned their public acts of violence as a way of claiming the privileges they thought they deserved as daughters of the soil. Antiguan women and men grabbed sticks and stones and assaulted Barbudans and other perceived antagonists in unison. Antiguan women's participation was essential to the spread and continuation of the uprising. Firsthand accounts of the violence located male bravado at the origin of these events, but colonial officers' correspondence, the press, and the court testimonies repeatedly state that women were equally if not more unruly than the men and, indeed, resembled them in their looks and comportment during the affray. Numerous witnesses described accused women rioters, such as Grace George, Rebecca Hazlewood, and Harriet Solomon, as wearing sack shirts "like men" or tying up their dresses or coats so they looked "like men" on those days.[38] Portrayals of women perpetrating violence while taking on the appearance of men overtly masculinized them, and the repetition of these descriptions in the press and official correspondence may have helped to justify the equally harsh punishments meted out to them. In fact, these rebellious women's modifications of their clothing may not have had a masculinizing intent; they may just have facilitated the very physical activities in which they were engaged. The white writer Mrs. Lanaghan described the loud speech, indecent dress, and "improper" carriage of black women at work in the town and country a decade earlier: "Many of the negro women, particularly those who live in the country, and are employed in agriculture, are so very masculine in their voice, manners, and appearance, that it is at times a matter of doubt to say which sex they belong." Ultimately, nonelite observers, unlike elites, would have presumed that the women rebels did not always dress "like men." But tales of disorderly demeanor and "manly" dress among the women echo the disparaging discourse, which members of all social groups knew well, about the masculine nature of women of African descent that had been prevalent since slavery in Antigua and the broader British Caribbean.[39]

The reported actions of women rebels confirm their calculated aggression over the four days. They beat as many Barbudan women and men as they could find, and they also targeted a number of local white elites, Madeirans, and policemen both verbally and physically. The descriptions of their subversive activities encourage a gendered approach to the politics that underlay the 1858 uprising. Their prominence in this revolt offers a rare opportunity to explore women's critical contributions to freedpeople's community formation and resistance in Antigua. Indeed, the 1858 uprising resembles many other historical instances of black popular resistance in Antigua and throughout the British Caribbean, from slavery through the early twentieth century, in which women consistently appear as "persistent rebels" on the front lines of conflict.[40]

Antiguan workingwomen functioned as informal organizers during the course of this revolt due to their consistent access to public spaces in St. John's. In many Caribbean societies, women based in towns engaged in both work and leisure activities in the street.[41] In such areas as the Point, where houses were too small and crowded to double as workplaces or shops, women primarily conducted their small-scale independent labor outside the home. Also, the streets were working people's chief spaces for socializing. Women regularly ran errands, sold their wares to other women and to men, and gathered with friends and loved ones as they went about their daily lives in the streets of St. John's. While the 1858 uprising unfolded spontaneously rather than from the execution of a conspiracy, and several participants rather than a few identifiable leaders determined the movements of the crowds, women were poised to assume crucial roles as organizers helping distinct dissident actions coalesce into a mass disturbance. For example, a witness recalled seeing Frances Gilliard, who actively participated in the assault on the police station on Friday, March 26: "I saw her on Friday morning between 6 and 7 o'clock. [The women] had gone within [the] railing of [the] arsenal and armed themselves with clubs and all they could find. They were about 1000 strong mostly all women. When that crowd went down, another crowd came up 500 or 600 headed by this woman, she headed them. Her coat was tied up and a club stick in her hand. A double crowd collected."[42] Another witness reported, "I saw [Charity Cole] on Thursday night 25th March. . . . Charity Cole's crowd was coming down. She called out 'our side.' She had a stick in her hand and her coat tied up."[43] When a crowd stormed a policeman's house, a witness heard Catharine Willis "sing out": "This is Mr. Knight's house. Boys[,] take possession." Willis "struck the door with a stick," and she and the rest of the throng "mashed up the things" in the home.[44]

As marketers, laundresses, and servants, as well as in any number of occupations that constantly placed them in the street, black working-women occupied what Sheller describes as "a special economic and social position as a link between town and country, between markets and fields, and between the state and the families it tried to control."[45] These women could easily become communicators of crucial information, bearers of weapons, and galvanizers of action during moments of mass mobilization. While some Antiguan women were heavily involved in the disturbance, many others were principal informants regarding the actions of other women and men during the trials. More often than not, women informants provided evidence that helped to convict the accused, but some testified that their friends or kin were in places other than where violence had unfolded, providing their loved ones with alibis.

Women's testimonies reveal their crucial historical role in the St. John's black working-class community as observers of street-based interactions. For example, Lidia Daniel testified that after returning from service at the Moravian church on St. John's Street on Thursday night, she met Georgiana Jackson, who lived with her, and the pair sat at their gate together most of the night watching and listening to the violence take place, but they left the premises only once, to visit Daniel's relative. They heard reports of people being killed but maintained that they never joined the crowds. Since Jackson, but not Daniel, was accused, Daniel pointedly declared: "If [Jackson] did any thing wrong I must have done the same."[46] Similarly, Jane Cole insisted that Quashy Phipps was not involved in the action on Thursday, as he had come from Dominica on a sloop that day bearing fruit that he then sold at the harbor. Cole went down to the wharf to purchase fruit from him. Declaring that, as Phipps's neighbor, she knew his whereabouts, Cole stated that although later on Thursday evening he was drunk, she was sure that he stayed home all night and did not participate in the violence.[47] The jury rarely considered the testimony of such witnesses to be sufficient evidence to nullify incriminating information and spare their loved ones jail time. Women's statements both for and against the accused show that their regular travels in the streets by day and at night made them well aware of any public interactions that took place.

The sources amply demonstrate *how* Antiguan women observed or participated in these events but offer no indications of *why* those who actively participated chose to do so. These women consistently perceived themselves and acted as "countrymen." Did women rioters mobilize this nativist discourse for gender-specific goals, or were they only upholding the broader ends of economic advancement and political voice for which men were also fighting? A look at the historical circumstances of Antiguan urban women's lives and their movements and utterances in this uprising offers some clues. Definitive conclusions cannot be drawn about what those who fomented this rebellion envisioned as their ultimate goals. But had their violence brought them a victory over the colonial power structure, as well as over the Barbudans, any economic or political spoils they won would likely have accrued solely to men. Most nineteenth-century Caribbean societies privileged men's interests over those of women, and it is quite likely that the parity between women and men visible on the front lines of the riot would not have continued afterward. Antiguan black workingwomen endured a number of everyday gender inequalities that this riot would not have undone.

The trial transcript features several testimonies of women rioters citing their multiple responsibilities that kept them from the revolt. For example, Margaret Carty insisted that she was at home with her four children and not in the crowds, as other witnesses testified. Similarly, Elizabeth McChand reported that by 7:00 or 7:30 a.m. on Friday, March 26, Rachael Richards, who was charged with assaulting a police officer during the battle at the station, was in her yard with a bundle of clothes, which McChand was assisting her in washing. McChand claimed that Richards never left her yard until that evening, after the violence had ended.[48] Antiguan workingwomen's private and public labors particular to their sex, ironically presented in the testimony as alibis for accused women seeking to exonerate themselves, illuminate some possible reasons for their prominence in the disturbance.

Black women in Antigua and throughout the British Caribbean historically balanced domestic duties, such as child care and keeping house, with income-producing labor outside the home, in the context of staggering poverty and violence.[49] The move from estates to free villages and towns did not relieve the pressures on women, given the instability of housing in each locale. Severe overcrowding, shoddy construction, and lack of access to fresh water all plagued black people who lived in the towns and villages during the 1850s.[50] In the mid-1850s, 21 percent of all children born alive died in infancy, a sure indicator of black families' dire living conditions.[51] Residence in St. John's may have enabled black families to escape from the watchful eyes of sugar estate managers, but the standard of living in town was abysmal. Freedwomen were hard-pressed to maintain their homes, keep their children fed, and garner an income, and thus directed their assaults in 1858 to outsiders perceived as exacerbating their community's already immense struggles.

Like their male countrymen, Antiguan workingwomen fought for the material benefits they felt were their due as natives. Antiguan workingwomen who attacked Barbudan women and their houses during the riot had the same reasons for regarding Barbudans as interlopers that Antiguan workingmen did. Antiguan women faced competition from Barbudan women in the gender-segregated labor market of St. John's. Barbudan women actually shared many of Antiguan women's socioeconomic grievances, but Antiguan women deemed them enemies rather than allies. Similarly, assaulting Madeiran merchants and vandalizing their properties may have seemed a just retribution for their rapid success amid black working people's blocked mobility. Stoning planters and policemen might have challenged the delimiting of women's access to public space and the criminalizing of their independent economic pursuits. Defending themselves and their loved ones against such aggressive policing involved complicated and costly legal proceedings that strained family resources. Constant troubles with the law also undermined certain basic material and social meanings of freedom, especially the right to earn a livelihood and keep their families intact.

The state's continued obstruction of black working people's progress and the absence of legitimate outlets to express their dissent resulted in extralegal forms of protest that used the street as a public theater and violence as political practice. Antiguan women's utterances, self-presentation, styles of leadership, and confrontations with authorities during the 1858 uprising show the broad-based nature of their political aims and practices, even as they expressed certain grievances and employed ways to degrade other black women that were gender specific.

Such gender-specific demands, opportunities, and constraints that may have led Antiguan women to incite riot were fused with their self-perception as workers, as natives, and even as citizen-subjects who deserved political and economic equality.

The appearance and conduct of women rebels, as the sources describe them, violated what elites recognized as appropriate "feminine" or "motherly" comportment. Their blackness already disqualified them from the status of "ladies," but their unruliness left them open to a more virulent masculinization. These women seemed well aware of whites' conceptions of femininity and masculinity in colonial Caribbean society and how these notions affected their particular positioning as gendered, racial, and class subjects in Antigua. Already construed through their blackness and their labor as masculine, these workingwomen did not hesitate to employ their physical strength and boldness to their advantage when taking to the streets alongside men. Aware that society and the state rewarded what whites regarded as appropriate feminine behavior, they deliberately adopted it in court and insisted to the authorities that, instead of participating in the affray, they were occupied with their motherly duties and minding their own business at home.[52] This violent episode and its aftermath show that black Antiguan women's acts of resistance, like their everyday lives, consistently blurred the notional divides between women's and men's public and private concerns.

The Expanding Scope of Rioters' Violence

Although the animosity of Antiguan countrymen against foreign-born Barbudans sparked this protracted episode of violence, the rioters expanded their focus over the four days, lashing out at many other social groups they believed were impeding their progress. Antiguan rioters deliberately attacked Portuguese immigrants from Madeira. Joaquim Marques reported that on the last day of rioting, Richard Ephraim, a black Antiguan, beat him and stole a handkerchief and a small amount of money.[53] Antonio Rodrigue, a rum shop owner in the Point, testified that a crowd of five local women stormed into his shop on the Tuesday of the uprising. They demanded that he give them bottles of rum, which they passed to the men outside. Then the women brandished sticks, threatened Rodrigue with bodily harm, and proclaimed: "The Portuguese were the next they intended to beat out of the island."[54] In the rebels' eyes, the Madeirans were an undesirable group of foreigners who competed with and surpassed them economically, as the privileges of whiteness enabled them to leave plantation labor and become petty merchants within a decade of their arrival on the island. Antiguans asserted their birthright over Madeirans as well, subjecting them to physical force and material dispossession, as they did Barbudans.

Local whites of influence were not spared either. Paul Horsford, a planter who owned a 235-acre estate and was the brother of Antigua's previous solicitor general, was bludgeoned when he came into St. John's on Wednesday evening to help quell the disturbance. In court, Horsford testified that two or three women came upon him in the Point near a house that he was renting to a policeman. They were planning to attack the house, as they had several other policemen's residences, and as Horsford tried to stop them, he was struck with a large stone by one of the women. She uttered the familiar words "our side!" and a crowd assembled to pelt him with stones before he got away.[55] Other rioters announced a general assault on white authority. Before the shootings on Friday afternoon, William Nanton, a boy of twelve, was reportedly seen running with "an armful of stones" toward the police station while shouting: "Now is the time, down with the Buckra!"[56] Buckra was the colloquial phrase that African-descended communities in the British West Indies used to refer to whites. This youth's utterance testifies to the radical political potential that the rebellion unleashed in the island's working people.

While Madeirans and whites of the planter class experienced freed-people's rage intermittently, these insurgents expressed even greater animosity toward the policemen attempting to suppress the riot. During their numerous encounters with policemen, black working-class Antiguans fused anger at the police's defense of the Barbudans with anger at their role as the forceful arm of oppressive white authority on the island. Antigua's police force was small and largely composed of mixed-race and black Antiguan-born men who enjoyed a limited degree of privilege and influence, and some were even related to participants in the riot.[57] Policemen were more vulnerable than the powerful whites of the planter class, since they were not so far removed from the rebels' station in life. But defeating the police may have been a stepping-stone to a more protracted attack on the island's whites, given the rebels' intent at the uprising's finale to penetrate the police station and seize the arsenal.

Black residents of the Point knew the policemen and where they lived, which allowed for the looting and destruction of many of their homes. A group led by Samuel Lafovey broke into the home of the officer William

Knight on the second night of the uprising and stole a watch and some clothes. Another crowd, led by Catharine Willis, eventually smashed all of the contents in Knight's home to pieces. The house of a policeman by the name of Chapman was attacked and the furniture inside destroyed.[58] The home of the mixed-race police sergeant, John Harley, was showered with stones on Thursday, March 25; then a crowd broke both the front door and a few windows before proceeding to demolish his furniture and clothing while his family fled.[59]

The white police chief, Edward Shorediche, also fell victim to an attack on his person and property, as a group of rioters led by John McKenzie Fisher reportedly ambushed Shorediche's horse-drawn gig just prior to the Friday morning shootings. The group broke the gig apart and threw it over the wharf and into the sea. Fisher was then said to have instructed the mob to "return and get out the carriage of Mr. Shorediche and give the ladies a drive who had been working hard all night."[60] Presumably, the hard work for which the women would be rewarded with a ride in Shorediche's carriage was their nightlong battle against the police. Black men's parading of black women in ways typically befitting privileged white women and men was a deliberate inversion of the social hierarchy. This flight of fancy indicates the solidarity between men and women rioters and the deep hostility they collectively harbored toward the police as enforcers of Antigua's discriminatory social order. As events progressed, the targeted attacks on Barbudans morphed into a mass revolt against the authorities, both white and black.

A continuous critique of the police and their tactics emerges from the actions and statements of the Antiguan aggressors. From the earliest moments of the uprising, black working people lashed out at the police and their proclamations as the persons and instruments of authority. For example, on Tuesday, March 23, as Shorediche and the justice of the peace John Lowry read the Riot Act, Nathaniel Francis reportedly shouted to the crowd that the proclamation was "a damned piece of paper." After he pitched stones at the justice, Francis then declared: "Damn Mr. Lowry, give it to Mr. Shorediche!" This led to the police chief receiving a torrent of stones.[61] The witness Charles Richards reported that on the same day (perhaps during that same confrontation), Joseph Henry attempted to throw Shordiche into the sea, but Shordiche made a narrow escape.[62]

Lower-ranking policemen were also the targets of physical and verbal assault. During the last two days of rioting, the mixed-race police sergeant John Harley was vilified and stoned. Many witnesses recalled episodes in which several rioters singled him out for attack. Rachael Richards was heard in the crowd outside the police station on Friday morning belittling Harley, asking, "What is that old man saying?" She then declared, "We don't care a damn what he's saying!"[63] As the crowd laid siege to the police station that Friday morning, Richards, as well as Rebecca Joseph, Mary Abel, and Letitia Frederick, along with several other women rioters, charged Harley with being a patron, if not a practitioner, of obeah.[64] For instance, Mary Moses was said to have held up a phial and declared to Harley: "You son of a bitch—we took this out of your bed and no wonder you had such power over [the] police."[65] All the accounts of the discovery of Harley's involvement in obeah are strikingly similar, with one woman finding a phial and alleging it to be a tool for his maintenance of authority over the rest of the force. While in each case the witness identified a single woman as having made the discovery, the aggregate of the testimonies suggests that a group may have found the phial during the collective attack on his home the night before, and they all made it their business to inform the rest of the rioters of Harley's secret. Alleging that the sergeant believed in obeah, the same illicit institution that he and the other members of the force were duty bound to police, must have given them extra confidence as they embarked on their attack on the police station that Friday.

Mary Gardiner, a relative of Harley, took the opportunity to target him during that final confrontation. Gardiner reportedly pitched a stone directly at Harley's head and knocked him unconscious. Several witness testified that she loudly exclaimed, "If Sergeant Harley died, I knocked him down with half a brick!" Gardiner declared the accusation unfounded, insisting that she would not have "lifted a stone" against Harley as "Mr. Harley and my father are relatives." This fact did not prevent the court from convicting her of attempted murder.[66] The specific episodes targeting Harley as a more powerful member of the force with direct ties to black working people of the Point reflect insurgents' general ire toward police authority, layered onto a personal vendetta, to remind Harley that he was no better than they were, despite his middle-class status.

The shootings at the police station on Friday morning inspired rioters' most vigorous condemnation of the force. Their statements expressed their pervasive dissatisfaction with the police's entrenched power over black working people's bodies, mobility, and livelihoods well before March 1858. Numerous rioters stated that the police chief did not authorize the officers to fire on the crowd, thus making the shootings legally punishable as wrongful deaths. Mary Abel reportedly declared: "The bodies should not be removed for Mr. Shorediche had given no orders to fire. . . . The police must fling away their guns for they could not live in Antigua." As with the Barbudans and Madeirans, rioters wished to rid Antigua of the police, as "the people's" perceived enemies, and claim the island as their own. She then exclaimed: "Shorediche ought to be killed and [Police Officer] Lake had no right to be here after this. Lake shot Rebecca Adam and after doing so took the butt of his gun and knocked out her brains!"[67] Many rioters tried to prevent the coroner from removing the dead bodies so they would remain as a public testament to what the rioters believed was unnecessary violence, and at least two rioters threatened to set the entire town of St. John's on fire during the standoff.[68] David Wilcox exclaimed to the crowd that they were "great fools" if they did not seek "satisfaction," since the police had shot the people like "dead sheep."[69] In the rebels' eyes, the victims' bodies proved the state's guilt.

Black working-class Antiguans also sought vengeance against the police through subterfuge. Christian Henry's actions reveal a strategic use of the colonial system of authority in order to subvert it and assist the insurgents. Henry feigned allegiance with the status quo to further the rebel cause by getting himself sworn in as a special constable during the uprising. Witnesses identified Henry encouraging the crowds as they continued their attacks on the last two days, and some saw him use the weapons he was given for subduing the crowd to shoot at the police at key moments. On Wednesday, March 24, Henry appeared at the police station to say that his employer, James Gordon, had sent him to be sworn in as a special constable. Henry was then supplied with a musket, but instead of reporting for duty, he joined the crowd in the Point in their search for the Barbudan stevedore Barnard. Henry sought to prevent the attorney Alexander Adlam from quelling the crowd and, along with several other individuals armed with sticks and stones, surrounded Adlam to force his retreat. On Thursday, Henry showed up for duty at the police station, but by Friday morning, Henry was seen outside the station firing his musket at other officers who were attempting to stop the crowd's attack. The sources do not indicate that Henry was able to injure anyone.[70]

Later on Friday, Henry appeared in the area of the public market, again harassing Adlam as the latter tried to proclaim martial law and disperse the crowd.[71] On Friday night, Henry was still performing his constabulary duties undetected, this time guarding apprehended rioters detained at the police station. He was heard instructing the detainees not to say anything, because "they had been brought in for nothing and the Buckras could do nothing to them." At that moment he was arrested by another police officer.[72] Henry took advantage of the upheaval to destabilize law and order from within. He moved about town with more audacity than the rest of his compatriots, because his appointment as a constable allowed him to bear arms, which was denied to most black workingmen under normal circumstances. His calculated seizure of power affirms his and others' desire to dominate their oppressors by force. His ready use of arms also implies what this mob might have done had the insurgents managed to take possession of the arsenal.

Henry's participation suggests that some black working people from the countryside may have been involved in the unrest in St. John's. James Gordon's testimony regarding Christian Henry does not offer any details about his employee, stating simply that Henry had worked for him for a year and a half and that Henry's "conduct was better than expected."[73] The trust his employer placed in him may have enabled Christian Henry to be enlisted as a special constable. A James Gordon appears in the sources as a proprietor of a plantation in the parish of St. Peter.[74] If this was indeed the same Gordon, and if Henry labored on his sugar estate, this fact belies the constant refrain in public and private correspondence regarding 1858 that rural working people did not participate in or sympathize with the uprising.[75]

Yet months after the rioting had ended, black working people in the countryside publicly distanced themselves from the rebellious actions of their town-based counterparts. They penned, signed, and sent to the authorities numerous statements denouncing the violence and insisting that they had no knowledge of the uprising until it had ended.[76] Male residents of free villages and plantations, such as Liberta, Bethesda, and Darby's Estate, endorsed six appeals to Governor Hamilton. These letters all shared similar language. For instance, the petition from All Saints Village declared the signatories' "devoted loyalty to Her Most Gracious Majesty the Queen" and their intent to maintain the peace, given their progress since "England conferred upon [them] the blessing of Freedom."[77] Petitioners sought to allay any suspicion that they were "wanting in loyalty and good conduct." The All Saints letter also alluded to a petition from local whites calling 1858 an island-wide conspiracy that country laborers were supporting, to which these formal protestations were probably a direct response.[78] Through these statements, spokesmen for rural black working people tried to counter the conclusion that local whites had quickly drawn: that the violent uprising attested to the failure of emancipation. Rural black working people may well have privately dissented from these sentiments, but this pointed public language sought to retain what little social capital they had at a time when whites distrusted the island's entire black population.

Other events suggest the possibility that, while it was unfolding, this town-based uprising inspired some workers in the countryside to take action. On Thursday, March 25, a property dispute arose on George Byam's Estate in St. Mary Parish between the proprietor, Mr. Foreman, and Mr. Rodin, the attorney representing Luckie Bros. & Co., a company to which Foreman was indebted. A fistfight ensued between Rodin and Foreman's brother, but by the time the police were summoned, an unspecified number of laborers had apparently become "riotous" themselves, "taking part on either side" of the dispute.[79] The laborers were only calmed when threatened with a reading of the Riot Act. Here, as in the larger conflagration in town, a personal clash sparked the conflict, but it quickly escalated until Byam's Estate stood on the brink of mass violence. Laborers who took part on Foreman's behalf may have sought to defend him against his creditors. But the few sources on this occurrence do not say whether the majority of laborers sided with or against the manager, or if their disturbance was even rooted in the management's debt dispute. The capital had been engulfed in an uprising for two days by the time of the dispute at Byam's, and black laboring people might have welcomed the violent conflict between the manager and his creditor as an excuse to voice their discontent with the structure of power on their estate. Moreover, although the record does not clearly indicate rural support for townspeople's rebellious actions, rioters in St. John's considered recruiting rural residents as the uprising continued. John Joseph reportedly exclaimed to a few policemen late Thursday night: "The police are nothing to us. . . . We are able to conquer the police with stones. . . . What will you do when we get the country people with us?"[80] The 1858 riot reverberated well beyond the city limits.

The conflicts that unfolded during this uprising signify that, while Barbudan working people were the initial objects of their rage, Antiguan working people had much broader aims than terrorizing and expelling their immediate neighbors from the Point. They claimed the freedom to move about public space in the town as they saw fit, defying the increasingly stringent regulations against their self-interested pursuits.

Moreover, the rebels targeted Antigua's power structure by attacking local policemen and, directly as well as indirectly, the whites whose interests they protected. Their angry exclamations and violent aggression against individuals of other social classes over the course of the riot articulated their deep-seated frustration with their degraded condition and the material and social inequities that produced it.

The rebellion dredged up the long-standing fear felt by the few hundreds of whites left in Antigua who were woefully outnumbered by thousands of freed but constrained black people. Whites tolerated widespread black dissent expressed through less belligerent everyday acts, but open rebellion, however short-lived, generated widespread panic. An absentee British proprietor, G. Estridge, conveyed these fears to Lord Carnarvon, the colonial undersecretary of state, after receiving a number of letters from the island relaying the threats to white control that surfaced during and after the uprising. One letter stated: "200 are now in the gaol, & say when they go they will serve the white people out. They had distributed the white women amongst those that shall fight the brunt."[81] White men in slave societies throughout the Americas had long circulated rumors that black men would take vengeance against white men and obtain unbridled sexual access to white women's bodies. Such hysteria, which inverted a pervasive pattern of racialized sexual violence actually perpetrated by white men against black women in slavery and freedom, resurfaced regularly in these societies to justify the punitive repression of free black men in times of crisis.[82] Estridge's letter also mentioned: "The laborers in the country were quiet, altho', had the others gained their ends, I think the country folk would have joined them."[83] While some public discourse and private correspondence endeavored to depoliticize the actions of rioters and label it a mere "boatsmen's row," many other whites were attuned to the uprising's broader and more menacing significance.

Conclusion

The 1858 uprising was a crucial turning point in black working people's progress. The rebels posed the most vociferous and powerful challenge to colonial Antigua's class and race order in the island's previous history. They threatened local authority by decrying police tactics and pressing these more powerful individuals to endure the degradation usually reserved for themselves, subjecting them to physical attack, material dispossession, and, in the case of Christian Henry, attempts to take their place. Throughout the uprising, black Antiguans also used other means of subversion that they often employed in times of relative quiet, such as identifying the tools of obeah, committing theft, and threatening fire. The actions and statements of participants indicate that the events of March 1858 capped black working people's everyday and more muted forms of resistance against oppression that had been at work since abolition.

These brutal episodes reveal the selective nature of resistance for galvanizing some oppressed peoples while simultaneously subduing others. Antiguan black working people's attempts to reshape the emancipation project were diffuse and, on occasion, self-contradictory. At the very same time that Antiguans were oppressed by colonial rule and aggressive policing, they played the role of oppressors, subjugating Barbudan working people who were similarly circumstanced. Furthermore, the rioters not only sought out Barbudan victims but also perpetrated cruel acts against Antiguan-born men and women who refused to join their campaign or attempted to prevent their actions. Amid their public and violent critique of local structures of domination, Antiguan working people participated in the domination of others and reified their own oppression.[84]

This case carries significance not only for its negative effects but also for its radical intentions. The events of 1858 demonstrate how Antiguan black working people seized opportunities that might have made them feel free after a period of economic downturn that shrank their freedoms to the barest of minimums. Freedom for formerly enslaved Antiguans meant more than increased access to living wages and better jobs on or off the plantation. Their use of force represented the freedom to delineate who was and who was not included in their sense of community, spatially as neighbors and discursively as "countrymen." Freedom also underlined the spectacle of hundreds of working people protesting in the streets when all other forms of political voice were blocked and public spaces were heavily policed because of their presence. The uprising intimated that Antiguans envisioned more far-reaching possibilities than what they had attained since 1834. The 1858 uprising demonstrates that, despite frequently contradictory modes of struggle on the ground, Antiguan black working people's broader objectives were to gain equality and transform the society in which they lived and labored.

During the uprising, black working people's language grew increasingly seditious as their encounters in the streets became more violent.

While Antiguans did not possess the means or political power to alter their social position, their actions show an acute awareness of the colony's intertwined systems of legal and customary class and racial discrimination that blocked their progress. The 1858 riot also strongly indicates that Antiguan freedpeople had a conscious framework for understanding the connection between their blackness and their poverty. The riot and its aftermath reveal the ways these inequities combined to thwart black working people's prospects. In the wake of these events, the militia was briefly resurrected on a volunteer basis, with the intent to police the black working-class community made obvious by the qualifications that blocked all but the most propertied of individuals from joining.[85] Even if they gained material security in postslavery Antigua, the racial ceiling worked in conjunction with class competition to prohibit their advancement to any degree that could undo planter dominance. Black working people's extreme poverty and the severe limitations on their rights would remain in place into the early twentieth century. Despite the unfavorable odds, Antigua's black working people would continuously struggle against subjugation long after 1858.

Emancipation's greatest contradiction lay in the fact that no one in the island's black working class, regardless of birthplace, received the expected material and social gains from freedom, given the stasis of the local economy and the exclusionary nature of the polity. These gains would continuously elude working people as they splintered their resistance efforts rather than forging broader allegiances among themselves. These divisions certainly benefited colonial officials and planters seeking to uphold their socioeconomic power. Antigua's 1858 uprising also offers a complicated example of gendered postslavery resistance. Workingwomen and -men who were oppressed in gender-specific ways rose up in defense of distinct but overlapping causes. Yet they shared common cause with many whom they construed as their opponents. Indeed, not only did oppressed women's and men's political goals both align and diverge in this instance but combative acts that the state typically associated with men were regularly perpetrated by women throughout the uprising. Antiguan women exacted violence upon both men and other women, Barbudan and Antiguan alike. The humiliation and torture of black women that was rife within slavery continued unabated after emancipation, and their easy reenactment during the uprising again reveals how oppressed people's resistance can reify their oppression. Antiguan women's experiences come to the fore in challenging ways despite imperfect colonial archives, troubling both gendered conventions and the methods and meaning of subaltern political expression.

Ultimately, the uprising reveals the complex ways in which freed-people envisioned and experienced freedom over the long term. Their violent rebellion indicted Antigua's authorities for imposing a freedom that remained contingent and incomplete. The events of 1858 produced both power and powerlessness for Antiguan men and women, as they unsuccessfully attempted to claim freedom as exclusively theirs through public protest and yet failed to expand it beyond its narrow, state-authored definition of social submission and low-wage labor.

....

"MY COLOR BROKE ME DOWN"

Postslavery Violence and Incomplete Freedom

in the British Caribbean

Mass revolt was a principal vehicle for Afro-Caribbean people to voice their discontent with the hollowness of emancipation. Black working people consistently used violence to publicly protest their condition, but the authorities in both the colony and the metropole were increasingly hostile to their aspirations. Postslavery resistance exposed the pitfalls of a partial, racially delimited freedom that fixed freedpeople in a position of economic, social, and political subordination. These spectacular uprisings and the brutal repression they engendered highlight the frustrations black people throughout the region faced as they continued to struggle against extremely adverse circumstances.

Antigua's 1858 uprising unfolded within a broader tide of explosive popular unrest in the British Caribbean. Most colonial territories experienced at least one major incident of popular unrest after 1834, and mass uprisings occurred at least twice a decade within the first forty years.[1] Freedpeople in St. Kitts, Montserrat, and Trinidad fomented disturbances upon the announcement of the apprenticeship. In Dominica the 1844 Guerre Negre (Black War, or census riots) occurred because freedpeople suspected census takers of "taking names" to reenslave them. In 1849 in St. Lucia, laboring people rose up against higher taxation on their provision grounds. The British Virgin Island of Tortola was convulsed by the Road Town Riots of 1853, when freedpeople assaulted magistrates and other propertied whites and scorched the town and surrounding areas in response to increased taxation on cattle; in the wake of the riots, all but three members of the white population of this small island fled to nearby St. Thomas. Guyana's 1856 Angel Gabriel Riots involved hundreds of black working people targeting Portuguese Madeiran merchants for their prosperity in the wake of black poverty. In 1862, a labor strike in St. Vincent exploded into a mass assault by freedpeople on planters' persons and property.

The historian Juanita De Barros suggests that earlier postslavery uprisings reflected popular concerns about "protecting freedom," while later revolts, which she says began with the turning point of Jamaica's 1865 Morant Bay Rebellion, were "animated by the attempt to establish new rights, to gain equality rather than to protect freedom."[2] Upon further examination, both the aims of protecting freedom and of attaining new rights coursed through all the postslavery rebellions in the Anglophone Caribbean. From the outset, emancipated people understood freedom to signify benefits that far exceeded mere legal release from bondage. Yet the Morant Bay Rebellion was a watershed in British Caribbean history. The culmination of many smaller riots that had unfolded in Jamaica over the previous two decades, it simultaneously expressed freedpeople's unfulfilled desire for land and their solidarity against detested white planters. The bloodiest of the region's post-1834 revolts, Morant Bay killed hundreds of Jamaicans, black and white, and caused widespread destruction of property.[3] Its reverberations were quickly felt in the metropole, as the Colonial Office restructured its approach to administering the Caribbean colonies. It prompted vehement debate among officials in London regarding both the use of excessive force to police black masses and the efficacy of electoral government in the West Indies.

In 1876, both Tobago and Barbados experienced collective uprisings. Tobago's Belmanna Riots unfolded after local police tried to quell a disturbance on a sugar estate, killing one of the workers; in response, angry crowds attacked the police station and later dismembered Belmanna, the police corporal who had led the suppression of unrest on the estate. Barbadian blacks launched the Federation Riot when the governor of Barbados proposed federation with the Windward Islands, a move that factionalized political elites because it threatened the limited advances that blacks had made in the electorate and also, as in Dominica in 1844, carried rumors of reestablishment of slavery. High-ranking estate workers took advantage of the political friction to launch a widespread strike, destroying much local property and prompting the flight of significant numbers of whites. During the severe economic depression of the 1880s and 1890s, the British Caribbean saw a continued stream of unrest that was precipitated by abysmal sugar prices in the world market. This tradition culminated in the massive strikes launched by sugar laborers in the 1930s across several islands, which contributed to the founding of the region's first trade unions and political parties.[4] Each successive riot stimulated similar uprisings elsewhere, forming a legacy of protest on which twentieth-century anticolonialism was built.

All of these revolts were swiftly and severely crushed, and considerable numbers of participants were jailed or killed. These uprisings all stemmed from a similar set of unresolved tensions. Such moments highlight black working people's politics as they attempted to seize the long-expected but consistently denied benefits of emancipation, including economic equity, political enfranchisement, and social autonomy. Furthermore, these revolts displayed a common consciousness among rebels of their multilayered deprivation and its origins in racial hierarchy. This trail of mass unrest unearthed black working people's continued development and articulation of race identity through their protests against the unyielding racial discrimination that was a hallmark of their compromised freedom. Antigua in 1858 is part of the regional trajectory of racial articulation through mass uprising. Yet unlike most other revolts that directly struck against the rule of white minorities, 1858 involved intraracial struggles that produced more complicated expressions of the rebels' understanding of their collective identity.

Shifting Conceptions of Identity

During the 1858 uprising, Antiguan rebels viewed race as a profoundly important category shaping their lives. Race framed their attempts to decipher their degraded position in the island's highly stratified social order. But rebels' racial politics emerged from an identity politics rooted first in other factors, such as class and birthplace. The conflict originated between black Antiguans and Barbudans and then expanded to include the local black and mixed-race police force, revealing the rebels' hostility against those with similar racial origins and, in the Barbudans' case, similar class status. Antiguan violence against whites in authority occurred only intermittently, while they routinely attacked others of African descent in their midst. But, eventually, participants enacted a racialized discourse that contested the dominance and legitimacy of Antigua's white oligarchy. Their utterances progressed from making Barbudans "beg pardon," to upholding their "side" against all who dared interfere, to proclamations of "down with the Buckra!" while attempting to break into the police station and seize its arsenal.

During the trial, an accused rioter, John Joseph, identified himself as the owner of a freehold near English Harbor worth five thousand pounds, which distinguished him, as a landowner and country dweller, from the large majority of the impoverished working people fighting in the streets of the Point. Joseph declared in court that the police apprehended him amid the fray because "my color broke me down."[5] His blackness dissolved any privileges that his material means might have afforded him to avoid arrest. Joseph, like many others, was identified several times in court as a central agitator of violence over the course of the four days. At that point in the trial, he and other accused participants were offering all possible alibis in order to avoid punishment. But Joseph's testimony strikingly suggests that, whether or not he had thrown stones, he knew that his presence in the street as a black man automatically rendered him subject to oppression, and in 1858's aftermath, prosecution. As he understood the colony's racial order, propertied blacks were just as powerless as the landless when whites' interests in law and order were at stake.

Black working Antiguans crafted a politicized sense of racial identity that expanded over the four days of conflict. They began with a circumscribed, nativist protest against their economic competitors, who under different circumstances might have been allies in their struggle against the inequities of the colonial social order. Antiguan insurgents distilled their political identities, however contradictory, from their everyday encounters with power, and the resulting articulations were unlike those present in postslavery uprisings elsewhere in the region. For example, the mostly black Guyanese who assaulted Madeirans en masse in 1856 were reportedly galvanized by not only a street preacher's anti-Portuguese rhetoric but also a rumor that the governor wanted black people to expel all Portuguese from the colony.[6] Jamaican insurgents during the Morant Bay Rebellion, shouting such slogans as "black cleave to black" and "color for color," delineated their racialized cohort in the broadest fashion from the start; anyone of African descent was a potential ally, including indentured African immigrant laborers, black policemen, mixed-race middling residents, and Maroons.[7] In 1858 black Antiguans ultimately rallied around their long-standing sense that local white elites were their most formidable enemy and the architects of their racially oppressed state, but showed hostility to other African-descended people along the way.

Regional and Imperial Inflections

Beyond their complicated and distinctive identity politics, the perpetrators of Antigua's 1858 uprising, along with many observers, perceived their protest as part of an imperial pattern of unrest. People in one place certainly knew about uprisings elsewhere, as information traveled quickly among island territories lying in close proximity within the same sea. Some rioters drew inspiration from earlier uprisings elsewhere in the British Caribbean as they launched their own struggle. Specifically, memories of Tortola's 1853 Road Town uprising encouraged participants in Antigua's 1858 riot. According to Governor Hamilton, "The case of Tortola destroyed in a tumult by fire . . . is frequently referred to by the rioters in this occasion."[8] During the standoff at the police station on Friday, March 26, Alexander Nanton reportedly urged people not to leave until the rioters had taken "every drop of [the policemen's] damned blood. They could do it at Tortola and why could [we] not do it here."[9] Rebels in Antigua drew strength from the example of their regional contemporaries as they articulated the political motivations of their violent acts.[10]

Conflicts brewing in more distant corners of the British Empire also made their way into the language of rebellion in Antigua, revealing more contradictions in the agitators' discourse. Their references to Tortola suggest their self-identification as anticolonial rebels, but they simultaneously employed a contradictory imperialist language to describe certain key elements of their mass action. The trial testimonies repeatedly mention that, as they tore down the Barbudan stevedore Thomas Barnard's home, Antiguan rebels exclaimed that "Sebastopol" had been taken.[11] The 1854–55 Siege of Sevastopol was a well-publicized and decisive battle in the hard-won victory of allied French and British forces in the Crimean War, waged against the Russians in defense of the Ottoman Empire.[12] Antiguans' use of "Sebastopol" as a metaphor for their attempts to terrorize Barnard and, by extension, all other Barbudans in their midst suggests their immersion in current events and their facility with imperial political dialogue. "Sebastopol" connoted British might in battle, hinting that Antiguans equated their violent acts with the wielding of power. This phrase also signaled to all those in earshot that they regarded their attacks on Barbudans and others as literal warfare, an escalation of the everyday struggles they waged in unstable times.

Ironically, the Crimean War also helped to deplete Britain's resources and weaken its military control over its imperial possessions around the globe. These lapses prompted rebellious colonial subjects to openly challenge British domination in the late 1850s, including in Ireland, South Africa, China, and, most prominently, India.[13] The 1857 Indian insurgency did not appear in freedpeople's utterances, but, as the empire's most recent and widely sensationalized rebellion, it clearly shaped elite whites' thinking about 1858. References to India surfaced in the flurry of anxious correspondence among Antigua's colonial officials, indicating the hysteria of whites as they faced unprecedented public upheaval. One letter stated that if rebels in St. John's had not been thwarted in time, "the atrocities could have rivaled those of Cawnpore [Kanpur]."[14] Comparisons to Road Town, Sevastopol, and Kanpur suggested local awareness among all social strata that 1858 fit into a broad spectrum of political upheaval mainly occasioned by colonial subjects' challenges to imperial rule.

Rebellions in the British Caribbean did not create positive changes in the status of black working people, but they did disrupt the functioning of the empire. In turn, local and metropolitan authorities had to restructure their administrative controls in the region to enforce peace. This stream of violence in the British Caribbean eventually prompted Britain to officially end electoral self-government, dashing any hope for legal political participation, which was already customarily denied to most freedpeople in the region. Jamaica's Morant Bay Rebellion, seen as a cautionary tale about the dangers of expanding the franchise among African-descended people, lay at the heart of Parliament's decision to establish Crown colony rule in most territories before 1900. Antigua instituted what Susan Lowes has termed "quasi–Crown Colony" rule in 1871. Most officials were directly appointed by Britain, as locally elected positions were reduced to a handful of members on a single legislative council that administered Antigua in conjunction with many other territories. The streamlining of governance via the reformation of the Leeward Islands Colony formalized and rescaled previous arrangements among the small eastern Caribbean isles, which at earlier points involved a shared governor seated in Antigua and individually functioning legislatures in the Leewards. The 1871 measure conjoined all aspects of

Antigua's and Barbuda's administration with Dominica, the British Virgin Islands (Tortola, Virgin Gorda, Anegada, and Jost Van Dyke), Montserrat, St. Kitts, Nevis, and Anguilla (the last three were already federated into a single unit).[15]

Crown colony rule stripped planter elites of administrative authority but did nothing to upset their social control or economic power over the black populace.[16] Thomas Holt argues that racial assumptions about the innate inefficacy of freedpeople that emerged in the years after 1834, compounded with the savagery that whites associated with the region's rash of black-led uprisings, helped dissuade colonial officials of the British Caribbean's readiness for self-rule.[17] Yet Antigua's history reveals that ideas about black backwardness underlaid officials' configuration of emancipation policy in 1833. As black communities pursued palpable change in their everyday lives in freedom through various means, local and metropolitan whites narrowed the possibilities for economic, political, and social equity. Public violence was freedpeople's most desperate attempt at change, which provoked retaliatory measures from the state, including violence, incarceration, increased community surveillance, and the dissolution of the franchise, effectively dealing more crushing blows to the hopes that emancipation had aroused.

A Dream Deferred

The politics behind Antigua's 1858 uprising, along with all of the British Caribbean's postslavery rebellions, signal that emancipation forged the conception but not the actualization of more inclusive forms of political and economic citizenship. These events should also draw attention to the longer history of mundane acts of resistance that undergirded them. The many tools that black working people used to navigate their subordination, including rumor and seditious speech, theft, spiritual practices, and physical assaults to the bodies and property of the more powerful, as well as each other, all played a role in postslavery uprisings. Freedom's significance emerges most plainly from sustained exploration of these quotidian rhythms of working-class life in the tumultuous context of this unprecedented social transformation.

The frequency of revolts, coupled with the regularity and variety of everyday violence among freedpeople, arose from the damaging legacy of enslavement and its basis in constant coercion. Brutality pervaded all elements of post-1834 Antiguan society, from the intimate partnerships between women and men to the regulatory relations between freedpeople and employers, missionaries, and state authorities, making violence the language of power. Acknowledging the pervasiveness of violence requires us to reconsider how emancipated people entered into and sustained their freedom across postslavery societies. Instead of being a time of jubilation, freedom continued a state of siege. Attention to violence also illuminates the gendered character of emancipation as a state project and a lived experience. Black women endured brutality from their male partners and each other amid the pressures of a besieged freedom that the plantation, church, and state collectively engineered. Consequently, violence was the tool that black working people seized on when their progress seemed entirely blocked. This aggression indicates the instability of life within societies that rendered them as expendable bodies in labor and suspected criminals in leisure.

A cursory review of Antigua's ill-fated trajectory after 1834 reveals not only the inhospitable context of postslavery societies for the fulfillment of black aspirations but also the crippling nature of Antigua's specific attributes as a small, impoverished island. This small island offered its black inhabitants little room for the exercise of freedom. In fact, the island's small size played a large part in how a limited and steadily declining number of whites were able to wield such inordinate power over the majority of the people. Freedpeople could not escape the island's spatial, social, and legal confines without great difficulty and were rarely able to completely evade the surveillance of authorities. The techniques of containment and control developed in this constrained context after 1834, such as vagrancy laws and rent and tenancy agreements, were widely adopted in 1838, when apprenticeship ended elsewhere in the British Caribbean. The full freedom that the region's former slaves received at that time was severely limited, as it had already been in Antigua.

The end of slavery in Antigua was not followed by unbroken domination, as emancipated people made dogged efforts to infuse freedom with broader and more substantive meanings. That under such repressive conditions freedpeople still eked out livelihoods, built communities, and engaged in culturally affirming forms of leisure remains remarkable. Every day, black workingwomen and -men attempted to live and move through their ever-changing worlds as free beings. They reunified their families, restructured their labors on estates, and engaged in a range of trades that allowed independence from sugar work. They scraped up the resources to settle in new homes, to educate themselves and their children, to dress in new fashions, to attend dances and festivals, and to enjoy their lives. They pursued all legal avenues to improve themselves and obtain the social respectability denied them while enslaved. When those efforts became unsustainable and the authorities grew more repressive, they fell back on the licit and illicit tactics that had always secured them slivers of freedom, even in the era of bondage. Provisioning during work hours, arson, petty theft, and obeah may have entered the record as punishable offenses, but they doubled as the lifeblood of black communities trying to protect themselves amid vehement efforts to deprive them of all the liberatory elements of freedom.

Despite all black working people's efforts, freedom was stripped of many of its crucial dimensions. Freedom, as a fluid construct, can expand or contract with the changing parameters of struggle. Yet even in its barest form, freedom still carries certain basic expectations. The story of freedom as told here defies a liberal narrative of increasing progress and inclusivity over time: things got much worse for black people before they got better, which withered their community-minded ethos. In Antigua, class relations did not exclusively determine the meanings of freedom. This story is as much if not more about race and the extreme tactics to which whites would resort to maintain racial supremacy, measures that would not have been applied to restive working-class whites anywhere in the British Empire. Whites never regarded African-descended people as part of the body politic. That they had no rights that any white person was required to respect guided the ways freedom was conceived and executed. Freedom's story must encompass the sobering fact that black people, taking cues from white-dominated colonial society, competed with and distrusted one other and, at moments, assailed one another. The human cost at which Antiguans obtained the limited freedom they did enjoy was substantial.

NOTES

....

Introduction

1. Mrs. Lanaghan (also known as Mrs. Flannigan), *Antigua and the Antiguans: A Full Account of the Colony and Its Inhabitants from the Time of the Caribs to the Present Day*, 2 vols. (London: Saunders & Otley, 1844), vol. 2, 43–44.

2. Ibid., 44.

3. Ibid., 21.

4. Ibid., 43; parenthetical insertion is Lanaghan's.

5. Most histories of abolition in the Caribbean and the Atlantic World are expressly concerned with the changes in labor and political culture that followed. Earlier studies often center on those managing the emancipation process rather than those who were being emancipated. See Douglas Hall, *Five of the Leewards, 1834–1870: The Major Problems of the Postemancipation Period in Antigua, Barbuda, Montserrat, Nevis and St. Kitts* (St. Laurence, Barbados: Caribbean Universities Press, 1971); William Green, *British Slave Emancipation: The Sugar Colonies and the Great Experiment, 1830–1865* (Oxford, UK: Clarendon Press, 1976); Eric Foner, *Nothing but Freedom: Emancipation and Its Legacy* (Baton Rouge: Louisiana State University Press, 1983); Robin Blackburn, *The Overthrow of Colonial Slavery, 1776–1848* (London: Verso, 1988). More recent studies tend to exhibit greater interest in freedpeople's experiences: Frederick Cooper, Thomas

Holt, and Rebecca Scott, *Beyond Slavery: Explorations of Race, Labor and Citizenship in Postemancipation Societies* (Chapel Hill: University of North Carolina Press, 2000); Mimi Sheller, *Democracy after Slavery: Black Publics and Peasant Radicalism in Haiti and Jamaica* (Gainesville: University Press of Florida, 2000); Demetrius L. Eudell, *The Political Languages of Emancipation in the British Caribbean and the U.S. South* (Chapel Hill: University of North Carolina Press, 2002); Laurent Dubois, *A Colony of Citizens: Revolution and Slave Emancipation in the French Caribbean, 1787–1804* (Chapel Hill: Published for the Omohundro Institute of Early American History and Culture by the University of North Carolina Press, 2004); Rebecca Scott, *Degrees of Freedom: Louisiana and Cuba after Slavery* (Cambridge, MA: Belknap Press of Harvard University Press, 2005). Studies of single Caribbean territories focus on the same themes of labor and politics: Rebecca Scott, *Slave Emancipation in Cuba: The Transition to Free Labor, 1860–1899* (Princeton, NJ: Princeton University Press, 1985); Thomas Holt, *The Problem of Freedom: Race, Labor, and Politics in Jamaica and Britain, 1832–1938* (Baltimore, MD: Johns Hopkins University Press, 1992); Howard Johnson, *The Bahamas from Slavery to Servitude, 1783–1933* (Gainesville: University Press of Florida, 1996); Hilary Beckles, *Great House Rules: Landless Emancipation and Workers' Protest in Barbados, 1838–1938* (Kingston, Jamaica: Ian Randle Publishers, 2004). Scholarship on the post–Civil War United States also frames the transition to freedom in terms of labor and politics; see, for example, Eric Foner, *Reconstruction: America's Unfinished Revolution, 1863–1877* (New York: Harper and Row, 1988); Steven Hahn, *A Nation under Our Feet: Black Political Struggles in the Rural South from Slavery to the Great Migration* (Cambridge, MA: Harvard University Press, 2003).

6. D. Hall, *Five of the Leewards, 1834–1870*, and Green, *British Slave Emancipation*, especially advance this argument about small islands. Compare with T. Holt, *The Problem of Freedom*, who suggests that freed Jamaicans' formation of an independent peasantry, due to greater land availability, critically informed their sense of political and economic freedom.

7. This book builds on and extends recent works that demonstrate black people's multilayered efforts to survive and contest the incomplete nature of freedom in the Caribbean. See Woodville Marshall, " 'We Be Wise to Many More Tings': Blacks' Hopes and Expectations of Emancipation," in *Caribbean Freedom: Economy and Society from Emancipation to the Present*, edited by Hilary McD. Beckles and Verene Shepherd (Princeton, NJ: Markus Wiener Publishers, 1996); Diana Paton, *No Bond but the Law: Punishment, Race, and Gender in Jamaican State Formation, 1780–1870* (Durham, NC: Duke University Press, 2004); Luis A. Figueroa, *Sugar, Slavery, and Freedom in Nineteenth-Century Puerto Rico* (Chapel Hill: University of North Carolina Press, 2005); Pamela Scully and Diana Paton, eds., *Gender and Slave Emancipation in the Atlantic World* (Durham, NC: Duke University Press, 2005); Roseanne Adderley, *"New Negroes from Africa": Slave Trade Abolition and Free African Settlement in the Nineteenth-Century Caribbean* (Bloomington: Indiana University Press, 2006); Melanie Newton, *The Children of Africa in the Colonies: Free People of Color in Barbados in the Age of Emancipation* (Baton Rouge: Louisiana State University Press, 2008). The concept

of *embodied freedom*, developed by Mimi Sheller to address informal and intimate practices of liberation, has especially inspired my arguments; see Mimi Sheller, *Citizenship from Below: Erotic Agency and Caribbean Freedom* (Durham, NC: Duke University Press, 2012), 10.

8. My thinking here is inspired by the classic study of James Scott, *Domination and the Arts of Resistance: Hidden Transcripts* (New Haven, CT: Yale University Press, 1990). He views acts of public protest by oppressed people as the revelation of previously covert oppositional sentiments, which he terms *hidden transcripts*.

9. Ben Highmore, *Everyday Life and Cultural Theory: An Introduction* (London: Routledge, 2002), 2. Also see Henri Lefebvre, *Critique of Everyday Life*, vol. 1: *Introduction*, reprint ed. (London: Verso, 1991).

10. I recognize the potential imprecision of and slippage between these terms, but such imprecision descends from and reinforces the instability of the sources that document these moments of popular unrest.

11. For critiques of the resistance paradigm, especially regarding the ways in which oppressed people's oppositional acts can generate new forms of oppression for themselves and for other oppressed groups, see Sherry Ortner, "Resistance and the Problem of Ethnographic Refusal," *Comparative Studies in Society and History* 37, no. 1 (January 1995); Lila Abu-Lughod, "The Romance of Resistance: Tracing Transformations of Power through Bedouin Women," *American Ethnologist* 17, no. 1 (February 1990).

12. David Scott, *Refashioning Futures: Criticism after Postcoloniality* (Princeton, NJ: Princeton University Press, 1999), 83. His critiques of freedom and modernity as analytical frameworks in Caribbean history in this text and in *Conscripts of Modernity: The Tragedy of Colonial Enlightenment* (Durham, NC: Duke University Press, 2004) have informed my thinking on the pitfalls of freedpeople's resistance.

13. Among the vast scholarship supporting this point, Stephanie Smallwood, *Saltwater Slavery: A Middle Passage from Africa to American Diaspora* (Cambridge, MA: Harvard University Press, 2007), provides an excellent treatment of this trajectory from capture to enslavement. *Seasoning* refers to the acclimatization of Africans to various facets of life on the plantations of the Americas during the first two to three years after their arrival, including the work routine, the environment, and the diseases that prevailed. Significant numbers of Africans did not survive this phase.

14. Paton, *No Bond but the Law*, argues for the direct links between abolitionism and penal reform in the English colonies and shows that the high incidence of violence in the state-run penal system mimicked the violence of slavery.

15. Cooper, Holt, and Scott, *Beyond Slavery*, 21, argues that state-controlled abolition in general, and British abolition in particular, became a "test" of the slaves: "Would slaves show themselves to be universal men and women, responsive to the rationality of the market? . . . The qualified hope that the former slave would prove to be Economic Man risked becoming instead proof of the peculiarity of the African."

16. This line of thinking is inspired by Uday Mehta, "Liberal Strategies of

Exclusion," *Politics and Society* 18 (December 1990), which explores liberalism's implicit expectations of cultural, spiritual, educational, and social immersion in an Anglo-Protestant nexus. Abolition was in many ways a liberal enterprise, fraught with the same expectations that underlay exclusionary customs and policies that hindered freedpeople.

17. See Pamela Scully and Diana Paton, "Introduction," and Bridget Brereton, "Family Strategies, Gender, and the Shift to Wage Labor in the British Caribbean," in Scully and Paton, *Gender and Slave Emancipation in the Atlantic World*, as well as Sheller, *Citizenship from Below*. In the more voluminous literature about the United States after slavery, recent works confirm the complexities of gender and family relations and elucidate the particular struggles that freedwomen faced. See, especially, Tera W. Hunter, *To 'Joy My Freedom: Southern Black Women's Lives and Labors after the Civil War* (Cambridge, MA: Harvard University Press, 1997); Leslie Schwalm, *A Hard Fight for We: Women's Transition from Slavery to Freedom in South Carolina* (Urbana: University of Illinois Press, 1997); Noralee Frankel, *Freedom's Women: Black Women and Families in Civil War Era Mississippi* (Bloomington: Indiana University Press, 1999); Elizabeth Regosin, *Freedom's Promise: Ex-Slave Families and Citizenship in the Age of Emancipation* (Charlottesville: University of Virginia Press, 2002); Thavolia Glymph, *Out of the House of Bondage: The Transformation of the Plantation Household* (Cambridge, UK: Cambridge University Press, 2008); and Hannah Rosen, *Terror in the Heart of Freedom: Citizenship, Sexual Violence, and the Meaning of Race in the Postemancipation South* (Chapel Hill: University of North Carolina Press, 2009). This literature offers exemplary models for my investigation of the wide range of social arenas in which black women engaged in the practice of freedom and encountered its limits.

18. O. Nigel Bolland, "Systems of Domination after Slavery: The Control of Land and Labor in the British West Indies after 1838," *Comparative Studies in Society and History* 23, no. 4 (October 1981).

19. The postslavery transition in Jamaica has been the subject of numerous studies. See T. Holt, *The Problem of Freedom*; Gad J. Heuman, *The Killing Time: The Morant Bay Rebellion in Jamaica* (Knoxville: University of Tennessee Press, 1994); Kathleen Butler, *The Economics of Emancipation: Jamaica and Barbados, 1823–1843* (Chapel Hill: University of North Carolina Press, 1995); Sheller, *Democracy after Slavery*; Catherine Hall, *Civilising Subjects: Metropole and Colony in the English Imagination, 1830–1867* (Chicago: University of Chicago Press, 2002); Paton, *No Bond but the Law*; Gale Kenny, *Contentious Liberties: American Abolitionists in Post-emancipation Jamaica, 1834–1866* (Athens: University of Georgia Press, 2010); Sheller, *Citizenship from Below*. Eudell, *The Political Languages of Emancipation in the British Caribbean and the U.S. South*, 14, calls Jamaica "synonymous with the West Indies."

20. Robin D. G. Kelley, *Freedom Dreams: The Black Radical Imagination* (Boston: Beacon Press, 2002), offers a valuable synopsis of past and present social and intellectual movements of Africa and its diaspora and their shared goal of black freedom.

21. The definitive study of mixed-race Antiguans remains Susan Lowes, "The Peculiar Class: The Formation, Collapse, and Reformation of the Middle Class in

Antigua, West Indies, 1834–1940" (PhD diss., Columbia University, 1994). Also see her article " 'They Couldn't Mash Ants': The Decline of the White and Non-white Elites in Antigua, 1834–1900," in *Small Islands, Large Questions: Society, Culture, and Resistance in the Post-emancipation Caribbean,* edited by Karen Fog Olwig (London: Frank Cass, 1995). On the sociopolitical influence of people of color who had been manumitted before general abolition in other parts of the British Caribbean, see Gad J. Heuman, *Between Black and White: Race, Politics, and the Free Coloreds in Jamaica, 1792–1865* (Westport, CT: Greenwood Press, 1981); Edward L. Cox, *Free Coloreds in the Slave Societies of St. Kitts and Grenada, 1763–1833* (Knoxville: University of Tennessee Press, 1984); Dayo Mitchell, "The Ambiguous Distinctions of Descent: Free People of Color and the Construction of Citizenship in Trinidad and Dominica 1800–1838" (PhD diss., University of Virginia, 2004); Newton, *The Children of Africa in the Colonies.*

22. For analyses of dialogues in the Atlantic World surrounding slavery and free labor at the turn of the nineteenth century, see Blackburn, *The Overthrow of Colonial Slavery;* Holt, *The Problem of Freedom,* especially chapter 1; Thomas Bender, ed., *The Antislavery Debate: Capitalism and Abolitionism as a Problem in Historical Interpretation* (Berkeley: University of California Press, 1992); Christopher Leslie Brown, *Moral Capital: Foundations of British Abolitionism* (Chapel Hill: Published for the Omohundro Institute of Early American History and Culture by the University of North Carolina Press, 2006).

23. Kim D. Butler, *Freedoms Given, Freedoms Won: Afro-Brazilians in Post-abolition Sao Paulo and Salvador* (New Brunswick, NJ: Rutgers University Press, 1998), 5, notes that most Atlantic nations were prompted to control the abolition process as a way to preempt uprisings and continue profitable production. T. Holt, *The Problem of Freedom,* 42–53, lays out the British vision of emancipation and the various ways policy makers sought to address their primary concern—how to compel freedpeople to continue performing plantation labor.

24. The history of the labor movement in Antigua and the broader British Caribbean, which began in the 1890s and peaked with the rebellions of the 1930s, also doubles as the history of citizenship and democracy in the region. Developments in international politics and commodity markets converged to foster sustained popular agitation for citizenship. The trade union movement simultaneously focused on protecting labor and expanding civil rights for the masses. Black working people stood at the helm of this process, which in the *longue durée* had its roots in labor struggles immediately following emancipation. O. Nigel Bolland's masterful work, *The Politics of Labour in the British Caribbean: The Social Origins of Authoritarianism and Democracy in the Labour Movement* (Kingston, Jamaica: Ian Randle Publishers, 2001), offers the most complete history of unionism and democracy across the Anglophone Caribbean. For specifics on Antigua's labor movement and its political effects, see Bolland, *The Politics of Labour in the British Caribbean,* chapters 5, 6, and 9; Keithlyn B. Smith, *No Easy Pushover: A History of the Working People of Antigua and Barbuda, 1836–1994* (Scarborough, ON: Edan's Publishers, 1994); Brian Dyde, *A History of Antigua: The Unsuspected Isle* (London: Macmillan Publishers, 2000), chapters 20–23; Christolyn A.

Williams, "Labor Organization, Political Leadership, and Gender Exclusion in Antigua and Barbuda, 1917–70" (PhD diss., Graduate Center, City University of New York, 2007); Paget Henry, *Shouldering Antigua and Barbuda: The Life of V. C. Bird* (Hertfordshire, UK: Hansib Publications, 2010).

25. Michel-Rolph Trouillot, *Silencing the Past: Power and the Production of History* (Boston: Beacon Press, 1995), 102–7, observes that the power to record any moment in history and to create a primary source depends on broader power relations in society, which afford elites greater literacy, access to print, and credibility than oppressed people and lead to a distorted archival record of the past. This relationship of power is reproduced when historians use these sources without questioning the circumstances of their creation and the other perspectives they may silence.

26. Many scholars who focus on questions of identity and community formation in the African diaspora have engaged equally limiting archival records in similar ways, providing insightful methodological models for my approach. See Trouillot, *Silencing the Past*; Michael Gomez, *Exchanging Our Country Marks: The Transformation of African Identities in the Colonial and Antebellum South* (Chapel Hill: University of North Carolina Press, 1998); James Sweet, *Recreating Africa: Culture, Kinship, and Religion in the African-Portuguese World, 1441–1770* (Chapel Hill: University of North Carolina Press, 2003); Jennifer Morgan, *Laboring Women: Reproduction and Gender in New World Slavery* (Philadelphia: University of Pennsylvania Press, 2004); Smallwood, *Saltwater Slavery*; Saidiya Hartman, *Lose Your Mother: A Journey along the Atlantic Slave Route* (New York: Farrar, Strauss and Giroux, 2007); Saidiya Hartman, "Venus in Two Acts," *Small Axe* 26 (June 2008); Sheller, *Citizenship from Below*.

27. See Melville Herskovits, *The Myth of the Negro Past* (New York: Harper & Bros., 1941); Sidney W. Mintz and Richard Price, *The Birth of African-American Culture: An Anthropological Perspective* (Philadelphia: Institute for the Study of Human Issues, 1976); John Thornton, *Africa and Africans in the Making of the Atlantic World, 1400–1650* (Cambridge, UK: Cambridge University Press, 1992); Paul Lovejoy, "The African Diaspora: Revisionist Interpretations of Ethnicity, Culture and Religion under Slavery," *Studies in the World History of Slavery, Abolition and Emancipation* 2 (1997); Ira Berlin, *Many Thousands Gone: The First Two Centuries of Slavery in North America* (Cambridge, MA: Belknap Press of Harvard University Press, 1998); Gomez, *Exchanging Our Country Marks*; Sweet, *Recreating Africa*.

28. Adderley, *"New Negroes from Africa"*; and Monica Schuler, *"Alas, Alas, Kongo": A Social History of Indentured African Immigration into Jamaica, 1841–1865* (Baltimore, MD: Johns Hopkins University Press, 1980), have chronicled the traffic in "liberated" Africans seized from illegal slave ships in British Caribbean territories, such as Trinidad, the Bahamas, and Jamaica, and discuss their indelible influences on postslavery culture. Numbers for Antigua were smaller than in these other places, so while newly arrived Africans had some influence in the mid-nineteenth century (for example, in the spread of obeah), they were not responsible for as significant a cultural transformation after the end of the slave trade.

29. Barbara J. Fields, *Slavery and Freedom on the Middle Ground: Maryland during the*

Nineteenth Century (New Haven, CT: Yale University Press, 1985), 193, coined this apt phrase.

30. Brown, *Moral Capital*, discusses the various agendas British abolition served in the metropole and the empire.

31. For thoughtful iterations of this argument, see T. Holt, *The Problem of Freedom*, especially chapters 1 and 2; and Cooper, Holt, and Scott's introduction in *Beyond Slavery*.

32. Mindie Lazarus-Black, *Legitimate Acts and Illegal Encounters: Law and Society in Antigua and Barbuda* (Washington, DC: Smithsonian Institution Press, 1994), 2–3.

33. Gad J. Heuman, "Riots and Resistance in the Caribbean at the Moment of Freedom," in *After Slavery: Emancipation and Its Discontents*, edited by Howard Temperley (London: Frank Cass, 2000), offers a succinct overview of many of these uprisings. Heuman's *The Killing Time* and T. Holt's *The Problem of Freedom* also detail the extreme violence of the Morant Bay Rebellion and the British government's response, which abolished elective government in Jamaica and eventually the entire region.

34. This phrasing was inspired by Walter Rodney, *A History of the Guyanese Working People, 1881–1905* (Baltimore, MD: Johns Hopkins University Press, 1981), who uses it to evoke the importance of labor to these people's lives while acknowledging their humanity as working people rather than reducing them to mere "laborers."

35. T. Holt, *The Problem of Freedom*, 175, uses the two interrelated terms, *semi-peasantry* and *unfinished proletariat*, to describe the state of emancipated black working people in Jamaica who labored simultaneously on estates and private provision grounds and in other occupations. In Antigua, self-provisioning was severely limited by freedpeople's lack of access to arable land.

1. "A Landscape That Continually Recurred in Passing"

1. Jamaica Kincaid, *A Small Place* (New York: Farrar, Straus, Giroux, 1988).

2. Antonio Benitez-Rojo, *The Repeating Island: The Caribbean and the Postmodern Perspective* (Durham, NC: Duke University Press, 1992), argues for the Caribbean's uniquely hybrid aesthetic and its centrality to the making of Western modernity.

3. Laurent Dubois, *Avengers of the New World: The Story of the Haitian Revolution* (Cambridge, MA: Belknap Press of Harvard University Press, 2004), 49–50, discusses slaves in colonial Saint-Domingue socializing after their Sunday market, despite long-standing prohibitions against such gatherings in the 1685 French slave law, the Code Noir, and the intermittent use of the *maréchaussée*, an extensive slave-catching force, to break them up.

4. According to Dubois, *Avengers of the New World*, 65–68, Saint-Domingue's militia and its *maréchaussée* were mainly composed of free men of color. Melanie Newton, *The Children of Africa in the Colonies: Free People of Color in Barbados in the Age of Emancipation* (Baton Rouge: Louisiana State University Press, 2008), 55–56, mentions the predominance of free men of color in the Barbadian militia. Mavis Campbell, *The Maroons of Jamaica, 1655–1796: A History of Resistance, Collaboration and Betrayal* (South

Hadley, MA: Bergin and Garvey, 1988), 139, mentions the agreements made in the 1730s between the Jamaican colonial government and two large Maroon polities to exchange militia and slave-catching services for the right to remain sovereign within the colony.

5. Newton, *The Children of Africa in the Colonies*, 28.

6. Ibid., 33.

7. Brian Dyde, *A History of Antigua: The Unsuspected Isle* (London: Macmillan Publishers, 2000), 6–7, reviews the generally accepted account that Arawak peoples occupied Antigua until 1100 CE, when they were ousted by the Caribs. From then until the 1500s, when the first Europeans arrived, the Caribs inhabited Antigua intermittently for hunting and lumbering but resided permanently on nearby islands such as Dominica, which boasted sources of fresh water. Barbuda shows no evidence of earlier Arawak settlement, but was also used by Caribs for hunting and gathering. See also Desmond V. Nicholson, *Antigua, Barbuda and Redonda: A Historical Sketch* (St. John's: Museum of Antigua and Barbuda, 1991).

8. See Dyde, *A History of Antigua*, chapters 3 and 4, for more details on early English struggles with the Caribs.

9. David Barry Gaspar, *Bondmen and Rebels: A Study of Master-Slave Relations in Antigua* (Baltimore, MD: Johns Hopkins University Press, 1985), 95.

10. The Leeward Islands was an amalgamated colony of the British Crown formed in 1671 that included Antigua, Barbuda, St. Kitts, Nevis, Montserrat, Anguilla, and the Virgin Islands. It shared a joint legislature and governorship, the seat of which was located in Antigua. It was dismantled in 1816 but reconstituted in 1832–33, when Dominica was brought into this administration. As Susan Lowes notes in "The Peculiar Class: The Formation, Collapse, and Reformation of the Middle Class in Antigua, West Indies, 1834–1940" (PhD diss., Columbia University, 1994), 73, "this was more a unification on paper than in reality," as each territory had its own local government that set its own legal codes, chose administrators, and set its own taxes, while the Antiguan governor, who ostensibly exercised authority over the entire Leeward Islands, mainly administered Antigua.

11. Lowes, "The Peculiar Class," 34.

12. Gaspar, *Bondmen and Rebels*, 89–92. Ports of embarkation did not always correspond to points of origin among African captives.

13. See table 1.8 in David Eltis and David Richardson, "A New Assessment of the Transatlantic Slave Trade," in *Extending the Frontiers: Essays on the New Transatlantic Slave Trade Database*, edited by David Eltis and David Richardson (New Haven, CT: Yale University Press, 2008), 51, for the total number of Africans Antigua received. David Eltis and Paul Lachance, "The Demographic Decline of Caribbean Slave Populations: New Evidence from the Transatlantic and Intra-American Slave Trades," in *Extending the Frontiers*, edited by David Eltis and David Richardson (New Haven, CT: Yale University Press, 2008), 335–64, point out that Antigua and Barbados were the only two islands with a positive birth rate among slaves in the British Caribbean region during the period 1800–1833.

14. See the population table in Lanaghan, *Antigua and the Antiguans*, vol. 2, 284, which covers the 1700s and early 1800s. Vere L. Oliver, *The History of the Island of Antigua, One of the Leeward Caribbees in the West Indies, from the First Settlement in 1635 to the Present Time*, vol. 1 (London: Mitchell and Hughes, 1894), cli, gives the 1821 figures.

15. For a succinct treatment of the sexual and social hierarchy of colonial race relations in the British Caribbean, see Hilary McD. Beckles, "Property Rights in Pleasure: The Marketing of Enslaved Women's Sexuality," in *Caribbean Slavery in the Atlantic World: A Student Reader*, edited by Verene Shepherd and Hilary Beckles (Princeton, NJ: Markus Wiener, 2000), 692–701, which details how this sexualized hierarchy came into being and explains that the concept of rape could not apply to women who did not own their own bodies. Beckles also mentions the passage of Antigua's 1644 antimiscegenation law.

16. Oliver, *The History of the Island of Antigua*, vol. 1, cli; Lanaghan, *Antigua and the Antiguans*, vol. 2, 284. Lowes, "The Peculiar Class," 127–28, details the complicated formulations of class, race, and social privilege among the free colored middle class in early nineteenth-century Antigua.

17. The 1725 figure is cited in Gaspar, *Bondmen and Rebels*, 80. The 1729 data come from Oliver, *The History of the Island of Antigua*, vol. 1, xcviii.

18. John Luffman, letter XX, St. John's, Antigua, July 20, 1787, in *A Brief Account of the Island of Antigua Together with the Customs and Manners of Its Inhabitants, as Well White as Black: As Also an Accurate Statement of the Food, Cloathing, Labor, and Punishment of Slaves; In Letters to a Friend, Written in the Years 1786, 1787, 1788* (London: T. Cadell, 1789). See Lanaghan, *Antigua and the Antiguans*, vol. 1, 62, for discussion of the ten-acre land scheme of 1700.

19. Lanaghan, *Antigua and the Antiguans*, vol. 2, 284, provides the 1805 and 1821 totals; the 1805 figure may include children, and the 1821 figure only includes adults.

20. Gaspar, *Bondmen and Rebels*, 119–24, discusses many instances in which Antiguan authorities took the risk of arming slaves when warfare between Britain and other European powers unfolded in the Caribbean basin in the 1700s. Christopher Leslie Brown and Philip D. Morgan, eds., *Arming Slaves: From Classical Times to the Modern Age* (New Haven, CT: Yale University Press, 2006), confirms such patterns throughout the Americas.

21. Gaspar, *Bondmen and Rebels*, 119.

22. Luffman, letter XXXIX, July 21, 1788, in *A Brief Account of the Island of Antigua*, 1789.

23. Gaspar, *Bondmen and Rebels*, chapters 8 and 9, discusses marronage in Antigua. See Neville A. T. Hall, "Maritime Maroons: 'Grand Marronage' from the Danish West Indies," *William and Mary Quarterly* 42, no. 4 (October 1985), for a discussion of the seaborne flight of slaves from smaller islands to larger territories.

24. Lanaghan, *Antigua and the Antiguans*, vol. 2, 78. Dyde, *A History of Antigua*, 44, suggests that Martin might have met such a violent death because he committed more egregious offenses than denying time off.

25. Lanaghan, *Antigua and the Antiguans*, vol. 1, 62.

26. Gaspar, *Bondmen and Rebels*, 134–44, discusses these regulations in depth.

27. Gaspar, *Bondmen and Rebels*, presents the most comprehensive treatment of the 1736 Akan conspiracy as it was informed by the 1729 conspiracy and the revolts and plots that occurred in several other slave territories at the time; for obeah's role in the conspiracy, see pp. 246–49.

28. On the antislavery debate in the British Empire, see Christopher Leslie Brown, *Moral Capital: Foundations of British Abolitionism* (Chapel Hill: Published for the Omohundro Institute of Early American History and Culture by the University of North Carolina Press, 2006).

29. Claude Levy, "Slavery and the Emancipation Movement in Barbados 1650–1833," *Journal of Negro History* 55, no. 1 (January 1970).

30. Oliver, *The History of the Island of Antigua*, cxlviii, mentions clandestine imports in 1807 and 1808.

31. Levy, "Slavery and the Emancipation Movement in Barbados."

32. Lowes, "The Peculiar Class," 34.

33. Dyde, *A History of Antigua*, chapter 5, discusses the governorship of Sir William Codrington in the 1670s, and the succession of his son Christopher to the post in the 1690s. Simon Gikandi, *Slavery and the Culture of Taste* (Princeton, NJ: Princeton University Press, 2011), chapter 3, analyzes the contradictory position of Christopher Codrington as both an enlightened Oxford-educated philanthropist and an exacting West Indian slave master. On the Codrington family's metropolitan political influence, see M. J. Williams and David R. Fisher, "Bethell Codrington, Christopher (1764–1843), of Dodington, nr. Chipping Sodbury, Glos," The History of Parliament Trust, accessed January 9, 2013, http://www.historyofparliamentonline.org/volume/1790-1820/member/bethell-codrington-christopher-1764-1843.

34. David Lowenthal and Colin G. Clarke, "Slave-Breeding in Barbuda: The Past of a Negro Myth," *Annals of the New York Academy of Sciences* 292 (1977): 517. Population statistics show a growth from about a hundred slaves in the early 1700s to a total of just under five hundred at the time of emancipation.

35. Lowenthal and Clarke, "Slave-Breeding in Barbuda," 514. A British traveler declared in the 1850s that "Sir W. Codrington derives but little benefit from Barbuda, as the expenses usually swallow up the receipts"; Charles William Day, *Five Years' Residence in the West Indies* (London: Colburn & Co., 1852), vol. 2, 269.

36. Day, *Five Years' Residence in the West Indies*, vol. 2, 288.

37. Douglas Hall, *Five of the Leewards, 1834–1870: The Major Problems of the Postemancipation Period in Antigua, Barbuda, Montserrat, Nevis and St. Kitts* (Barbados: Caribbean Universities Press, 1971), 60.

38. Lowenthal and Clarke, "Slave-Breeding in Barbuda," 516. See Barry W. Higman, *Slave Populations of the British Caribbean, 1807–1834* (Baltimore, MD: Johns Hopkins University Press, 1984), 26–30, for an analysis of the high levels of infant mortality in the British Caribbean islands during the late slavery period.

39. Lowenthal and Clarke, "Slave-Breeding in Barbuda," 517, 529.

40. Ibid., 535, note 127.

41. Ibid., 528–29.

42. Ibid., 523.

43. See Mindie Lazarus-Black, *Legitimate Acts and Illegal Encounters: Law and Society in Barbuda and Antigua* (Washington, DC: Smithsonian Institution Press, 1994), 5, for discussion of the oral tradition of Barbudan slave breeding. In my own conversations with Antiguans and Barbudans on both islands and in New York City, I have heard many affirmations of Barbuda's reputation as a stud farm during slavery.

44. National Archives of Antigua and Barbuda, Victoria Park, St. John's, Antigua (hereafter NAAB), Codrington Papers, R.P. 2616, Roll 26, Robert Jarritt to Sir Christopher Bethell Codrington, December 8, 1829.

45. NAAB, Codrington Papers, R.P. 2616, Roll 3, Sir Christopher Bethell Codrington to Lord Stanley, June 1, 1834.

46. Dyde, *A History of Antigua*, 201–2, details the decline in English Harbour's importance over the mid-1800s.

47. Daniel McKinnen, *A Tour through the British West Indies, in the Years 1802 and 1803, Giving a Particular Account of the Bahama Islands* (London: J. White, 1804), 59.

48. See David Farquhar, *Missions and Society in the Leeward Islands, 1810–1850: An Ecclesiastical and Social Analysis* (Boston: Mount Prospect Press, 1999), 37–42, for more on the history of missions in Antigua and the racial composition of each denomination. Lanaghan, *Antigua and the Antiguans*, vol. 1, 218–34, 245–46, and 250, describes the origins of the St. John's branches of the Anglican, Methodist, and Moravian churches. Additional details on the Methodist church can be found at "Ebenezer," Methodist Church of Antigua & Barbuda, accessed May 7, 2013, http://methodistchurchantigua.org/new/congregations/ebenezer.

49. Lanaghan, *Antigua and the Antiguans*, vol. 1, 202–52, describes St. John's in detail.

50. Lowes, "The Peculiar Class," 72–88.

51. Day, *Five Years' Residence in the West Indies*, vol. 2, 269.

52. Lanaghan, *Antigua and the Antiguans*, vol. 1, 234–35, notes that the market was moved to a "street nearly facing the court house," which means it was likely on Gutter Lane, Market Street, or the back side of High Street.

53. Mary Prince, *The History of Mary Prince, A West Indian Slave* (London: F. Westley and A. H. Davis, 1831); reprinted as Mary Prince, *The History of Mary Prince: A West Indian Slave*, edited by Sara Salih (New York: Penguin Classics, 2000), 25–26.

54. On urban slavery in the United States and the Caribbean, see Richard C. Wade, *Slavery in the Cities: The South, 1820–1860* (New York: Oxford University Press, 1964); Higman, *Slave Populations of the British Caribbean*, 226–59. On town-based slaves in Antigua, especially the flexibility in their routines, see Gaspar, *Bondmen and Rebels*, 107–9; and Prince, *The History of Mary Prince*. Marisa Fuentes, "Power and Historical Figuring: Rachael Pringle Polgreen's Troubled Archive," *Gender and History* 22 (2010), analyzes the difficulties that urban enslaved women faced in the sexual economy of colonial cities and towns in the Americas.

55. Lanaghan, *Antigua and the Antiguans*, vol. 1, 213–14.

56. Ibid., 62.

57. Prince, *The History of Mary Prince*, 26.

58. Luffman, letter XXIV, November 9, 1787, in *A Brief Account of the Island of Antigua*, 1789.

59. Lowes, "The Peculiar Class," 33, points out that many current place names in Antigua descend from the first generation of planters, who began their enterprises in the late 1600s.

60. McKinnen, *A Tour through the British West Indies*, 57–58.

61. Luffman, letter XXIV, November 9, 1787, in *A Brief Account of the Island of Antigua*, 1789.

62. D. Hall, *Five of the Leewards*, appendix A, 187–203, lists all the operational sugar estates on the island in 1829, 1843, 1878, 1891, and 1921. Lanaghan, *Antigua and the Antiguans*, vol. 1, 23–25; and Gaspar, *Bondsmen and Rebels*, 22–26, vividly describe these methods of torture.

63. This summary follows Gaspar, *Bondsmen and Rebels*, chapter 5.

64. Daina Raimey Berry, *"Swing the Sickle for the Harvest Is Ripe": Gender and Slavery in Antebellum Georgia* (Urbana: University of Illinois Press, 2007), especially chapter 1, offers a thoughtful analysis of the false divide created by the distinction between "skilled" and "unskilled" labor in plantation societies, which invariably disadvantaged enslaved women, as they were relegated to the majority of "unskilled" tasks, especially given their overwhelming representation in the ranks of field laborers.

65. Prince, *The History of Mary Prince*, recalls sexualized services she was compelled to perform for one of her owners in Bermuda in the early 1800s; his "indecency" prompted Prince to urge him to sell her to an owner in Antigua. Deborah Gray White, *Ar'n't I a Woman: Female Slaves in the Plantation South* (New York: W. W. Norton, 1985), offers one of the earliest and strongest refutations of the common notion that domestic servitude was "easier" than field labor.

66. Hilary McD. Beckles, "Old Doll's Daughters: Slave Elitism and Freedom," in *Centering Woman: Gender Discourses in Caribbean Slave Society* (Kingston, Jamaica: Ian Randle Publishers; Princeton, NJ: Markus Wiener Publishers, 1998), 125–39, discusses an extraordinary example of this phenomenon in late eighteenth-century Barbados.

67. Lanaghan, *Antigua and the Antiguans*, vol. 1, 114, notes that in 1778 regulations were passed locally to allow slaves holidays from Christmas Eve through December 28 annually, which owners were mandated to uphold under penalty of one hundred pounds. Dyde, *A History of Antigua*, 91, says that an earlier act of 1723 mandated Christmas and the two days following as legal slave holidays; owners who violated the law risked a twenty-pound fine. Dyde emphasizes that these were the only days off to which slaves were entitled by law, implying that all other days off slaves enjoyed, including the weekly half-day on Saturday and all of Sunday, were upheld only by custom.

68. Dyde, *A History of Antigua*, 44–45.

69. Gaspar, *Bondmen and Rebels*, 109.

70. Ibid., chapter 6. Gaspar states that the Antiguan legislature passed acts in 1702, 1714, 1723, and 1757 aimed at curtailing the market and other Sunday amusements of enslaved people and regulating the items they could sell.

71. Stephanie M. H. Camp, *Closer to Freedom: Enslaved Women and Everyday Resistance in the Plantation South* (Chapel Hill: University of North Carolina Press, 2004), 7.

72. Important discussions of enslaved people's marketing and its potentially subversive implications in the United States and the Caribbean include Sidney Mintz and Douglas Hall, "The Origins of the Jamaican Internal Marketing System," *Yale University Publications in Anthropology* 57 (1960); Sidney Mintz, *Caribbean Transformations* (Chicago: Aldine Publishers, 1974); Ira Berlin and Philip Morgan, eds., *The Slaves' Economy: Independent Production by Slaves in the Americas* (London: Frank Cass, 1991), especially Hilary McD. Beckles, "An Economic Life of Their Own: Slaves as Commodity Producers and Distributors in Barbados," 31–47; Ira Berlin and Philip Morgan, eds., *Cultivation and Culture: Labor and the Shaping of Black Life in the Americas* (Charlottesville: University of Virginia Press, 1993), especially Woodville Marshall, "Provision Ground and Plantation Labor in Four Windward Islands: Competition for Resources during Slavery," 203–20; Dale Tomich, "*Une Petite Guinee*: Provision Ground and Plantation in Martinique, 1830–1848," 221–42; John Campbell, "As 'A Kind of Freeman'? Slaves' Market-Related Activities in the South Carolina Up Country, 1800–1860," 243–74; and Roderick MacDonald, "Independent Economic Production by Slaves on Antebellum Louisiana Sugar Plantations," 275–301; Dale Tomich, *Slavery in the Circuit of Sugar: Martinique and the World Economy, 1830–1848* (Baltimore, MD: Johns Hopkins University Press, 1990). For Brazil, see B. J. Barickman, "'A Bit of Land, Which They Call Roca': Slave Provision Grounds in the Bahian Reconcavo, 1780–1860," *Hispanic American Historical Review* 74, no. 4 (November 1994).

73. Campbell, "As 'A Kind of Freeman,'" shows that U.S. slave owners increasingly monitored and even curtailed slaves' independent production and marketing. In contrast, Mintz, *Caribbean Transformations*, demonstrates that in the British Caribbean, slave marketing was publicly decried but allowed to persist because it was recognized as necessary to keep enslaved people fed.

74. Ibid., 6–7, 10.

75. For precolonial agricultural production and marketing among African women, see Claire Robertson and Martin Klein, eds., *Women and Slavery in Africa* (Madison: University of Wisconsin Press, 1983); Bessie House-Midamba and Felix K. Ekechi, eds., *African Market Women and Economic Power: The Role of Women in African Economic Development* (Westport, CT: Greenwood Press, 1995). For the African origins of enslaved people's marketing activities, see Mintz and Hall, "The Origins of the Jamaican Internal Marketing System," 23–24; and Jennifer Morgan, *Laboring Women: Reproduction and Gender in New World Slavery* (Philadelphia: University of Pennsylvania Press, 2004), chapter 2.

76. Luffman, letter XXII, September 15, 1787, in *A Brief Account of the Island of Antigua*, 1789.

77. David Barry Gaspar, "Slavery, Amelioration, and Sunday Markets in Antigua, 1823–1831," *Slavery & Abolition* 9, no. 1 (1988): 5.

78. Beckles, "An Economic Life of Their Own," 33. He argues that slaves on Barbados had a significant enough measure of economic autonomy that they can be termed "petty proto-peasants."

79. Johnston Browne to unknown recipient, "Antigua in the West Indies, April 1832: Details Written for a Stranger Travelling through the West Indies," April 1, 1832, unpublished letter enclosed in Great Britain, Colonial Office Papers, British Public Record Office, National Archives, Kew, London, UK (hereafter PRO, CO) 7/40, 2–3.

80. Browne, "Antigua in the West Indies, April 1832," 7.

81. Kenneth Morgan, *Slavery and the British Empire: From Africa to America* (Oxford, UK: Oxford University Press, 2007), chapters 4 and 5, discusses how slaves' labor and demography were affected by amelioration and planters' reluctance to uphold its mandates.

82. For detailed descriptions, see K. Morgan, *Slavery and the British Empire*, chapter 4; and J. Morgan, *Laboring Women*, chapter 3.

83. Gaspar, "Slavery, Amelioration, and Sunday Markets in Antigua," 6.

84. Gaspar, *Bondmen and Rebels*, 109.

85. Lanaghan, *Antigua and the Antiguans*, vol. 2, 32–33.

86. Prince, *The History of Mary Prince*, 27.

87. Gaspar, "Slavery, Amelioration, and Sunday Markets in Antigua," 6–7.

88. Browne, "Antigua in the West Indies, April 1832," 6 and 9, mentions the distances slaves traveled to market. Luffman, Letter XXXI, March 28, 1788, in *A Brief Account of the Island of Antigua*, 1789, discusses the central location of Otto's.

89. Both Gaspar, *Bondmen and Rebels*, 137; and Dyde, *A History of Antigua*, 95, offer detailed descriptions of the market at Otto's. They suggest that pass laws were generally not enforced by the late 1700s and that slaves took advantage of that laxity to make Sunday a full day of amusement in town.

90. Luffman, letter XXXI, March 28, 1788, in *A Brief Account of the Island of Antigua*, 1789.

91. Ibid.

92. Lanaghan, *Antigua and the Antiguans*, vol. 1, 146.

93. Gaspar, *Bondmen and Rebels*, 138.

94. For the quote from the Barbadian catechist, see Beckles, "An Economic Life of Their Own," 34. For the quotes from the Jamaican missionary and the Edward Long text, see Mintz, *Caribbean Transformations*, 204. Note the similarity in the negative language used by Lanaghan and Long to describe slave amusements.

95. Gaspar, *Bondmen and Rebels*, 138. However, the requirement that the militia be present at the market was probably not enforced, as evidenced by the need to assemble local troops in response to the 1831 uprising. Whites' complaints about the

inadequacies of the militia and police force can be found in the press and in private correspondence during the late slavery and early postemancipation periods.

96. See Luffman, letter XXX, March 14, 1788, in *A Brief Account of the Island of Antigua,* 1789.

97. See Stephanie Smallwood, *Saltwater Slavery: A Middle Passage from Africa to American Diaspora* (Cambridge, MA: Harvard University Press, 2007), especially chapter 2, for a recent and thoughtful take on the process of stripping slaves' social ties to make them into commodified units of labor. The classic argument is Orlando Patterson, *Slavery and Social Death: A Comparative Study* (Cambridge, MA: Harvard University Press, 1982).

98. Recent studies have confirmed the critical contribution of free people of color and urban slaves in the fomenting of revolt in slave societies in the Americas: Joao Jose Reis, *Slave Rebellion in Brazil: The Muslim Uprising of Bahia in 1835* (Baltimore, MD: Johns Hopkins University Press, 1993); Laurent Dubois, *A Colony of Citizens: Revolution and Slave Emancipation in the French Caribbean, 1787–1804* (Chapel Hill: Published for the Omohundro Institute of Early American History and Culture by the University of North Carolina Press, 2004); Matt Childs, *The 1812 Aponte Rebellion in Cuba and the Struggle against Atlantic Slavery* (Chapel Hill: University of North Carolina Press, 2008).

99. Gaspar, *Bondmen and Rebels,* 16.

2. "So Them Make Law for Negro, So Them Make Law for Master"

1. In calling this combination of the market protest and the subsequent fires an uprising or a rebellion, I mean to indicate both that the event involved numerous enslaved people acting simultaneously and that it raised fundamental issues regarding enslavement and the rights of people of African descent in the British Empire. However, I invoke such labels with caution, as the fragmentary nature of the archival record makes it difficult to ascertain the scale of this uprising and define the specific political ideologies that animated participants.

2. On enslaved people making legal claims against colonial states, including petitioning for the right to self-manumission, see Sue Peabody, "*Negresse, Mulatresse, Citoyenne:* Gender and Emancipation in the French Caribbean, 1650–1848," in *Gender and Slave Emancipation,* edited by Pamela Scully and Diana Paton (Durham, NC: Duke University Press, 2005); Alejandro de la Fuente, "Slave Law and Claims-Making in Cuba: The Tannenbaum Debate Revisited," *Law and History Review* 22, no. 2 (May 2004). Like Frank Tannenbaum, *Slave and Citizen: The Negro in the Americas* (New York: Vintage Books, 1946), de la Fuente argues that slaves within the British system did not have the spectrum of codified rights that enslaved people did in the Spanish colonies.

3. David Barry Gaspar, "Slavery, Amelioration, and Sunday Markets in Antigua, 1823–1831," *Slavery & Abolition* 9, no. 1 (1988), inspired the arguments in this chapter.

4. Gaspar, "Slavery, Amelioration, and Sunday Markets in Antigua," 2.

5. Michael Craton, *Empire, Enslavement and Freedom in the Caribbean* (Kingston, Jamaica: Ian Randle Publishers, 1997), 310–11.

6. Brian Dyde, *A History of Antigua: The Unsuspected Isle* (London: Macmillan Publishers, 2000), 106.

7. Gaspar, "Slavery, Amelioration, and Sunday Markets in Antigua," 3–5, 22.

8. See Dyde, *A History of Antigua*, 92–94, for estimates of the size of various Christian congregations. By 1800, Methodists and Moravians had attracted about twelve thousand congregants, or about two-fifths of the total enslaved population. See also David Farquhar, *Missions and Society in the Leeward Islands, 1810–1850: An Ecclesiastical and Social Analysis* (Boston: Mount Prospect Press, 1999), 37–42.

9. Two more acts were passed in 1824; see Gaspar, "Slavery, Amelioration, and Sunday Markets in Antigua," 12.

10. Ibid., 2.

11. *Substance of the Debate in the House of Commons, on the 15th May, 1823* (London: HMSO, 1823), cited in Gaspar, "Slavery, Amelioration, and Sunday Markets in Antigua," 3.

12. Bertie Jarvis quoted in Vere L. Oliver, *The History of the Island of Antigua, One of the Leeward Caribbees in the West Indies, from the First Settlement in 1635 to the Present Time*, 2 vols. (London: Mitchell and Hughes, 1894), vol. 1, cli. Jarvis referred to *An Appeal in Behalf of the Negro Slaves in the West Indies* (1823), by Member of Parliament William Wilberforce.

13. Gaspar, "Slavery, Amelioration, and Sunday Markets in Antigua," 10.

14. Ibid., 11.

15. Emilia Viotti Da Costa, *Crowns of Glory, Tears of Blood: The 1823 Demerara Slave Rebellion* (New York: Oxford University Press, 1994), 174–206; Craton, *Empire, Enslavement and Freedom in the Caribbean*, 311–14.

16. Claude Levy, "Slavery and the Emancipation Movement in Barbados 1650–1833," *The Journal of Negro History* 55, no. 1 (January 1970): 7.

17. Viotti da Costa, *Crowns of Glory, Tears of Blood*; Craton, *Empire, Enslavement and Freedom in the Caribbean*, 315.

18. Gaspar, "Slavery, Amelioration, and Sunday Markets in Antigua," 11–13.

19. Craton, *Empire, Enslavement and Freedom in the Caribbean*, 316.

20. Gelien Matthews, *Caribbean Slave Revolts and the British Abolitionist Movement* (Baton Rouge: Louisiana State University Press, 2006).

21. PRO, CO 7/31, Ross to Goderich, March 4, 1831; also quoted in Gaspar, "Slavery, Amelioration, and Sunday Markets in Antigua," 14. A petition dated the same day as the Sunday market act that refers to the need for military protection and "securing the Negro population from the horrid evils of Anarchy" after emancipation indicates that whites feared possible upheaval not just from freedom but also because of the Sunday market act itself.

22. Thomas Holt, *The Problem of Freedom: Race, Labor, and Politics in Jamaica and Britain, 1832–1938* (Baltimore, MD: Johns Hopkins University Press, 1992), 39, argues for strong links between the debates in Parliament concerning control of

blacks in the aftermath of slavery and those concerning control of the white working classes.

23. Langford Lovell Hodge, an estate proprietor then serving as a magistrate, saw the possibilities for slave discipline that lay within this once-dreaded measure and ignored the governor's request. Duke Humfrey's Library, Bodleian Library, Oxford University, Oxford, UK, papers of Langford Lovell Hodge (hereafter LLH), Ms.Eng.Lett.c.217, Langford Lovell Hodge to Messrs. Pulford, March 13, 1831.

24. See George Gillanders Findlay, *History of the Wesleyan Methodist Missionary Society*, 5 vols. (London: Epworth Press, 1921–1924), vol. 2, 168, 170, for recollections of Cadman's work in St. Barthelemy and Anguilla; and William Moister, *Missionary Anecdotes: Sketches, Facts, and Incidents Relating to the Heathen and the Effects of the Gospel in Various Parts of the World* (London: Wesleyan Conference Office, 1875), 299, for his work in St. Kitts.

25. Wesleyan Methodist Missionary Society Papers, West Indies Province, School of Oriental and African Studies Library, London, UK (hereafter WMMSPWIP), Box 9, Fiche 419, Brother Jonathan Cadman to the Wesleyan Methodist Missionary Society secretaries, March 31, 1831.

26. Ibid.; emphasis in the original.

27. British plebeians and workers had also asserted that "customary" rights were based on laws when they knew otherwise and cloaked new claims under the cover of customary practice as indisputable rights. Peter King, *Crime and Law in England, 1750–1840: Remaking Justice from the Margins* (Cambridge, UK: Cambridge University Press, 2006).

28. Craton, *Empire, Enslavement and Freedom in the Caribbean*, 341; and Viotti da Costa, *Crowns of Glory, Tears of Blood*, make this argument for Demerara. Craton notes that when Demerara's governor encountered a group of enslaved rebels on the first morning of the uprising and asked what they wanted, they responded, "Our rights" (341).

29. WMMSPWIP, Box 9, Fiche 419, Brother Jonathan Cadman to the Wesleyan Methodist Missionary Society secretaries, March 31, 1831.

30. See NAAB, CO 372, Antigua Council Minutes, 1831–1833, Governor Patrick Ross to Lord Viscount Goderich, March 12, 1831, as well as the council minutes from February 17, 1831. The act in its entirety is enclosed in Ross's letter.

31. WMMSPWIP, Box 9, Fiche 420, Brothers William Dowson, John Felvus, John Floodge, and William Blough to the Wesleyan Methodist Missionary Society secretaries, April 5, 1831. The reported violence likely unfolded at the slaves' market at Otto's rather than the public market on Long Street.

32. PRO, CO 7/31, Ross to Goderich, April 1, 1831.

33. WMMSPWIP, Box 9, Fiche 420, Dowson et al. to the Wesleyan Methodist Missionary Society secretaries, April 5, 1831.

34. See Swithin Wilmot, "'Females of Abandoned Character'? Women and Protest in Jamaica, 1838–65," in *Engendering History: Caribbean Women in Historical Perspective*, edited by Verene Shepherd, Bridget Brereton, and Barbara Bailey (Kingston,

Jamaica: Ian Randle; London: James Currey, 1995); Mimi Sheller, "Quasheba, Mother, Queen: Black Women's Public Leadership and Political Protest in Post-emancipation Jamaica, 1834–65," *Slavery & Abolition* 19, no. 3 (1998), 90–117.

35. PRO, CO 7/31, "List of Estates in Antigua Which Have Suffered More or Less by Conflagration," enclosure in Governor Patrick Ross to Lord Viscount Goderich, Colonial Secretary, April 5, 1831; Dyde, *A History of Antigua*, 127.

36. PRO, CO 7/31, Governor James Lyon to Goderich, March 28, 1831; PRO, CO 7/31, Governor James Lyon to Goderich, April 2, 1831.

37. PRO, CO 7/31, Governor James Lyon to Goderich, April 2, 1831.

38. See John Anderson, *Between Slavery and Freedom: Special Magistrate John Anderson's Journal of St. Vincent during the Apprenticeship*, edited by Roderick McDonald (Philadelphia: University of Pennsylvania Press, 2001), 75, note 23.

39. PRO, CO 7/31, "List of Slaves Tried by the Court Martial Appointed under 'An Act for the Punishment of Offences Committed by Slaves during Times of Actual Alarms,'" enclosure in Ross to Goderich, April 16, 1831.

40. Claire Midgley, *Women against Slavery: The British Campaigns, 1780–1870* (London: Routledge, 1995), 95, 102–3, describes the tendency of British women antislavery activists to represent enslaved women in the colonies as "the ultimate passive victims." Midgley argues that the 1823 amelioration code contained prohibitions against the flogging of slave women largely because of the campaigns of white women activists. While Midgley mentions local colonial officials' reluctance to follow all the metropolitan recommendations, it is possible that the special interest shown by the British public in slave women's conditions prompted the colonies to overlook their subversive activities more readily than those of slave men.

41. Robert Marsh Hughes, *The Duties of Judge Advocates, Compiled from Her Majesty's and the Hon. East India Company's Military Regulations and from the Works of Various Writers of Military Law* (London: Smith, Elder and Co., 1845), 112.

42. See PRO, CO 7/31, "Proceedings of a Court Martial for the Trial of All Offenders Being Slaves during the Existence of the Present Actual Alarm," March 26–29, 1831; and NAAB, CO 372, Antigua Council Minutes, 1831–1833.

43. Hughes, *The Duties of Judge Advocates*, 10–11.

44. Walter Johnson, "Time and Revolution in African America," in *Rethinking American History in a Global Age*, edited by Thomas Bender (Berkeley: University of California Press, 2002), 155.

45. WMMSPWIP, Box 9, Fiche 420, Dowson et al. to the Wesleyan Methodist Missionary Society secretaries, April 5, 1831. David Barry Gaspar, *Bondmen and Rebels: A Study of Master-Slave Relations in Antigua* (Baltimore, MD: Johns Hopkins University Press, 1985), shows that African cultural rituals played a critical role in how Antigua's slaves organized some rebellions, but in this case we have no evidence regarding African-derived practices.

46. WMMSPWIP, Box 9, Fiche 419, Brother Jonathan Cadman to the Wesleyan Methodist Missionary Society secretaries, March 31, 1831.

47. "Proceedings of a Court Martial," March 26, 1831.

48. Ibid.

49. Ibid.

50. See Mary Lyndon Shanley, *Feminism, Marriage, and the Law in Victorian England, 1850–1895* (Princeton, NJ: Princeton University Press, 1993).

51. "Proceedings of a Court Martial," March 26, 1831.

52. Ibid.

53. PRO, CO 7/31, Ross to Goderich, April 31, 1831, quoted in Gaspar, "Slavery, Amelioration, and Sunday Markets in Antigua," 17.

54. Cadman to Wesleyan Society secretaries, March 31, 1831. Friars' Hill was an estate located about a mile from the center of St. John's. "French's Estate" is likely the estate known as Elliot's, listed in Douglas Hall, *Five of the Leewards, 1834–1870: The Major Problems of the Postemancipation Period in Antigua, Barbuda, Montserrat, Nevis and St. Kitts* (St. Laurence, Barbados: Caribbean Universities Press, 1971), appendix A, as belonging to the "Heirs of French" in the parish of St. Philip's.

55. PRO, CO 7/31, Ross to Goderich, April 5, 1831. Browne mentions a proprietor named Gilchrist who was known for reducing food rations in a side note in "Antigua in the West Indies, April 1832," 8; D. Hall, *Five of the Leewards*, 18, says that a Gilchrist was found guilty of this offense.

56. Paraphrase of Robert Jarritt to Christopher Codrington, June 6, 1831, in Robeson Lowe, ed., *The Codrington Correspondence, 1743–1851, Being a Study of a Recently Discovered Dossier of Letters from the West Indian Islands of Antigua and Barbuda Mostly Addressed to the Codringtons of Dodington with Especial Reference to the History of Those Adventurous Times and the Hitherto Unrecorded Postal History of the Antiguan Mail* (London: Robeson Lowe, 1951), 70.

57. Dyde, *A History of Antigua*, 118, 130. Oliver, *The History of the Island of Antigua*, clii, has a copy of the cover letter for the 1830 sheaf petition; Hill and Loving are the leading signatories.

58. Henry Loving, *Correspondence with the Right Hon. Viscount Goderich, Secretary of State for the Colonies, on the Subject of the Political Rights of the Free Coloured and Black Inhabitants of the Island of Antigua, by Henry Loving, a Man of Colour and the Delegate of His Brethren* (London: S. Bagster, 1832).

59. Susan Lowes, "The Peculiar Class: The Formation, Collapse, and Reformation of the Middle Class in Antigua, West Indies, 1834–1940" (Ph.D. diss., Columbia University, 1994), chapter 4.

60. Susan Lowes, " 'They Couldn't Mash Ants': The Decline of the White and Non-white Elites in Antigua, 1834–1900," in *Small Islands, Large Questions: Society, Culture and Resistance in the Post-emancipation Caribbean*, edited by Karen Fog Olwig (London: Frank Cass, 1995), 39, details Loving's career.

61. Lowe, *The Codrington Correspondence*, 70.

62. *Antigua Weekly Register*, May 24, 1831.

63. Ibid.

64. WMMSPWIP, Box 9, Fiche 425, Brother John Felvus to Wesleyan Methodist Missionary Society Secretaries, July 7, 1831.

65. PRO, CO 7/31, proclamation by King William IV (communicated to Ross by Goderich) addressed to the general population of Antigua, August 12, 1831.

66. PRO, CO 7/31, proclamation by King William IV (communicated to Ross by Goderich) addressed to the general population of Antigua, August 12, 1831. (Note that this is a different proclamation from the proclamation in the previous note.)

67. Dyde, *A History of Antigua*, 127; Gaspar, "Slavery, Amelioration, and Sunday Markets in Antigua," 20; Browne, "Antigua in the West Indies, April 1832."

68. Gaspar, "Slavery, Amelioration, and Sunday Markets in Antigua," 21; Craton, *Empire, Enslavement and Freedom in the Caribbean*, 322. See also Craton, "Proto-Peasant Revolts? The Late Slave Rebellions in the British West Indies, 1816–1832," in his *Empire, Enslavement and Freedom in the Caribbean*, 299.

69. Johnson, "Time and Revolution in African America," 155.

70. De la Fuente, "Slave Law and Claims-Making in Cuba," 349.

71. Matthews, *Caribbean Slave Revolts and the British Abolitionist Movement*, argues that the rebellions in Barbados, Demerara, and Jamaica changed the discourse of the abolitionist movement.

3. *"But Freedom till Better"*

1. James Thome and Joseph Horace Kimball, *Emancipation in the West Indies: A Six Month's Tour in Antigua, Barbados and Jamaica, in the Year 1837* (New York: Anti-slavery Society, 1838), 64.

2. Ibid., 65. Antigua's Contract Act required all estate laborers to enter into a yearlong contract that could not be ended early without a month's notice by employer or employee.

3. Ibid., 64; emphasis in the original.

4. Woodville Marshall, " 'We Be Wise to Many More Tings': Blacks' Hopes and Expectations of Emancipation," in *Caribbean Freedom*, edited by Hilary McD. Beckles and Verene Shepherd (Kingston, Jamaica: Ian Randle Publishers, 1993).

5. On the concept of the moral economy, see Karl Polanyi, *The Great Transformation* (Boston: Beacon Press, 1957); Edward P. Thompson, "The Moral Economy of the English Crowd in the Eighteenth Century," *Past and Present* 50 (February 1971); James Scott, *The Moral Economy of the Peasant: Rebellion and Subsistence in Southeast Asia* (New Haven, CT: Yale University Press, 1976).

6. For details, see William Green, *British Slave Emancipation: The Sugar Colonies and the Great Experiment, 1830–1865* (Oxford, UK: Clarendon Press, 1976), 121–22; Sheena Boa, "Experiences of Women Estate Workers during the Apprenticeship Period in St. Vincent, 1834–38: The Transition from Slavery to Freedom," *Women's History Review* 10, no. 3 (October 2001): 382–83. Bridget Brereton, "Family Strategies, Gender, and the Shift to Wage Labor in the British Caribbean," in *Gender and Slave Emancipation in the Atlantic World*, edited by Pamela Scully and Diana Paton (Durham, NC: Duke University Press, 2005), 144–45, discusses the conflicts that arose between planters and apprenticed freedwomen in Grenada and the other Windward Islands

over the requirement that they work extra days to cover the expenses of maintaining their "free" children under the age of six.

7. Thomas Holt, *The Problem of Freedom: Race, Labor, and Politics in Jamaica and Britain, 1832–1938* (Baltimore, MD: Johns Hopkins University Press, 1992), 56.

8. *Antigua Herald & Gazette*, October 26, 1833.

9. *Antigua Herald & Gazette*, March 1, 1834, contains a reprint of the February 11, 1834, issue of the *Bermuda Royal Gazette*, which covers the decision to skip apprenticeship.

10. *Antigua Herald & Gazette*, March 29, 1834.

11. NAAB, Antigua Council Minutes, 1831–33, CO 372, petition from John Duncombe Taylor, Francis Shand, and Samuel Otto Baijer to the Council and Assembly of Antigua, February 19, 1833. Samuel Otto Baijer was also an assemblyman; notably, he owned the property on which the slaves' market at Otto's was established.

12. Ibid. As Green, *British Slave Emancipation*, 121, points out, when the program was initially formulated in Parliament, the workweek for apprentices was set at forty-five hours. In its final form, however, the apprenticeship program mandated a workweek of forty and one-half hours for all freedpeople; see Douglas Hall, *Five of the Leewards, 1834–1870: The Major Problems of the Postemancipation Period in Antigua, Barbuda, Montserrat, Nevis and St. Kitts* (St. Laurence, Barbados: Caribbean Universities Press, 1971), 16; and Boa, "Experiences of Women Estate Workers during the Apprenticeship Period in St. Vincent," 383.

13. Green, *British Slave Emancipation*, 124–25.

14. NAAB, Antigua Council Minutes, 1831–33, CO 372, report of Joint Committee to Governor Evan McGregor, October 31, 1833 (hereafter referred to as Joint Committee Report).

15. Kathleen Butler, *The Economics of Emancipation: Jamaica and Barbados, 1823–1843* (Chapel Hill: University of North Carolina Press, 1995), chapters 1 and 2.

16. Ibid., 27–29. Butler notes that for each colony, "they calculated [the absolute value] as a percentage of the total value of all slaves [in the British Empire], which the government had estimated at £45,281,738 sterling. Each colony then received a percentage of the indemnity equal to the ratio that the value of its slaves bore to the total value of all slaves covered by the act" (27).

17. D. Hall, *Five of the Leewards*, 15, 21; and Joint Committee Report.

18. Lord Stanley to MacGregor, December 13, 1833, reprinted in *Antigua Herald & Gazette*, February 15, 1834.

19. D. Hall, *Five of the Leewards*, 10, says that Antigua received about £425,000 in compensation, indicating an average compensation of roughly £14 per slave. Approximately £7,250 went to the Codringtons, who owned all five hundred slaves in Barbuda. See p. 15 for the failure of the proposal for duty repeal and p. 24 for the troubling consequences of reversing the plans for immediate freedom.

20. Statement by Samuel Otto Baijer, Minutes of the House of Assembly, February 6, 1834, reprinted in *Antigua Herald & Gazette*, February 15, 1834.

21. Statement by Speaker of the House, Minutes of the House of Assembly, February 6, 1834, reprinted in *Antigua Herald & Gazette*, February 15, 1834.

22. In England, the authorities expressed similar fears of wandering paupers; see A. L. Beier, *Masterless Men: The Vagrancy Problem in England, 1560–1640* (London: Methuen, 1985). For a comparison of the categories "gypsies" (whose independence gained them a modicum of legitimacy) and "vagrants" (who were seen as burdening the public coffers), see Mark Netzloff, *England's Internal Colonies: Class, Capital, and the Literature of Early Modern English Colonialism* (London: Palgrave Macmillan, 2003), 146–64. The connections between the two categories may explain why Nugent specifically chose the labeling of freedpeople as "gypsies."

23. Joint Committee Report. *Cachetic* is the medical term used to describe a person afflicted with cachexia, which *Merriam-Webster* defines as "general physical wasting and malnutrition, usually associated with chronic disease." See the entry for cachexia at www.merriam-webster.com (accessed October 18, 2012).

24. *Antigua Herald & Gazette*, February 22, 1834.

25. *Antigua Herald & Gazette*, October 26, 1833.

26. See Swithin Wilmot, " 'Not Full Free': The Ex-Slaves and the Apprenticeship System in Jamaica, 1834–38," *Jamaica Journal* 17 (1984); Woodville Marshall, "Apprenticeship and Labour Relations in Four Windward Islands," in *Abolition and Its Aftermath: The Historical Context, 1790–1916*, edited by David Richardson (London: Frank Cass, 1985); Richard Frucht, "Emancipation and Revolt in the West Indies: St. Kitts, 1834," *Science and Society* 39 (1975); T. Holt, *The Problem of Freedom*, chapters 2 and 3.

27. PRO, CO 7/39, Loving to MacGregor, August 27, 1834.

28. PRO, CO 7/39, James Warner to MacGregor, August 4, 1834. See also Frucht, "Emancipation and Revolt in the West Indies."

29. According to Brian Dyde, *A History of Antigua: The Unsuspected Isle* (London: Macmillan Publishers, 2000), 152–53, the 1834 Police Act established a police force of twenty-four officers and authorized the appointment of 250 rural constables by parish magistrates. The militia was finally abolished in 1838.

30. PRO, CO 7/39, Loving to MacGregor, August 27, 1834. In calling the landless wage laborers *peasants*, Loving adopted the misnomer used by British civil servants.

31. NAAB, Codrington Papers, Roll 2616/3, Robert Jarritt to Christopher Codrington, September 4, 1834.

32. PRO, CO 7/39, Loving to MacGregor, August 27, 1834.

33. Holt, *The Problem of Freedom*, 63.

34. PRO, CO 7/43, Richard Wickham to Samuel Warner, May 20, 1836.

35. NAAB, Codrington Papers, Roll 2616/3, Robert Jarritt to Christopher Bethell Codrington, March 16, 1835.

36. On "Saint Monday" and the problem of work discipline, see Kirstin Olsen, *Daily Life in 18th Century England* (Westport, CT: Greenwood Publishing, 1999), 115–16. Douglas Reid, "The Decline of Saint Monday, 1766–1866," *Past and Present* 71 (May 1976), explains that English industrialists adopted a half-day on Saturdays in order to ensure that workers would show up on Monday morning.

37. PRO, CO 7/57, Colebrooke to Normanby, June 12, 1839.

38. D. Hall, *Five of the Leewards*, 60. Codrington eventually received approximately £7,250 in compensation for the five hundred slaves on Barbuda.

39. PRO, CO 7/41, Loving to MacGregor, May 15, 1835, enclosure no. 5 in MacGregor to Aberdeen, May 16, 1835. This arrangement initially failed them when severe drought laid waste to their crops later in 1835.

40. D. Hall, *Five of the Leewards*, 68.

41. PRO, CO 7/41, Barbuda Laborers' Agreement, May 4, 1835, enclosure no. 6 in MacGregor to Aberdeen, May 16, 1835.

42. PRO, CO 7/41, Loving to MacGregor, May 16, 1835. See also David Lowenthal and Colin G. Clarke, "Slave-Breeding in Barbuda: The Past of a Negro Myth," *Annals of the New York Academy of Sciences* 292 (1977): 526–27.

43. PRO, CO 7/41, *Antigua Weekly Register*, April 21, 1835, and *Antigua Free Press*, April 23, 1835, enclosures nos. 2 and 3 in MacGregor to Aberdeen, May 16, 1835.

44. PRO, CO 7/64, Colebrooke to Russell, June 19, 1840.

45. "An Act for the Better Adjusting and More Easy Recovery of the Wages of Servants in Husbandry and of Artificers, Handicraftsmen, and Other Labourers Employed upon Estates; And for the Better Regulation of Such Servants, Artificers and Other Labourers." See PRO, CO 7/42, MacGregor to Glenelg, August 10, 1835.

46. PRO, CO 7/39, MacGregor to Thomas Spring-Rice, MP, secretary of state for the colonies, December 30, 1834.

47. PRO, CO 7/39, MacGregor to Spring-Rice, December 30, 1834.

48. PRO, CO 7/39, Spring-Rice to MacGregor, February 26, 1835.

49. See Jennifer Morgan, *Laboring Women: Reproduction and Gender in New World Slavery* (Philadelphia: University of Pennsylvania Press, 2004).

50. PRO, CO 7/39, Spring-Rice to MacGregor, February 26, 1835.

51. This conclusion is based on my assessment of documents currently housed at the British National Archives that were transmitted between Antiguan officials and the Colonial Office during the period 1830–60, which show a considerable time lag between when legislation was devised in the colony and when it was approved in London. This delay likely resulted from the slow shipping of mail, the bureaucratic procedures of the Colonial Office, and frequent turnover among administrators in both Antigua and London.

52. As D. Hall, *Five of the Leewards*, 148, points out, the colonial secretary had no power to formulate laws; he could only negate legislation devised in the colonies and negotiate with local officials over changes that would make it meet with his approval.

53. PRO, CO 7/41, Loving to MacGregor, February 25, 1835.

54. PRO, CO 7/42, MacGregor to Lord Glenelg, baronet, secretary of state for the colonies, August 10, 1835.

55. See Dyde, *A History of Antigua*, 151, 154. PRO, CO 7/57, Lord Glenelg, secretary of state for the colonies, to Governor William Colebrooke of Antigua, February 2, 1839, explains the amended act of August 6, 1835. See PRO, CO 7/39, Spring-Rice to MacGregor, February 26, 1835, for the former's objections.

56. PRO, CO 7/57, Nibbs to Walker, August 23, 1838. The penalties to which employers were liable were higher in the amended act than in the original version; see PRO, CO 7/39, Spring-Rice to MacGregor, February 26, 1835.

57. WMMSPWIP, Box 21, Fiche 990, Rev. Matthew Banks to Rev. John Beecham, January 6, 1835; emphasis in the original.

58. PRO, CO 7/39, MacGregor to Spring-Rice, December 1, 1834.

59. Mindie Lazarus-Black, *Legitimate Acts and Illegal Encounters: Law and Society in Barbuda and Antigua* (Washington, DC: Smithsonian Institution Press, 1994), 22–23. Before emancipation, this court functioned exclusively to try the cases of criminally accused slaves; it still presided over criminal cases afterward, even when black working people were appealing magistrates' decisions in employment disputes.

60. PRO, CO 7/39, MacGregor to Spring-Rice, August 29, 1834.

61. PRO, CO 7/39, Loving to MacGregor, October 1, 1834. Also see Dyde, *A History of Antigua*, 154.

62. O. Nigel Bolland, "Systems of Domination after Slavery: The Control of Land and Labor in the British West Indies after 1838," *Comparative Studies in Society and History* 23, no. 4 (1981): 594–95, discusses how Antigua's Contract Act functioned as a regional model.

63. Bodleian Library, Oxford University, Oxford, UK , Papers Relating to the Estates of Langford Lovell Hodge (hereafter LLH), Ms.Eng.Lett.c.218, Langford Lovell Hodge to John H. Forbes, Esq., March 8, 1835.

64. Wickham to Warner, May 20, 1836.

65. PRO, CO 7/41, Loving to MacGregor, February 28, 1835.

66. PRO, CO 7/41, Loving to MacGregor, January 31, 1835.

67. PRO, CO 7/48, James Baker to Colebrooke, August 21, 1837; PRO, CO 7/48, Robert Horsford to Colebrooke, August 20, 1837.

68. PRO, CO 7/48, Glenelg to Colebrooke, November 14, 1837.

69. PRO, CO 7/56, Colebrooke to Glenelg, January 12, 1839.

70. PRO, CO 7/39, report of the committee of the council formed to observe emancipation, Councilmen William Byam, Paul Horsford, and George Savage Martin to MacGregor, November 22, 1834. Also see PRO, CO 7/39, Loving to MacGregor, October 1, 1834.

71. Frances Lanaghan, *Antigua and the Antiguans: A Full Account of the Colony and Its Inhabitants from the Time of the Caribs to the Present Day*, vol. 1 (London: Saunders & Otley, 1844), 204, italics in original.

72. Byam, Horsford, and Savage Martin to MacGregor, November 22, 1834; also Loving to MacGregor, October 1, 1834.

73. Notable contributions to the literature on freedpeople's flight from sugar plantations include Douglas Hall, *Free Jamaica, 1838–1865: An Economic History* (New Haven, CT: Yale University Press, 1959); Douglas Hall, "The Flight from the Estates Reconsidered: The British West Indies, 1838–42," *Journal of Caribbean History* 10–11 (1978); Sidney Mintz, *Caribbean Transformations* (Chicago: Aldine Publishing, 1974); W. Green, *British Slave Emancipation*; Bolland, "Systems of Domination after

Slavery"; Michel-Rolph Trouillot, "Labour and Emancipation in Dominica: Contribution to a Debate," *Caribbean Quarterly* 30, nos. 3–4 (1984); Jean Besson, "Freedom and Community: The British West Indies," in *The Meaning of Freedom: Economics, Politics, and Culture after Slavery*, edited by Frank McGlynn and Seymour Drescher (Pittsburgh: University of Pittsburgh Press, 1992); Woodville Marshall, "The Post-slavery Labour Problem Revisited," in *Slavery, Freedom, and Gender: The Dynamics of Caribbean Society*, edited by Brian Moore (Kingston, Jamaica: University of the West Indies Press, 2001).

74. Brereton, "Family Strategies, Gender, and the Shift to Wage Labor in the British Caribbean."

75. PRO, CO 7/57, William Walker to Thomas Nibbs, August 23, 1838.

76. Ibid. Also see PRO, CO 7/57, Nibbs to Walker, August 23, 1838; and PRO, CO 7/57, Walker to Nibbs, August 21, 1838.

77. Loving to MacGregor, October 1, 1834.

78. WMMSPWIP, Box 21, Fiche 997, Charles Thwaites to Rev. John Beecham, February 28, 1838.

79. Joseph Sturge and Thomas Harvey, *The West Indies in 1837; Being the Journal of a Visit to Antigua, Montserrat, Dominica, St. Lucia, Barbadoes, and Jamaica; Undertaken for the Purpose of Ascertaining the Actual Condition of the Negro Population of Those Islands* (London: Hamilton, Adams, and Co., 1838), 356–57.

80. WMMSPWIP, Box 21, Fiche 999, Charles Thwaites to Rev. John Beecham, July 9, 1838. Also see Sturge and Harvey, *The West Indies in 1837*, 357.

81. Thwaites to Beecham, July 9, 1838.

82. Byam, Horsford, and Savage Martin to MacGregor, November 22, 1834.

83. Keithlyn B. Smith and Fernando C. Smith, *To Shoot Hard Labour: The Life and Times of Samuel Smith, an Antiguan Workingman, 1877–1982* (Scarborough, ON: Edan's Publishers, 1986), 28–32.

84. Thome and Kimball, *Emancipation in the West Indies*, 82.

85. PRO, CO 7/42, notes from a meeting of the Privy Council, August 3, 1835. Richard Nanton reported that about 1,800 slaves in his vicinity were not at work. According to D. Hall, *Five of the Leewards*, appendix A, 200, the planter Richard Nanton owned Smith's estate in the southern parish of St. Mary's.

86. PRO, CO 7/42, Richard W. Nanton to MacGregor, August 3, 1835.

87. PRO, CO 7/42, MacGregor to Glenelg, August 10, 1835.

88. This statement from William Byam, planter and Privy Council member, was contained in PRO, CO 7/42, notes from a meeting of the Privy Council, August 3, 1835. Byam is listed in D. Hall, *Five of the Leewards*, appendix A, 192, as the owner of Crabbs Hill Estate between the late 1820s and the early 1840s in St. Peter's Parish in the eastern section of the island. The "heirs of Byam" are also listed as proprietors of Jarvis's and Blizard's estates in St. George's, the northernmost parish that borders St. Peter Parish. Workers at Jarvis's and Blizard's struck and were subsequently coerced to return to work, so Byam could be referring to those plantations; alternatively, he could be referring to Crabbs Hill, which would suggest a more widespread strike.

89. PRO, CO 7/42, Loving to MacGregor, August 3, 1835. The "southern district" of the island to which Loving refers comprises either St. Paul or St. Mary Parish. The "Popeshead Division" likely corresponds to an area that eventually included a Moravian church chapel and schoolhouse; Popeshead was in St. John's Parish about three and a half miles outside the town of St. John's. See PRO, CO 318/138, report on Negro education in the Windward and Leeward Islands, C. J. Latrobe to Lord Glenelg, April 14, 1838.

90. PRO, CO 7/42, Loving to MacGregor, August 5, 1835.

91. PRO, CO 7/42, notes from a meeting of the Privy Council, August 3, 1835.

92. Ibid.

93. In PRO, CO 7/43, MacGregor to Glenelg, May 30, 1836, the governor outlines the requirements for the franchise.

94. PRO, CO 7/42, MacGregor to Glenelg, August 3, 1835. Carty's statement is contained in the enclosures, which also include minutes from an emergency meeting of the Privy Council in response to the strikes.

95. Ibid.

96. See the letter from Lord Glenelg to J. Carmichael Smyth, October 31, 1836, in Great Britain, Parliament, House of Commons, *Papers Presented to Parliament, by Her Majesty's Command, in Explanation of the Measures Adopted by Her Majesty's Government, for Giving Effect to the Act for the Abolition of Slavery throughout the British Colonies*, part IV, Jamaica. Barbados. British Guiana ([London]: n.p., 1837), 442–43. In this letter, Colonial Secretary Glenelg warns Guyana's Governor Smyth that indentures were unfairly being extended past the time required to pay back the cost of the voyage and mentions the false representation of better wages and a better life in Guyana to induce black working people from other islands, including Antigua, to emigrate there.

97. D. Hall, *Five of the Leewards*, 40.

98. Glenelg to Smyth, October 31, 1836.

99. D. Hall, *Five of the Leewards*, 8. Hall notes on p. 41 that the officially recorded number of emigrants from Antigua in the years 1839–46 totaled 203, while during the same period 963 emigrants left from St. Kitts, 2,609 from Nevis, and 2,218 from Montserrat, despite their considerably smaller population totals than Antigua. In 1834, relative to Antigua's 30,000 newly freedpeople, St. Kitts had about 20,000, Nevis had 8,800, and Montserrat only 5,000.

100. Sylvester Hovey, *Letters from the West Indies: Relating Especially to the Danish Island St. Croix, and to the British Islands Antigua, Barbadoes, and Jamaica* (New York: Gould and Newman, 1838), 67; and Lanaghan, *Antigua and the Antiguans*, vol. 2, 157, both describe the drought and its economic consequences.

101. PRO, CO 7/43, Richard Wickham to Samuel Warner, July 6, 1836, enclosed in MacGregor to Glenelg, July 25, 1836. See Dyde, *A History of Antigua*, 155, for the January 1837 correspondence of Samuel Auchinlech, a Codrington estate manager, who described any freedperson's travel to Guyana via Montserrat as a "sort of kidnapping practice" on the part of recruiting agents.

102. PRO, CO 7/46, Light to Glenelg, January 25, 1837, with enclosures regarding

Antiguan laborers detained in Montserrat for attempting to flee to Guyana. That practice probably contributed to the disproportionately high rate of emigration from Montserrat.

103. Neville A. T. Hall, "Maritime Maroons: 'Grand Marronage' from the Danish West Indies," *William and Mary Quarterly* 42, no. 4 (October 1985).

104. PRO, CO 7/44, Light to Glenelg, October 19, 1836. The enclosures include excerpts from the text of the act, along with considered responses highlighting how unreasonable many of its provisions were. It is unclear whether these responses were composed by the Colonial Office in London or by dissenting legislators in Antigua, as that document is unsigned.

105. Sturge and Harvey, *The West Indies in 1837*, 15–16.

106. Ibid.

107. PRO, CO 7/46, Light to Glenelg, January 25, 1837.

108. Ord must have appeared to be a rabble-rouser to local authorities since he was associated with the mixed-race faction agitating for political change. As a signatory on the 1830 mixed-race middle-class petition for political rights, Ord was likely clued into the numerous constraints that made many Antiguans of African descent frustrated enough to want to leave the island. See Vere L. Oliver, *The History of the Island of Antigua, One of the Leeward Caribbees in the West Indies, from the First Settlement in 1635 to the Present Time*, vol. 1 (London: Mitchell and Hughes, 1894), cli–cliii, for a copy of this petition and a list of its signatories.

109. PRO, CO 7/44, Light to Glenelg, October 19, 1836.

110. For analysis of the postslavery economy, race relations, and working people's resistance in Guyana and Trinidad, see Alan H. Adamson, *Sugar without Slaves: The Political Economy of British Guiana, 1838–1904* (New Haven, CT: Yale University Press, 1972); Walter Rodney, *A History of the Guyanese Working People, 1881–1905* (Baltimore, MD: Johns Hopkins University Press, 1981); Brian Moore, *Race, Power, and Social Segmentation in Colonial Society: Guyana after Slavery, 1838–1891* (New York: Gordon and Breach Science Publishers, 1987); and Juanita De Barros, *Order and Place in a Colonial City: Patterns of Struggle and Resistance in Georgetown, British Guiana, 1889–1924* (Montreal: McGill-Queen's University Press, 2003); Donald Wood, *Trinidad in Transition: The Years after Slavery* (Oxford, UK: Oxford University Press, 1968); Bridget Brereton, *Race Relations in Colonial Trinidad, 1870–1900* (Cambridge, UK: Cambridge University Press, 1979); and David Trotman, *Crime in Trinidad: Conflict and Control in a Plantation Society, 1838–1900* (Knoxville: University of Tennessee Press, 1986).

111. PRO, CO 7/48, Colebrooke to Glenelg, November 16, 1837.

112. Marshall, " 'We Be Wise to Many More Tings,' " 15.

4. "An Equality with the Highest in the Land"?

1. Mrs. Lanaghan, *Antigua and the Antiguans*, vol. 2, 140.

2. For examples of black consumption and social practices elsewhere in the black Atlantic, see Marc Hertzman, *Making Samba: A New History of Race and Music*

in Brazil (Durham, NC: Duke University Press, 2013), chapters 1 and 2; Steve O. Buckridge, *The Language of Dress: Resistance and Accommodation in Jamaica, 1760–1890* (Kingston, Jamaica: University of the West Indies Press, 1998), chapter 2; Camp, *Closer to Freedom*, chapter 3; Hunter, *To 'Joy My Freedom*, chapter 7; Shane White and Graham White, *Stylin': African-American Expressive Culture from Its Beginnings to the Zoot Suit* (Ithaca, NY: Cornell University Press, 1997), chapter 4.

3. Richard Burton, *Afro-Creole: Power, Opposition, and Play in the Caribbean* (Ithaca, NY: Cornell University Press, 1997), 5.

4. Brian Moore, *Cultural Power, Resistance, and Pluralism: Colonial Guyana, 1838–1900* (Montreal: McGill-Queen's University Press, 1995), 91.

5. Stephanie Smallwood, "Commodified Freedom: Interrogating the Limits of Anti-slavery Ideology in the Early Republic," *Journal of the Early Republic* 24, no. 2 (2004): 297. Also see Stephanie Smallwood, *Saltwater Slavery: A Middle Passage from Africa to American Diaspora* (Cambridge, MA: Harvard University Press, 2007).

6. Homi Bhabha, "Of Mimicry and Man: The Ambivalence of Colonial Discourse," in *The Location of Culture* (Oxford, UK: Routledge, 1994), 122.

7. Sheena Boa, "Young Ladies and Dissolute Women: Conflicting Views of Culture and Gender in Public Entertainment, Kingstown, St. Vincent, 1838–1888," in *Gender and Slave Emancipation in the Atlantic World*, edited by Pamela Scully and Diana Paton (Durham, NC: Duke University Press, 2005), 248.

8. For Antigua, see Susan Lowes, "'They Couldn't Mash Ants': The Decline of the White and Non-white Elites in Antigua, 1834–1900," in *Small Islands, Large Questions: Society, Culture and Resistance in the Post-emancipation Caribbean*, edited by Karen Fog Olwig (London: Frank Cass, 1994), 41–42. See also Boa, "Young Ladies and Dissolute Women"; and Ann Laura Stoler, "Rethinking Colonial Categories: European Communities and the Boundaries of Rule," *Comparative Studies in Society and History* 31, no. 1 (1989).

9. Susan Lowes, "The Peculiar Class: The Formation, Collapse, and Reformation of the Middle Class in Antigua, West Indies, 1834–1940" (Ph.D. diss., Columbia University, 1994), 37, note 11, speculates that Lanaghan was possibly married to Robert Lenaghan, a town merchant in the 1840s, given the text's exhaustive details about St. John's. Edgar Lake, "*Antigua and the Antiguans*: The Question of Its Authorship," *The Antigua and Barbuda Review of Books* 6, no. 1 (Summer 2013), 137–39 notes 35 and 36, proposes that Lanaghan may have been the wife of either William or Patrick Lenaghan, Antigua merchants-turned-planters in the early 1800s. He also questions whether Lanaghan even authored the text, suggesting that instead a male descendant of the Antigua Lenaghans, a London-based barrister also named Patrick, may have composed it from family papers. I contend that such attention to the intimate aspects of freedpeople's social lives in the passages featured in this chapter suggest the perspective, if not the authorship, of a literate elite woman resident on the island.

10. On the emergence of free villages in Jamaica, Guyana, and Trinidad, see Jean Besson, "Freedom and Community: The British West Indies," in *The Meaning of Free-*

dom: *Economics, Politics and Culture after Slavery,* edited by Frank McGlynn and Seymour Drescher (Pittsburgh, PA: University of Pittsburgh Press, 1992), 191–95.

11. Lanaghan, *Antigua and the Antiguans,* vol. 2, 130–31.

12. Keithlyn B. Smith and Fernando C. Smith, *To Shoot Hard Labour: The Life and Times of Samuel Smith, an Antiguan Workingman, 1877–1982* (Scarborough, ON: Edan's Publishers, 1986), 38, 41. Samuel Smith, the grandchild of slaves, was born on a plantation in St. Peter Parish in 1877 and spent most of his childhood and early adulthood living in former slave barracks.

13. Numerous enclosures in PRO, CO 7/58, Gov. William Colebrooke to Lord Normanby, Colonial Secretary of State, August 10, 1839, pertain to the state of newly created free villages and discuss free villagers' legal rights.

14. The "ten-acre" settlement program is described in Lanaghan, *Antigua and the Antiguans,* vol. 1, 62. Lanaghan did not specify where this land was located, but David Barry Gaspar, *Bondmen and Rebels: A Study of Master-Slave Relations in Antigua* (Baltimore, MD: Johns Hopkins University Press, 1985), 98, mentions that in the mid-eighteenth century, "in the neck of land on the south coast of the volcanic district, between Indian Creek and English Harbour in St. Paul Parish, was an apparent concentration of small farms, with those from the area labeled 'Ten Acre' Men."

15. Douglas Hall, *Five of the Leewards, 1834–1870: The Major Problems of the Postemancipation Period in Antigua, Barbuda, Montserrat, Nevis and St. Kitts* (Barbados: Caribbean Universities Press, 1971), 41–42. Also see PRO, CO 7/42, MacGregor to Glenelg, August 1, 1835, for Loving's and Scotland's statements.

16. WMMSPWIP, Rev. Matthew Banks to Rev. John Beecham, January 6, 1835; emphasis in the original. In this letter, Banks states that he is sending to Beecham, general secretary of the Wesleyan Methodist Missionary Society in London, a copy of his letter to Governor Evan MacGregor containing his "sentiments as to the best means of promoting the prosperity of this country &c."

17. Brian Dyde, *A History of Antigua: The Unsuspected Isle* (London: Macmillan Publishers, 2000), 155. D. Hall, *Five of the Leewards,* dates the move off estates a year earlier but provides no specific information about the new villages.

18. Dyde, *A History of Antigua,* 155.

19. D. Hall, *Five of the Leewards,* 44.

20. PRO, CO 7/58, Colebrooke to Lord Normanby, August 8, 1839, with enclosures. The leading Anglican clergyman, Reverend Robert Holberton, refused to submit a report to Governor Colebrooke, which may indicate that the Anglican Church was less involved in the creation of free villages. David Farquhar, *Missions and Society in the Leeward Islands, 1810–1850: An Ecclesiastical and Social Analysis* (Boston: Mount Prospect Press, 1999), 70–74, describes the surge in missionary activity but does not mention the Anglican clergy.

21. PRO, CO 7/58, Martin Nanton to Walker, June 11, 1839, enclosed in Colebrooke to Normanby, August 8, 1839.

22. K. Smith and F. Smith, *To Shoot Hard Labour,* 57–58.

23. Samuel Smith describes village homes as made of wattle and daub, a

centuries-old construction technique that involves the use of mud, animal dung, or other clayey material as adhesive or coating for walls made of woven or slatted wood. Lanaghan, *Antigua and the Antiguans*, vol. 2, 131, mentions the prevalence of wattle-and-daub houses in free villages.

24. Lanaghan, *Antigua and the Antiguans*, vol. 2, 132–34.

25. PRO, CO 7/58, Martin Nanton to Walker, June 11, 1839.

26. Lanaghan, *Antigua and the Antiguans*, vol. 1, 267; Joseph Sturge and Thomas Harvey, *The West Indies in 1837; Being the Journal of a Visit to Antigua, Montserrat, Dominica, St Lucia, Barbados and Jamaica; Undertaken for the Purpose of Ascertaining the Actual Condition of the Negro Population of Those Islands* (London: Hamilton, Adams & Co., 1838), 32.

27. PRO, CO 7/58, Martin Nanton to Walker, June 11, 1839 (enclosed in Colebrooke to Normanby, August 8, 1839).

28. PRO, CO 7/58, Rev. John Cameron to Governor Colebrooke, June 15, 1839, enclosed in Colebrooke to Normanby, August 8, 1839.

29. PRO, CO 7/58, Cameron to Colebrooke, June 15, 1839; Rev. John Parkes to Colebrooke, June 20, 1839; and Rev. C. Henry Warner to Colebrooke, June 26, 1839 (all enclosed in Colebrooke to Normanby, August 8, 1839).

30. PRO, CO 7/58, Cameron to Colebrooke, June 15, 1839.

31. PRO, CO 7/58, Warner to Colebrooke, June 26, 1839.

32. Diane Austin-Broos, *Jamaica Genesis: Religion and the Politics of Moral Orders* (Chicago: University of Chicago Press, 1997), 37–38. See also Catherine Hall, *Civilising Subjects: Colony and Metropole in the English Imagination, 1830–1867* (Chicago: University of Chicago Press, 2002), 120–39; and Gale Kenny, *Contentious Liberties: American Abolitionists in Post-emancipation Jamaica* (Athens: University of Georgia Press, 2010).

33. Pamela Scully and Diana Paton, "Introduction: Gender and Slave Emancipation in Comparative Perspective," in Scully and Paton, *Gender and Slave Emancipation*, 13, 19.

34. PRO, CO 7/58, Magistrate James Scotland, Jr., Police Chief Martin Nanton, and Magistrate William Walker to Governor Colebrooke, July 23, 1839, and notes dated July 17, 1839 (all enclosed in Colebrooke to Normanby, August 8, 1839).

35. PRO, CO 7/58, Warner to Colebrooke, June 26, 1839.

36. Bridget Brereton, "Family Strategies, Gender, and the Shift to Wage Labor in the British Caribbean," in Scully and Paton, *Gender and Slave Emancipation*, 156.

37. PRO, CO 7/58, Scotland, Nanton, and Walker to Colebrooke, July 23, 1839.

38. Letter from "An Agriculturist" to the editor, *Antigua Weekly Register*, June 18, 1839. The mountain villages to which this letter refers were mainly in the southern part of the island. The Moravian missionary C. Henry Warner said that his remarks regarding the honest and moral conduct of village residents "don't apply to the settlers in the mountains"; PRO, CO 7/58, Warner to Colebrooke, June 26, 1839.

39. LLH, Ms. Eng.Lett.c.215/1, Folder 4–5, W. H. Martin to Langford Lovell Hodge, August 26, 1844.

40. See PRO, CO 7/64, William Walker to Colebrooke, January 31, 1840, for descriptions of independent gangs.

41. Monica Schuler, "Liberated Africans in Nineteenth-Century Guyana," in *Slavery, Freedom and Gender: The Dynamics of Caribbean Society*, edited by Brian Moore, Barry Higman, and Patrick Bryan (Kingston, Jamaica: The University of the West Indies Press, 2001), 139. Moon-Ho Jung, *Coolies and Cane: Race, Labor and Sugar in the Age of Emancipation* (Baltimore, MD: Johns Hopkins University Press, 2006), 89, found that on Cuban sugar plantations, Chinese immigrant laborers formed similar gangs after their indentures ended.

42. D. Hall, *Five of the Leewards*, 45.

43. PRO, CO 7/69, Walker to MacPhail, November 13, 1841.

44. PRO, CO 7/74, William Walker to Governor Charles Fitzroy, September 30, 1842, with enclosures containing the third-quarter stipendiary magistrate's report for 1842, enclosed in Fitzroy to Stanley, January 20, 1843.

45. PRO, CO 7/69, William Walker to Lt. Governor John MacPhail, October 23, 1841, enclosed in MacPhail to Lord Stanley, November 13, 1841.

46. Ibid. See also Lanaghan, *Antigua and the Antiguans*, vol. 2, 160.

47. PRO, CO 7/74, Walker to Fitzroy, September 30, 1842.

48. PRO, CO 7/74, "Papers Relative to the Earthquake in the West Indies," Governor Charles Fitzroy to Lord Stanley, February 10, 1843.

49. PRO, CO 7/76, Robert Horsford to Governor Fitzroy, Quarterly Magistrate's Report from April 1 to June 30, 1843; Lanaghan, *Antigua and the Antiguans*, vol. 2, 160.

50. LLH, Ms. Eng.Lett.c.215/1 Folder 1–3; Letter from W. H. Martin to Langford Lovell Hodge, August 10, 1844.

51. PRO, CO 7/76, Quarterly Magistrate's Report from April 1 to June 30, 1843.

52. William Sewell, *The Ordeal of Free Labour in the British West Indies* (London: Sampson Low & Co, 1862; reprint, London: Frank Cass & Co., 1968), 148.

53. PRO, CO 7/78, Robert Horsford to Governor Fitzroy, stipendiary magistrate's half-yearly report from June 30 to December 31, 1844.

54. Lanaghan, *Antigua and the Antiguans*, vol. 2, 102.

55. Ibid., 130.

56. See Janet Schaw, *Journal of a Lady of Quality, Being the Narrative of a Journey from Scotland to the West Indies, North Carolina, and Portugal, in the Years 1774–1776*, edited by Evangeline W. Andrews (New Haven, CT: Yale University Press, 1921), 107–8, where she describes the Christmastime procession of enslaved men and women to the local market in Antigua.

57. Camp, *Closer to Freedom*, chapter 3, argues that such forms of resistance were at work in slaves' socializing at illicit dances and dressing in a festive manner in the U.S. South.

58. Lanaghan, *Antigua and the Antiguans*, vol. 2, 127–28.

59. Ibid., 128.

60. Jennifer Morgan, " 'Some Could Suckle over Their Shoulder': Male Travelers, Female Bodies, and the Gendering of Racial Ideology, 1500–1770," *William and Mary Quarterly* 54, no. 1 (January 1997).

61. Boa, "Young Ladies and Dissolute Women," 252.

62. Lanaghan, *Antigua and the Antiguans*, vol. 2, 110–11; emphasis in the original.

63. Ibid., 107–8.

64. Ibid., 108–14.

65. PRO, CO 7/68, Lt. Governor John MacPhail to Lord Russell, August 26, 1841, with enclosures, including Graeme's letter.

66. Ibid., 125.

67. Deborah Gray White, *Ar'n't I a Woman: Female Slaves in the Plantation South* (New York: W. W. Norton, 1985), 17–20, discusses the "Sambo" character's problematic influence on the historiography of U.S. slavery. Thomas Holt, *The Problem of Freedom: Race, Labor, and Politics in Jamaica and Britain, 1832–1938* (Baltimore, MD: Johns Hopkins University Press, 1992), chapters 5 and 8, explores "Quashee" as a troublesome trope in English West Indian slavery.

68. Lanaghan, *Antigua and the Antiguans*, vol. 2, 118–20.

69. Joseph John Gurney, *A Winter in the West Indies, Described in Familiar Letters to Henry Clay, of Kentucky* (London: John Murray; Norwich: Josiah Fletcher, 1840), 66, 62.

70. Lanaghan, *Antigua and the Antiguans*, vol. 2, 121; emphasis in the original.

71. Ibid., 121; emphasis in the original.

72. Robin D. G. Kelley, *Race Rebels: Culture, Politics, and the Black Working Class* (New York: The Free Press, 1994), 50.

73. Bhabha, "Of Mimicry and Man." See also Kelley, *Race Rebels*, 50.

74. Gurney, *A Winter in the West Indies*, 60; emphasis in the original.

75. Wesleyan Methodist Missionary Society, *Rules and Regulations of the Wesleyan Methodist Sunday School Institution of Saint John's, Antigua* (London: D. Marples and Co., 1836), 13.

76. Moravian Church Archives, Eastern West Indies Province, Bethlehem, PA, United States (hereafter MCA, EWI), Box A11, Folder 10, "Exclusions October 1833–November 1856, Antigua," October 1845 entry for Henry Edward and Thomas, Grace Hill Congregation.

77. Charles William Day, *Five Years' Residence in the West Indies*, vol. 2 (London: Colburn & Co., 1852), 277.

78. Lanaghan, *Antigua and the Antiguans*, vol. 1, 205.

79. John Luffman, letter XXXI, March 28, 1788, in *A Brief Account of the Island of Antigua Together with the Customs and Manners of Its Inhabitants as Well White as Black: As Also an Accurate Statement of the Food, Clothing, Labor, and Punishment, of Slaves; In Letters to a Friend, Written in the Years 1786, 1787, 1788* (London: T. Cadell, 1789).

80. Lanaghan, *Antigua and the Antiguans*, vol. 2, 116–17.

81. PRO, CO 7/67, MacPhail to Russell, May 20, 1841, with enclosures, including a letter from the stipendiary magistrate William Walker to MacPhail discussing the dances.

82. Hunter, *'To Joy My Freedom*, 168, makes a similar argument regarding the U.S. South.

83. Ibid., 183.

84. Day, *Five Years' Residence in the West Indies*, vol. 2, 281.

85. PRO, CO 7/81, Fitzroy to Stanley, May 12, 1845. Enclosures include a report from Horsford on Antigua. Also quoted in D. Hall, *Five of the Leewards*, 45; and Dyde, *A History of Antigua*, 161.

86. WMMSPWIP, Box 22, Fiche 1042, Rev. Jesse Pilcher to Rev. Elijah Hoole, October 8, 1845.

87. Frederick Cooper, Thomas Holt, and Rebecca Scott, *Beyond Slavery: Explorations of Race, Labor, and Citizenship in Postemancipation Societies* (Chapel Hill: University of North Carolina Press, 2000), 21; also see Holt's chapter in *Beyond Slavery*, "The Essence of the Contract: The Articulation of Race, Gender, and Political Economy in British Emancipation Policy, 1838–1866," 45–47.

5. "Sinful Conexions"

1. *Periodical Accounts Relating to the Missions of the Church of the United Brethren Established among the Heathen*, vol. 20 (London: W. J. M'Dowall for the Brethren's Society for the Furtherance of the Gospel among the Heathen, 1851), 471.

2. On Christian churches' interventions in black families in other territories, see Newton, *Children of Africa*, 161-172 (Barbados); and Austin-Broos, *Jamaica Genesis*, chapter 2 (Jamaica). On the British colonial state's focus on marriage as part of the post-slavery civilizing mission in Jamaica, Guyana and Barbados, see Juanita De Barros, *Reproducing the British Caribbean: Sex, Gender and Population Politics after Slavery* (Chapel Hill: University of North Carolina Press, 2014), 13, 55–58.

3. For the Catholic Church's unsuccessful attempts to promote monogamous marriage in Brazil, see James Sweet, *Recreating Africa: Culture, Kinship, and Religion in the African-Portuguese World, 1441–1770* (Chapel Hill: University of North Carolina Press, 2003), 43–45. Barry W. Higman, *Slave Populations of the British Caribbean, 1807–1834* (Kingston: University of the West Indies Press, 1995), 364–71, finds that female-headed families prevailed among slaves on sugar plantations and argues that urban slavery, as well as the influence of the churches after 1800, created tendencies toward monogamous marriage.

4. Texts in the 1970s showing an intact African American slave family and community, such as John Blassingame, *The Slave Community: Plantation Life in the Antebellum South* (New York: Oxford University Press, 1972); and Herbert Gutman, *The Black Family in Slavery and Freedom, 1750–1925* (New York: Pantheon Books, 1976), were penned partly in response to social science and public policy beliefs at the time about the ills of pathological black family development, including absentee fathers and domineering single mothers. This work contributed to an overarching sense of domestic life in slavery and early freedom as featuring harmonic relations between black men and women, and a nuclear family structure with a patriarchal cast. Anglophone Caribbean historiography also evidenced similar trends, not coincidentally, on the heels of similar analyses of family pathology in the West Indies, which were prevalent in the 1960s and 1970s. Such works as Lucille Mair, *The Rebel Woman in the British West Indies* (Kingston: Institute of Jamaica, 1975); or such later

texts as Barbara Bush, *Slave Women in Caribbean Society: 1650–1838* (London: James Currey, 1990), were more intent on demonstrating the resistance and leadership of enslaved women than the U.S. studies, but they still framed their discussions within the discourse of marriage and family. In these texts, black women resisted white domination but not that of their male counterparts.

5. Hilary McD. Beckles, *Centering Woman: Gender Discourses in Caribbean Slave Society* (Kingston, Jamaica: Ian Randle Press, 1999), 55. See also Jennifer Morgan, *Laboring Women: Reproduction and Gender in New World Slavery* (Philadelphia: University of Pennsylvania Press, 2004), chapter 1; and Alexander X. Byrd, *Captives and Voyagers: Black Migrants across the Eighteenth-Century British Atlantic World* (Baton Rouge: Louisiana State University Press, 2008), 98.

6. Maarit Forde and Diana Paton, "Introduction," in *Obeah and Other Powers: The Politics of Caribbean Religion and Healing*, edited by Diana Paton and Maarit Forde (Durham, NC: Duke University Press, 2012), 5–6.

7. For discussions of obeah's multiple significance, see Orlando Patterson, *The Sociology of Slavery: An Analysis of the Origins, Development and Structure of Negro Slavery in Jamaica* (London: MacGibbon and Kee, 1967), 183–89; Higman, *Slave Populations of the British Caribbean*, 271; David Barry Gaspar, *Bondmen and Rebels: A Study of Master-Slave Relations in Antigua* (Baltimore, MD: Johns Hopkins University Press, 1985), 246–47; Mindie Lazarus-Black, *Legitimate Acts and Illegal Encounters: Law and Society in Barbuda and Antigua* (Washington, DC: Smithsonian Institution Press, 1994), 43–45; Joseph Murphy, *Working the Spirit: Ceremonies of the African Diaspora* (New York: Beacon Press, 1994); Margarite Fernandez Olmos and Lizabeth Paravisini-Gebert, *Sacred Possessions: Vodou, Santeria, Obeah, and the Caribbean* (New Brunswick, NJ: Rutgers University Press, 1997), esp. 6–7; Jerome S. Handler, "Slave Medicine and Obeah in Barbados, ca. 1650 to 1834," *New West Indian Guide* 74 (2000); Diana Paton, *No Bond but the Law: Punishment, Race, and Gender in Jamaican State Formation, 1780–1870* (Durham, NC: Duke University Press, 2004), 184–86.

8. Lazarus-Black, *Legitimate Acts and Illegal Encounters*, 47.

9. Wesleyan Methodist Missionary Society Papers, School of Oriental and African Studies Library, London, UK (hereafter WMMSP), Fiche 3–4, Anne Gilbert to Rev. Richard Pattison, June 1, 1804.

10. Lazarus-Black, *Legitimate Acts and Illegal Encounters*, 44.

11. Mrs. Lanaghan, *Antigua and the Antiguans: A Full Account of the Colony and Its Inhabitants from the Time of the Caribs to the Present Day*, vol. 2 (London: Saunders & Otley, 1844), 50.

12. Joseph Sturge and Thomas Harvey, *The West Indies in 1837; Being the Journal of a Visit to Antigua, Montserrat, Dominica, St. Lucia, Barbados and Jamaica; Undertaken for the Purpose of Ascertaining the Actual Condition of the Negro Population of Those Islands* (London: Hamilton, Adams & Co., 1838), 32.

13. Ibid., 51–55. See also Robert Farris Thompson, *Flash of the Spirit: African and Afro-American Art and Philosophy* (New York: Vintage Books, 1984), 142–45.

14. Paton observes the same of Jamaican obeah patrons in "The Trials of Inspec-

tor Thomas: Policing and Ethnography in Jamaica," in Paton and Forde, *Obeah and Other Powers*, 172–97.

15. PRO, CO 7/68, MacPhail to Russell, August 26, 1841, with enclosures.

16. Sturge and Harvey, *The West Indies in 1837*, 30.

17. On the question of spiritual practices in the African diaspora, see Roseanne Adderley, *"New Negroes from Africa": Slave Trade Abolition and Free African Settlement in the Nineteenth-Century Caribbean* (Bloomington: Indiana University Press, 2006), chapters 5 and 6; and Sweet, *Recreating Africa*.

18. David Farquhar, *Missions and Society in the Leeward Islands, 1810–1850* (Boston: Mount Prospect Press, 1999), 8–9, 32–35, 50–51.

19. See Great Britain, Parliamentary Papers, *Tables of the Revenue, Population, Commerce, &c. of the United Kingdom, and Its Dependencies: Supplement to Part VIII; Colonies—1837 to 1839, Compiled from Official Returns* (Great Britain: Her Majesty's Stationery Office, 1840), 35, for a table of total Moravian church membership in Antigua.

20. PRO, CO 7/83, Robert Horsford to Lt. Governor Charles Cunningham, March 21, 1846, with the enclosures "Statistical Summary for the Half-Year Ending 31 December 1845." Douglas Hall, *Five of the Leewards, 1834–1870: The Major Problems of the Postemancipation Period in Antigua, Barbuda, Montserrat, Nevis and St. Kitts* (St. Laurence, Barbados: Caribbean Universities Press, 1971), 49, table 6, has most of these figures. On working-class membership in the Moravian church, see, for example, PRO, CO 7/83, 1845 Blue Book for Antigua, Cunningham to Gladstone, April 27, 1846.

21. Lazarus-Black, *Legitimate Acts and Illegal Encounters*, 156.

22. Inadequate schools were the norm throughout the British Caribbean; see Hilary McD. Beckles, *Great House Rules: Landless Emancipation and Workers' Protest in Barbados, 1838–1938* (Kingston, Jamaica: Ian Randle Publishers, 2004), 60; Thomas Holt, *The Problem of Freedom: Race, Labor, and Politics in Jamaica and Britain, 1832–1938* (Baltimore, MD: Johns Hopkins University Press, 1992), 195; Howard Fergus, A History of Education in the British Leeward Islands, 1835–1945 (Kingston, Jamaica: University of the West Indies Press, 2003), 16.

23. Farquhar, *Missions and Society in the Leeward Islands*, 104–5. Also see Fergus, *A History of Education in the British Leeward Islands*, 11.

24. Brian Dyde, *A History of Antigua: The Unsuspected Isle* (London: Macmillan Publishers, 2000), 151.

25. Farquhar, *Missions and Society in the Leeward Islands*, 121, 118. Also see Clare Midgley, *Women against Slavery: The British Campaigns, 1780–1870* (New York: Routledge, 1992), 55, for more on the Ladies Negro Education Society. On the Mico bequest, which funded teacher training in Antigua, see Robert Proctor, "Early Developments in Barbadian Education," *Journal of Negro Education* 49, no. 2 (1980): 191.

26. PRO, CO 318/138, "Report on Negro Education," Charles J. Latrobe to Lord Glenelg, April 14, 1838, pp. 68–69, 80–84.

27. Sylvester Hovey, *Letters from the West Indies: Relating Especially to the Danish Island St. Croix, and to the British Islands Antigua, Barbadoes, and Jamaica* (New York: Gould and Newman, 1838), 85.

28. WMMSPWIP, Box 21, Fiche 1001, Rev. James Cameron to Wesleyan Methodist Missionary Society secretaries, December 20, 1838.

29. James A. Thome and Joseph Horace Kimball, *Emancipation in the West Indies: A Six Month's Tour in Antigua, Barbados and Jamaica in the Year 1837* (New York: American Anti-slavery Society, 1838), 128; emphasis in the original.

30. WMMSPWIP, Box 21, Fiche 997, Rev. James Cox to Wesleyan Methodist Missionary Society secretaries, February 15, 1838; emphasis in the original.

31. Lanaghan, *Antigua and the Antiguans*, vol. 1, 319.

32. PRO, CO 7/74, Fitzroy to Stanley, January 20, 1843, with the enclosure "Rules and Regulations of the Spring-Gardens' Benevolent Society," Antigua's *Herald* newspaper office, 1838. See also John Gurney, *A Winter in the West Indies, Described in Familiar Letters to Henry Clay of Kentucky* (London: John Murray; Norwich: Josiah Fletcher, 1840), 62.

33. Dyde, *A History of Antigua*, 118–19. Also see Farquhar, *Missions and Society in the Leeward Islands*, 92–95.

34. See PRO, CO 7/74, "Rules and Regulations of the Spring-Gardens' Benevolent Society"; PRO, CO 7/74, Fitzroy to Stanley, January 20, 1843, with the enclosure "Consolidated Rules and Regulations of the Wesleyan Methodist Friendly Club" of Willoughby Bay.

35. PRO, CO 7/83, Robert Horsford to Lt. Governor Charles Cunningham, March 21, 1846, with enclosures of the "Statistical Summary for the Half-Year Ending 31 December 1845." D. Hall, *Five of the Leewards*, 49, has related figures.

36. The 1842 annual report of the Moravian friendly societies was enclosed in PRO, CO 7/74, Fitzroy to Stanley, January 20, 1843. On charitable donations after the earthquake, see PRO, CO 7/78, Harris to Fitzroy, magistrate's report for second half of 1843, January 19, 1844.

37. Mimi Sheller, *Democracy after Slavery: Black Publics and Peasant Radicalism in Haiti and Jamaica* (Gainesville: University Press of Florida, 2000), 157.

38. PRO, CO 7/74, "Rules and Regulations of the Spring-Gardens' Benevolent Society," pp. 7–8. Also see Farquhar, *Missions and Society in the Leeward Islands*, 94.

39. Farquhar, *Missions and Society in the Leeward Islands*, 94.

40. PRO, CO 7/74, "Rules and Regulations of the Spring-Gardens' Benevolent Society," p. 8.

41. PRO, CO 7/68, Lt. Governor John MacPhail to Lord John Russell, August 26, 1841, with enclosures.

42. Farquhar, *Missions and Society in the Leeward Islands*, 61–67.

43. *Instructions for the Missionaries of the Church of the Unitas Fratrum, or United Brethren*, 2nd ed. (London: Printed for the Brethren's Society for the Furtherance of the Gospel among the Heathen, 1840), 45.

44. PRO, CO 7/74, enclosures *Rules for the Tenantry of the Moravian Settlements at Antigua* (pamphlet, n.d.), and *Articles of the Friendly Society in Connexion with the Church of the United Brethren at (Moravian Settlements) Antigua* (pamphlet, 1836).

45. *Instructions for the Missionaries of the Church of the Unitas Fratrum*, 51.

46. MCA, EWI, Moravian Church Eastern West Indies Conference File A11, Folder 9, Five Islands Book of Remarks, manuscript ledger, exclusions for 1839–62.

47. Ibid.

48. J. C. S. Mason, *The Moravian Church and the Missionary Awakening in England, 1760–1800* (Suffolk, UK: Boydell & Brewer, 2001), 99–100.

49. According to Jon Sensbach, "Slavery, Race, and the Global Fellowship: Religious Radicals Confront the Modern Age," in *Pious Pursuits: German Moravians in the Atlantic World*, edited by Michele Gillespie and Robert Beachey (Oxford, UK: Berghahn Books, 2007), 212, slaves in the Danish colony of St. Thomas loathed the helpers and called for their removal for many of the same reasons.

50. Jon Sensbach, *A Separate Canaan: The Making of an Afro-Moravian World in North Carolina, 1763–1840* (Chapel Hill, NC: Omohundro Institute of Early American History and Culture, 1998), 128–29; and Herman Bennett, *Africans in Colonial Mexico: Absolutism, Christianity, and Afro-Creole Consciousness, 1570–1640* (Bloomington: Indiana University Press, 2004), chapter 6, point out that blacks' denunciation of whites' moral lapses might be used to undermine the racial hierarchy or to settle scores with enemies.

51. MCA, EWI, Moravian Church Eastern West Indies Conference File A11, Folder 9, Five Islands Book of Remarks, exclusions for 1839–62.

52. It remains unclear whether this woman was referred to in a belittling manner as a "girl" or was actually quite young. If Lucy were as elderly as the record suggests, she might have called someone who was in Ambrose's age range a girl. According to Moravian exclusion records, adolescent girls were frequently involved in sexual relations.

53. MCA, EWI, Moravian Church Eastern West Indies Conference File A11, Folder 9, Five Islands Book of Remarks, exclusions for 1839–62.

54. Ibid.

55. *Instructions for the Missionaries of the Church of the Unitas Fratrum*, 49. Lanaghan, *Antigua and the Antiguans*, vol. 1, 320, also confirms that Methodists had a similar approach, as their night and Sunday schools on estates, which tended to elder teens aged out of day schools and adult learners, offered religious instruction to counteract "those temptations to which their age and sex are most subject."

56. MCA, EWI, Moravian Church Eastern West Indies Conference File A11, Folder 9, Five Islands Book of Remarks, exclusions for 1839–62.

57. MCA, EWI, Moravian Church Eastern West Indies Conference File A11, Folder 10, Five Islands Book of Remarks, exclusion list, St. John's, Antigua, exclusions for October 1833–November 1856 (island-wide).

58. Mary Prince, *The History of Mary Prince: A West Indian Slave*, edited by Sara Salih (New York: Penguin Classics, 2000), 30, discusses her wedding to Daniel James at the Spring Gardens Moravian Church in St. John's and her owners' disapproval of the marriage. See Thomas Pringle, "Supplement to the History of Mary Prince by the Editor," in Prince, *The History of Mary Prince*, 39–63, for his trial for libel in a suit brought by Prince's owners in 1833.

59. D. Hall, *Five of the Leewards*, 55–57, documents the downward trend in wage rates and the inflation in the prices of most staples after 1845.

60. MCA, EWI, Moravian Church Eastern West Indies Conference File A11, Folder 9, Five Islands Book of Remarks, exclusions for 1839–62.

61. Byrd, *Captives and Voyagers*, 98, remarked that slave owners in Jamaica knew that in order to protect their "investment" in slave women that it was "in [their] interest to provide for them some degree of independence" from slave men, including separate provision grounds and quarters, even when they were married.

62. MCA, EWI, Moravian Church Eastern West Indies Conference File A11, Folder 9, Five Islands Book of Remarks, exclusions for 1839–62.

63. Ibid.

64. MCA, EWI, Moravian Church Eastern West Indies Conference File A11, Folder 10, Five Islands Book of Remarks, exclusion list, St. John's, Antigua, exclusions for October 1833–November 1856 (island-wide).

65. MCA, EWI, Moravian Church Eastern West Indies Conference File A11, Folder 9, Five Islands Book of Remarks, exclusions for 1839–62.

66. On the prevalence of prostitution in the urban Caribbean and the continuities between enslavement and postemancipation sex work in terms of sexual violence and the devaluation of black women's bodies, see Hilary McD. Beckles, "Property Rights in Pleasure: The Marketing of Enslaved Women's Sexuality," in *Caribbean Slavery in the Atlantic World: A Student Reader*, edited by Verene Shepherd and Hilary Beckles (Princeton, NJ: Markus Wiener, 2000); Newton, *The Children of Africa in the Colonies*; Marisa Fuentes, "Power and Historical Figuring: Rachael Pringle Polgreen's Troubled Archive," *Gender and History* 22 (2010); Paulette A. Kerr, "Victims or Strategists? Female Lodging-House Keepers in Jamaica," in *Engendering History: Caribbean Women in Historical Perspective*, edited by Verene A. Shepherd, Bridget Brereton, and Barbara Bailey (Kingston, Jamaica: Ian Randle Publishers, 1995).

6. *"Mashing Ants"*

1. WMMSPWIP, Box 22, Fiche 1050, Rev. James Cox to Methodist Missionary Society secretaries, Rev. Dr. Bunting, Rev. Dr. Alder, Rev. Beecham, and Rev. Elijah Hoole, October 25, 1847.

2. See Susan Lowes, " 'They Couldn't Mash Ants': The Decline of the White and Non-white Elites in Antigua, 1834–1900," in *Small Islands, Large Questions: Society, Culture and Resistance in the Post-emancipation Caribbean*, edited by Karen Fog Olwig (London: Frank Cass, 1994).

3. Douglas Hall, *Five of the Leewards, 1834–1870: The Major Problems of the Postemancipation Period in Antigua, Barbuda, Montserrat, Nevis and St. Kitts* (Barbados: Caribbean Universities Press, 1971), 155.

4. Thomas Carlyle, "Occasional Discourse on the Negro Question," *Fraser's Magazine for Town and Country* 40 (February 1849); reprinted in pamphlet form as "Occasional Discourse on the Nigger Question" (London: Thomas Bosworth, 1853).

5. According to Kwasi Konadu, *The Akan Diaspora in the Americas* (New York: Oxford University Press, 2010), 266, notes 37 and 40, *Quashee* was an Anglicized bastardization of either the Akan male day name given at birth on a Sunday, Kwesi, or *kwasea*, the Akan term for "fool." Many slaves appear in plantation records with the name Quashee in Antigua and other Caribbean territories that likely had Akan (Coromantee) heritage. On the association of this name with the stereotype of an idle or disobedient slave or black workingman, see Thomas Holt, *The Problem of Freedom: Race, Labor, and Politics in Jamaica and Britain, 1832–1938* (Baltimore, MD: Johns Hopkins University Press, 1992), chapters 5 and 8. Mimi Sheller, "Quasheba, Mother, Queen: Black Women's Public Leadership and Political Protest in Jamaica, 1834–65," *Slavery & Abolition* 19, no. 3 (1998): 91–93, explicates the defiance connoted by its female iteration. *Quashee* also figured in U.S. proslavery rhetoric; see Edward Rugemer, *The Problem of Emancipation: The Caribbean Roots of the American Civil War* (Baton Rouge: Louisiana State University Press, 2008), 263–64. Also note that the English sometimes used *quashey* for squash and pumpkins. See Mark Cumming, ed., *The Carlyle Encyclopedia* (Madison, NJ: Farleigh Dickinson University Press, 2004), 385–87.

6. See Eric Hobsbawm, *Primitive Rebels: Studies in Archaic Forms of Social Movement in the 19th and 20th Centuries* (New York: W. W. Norton and Co., 1965); Edward P. Thompson, *The Making of the English Working Class* (1963); Ranajit Guha, *Elementary Aspects of Peasant Insurgency in Colonial India* (New Delhi: Oxford University Press, 1983); Richard Slatta, ed., *Bandidos: The Varieties of Latin American Banditry* (New York: Greenwood Press, 1987); Gilbert Joseph, "On the Trail of Latin American Bandits: A Reexamination of Peasant Resistance," *Latin American Research Review* 25, no. 3 (1990); Peter Linebaugh, *The London Hanged: Crime and Civil Society in the Eighteenth Century* (New York: Penguin, 1992); Tera W. Hunter, *To 'Joy My Freedom: Southern Black Women's Lives and Labors after the Civil War* (Cambridge, MA: Harvard University Press, 1997); Robin D. G. Kelley, *Race Rebels: Culture, Politics, and the Black Working Class* (New York: The Free Press, 1994); Eileen Suarez-Findlay, *Imposing Decency: The Politics of Sexuality and Race in Puerto Rico, 1870–1920* (Durham, NC: Duke University Press, 1999); Pablo Piccato, *City of Suspects: Crime in Mexico City, 1900–1931* (Durham, NC: Duke University Press, 2001); Diana Paton, *No Bond but the Law: Punishment, Race, and Gender in Jamaican State Formation, 1780–1870* (Durham, NC: Duke University Press, 2004).

7. See William Green, *British Slave Emancipation: The Sugar Colonies and the Great Experiment, 1830–1865* (Oxford, UK: Clarendon Press, 1976), chapter 8, esp. 234–45.

8. WMMSPWIP, Box 22, Fiche 1050, Rev. James Cox to Methodist Missionary Society Secretaries, Rev. Dr. Bunting, Rev. Dr. Alder, Rev. Beecham, and Rev. Elijah Hoole, October 25, 1847.

9. PRO, CO 7/87, Governor James M. Higginson to Rt. Hon. Earl Grey, secretary of state for the colonies, December 26, 1847, with petition enclosed.

10. PRO, CO 7/92, Higginson to Grey, February 25, 1849, with petition enclosed. See Keith Hamilton and Patrick Salmon, eds., *Slavery, Diplomacy, and Empire: Britain and the Suppression of the Slave Trade, 1807–1975* (Eastbourne, UK: Sussex Academic Press, 2009); Leslie Bethell, *The Abolition of the Brazilian Slave Trade: Britain, Brazil, and*

the *Slave Trade Question*, reprint ed. (Cambridge, UK: Cambridge University Press, 2009); David Murray, *Odious Commerce: Britain, Spain, and the Abolition of the Cuban Slave Trade* (Cambridge, UK: Cambridge University Press, 2002).

11. *Antigua Observer*, November 4, 1847; emphasis in the original.

12. According to D. Hall, *Five of the Leewards*, 123, wages reportedly represented half of the cost of sugar production.

13. PRO, CO 7/79, "Statistical Information from the 1st Jan to the 30th June 1844," Horsford to Fitzroy, June 30, 1844; PRO, CO 7/83, "Statistical Summary for the Half-Year Ending 31 December 1845," Horsford to Cunningham, March 31, 1846. In British currency, 20 pence equaled a shilling.

14. PRO, CO 7/89, "Statistical Summary for the Half-Year Ending 31 December 1847," Black to Higginson, December 31, 1847.

15. D. Hall, *Five of the Leewards*, 55, 57, 115, 124.

16. "Statistical Summary for the Half-Year Ending 31 December 1847."

17. See PRO, CO 7/83, Cunningham to Gladstone, June 27, 1846, for Lt. Gov. Cunningham's extended discussion of the perceived labor shortage among Antiguan planters.

18. For discussion of whitening policies in the Caribbean and Latin America, see Ana Margarita Cervantes-Rodríguez, *International Migration in Cuba: Accumulation, Imperial Designs, and Transnational Social Fields* (University Park: Pennsylvania State University Press, 2010), chapter 2; George Reid Andrews, *Afro-Latin America, 1800–2000* (Oxford, UK: Oxford University Press, 2004), chapter 4.

19. PRO, CO 7/84, "Statistical Summary for the Half-Year Ending 30 June 1846," Horsford to Cunningham, June 30, 1846.

20. See T. Holt, *The Problem of Freedom*, chapter 9.

21. PRO, CO 7/83, Cunningham to Gladstone, April 27, 1846; Dyde, *A History of Antigua*, 162.

22. British merchants and traders in Madeira helped to negotiate contractual labor emigration schemes; see Desmond Gregory, *The Beneficent Usurpers: A History of the British in Madeira* (Cranbury, NJ: Associated University Presses, 1988).

23. W. Green, *British Slave Emancipation*, 287.

24. Dyde, *A History of Antigua*, 162.

25. Allusions to the government paying the cost of transporting these immigrants appear in Great Britain, Parliament, House of Commons, *The Reports Made for the Year 1846 to the Secretary of State Having the Department of the Colonies in Continuation of the Reports Annually Made by the Governors of the British Colonies . . . Transmitted with the Blue Books for the Year 1846* ([London]: n.p., 1847), 46–49, dispatch no. 37, Higginson to Grey, May 25 1847; and Governor Higginson's speech to the legislature, reprinted in the *Antigua Observer*, November 25, 1847.

26. PRO, CO 7/90, Higginson to Grey, Blue Book of 1847, June 1, 1848.

27. D. Hall, *Five of the Leewards*, 156.

28. PRO, CO 7/83, Cunningham to Gladstone, June 27, 1846.

29. Higginson to Grey, Blue Book of 1847.

30. *Antigua Observer*, July 8, 1847.

31. David Farquhar, *Missions and Society in the Leeward Islands, 1810–1850: An Ecclesiastical and Social Analysis* (Boston: Mount Prospect Press, 1999), 136–37; Vere L. Oliver, *The History of the Island of Antigua, One of the Leeward Caribbees in the West Indies, from the First Settlement in 1635 to the Present Time*, vol. 2 (London: Mitchell and Hughes, 1894), 104.

32. Fidelis Brennan, "A Brief History of the Catholic Church in Antigua," Diocese of St. John's-Basseterre, accessed December 19, 2012, http://diocesesjb.org/site-map /contacts/16-sample-data-contact/35-shop-site/37-fruit-encyclopedia/57-t.

33. PRO, CO 7/92, Higginson to the Antigua Legislative Council and Assembly, February 15, 1849.

34. Mary Noel Menezes, "The Madeiran Portuguese Woman in Guyanese Society, 1830–1930," in *The Colonial Caribbean in Transition: Essays on Post-Emancipation Social and Cultural History*, edited by Bridget Brereton and Kevin Yelvington (Gainesville: University of Florida Press, 1999).

35. Dyde, *A History of Antigua*, 165–66; Oliver, *The History of the Island of Antigua*, vol. 2, 163.

36. Lowes, "The Peculiar Class," chapter 10.

37. See PRO, CO 7/82, Lt. Governor Cunningham to Stanley, December 23, 1845.

38. PRO, CO 7/82, Lord Stanley to Gov. Charles Fitzroy, August 26, 1845.

39. See the letters enclosed in PRO, CO 7/82, Fitzroy to Stanley, November 4, 1845. The quotation is from WMMSPWIP, Box 22, Fiche 1042, Rev. Jesse Pilcher to Methodist Missionary Society secretaries, October 25, 1845. The governor's reiteration of this recommendation five years later indicates that nothing had been done; see PRO, CO 7/95, Higginson to Grey, Blue Book for 1849, March 26, 1850.

40. PRO, CO 7/90, Higginson to Grey, Blue Book of 1847, June 1, 1848.

41. WMMSPWIP, Box 22, Fiche 1051, Rev. James Cox to Methodist Missionary Society secretaries, April 5, 1848; emphasis in the original. The privately funded Mico charity schools managed to stay open without charging fees; PRO, CO 7/92, Higginson to Grey, Blue Book for 1848, April 5, 1849.

42. PRO, CO 7/92, Stipendiary Magistrate Frederick Seymour to Higginson, "Statistical Summary for the Half-Year Ending 31 December 1848," March 10, 1849.

43. PRO, CO 7/92, Higginson to Grey, Blue Book for 1848, April 5, 1849; see also PRO, CO 7/95, Higginson to Grey, Blue Book for 1849, March 26, 1850.

44. WMMSPWIP, Box 22, Fiche 1052, Cox to Methodist Missionary Society secretaries, September 4, 1848.

45. PRO, CO 7/89, "Statistical Summary for the Half-Year Ending 31 December 1847," Black to Higginson, December 31, 1847; PRO, CO 7/90, Higginson to Grey, Blue Book of 1847, June 1, 1848; PRO, CO 7/92, Seymour to Higginson, "Statistical Summary for the Half-Year Ending December 31, 1848," March 10, 1849.

46. John Horsford, *A Voice from the West Indies: Being a Review of the Character and Results of Missionary Efforts in the British and Other Colonies in the Charibbean Sea, with Some Remarks on the Usages, Prejudices, &c. of the Inhabitants* (London: Alexander Heylin, 1856), 97.

47. Mimi Sheller, "Acting as Free Men: Subaltern Masculinities and Citizenship in Postslavery Jamaica," in *Gender and Slave Emancipation in the Atlantic World*, edited by Pamela Scully and Diana Paton (Durham, NC: Duke University Press, 2005). The *Antigua Observer*, October 14, 1847, reprinted a memorial from artisans, laborers, and other workmen in Grenada to Parliament that has comparable form and content to those composed a few weeks later in Antigua.

48. "Petition of the Inhabitants of St. George's Parish," *Antigua Observer*, December 16, 1847, had fifty signatures. The *Observer* printed similar petitions from All Saints Village, with 119 signatures, on December 23, and from the rural area of St. John's Parish, with 117 signatures, on December 30. The December 9 issue mentions the submission of the other parishes' petitions in the House of Assembly minutes.

49. "Petition of the Inhabitants of St. George's Parish."

50. Ibid.

51. See Eric Foner, *Free Soil, Free Labor, Free Men: The Ideology of the Republican Party before the Civil War*, reprint ed. (New York: Oxford University Press, 1995).

52. Sheller, "Acting as Free Men," observes missionary influence in the Jamaican petitions.

53. Joseph Sturge and Thomas Harvey, *The West Indies in 1837; Being the Journal of a Visit to Antigua, Montserrat, Dominica, St Lucia, Barbados and Jamaica; Undertaken for the Purpose of Ascertaining the Actual Condition of the Negro Population of Those Islands* (London: Hamilton, Adams & Co, 1838), 41. According to W. Green, *British Slave Emancipation*, 79–80, magistrates sat on vestries ex officio, but those bodies exercised no judicial powers.

54. See Susan Lowes, "The Peculiar Class: The Formation, Collapse, and Reformation of the Middle Class in Antigua, West Indies, 1834–1940" (PhD diss., Columbia University, 1994), chapter 5, esp. 147–50.

55. White Protestant dissenters in Britain and elsewhere in the empire regularly voiced the same complaints. See W. R. Ward, "The Tithe Question in England in the Early Nineteenth Century," *Journal of Ecclesiastical History* 14, no. 1 (April 1965); and Marjoleine Kars, *Breaking Loose Together: The Regulator Rebellion in Pre-revolutionary North Carolina* (Chapel Hill: University of North Carolina Press, 2002), 107–8.

56. D. Hall, *Five of the Leewards*, 155–58.

57. *Antigua Herald and Gazette*, April 10, 1847.

58. Ibid.

59. PRO, CO 7/89, Higginson to Grey, February 8, 1848.

60. PRO, CO 7/89, Attorney General James Sherriff to Private Secretary Charles Higginson, February 9, 1848.

61. Ibid.

62. PRO, CO 7/89, "The Humble Memorial of the Undersigned Freeholders of the Island of Antigua for Themselves and Others," to Earl Grey, n.d., enclosed in PRO, CO 7/89, Higginson to Grey, February 8, 1848, italics in original.

63. On the supposed inferiority of West Indian white society to proper En-

glishness, especially its reputation for impropriety and for financial, social, and sexual excess as a result of immersion in mainly black communities, see, for instance, David Lambert, *White Creole Culture, Politics and Identity during the Age of Abolition* (Cambridge, UK: Cambridge University Press, 2005), chapter 1.

64. PRO, CO 7/89, Grey to Higginson, April 18, 1848.

65. Hilary McD. Beckles, *Great House Rules: Landless Emancipation and Workers' Protest in Barbados, 1838–1938* (Kingston, Jamaica: Ian Randle Publishers, 2004), 88–90; Melanie Newton, *The Children of Africa in the Colonies: Free People of Color in Barbados in the Age of Emancipation* (Baton Rouge: Louisiana State University Press, 2008), chapter 6; Swithin Wilmot, "Politics at the 'Grassroots' in Free Jamaica, St. James 1838–1865," in *Working Slavery, Pricing Freedom: Perspectives from the Caribbean, Africa, and the African Diaspora*, edited by Verene Shepherd (New York: Palgrave MacMillan, 2002); T. Holt, *The Problem of Freedom*, 99–102, 215–32; Mimi Sheller, *Democracy after Slavery: Black Publics and Peasant Radicalism in Haiti and Jamaica* (Gainesville: University Press of Florida, 2000), 176.

66. PRO, CO 7/100, Lieutenant Governor Mackintosh to Earl Grey, colonial secretary, January 24, 1852, with enclosures; the enclosed issue of the *Antigua Weekly Times*, January 23, 1852, has a synopsis of this report.

67. John Davy, *The West Indies, Before and Since Slave Emancipation, Comprising the Windward & Leeward Islands' Military Command Founded on Notes and Observations Collected During a Three Years' Residence* (London: W. F. G. Cash, 1854), 397–98.

68. *Antigua Weekly Times*, January 23, 1852. T. Holt, *The Problem of Freedom*, 175, describes freedpeople in Jamaica in the early 1840s as a "semi-peasantry."

69. D. Hall, *Five of the Leewards*, 128–31.

70. PRO, CO 7/100, Blue Book for 1851, Mackintosh to Sir John Pakington, secretary of state for the colonies, April 12, 1852.

71. Charles William Day, *Five Years' Residence in the West Indies*, vol. 2 (London: Colburn & Co., 1852), 307.

72. For details of the fires, see the *Antigua Weekly Register*, April 9, April 16, and April 23, 1850, and the *Antigua Observer*, April 25, 1850. Megass, the dry residue that remained after the extraction of juice from sugar cane stalks, was often used as fuel by the sugar mills.

73. *Antigua Observer*, April 25, 1850.

74. Bonham Richardson, *Igniting the Caribbean's Past: Fire in British West Indian History* (Chapel Hill: University of North Carolina Press, 2004), 1.

75. Ibid., 1–2.

76. PRO, CO 7/98, "An Act to Repeal a Part of the Second Clause of an Act, entitled, 'An Act for the Punishment of Idle and Disorderly Persons, Rogues and Vagabonds, Incorrigible Rogues or Other Vagrants in This Island,'" March 27, 1851; also see the House of Assembly Minutes, January 9, 1851, reprinted in the *Antigua Weekly Register*, January 14, 1851, for lawmakers' debate over the issue.

77. Paton, *No Bond but the Law*, esp. chapter 4.

78. PRO, CO 7/98, Mackintosh to Grey, April 5, 1851.

79. Horsford, *A Voice from the West Indies*, 93.

80. *Antigua Weekly Register*, January 29, 1850.

81. Day, *Five Years' Residence in the West Indies*, 309.

82. Letter from "Oedipus, Jr." to the editor, *Antigua Weekly Register*, April 21, 1857.

83. Ibid. See also Monica Schuler, *"Alas, Alas, Kongo": A Social History of Indentured African Immigration into Jamaica, 1841–1865* (Baltimore, MD: Johns Hopkins University Press, 1980); Roseanne Adderley, *"New Negroes from Africa": Slave Trade Abolition and Free African Settlement in the Nineteenth-Century Caribbean* (Bloomington: Indiana University Press, 2006).

84. Letter from "Oedipus, Jr." to the editor, *Antigua Weekly Register*, April 21, 1857. The letter does not specify where these troops came from.

85. *Antigua Weekly Register*, September 30, 1856, stated that the *Observer* at the time had "undergone a sudden conversion to a contrary opinion. In the last number of that paper the population, 'especially of the towns,' is characterised as 'idle and disorderly,' a set of 'blood-craving' 'rabble,' 'lawless' 'semi-savages'; and that at any time property, life itself, 'is at the mercy of a collection of miscreants.'" The *Antigua Weekly Register* condemned the *Observer's* assessment as biased, but continued: "It must, however, be admitted that [the townspeople] are not so well behaved and peaceable as they were some years since, if any reliance can be placed on criminal statistics. That a lower moral tone now pervades the people generally must be admitted by all who take the trouble to examine the subject."

86. PRO, CO 7/110, Governor Hamilton to Edward Bulwer Lytton, MP, July 28, 1858.

87. PRO, CO 7/87, "Statistical Summary for the Half-Year Ending June 30, 1847," Magistrate G. Black to Governor Higginson, June 30, 1847.

88. PRO, CO 7/98, "Statistical Summary for the Half-Year Ending 31 December 1850," Stipendiary Magistrate G. Black to Governor Mackintosh, March 1, 1851.

89. "Twenty-Third Report of the Daily Meal Society's Infirmary and Lazaretto," reprinted in the *Antigua Weekly Register*, July 15, 1851.

90. *Antigua Weekly Register*, September 13, 1853, reported that 370 individuals were on poor relief and that 28 more sought shelter in addition to public assistance. This article states that the *Antigua Observer* reported a total of 771 on relief in the six parishes.

91. "Thomas Price to W. M. Ledeatt, Esq., MD, on the Propriety of Forming an Antigua Industrial Association, 30 November 1853," reprinted in the *Antigua Weekly Register*, December 6, 1853. D. Hall, *Five of the Leewards*, 145–46, argues that very few sustained attempts were made to move away from sugar, except for a temporary focus on cotton during the U.S. Civil War.

92. *Antigua Weekly Register*, December 6, 1853.

93. "Address of His Honor Sir Robert Horsford, C.B., at the Opening of the March Sessions of the Court of Queen's Bench and Grand Sessions," reprinted in *Antigua Weekly Register*, March 11, 1856.

94. See E. Thompson, "The Moral Economy of the English Crowd in the Eighteenth Century"; Linebaugh, *The London Hanged*, 250–55; Kelley, *Race Rebels*, 19.

95. Hunter, To 'Joy My Freedom, 60–61.

96. PRO, CO 7/104, Mackintosh to Newcastle, June 20, 1854; PRO, CO 7/100, Mackintosh to Pakington, April 13, 1852; D. Hall, *Five of the Leewards*, 75.

97. PRO, CO 7/87, Perru to Governor General of Guadeloupe, April 18, 1847, enclosed in Higginson to the Governor General of Guadeloupe, September 9, 1847; PRO, CO 7/100, Mackintosh to Pakington, April 13, 1852; D. Hall, *Five of the Leewards*, 76.

98. Sessions of the Court of Queen's Bench, June 14, 1850, reprinted in the *Antigua Weekly Register*, June 25, 1850.

99. House of Assembly Minutes, February 7, 1856, reprinted in *Antigua Weekly Register*, February 12, 1856.

100. Address of Sir Robert Horsford.

101. Paton, *No Bond but the Law*, 145.

102. *Antigua Weekly Register*, February 19, 1856.

103. Address of Sir Robert Horsford; emphasis in the original.

104. Paton, *No Bond but the Law*, 151.

105. *Antigua Weekly Register*, December 6, 1853.

106. Frances Lanaghan, *Antigua and the Antiguans: A Full Account of the Colony and Its Inhabitants from the Time of the Caribs to the Present Day*, vol. 2 (London: Saunders & Otley, 1844), 162–64.

7. "Our Side"

1. LLH, Ms.Eng.Lett.c.216, Folder 120–1, Adam Nicholson to Langford Lovell Hodge, October 28, 1858. This is the only reference to the term *nigger* that I have seen in Antiguan sources. It could either indicate Nicholson's exceptional severity as an estate manager or exemplify white elites' hardening views toward freedpeople.

2. Multiple issues in of the *Dominican* (Roseau, Dominica) in April 1858 featured details of the five-day riot in Antigua. The April 7 issue states that its story of the riot was based on the *Antigua Weekly Times* issue of March 27. The April 10 issue of *Port of Spain Gazette* (Port of Spain, Trinidad) carried coverage of the disturbances but gave no specific Antiguan newspaper as its source; the article instead cites "a friend with Antigua newspapers from 29th ult." The claim that the Barnard-Jarvis conflict began in a rum shop comes from an opinion column in the April 14, 1858, issue of *Dominican*.

3. *Dominican*, April 7, 1858. PRO, CO 7/110, Court of Oyer and Terminer, May 10, 1858–June 11, 1858, contains transcripts of the rioters' trials. Barbudan male and female victims testified to the violence of the rioters, who inflicted physical beatings and injured their property. Figures for the total number of rioters vary significantly, but even conservative estimates indicate that several hundred people took to the streets during the course of the four days.

4. The *Port of Spain Gazette*, April 10, 1858, also said that the police fired shots on Tuesday the twenty-third without injuring those in the crowd.

5. PRO, CO 7/109, Governor Ker Bailie Hamilton to Colonial Secretary Lord Stanley, MP, March 27, 1858.

6. Brian Dyde, *A History of Antigua: The Unsuspected Isle* (London: Macmillan Publishers, 2000), 163.

7. PRO, CO 7/109, Hamilton to Stanley, March 27, 1858, gives the total numbers killed and wounded. For the number of people who were tried and convicted, as well as their sentences, see PRO, CO 7/110, Court of Oyer and Terminer, May 10, 1858–June 11, 1858, both the opening statement and p. 245.

8. Governor Hamilton believed any suspicions of a premeditated plot to be unfounded but acknowledged that his sentiments were not shared by many officials at the time; see PRO, CO 7/110, Hamilton to Edward Bulwer Lytton, MP, July 28, 1858.

9. See the *Antigua Times*, June 26, July 17, September 18, and October 9, 1858, for articles, House of Assembly minutes, and reprints of private correspondence concerning Hamilton's performance during the riots, investigations, and trials. PRO, CO 7/110, "Petition to Her Majesty Queen Victoria," November 26, 1858, which carries more than 150 signatures from men in the planter and merchant classes, expressly seeks Hamilton's removal.

10. One printed primary source, William G. Sewell, *The Ordeal of Free Labour in the British West Indies* (1862; repr. London: Frank Cass & Co., 1968), 149–50, discusses the riot in some detail. Douglas Hall, *Five of the Leewards, 1834–1870: The Major Problems of the Postemancipation Period in Antigua, Barbuda, Montserrat, Nevis and St. Kitts* (St. Laurence, Barbados: Caribbean Universities Press, 1971), 83–84; and Dyde, *A History of Antigua*, 163, briefly mention these events.

11. Estimates ranged widely. One witness (p. 178) stated that on Thursday evening, three hundred or four hundred people were assembled by one rebel's blow of a whistle, and then the crowd proceeded to the police station. Two others (p. 69 and p. 116) reported seeing "600 or 800" in the streets on Thursday, March 25, and Friday, March 26. Another (p. 142) said that he saw a crowd of one thousand proceed up a street in the Point and another crowd of five hundred or six hundred women assembled on Friday morning. Estimates also appear of one thousand people (p. 107 and p. 180), two thousand people (p. 135), and two thousand to three thousand people (p. 102). All page numbers are from PRO, CO 7/110, Court of Oyer and Terminer, May 10–June 11, 1858.

12. On the Point's reputation as a lawless neighborhood, see Susan Lowes, "The Peculiar Class: The Formation, Collapse, and Reformation of the Middle Class in Antigua, West Indies, 1834–1940" (PhD diss., Columbia University, 1994), 282.

13. References to some rebels' occupations appear in PRO, CO 7/110, Court of Oyer and Terminer, May 10–June 11, 1858.

14. Ibid., 226 (an Antiguan woman), 175 (a Barbudan man).

15. PRO, CO 7/110, opening speech of Chief Justice William Snagg to Court of Oyer and Terminer, May 10, 1858.

16. PRO, CO 7/110, Court of Oyer and Terminer, May 10–June 11, 1858, p. 37. Bar-

budian seems to have been an alternative term for *Barbudan* in nineteenth-century parlance; it appeared periodically in the transcripts.

17. Ibid., 29.

18. Ibid., 26–27.

19. Ibid., 52.

20. Ibid., 38, 48.

21. Ibid., 48.

22. Ibid., 50.

23. Ibid., 210–11, 216, 217, 220.

24. Stephanie Smallwood, *Saltwater Slavery: A Middle Passage from Africa to American Diaspora* (Cambridge, MA: Harvard University Press, 2007), 36, identifies the slave trade as the site of "an enduring project in the modern Western world: probing the limits up to which it is possible to discipline the body without extinguishing the life within," which rings true for labor regimes in slavery and freedom as well.

25. PRO, CO 7/110, Court of Oyer and Terminer, May 10–June 11, 1858, 106; other examples of rioters exclaiming "our side!" appear on 32, 48, 54, 140, 143, 193, 195.

26. See D. Hall, *Five of the Leewards*, 84–85; and Dyde, *A History of Antigua*, 192, for explanations of Barbuda's annexation to Antigua and continued public complaints about Barbudans' lawlessness in both Barbuda and Antigua.

27. PRO, CO 7/110, Court of Oyer and Terminer, May 10–June 11, 1858, p. 209.

28. Ibid., 208.

29. Ibid., 90.

30. PRO, CO 7/110, address of Chief Justice William Snagg to grand jury, Court of Oyer and Terminer opening statement, May 10, 1858.

31. Juanita De Barros, *Order and Place in a Colonial City: Patterns of Struggle and Resistance in Georgetown, British Guiana, 1889–1924* (Montreal: McGill-Queen's University Press, 2003), 99, 139.

32. PRO, CO 7/110, Court of Oyer and Terminer, May 10–June 11, 1858, p. 52.

33. Ibid., 175.

34. Ibid., 41.

35. Ibid., 121.

36. Ibid., 49.

37. Mimi Sheller, "Acting as Free Men: Subaltern Masculinities and Citizenship in Postslavery Jamaica," in *Gender and Slave Emancipation in the Atlantic World*, edited by Pamela Scully and Diana Paton (Durham, NC: Duke University Press, 2005), 82. In Jamaica, Sheller sees this discourse as entirely masculinized and heavily identified with the Baptist Church; this Christianized version of manhood charged men to act as upstanding, free citizens on behalf of their families and subsumed women's freedom under that of men. Antiguan women's articulation of their rights as countrymen suggests that they did not subscribe to the gendered, Christianized discourse of freedom as men's domain, at least during this violent outbreak.

38. PRO, CO 7/110, Court of Oyer and Terminer, May 10–June 11, 1858, p. 27; see also pp. 52, 142.

39. Frances Lanaghan, *Antigua and the Antiguans: A Full Account of the Colony and Its Inhabitants from the Time of the Caribs to the Present Day*, vol. 2 (London: Saunders & Otley, 1844), 146. Richard Burton, *Afro-Creole: Power, Opposition, and Play in the Caribbean* (Ithaca, NY: Cornell University Press, 1997), 164, discusses the "street woman par excellence" in the West Indies as "manlike" and an object of fascination and ridicule among white observers.

40. Hilary McD. Beckles, *Natural Rebels: A Social History of Enslaved Black Women in Barbados* (New Brunswick, NJ: Rutgers University Press, 1990), chapter 8, calls enslaved African women "persistent rebels." Swithin Wilmot, "'Females of Abandoned Character'? Women and Protest in Jamaica, 1838–65," in *Engendering History: Caribbean Women in Historical Perspective*, edited by Verene Shepherd, Bridget Brereton, and Barbara Bailey (Kingston, Jamaica: Ian Randle Publishers; London: James Currey, 1995); and Mimi Sheller, "Quasheba, Mother, Queen: Black Women's Public Leadership and Political Protest in Postemancipation Jamaica," *Slavery & Abolition* 19, no. 3 (1998): 91, use the same characterization to describe Jamaican freedwomen engaging in public resistance. These and other works insist on the centrality of women to popular street protest.

41. For descriptions of nineteenth-century Afro-Caribbean women's street activity, see Félix V. Matos-Rodríguez, "Street Vendors, Peddlers, Shop-Owners and Domestics: Some Aspects of Women's Economic Roles in Nineteenth-Century San Juan, Puerto Rico, 1820–1870," in *Engendering History: Caribbean Women in Historical Perspective*, edited by Verene Shepherd, Bridget Brereton, and Barbara Bailey (Kingston, Jamaica: Ian Randle Publishers; London: James Currey, 1995); Sheller, "Quasheba, Mother, Queen," 103–11; and Sheena Boa, "Young Ladies and Dissolute Women: Conflicting Views of Culture and Gender in Public Entertainment, Kingstown, St. Vincent, 1838–1888," in *Gender and Slave Emancipation in the Atlantic World*, edited by Pamela Scully and Diana Paton (Durham, NC: Duke University Press, 2005), 252–59.

42. PRO, CO 7/110, Court of Oyer and Terminer, May 10–June 11, 1858, p. 142.

43. Ibid., 143.

44. Ibid., 134.

45. Sheller, "Quasheba, Mother, Queen," 103.

46. PRO, CO 7/110, Court of Oyer and Terminer, May 10–June 11, 1858, p. 226.

47. Ibid., 128.

48. PRO, CO 7/110, Court of Oyer and Terminer, May 10–June 11, 1858, pp. 28, 139.

49. A discussion of the balance between production and reproduction for Afro-Caribbean slave women under precarious circumstances features prominently in Barry W. Higman, *Slave Populations of the British Caribbean, 1807–1834* (Baltimore, MD: Johns Hopkins University Press, 1984); Marietta Morrissey, *Slave Women in the New World: Gender Stratification and the Caribbean* (Lawrence: University Press of Kansas, 1989); Barbara Bush, *Slave Women in Caribbean Society: 1650-1838* (London: James Currey, 1990); Hilary McD. Beckles, *Centering Woman: Gender Discourses in Caribbean Slave Society* (Kingston, Jamaica: Ian Randle Publishers; Princeton, NJ: Markus Wiener

Publishers, 1998); Mary Turner, "The 11 O'clock Flog: Women, Work and Labour Law in the British Caribbean," *Slavery & Abolition* 20, no. 1 (1999); and Jennifer Morgan, *Laboring Women: Reproduction and Gender in New World Slavery* (Philadelphia: University of Pennsylvania Press, 2004). For how the balance continued in freedom, see Wilmot, "'Females of Abandoned Character'?"; Bridget Brereton, "Family Strategies, Gender, and the Shift to Wage Labor in the British Caribbean," in *Gender and Slave Emancipation in the Atlantic World*, edited by Pamela Scully and Diana Paton (Durham, NC: Duke University Press, 2005); and Sheller, "Quasheba, Mother, Queen."

50. While Dyde describes housing of the early 1860s, this characterization clearly applies to the late 1850s; Dyde, *A History of Antigua*, 177–78.

51. Mindie Lazarus-Black, *Legitimate Acts and Illegal Encounters: Law and Society in Barbuda and Antigua* (Washington, DC: Smithsonian Institution Press, 1994), 112.

52. Sheller, "Quasheba, Mother, Queen," 95, concludes that Afro-Jamaican women knew that the "suffering mother" genre would serve as the most palatable explanation to white officials for their labor protests.

53. PRO, CO 7/110, Court of Oyer and Terminer, May 10–June 11, 1858, p. 15.

54. Ibid., 43.

55. Ibid., 54.

56. Ibid., 74. Nanton's age is stated on p. 89, where it is noted that he cried in the court when charged. He was eventually acquitted of all charges.

57. According to Susan Lowes, "'They Couldn't Mash Ants': The Decline of the White and Non-white Elites in Antigua, 1834–1900," in *Small Islands, Large Questions: Society, Culture and Resistance in the Post-emancipation Caribbean*, edited by Karen Fog Olwig (London: Frank Cass, 1994), 37–38, in 1832 free colored men composed two-thirds of the militia but were denied any positions of rank. After 1834, when the militia was replaced by a smaller police force, the police force was also primarily composed of men of African descent, and by the mid-1840s, mixed-race men of some prominence had managed to secure some public service jobs, including the police magistracy. Henry Loving was the first nonwhite chief.

58. PRO, CO 7/110, Court of Oyer and Terminer, May 10–June 11, 1858, pp. 31–34.

59. Ibid., 135.

60. Ibid., 132. Shorediche is identified as white in PRO, CO 7/76, "A Confidential Report of the Claims of Candidates for Government Offices in Antigua as Called for by Lord Stanley's Circular Dispatch Dated the 13th of June 1842," which lists all of the candidates by name and racial background.

61. PRO, CO 7/110, Court of Oyer and Terminer, May 10–June 11, 1858, p. 23.

62. Ibid., 135.

63. Ibid., 138.

64. See ibid., 138, for a retelling of Richards's discovery of the phial; see p. 106 for Rebecca Joseph, p. 134 for Mary Abel, and p. 146 for Letitia Frederick.

65. Ibid., 143.

66. See ibid., 73–74. Gardiner's statement resurfaced in much of the correspondence following the events of March 1858. For example, PRO, CO 7/110,

Hamilton to Bulwer Lytton, MP, July 28, 1858. Also see NAAB, Antigua Despatch no. 112, Hamilton to Sir E. Bulwer Lytton, MP, December 9, 1858. The second letter expresses some doubt as to whether or not Gardiner actually struck Harley or whether Harley was hit at random by flying stones. But three witnesses offering parallel testimony about Gardiner's words and actions suggests some further certainty that she likely was the culprit. Another witness, on p. 74 of the transcript, reported that Gardiner knocked out two windowpanes at the police station as well, indicating that she was possessed of good aim.

67. PRO, CO 7/110, Court of Oyer and Terminer, May 10–June 11, 1858, pp. 133–34.

68. Ibid.; see pp. 75 and 116 for threats of fire and p. 152 for an account of one attempt to prevent the removal of the bodies.

69. Ibid., 150.

70. Ibid., 154–58.

71. An article in the *Antigua Weekly Register*, June 15, 1858, also describes his whereabouts during the last day of the riot in detail. The article calls him "Christopher" rather than Christian Henry, as he was identified in the courtroom, but this is definitely the same individual.

72. PRO, CO 7/110, Court of Oyer and Terminer, May 10–June 11, 1858, p. 157.

73. Ibid., 155.

74. D. Hall, *Five of the Leewards*, appendix A, 194.

75. See declarations of country people's disassociation with the uprising in PRO, CO 7/109, Hamilton to Lord Stanley, MP, April 7, 1858.

76. See PRO, CO 7/110, December 1858 section, which contains the petitions.

77. PRO, CO 7/110, undated letter to Governor Hamilton from Michael McDonough, which was signed by several All Saints Village residents.

78. Ibid.

79. PRO, CO 7/110, Shorediche to Grantun (two letters), March 25, 1858; also see PRO, CO 7/110, Shorediche to Humphreys, July 7, 1858.

80. PRO, CO 7/110, Court of Oyer and Terminer, May 10–June 11, 1858, p. 153.

81. PRO, CO 7/110, G. Estridge, Esq. to Lord Carnarvon, May 7, 1858. *Gaol* is a British English spelling of the word *jail*.

82. Susan Dwyer Amussen, *Caribbean Exchanges: Slavery and the Transformation of English Society, 1640–1700* (Chapel Hill: University of North Carolina Press, 2007), 148, discusses this particularly sexualized strain of white hysteria, which was evident in the aftermath of the colonial Caribbean's earliest slave plots.

83. Estridge to Carnarvon.

84. Sherry Ortner, "Resistance and the Problem of Ethnographic Refusal," *Comparative Studies in Society and History* 37, no. 1 (1995): 182. Also see Lila Abu-Lughod, "The Romance of Resistance: Tracing Transformations of Power through Bedouin Women," *American Ethnologist* 17, no. 1 (February 1990): 47, which discusses how Bedouin women both "resist and support the existing system of power" in their various subversive practices.

85. Dyde, *A History of Antigua*, 164, states that the militia faded out of existence within a few years of its reestablishment.

Conclusion

1. See Hilary McD. Beckles, *Great House Rules: Landless Emancipation and Workers' Protest in Barbados, 1838–1938* (Kingston, Jamaica: Ian Randle Publishers, 2004), 34, on the 1834 disturbances in St. Kitts, Montserrat, and Trinidad, and chapter 4 for Barbados's 1876 Federation Riot. Also see PRO, CO 7/39, Governor James Warner of St. Kitts to Governor Evan MacGregor of Antigua, August 4, 1834. For Dominica's 1844 Guerre Negre Riot, see Michel-Rolph Trouillot, *Peasants and Capital: Dominica in the World Economy* (Baltimore, MD: Johns Hopkins University Press, 1988), 101–3; on the 1849 St. Lucia riots, see Michael Louis, " 'An Equal Right to the Soil': The Rise of a Peasantry in St. Lucia" (PhD diss., Johns Hopkins University, 1982), chapter 3. For the Road Town uprising of 1853, see Eugenia O'Neal, *From the Field to the Legislature: A History of Women in the Virgin Islands* (Westport, CT: Greenwood Press, 2001), 40–41. See also Gad J. Heuman, "Post-emancipation Resistance in the Caribbean: An Overview," in *Small Islands, Large Questions: Society, Culture and Resistance in the Post-emancipation Caribbean*, edited by Karen Fog Olwig (London: Frank Cass, 1994), 123–34; Woodville Marshall, " 'Vox Populi': The St. Vincent Riots and Disturbances of 1862," in *Trade, Government and Society in Caribbean History: Essays Presented to Douglas Hall*, edited by Barry Higman (Kingston, Jamaica: Caribbean Universities Press, 1983), 83–115; Bridget Brereton, "Post-emancipation Protest in the Caribbean: The 'Belmanna Riots' in Tobago, 1876," *Caribbean Quarterly* 30, no. 4 (1984); on Guyana's 1856 uprising, see Juanita De Barros, *Order and Place in a Colonial City: Patterns of Struggle and Resistance in Georgetown, British Guiana, 1889–1924* (Montreal: McGill-Queen's University Press, 2003), 99, 139; Michael Craton, *Empire, Enslavement and Freedom in the Caribbean* (Kingston, Jamaica: Ian Randle, 1997), 324–47.

2. De Barros, *Order and Place in a Colonial City*, 13.

3. For the public protests and political maneuvers of the black working and colored middle classes in Jamaica up to and during the 1865 Morant Bay Rebellion, see Thomas Holt, *The Problem of Freedom: Race, Labor, and Politics in Jamaica and Britain, 1832–1938* (Baltimore, MD: Johns Hopkins University Press, 1992), chapter 8; Gad J. Heuman, *The Killing Time: The Morant Bay Rebellion in Jamaica* (Knoxville: University of Tennessee Press, 1994); Swithin Wilmot, " 'Females of Abandoned Character'? Women and Protest in Jamaica, 1838–65," in *Engendering History: Caribbean Women in Historical Perspective*, edited by Verene Shepherd, Bridget Brereton, and Barbara Bailey (Kingston, Jamaica: Ian Randle Publishers; London: James Currey, 1995); Mimi Sheller, "Quasheba, Mother, Queen: Black Women's Public Leadership and Political Protest in Post-emancipation Jamaica," *Slavery & Abolition* 19, no. 3 (1998); and Mimi Sheller, *Democracy after Slavery: Black Publics and Peasant Radicalism in Haiti and Jamaica* (Gainesville: University Press of Florida, 2000), chapters 6–8.

4. O. Nigel Bolland, *The Politics of Labour in the British Caribbean: The Social Origins of*

Authoritarianism and Democracy in the Labour Movement (Kingston, Jamaica: Ian Randle Publishers, 2001), details the historical trajectory of twentieth-century unions in the British Caribbean as beginning in the informal popular uprisings after slavery.

5. PRO, CO 7/110, Court of Oyer and Terminer, May 10–June 11, 1858, p. 88.

6. De Barros, *Order and Place in a Colonial City*, 139.

7. See Heuman, *Killing Time*; and Sheller, *Democracy after Slavery*, for further discussion. In her conclusion, Sheller reflects on the many Afro-Jamaicans involved in agitations of Haitian exiles on the island who sought to oust the current Haitian president at the time, showing the potential linkage between Afro-Jamaicans and other black "foreigners," such as the Haitians, as resistance movements were built on both islands.

8. PRO, CO 7/109, Hamilton to Stanley, March 27, 1858.

9. PRO, CO 7/110, Court of Oyer and Terminer, May 10–June 11, 1858, p. 75.

10. The rebels' drawing on Tortola's example evokes the substantial inspiration drawn from Haiti within several Atlantic World revolts, as antislavery and anticolonial movements in the Caribbean, Latin America, and the United States heavily referenced the Haitian Revolution of 1791–1804 for most of the nineteenth century. See, for example, Sheller, *Democracy after Slavery*, 77–86; Julius S. Scott, "The Common Wind: Currents of Afro-Caribbean Political Communication in the Era of the Haitian Revolution" (PhD diss., Duke University, 1986); Rebecca J. Scott, *Degrees of Freedom: Louisiana and Cuba after Slavery* (Cambridge, MA: Belknap Press of Harvard University Press, 2005); Matt Childs, *The 1812 Aponte Rebellion in Cuba and the Struggle against Atlantic Slavery* (Chapel Hill: University of North Carolina Press, 2006); Ada Ferrer, "Talk about Haiti: The Archive and the Atlantic's Haitian Revolution," in *Tree of Liberty: Cultural Legacies of the Haitian Revolution*, edited by Doris Garraway (Charlottesville: University of Virginia Press, 2008).

11. For instance, see PRO, CO 7/110, Court of Oyer and Terminer, May 10–June 11, 1858, pp. 134, 206, 220, 221.

12. A plethora of historical works covers the significance of the Crimean War to British imperial history and the decisive siege of Sevastopol (also widely spelled "Sebastopol" in the 1800s) that ended with the victory of the French and the British. See, for instance, Orlando Figes, *The Crimean War: A History* (London: Macmillan, 2010), chapters 8 and 11. The war's multiple failures and its unnecessary exhaustion of Britain's human and material resources also are well documented. The war had a critical impact on popular culture within Britain and throughout the colonies. It was marked by the development of rapid communications through electric telegraph from the war front and an unprecedented publication of events in real time, in the form of photographs and newspaper reporting. See Stephanie Markovits, *The Crimean War in the British Imagination* (Cambridge, UK: Cambridge University Press, 2009). News of this siege was widely circulated in metropolitan and colonial newspapers, and it was memorialized in visual art and literature, including Leo Tolstoy's famed memorial of his days as a Russian soldier, *The Sebastopol Sketches*, trans. Frank D. Millet (1855; repr., New York: Harper and Bros., 1887). Antiguan working

people would very likely have known about Sevastopol and thus employed it as a timely metaphor amid their own rebellion.

13. See Richard Gott, *Britain's Empire: Resistance, Repression and Revolt* (London: Verso, 2011), parts IX and X, for a sense of how fraying controls in the British Empire figured into a succession of colonial revolts from the late 1840s through the late 1850s.

14. PRO, CO 7/110, Governor Ker Baillie Hamilton to the Right Honorable Edward Bulwer-Lytton, MP, July 28, 1858. Hamilton quotes the solicitor general of Antigua as having stated with respect to the 1858 riots: "Under Providence, we were indebted to the Police Force for the restoration of order, and the prevention of deeds which would have rivaled the atrocities of *Cawnpore*" (emphasis in the original). "Cawnpore" was the Victorian English spelling of "Kanpur," a town where hundreds of European hostages were killed at the hands of Indian insurgents in July 1857. See Barbara English, "The Kanpur Massacres in India in the Revolt of 1857," *Past and Present* 142 (February 1994), for a useful overview of the historiographical debates since the nineteenth century regarding Kanpur's significance as a turning point in this insurgency.

15. Susan Lowes, "'They Couldn't Mash Ants': The Decline of the White and Non-white Elites in Antigua, 1834–1900," in *Small Islands, Large Questions: Society, Culture and Resistance in the Post-emancipation Caribbean*, edited by Karen Fog Olwig (London: Frank Cass, 1994), 50, note 32; also see Douglas Hall, *Five of the Leewards, 1834–1870: The Major Problems of the Postemancipation Period in Antigua, Barbuda, Montserrat, Nevis and St. Kitts* (Barbados: Caribbean Universities Press, 1971), 175–77; and Brian Dyde, *A History of Antigua: The Unsuspected Isle* (London: Macmillan Caribbean, 2000), 175–76.

16. Patrick Bryan, *The Jamaican People, 1880–1902: Race and Social Control* (London: MacMillan Caribbean, 1991), 12.

17. T. Holt, *The Problem of Freedom*, 8, 307–9.

BIBLIOGRAPHY

....

Archives and Manuscript Collections

Antigua Council Meeting Minutes, 1831–1833, National Archives of Antigua and Barbuda, Victoria Park, St. John's, Antigua.

Codrington Papers, R.P. 2616, National Archives of Antigua and Barbuda, Victoria Park, St. John's, Antigua.

Great Britain, Colonial Office Papers, British Public Record Office, National Archives, Kew, London, UK (Colonial Office Series 7/31–111, Papers Pertaining to Antigua, 1831–1858).

Moravian Church Archives, Eastern West Indies Province, Bethlehem, PA, United States.

Papers of Langford Lovell Hodge, Duke Humfrey's Library, Bodleian Library, Oxford University, Oxford, UK.

Wesleyan Methodist Missionary Society Papers, School of Oriental and African Studies Library, London, UK.

West Indian Newspaper Collection, American Antiquarian Society, Worcester, MA, U.S.

Newspapers

Antigua Herald & Gazette (St. John's, Antigua)
Antigua Observer (St. John's, Antigua)
Antigua Times (St. John's, Antigua)
Antigua Weekly Register (St. John's, Antigua)
The Dominican (Roseau, Dominica)
Port of Spain Gazette (Port of Spain, Trinidad)

Published Primary Sources

Candler, John. "John Candler's Visit to Antigua." *Caribbean Studies* 5, no. 3 (1965): 51–57.

Carlyle, Thomas. "Occasional Discourse on the Negro Question." *Fraser's Magazine for Town and Country* 40 (1849): 670–79. Reprinted as "Occasional Discourse on the Nigger Question." London: Thomas Bosworth, 1853.

Davy, John. *The West Indies, Before and Since Slave Emancipation, Comprising the Windward & Leeward Islands' Military Command Founded on Notes and Observations Collected During a Three Years' Residence.* London: W. & F. G. Cash, 1854.

Day, Charles William. *Five Years' Residence in the West Indies.* 2 vols. London: Colburn & Co., 1852.

Findlay, George Gillanders. *History of the Wesleyan Methodist Missionary Society.* 5 vols. London: Epworth Press, 1921–1924.

Great Britain, Parliament, House of Commons. *Papers Presented to Parliament, by Her Majesty's Command, in Explanation of the Measures Adopted by Her Majesty's Government, for Giving Effect to the Act for the Abolition of Slavery throughout the British Colonies. Part IV, Jamaica. Barbados. British Guiana* [London]: n.p., 1837.

————. *The Reports Made for the Year 1846 to the Secretary of State Having the Department of the Colonies in Continuation of the Reports Annually Made by the Governors of the British Colonies . . . Transmitted with the Blue Books for the Year 1846.* [London]: n.p., 1847.

Great Britain, Parliamentary Papers. *Tables of the Revenue, Population, Commerce, &c. of the United Kingdom, and Its Dependencies: Supplement to Part VIII; Colonies—1837 to 1839, Compiled from Official Returns.* [London]: Her Majesty's Stationery Office, 1840.

Gurney, Joseph John. *A Winter in the West Indies, Described in Familiar Letters to Henry Clay, of Kentucky.* London: John Murray; Norwich: Josiah Fletcher, 1840.

Horsford, John. *A Voice from the West Indies: Being a Review of the Character and Results of Missionary Efforts in the British and Other Colonies in the Charibbean Sea with Some Remarks on the Usages, Prejudices, Etc. of the Inhabitants.* London: Alexander Heylin, 1856.

Hovey, Sylvester. *Letters from the West Indies: Relating Especially to the Danish Island St. Croix, and to the British Islands Antigua, Barbadoes, and Jamaica.* New York: Gould and Newman, 1838.

Hughes, Robert Marsh. *The Duties of Judge Advocates, Compiled from Her Majesty's and the Hon. East India Company's Militia Regulations and from the Works of Various Writers of Military Law.* London: Smith, Elder and Co., 1845.

Instructions for the Missionaries of the Church of the Unitas Fratrum, or United Brethren. 2nd ed. London: Printed for the Brethren's Society for the Furtherance of the Gospel among the Heathen, 1840.

Lanaghan, Mrs. [Frances]. *Antigua and the Antiguans: A Full Account of the Colony and Its Inhabitants from the Time of the Caribs to the Present Day.* 2 vols. London: Saunders & Otley, 1844.

Loving, Henry. *Correspondence with the Right Hon. Viscount Goderich, Secretary of State for the Colonies, on the Subject of the Political Rights of the Free Coloured and Black Inhabitants of the Island of Antigua by Henry Loving, a Man of Colour.* London: S. Bagster, 1832.

Lowe, Robeson, ed. *The Codrington Correspondence, 1743–1851, Being a Study of a Recently Discovered Dossier of Letters from the West Indian Islands of Antigua and Barbuda Mostly*

Addressed to the Codringtons of Dodington with Especial Reference to the History of Those Adventurous Times and the Hitherto Unrecorded Postal History of the Antiguan Mail. London: Robeson Lowe, 1951.

Luffman, John. A Brief Account of the Island of Antigua Together with the Customs and Manners of Its Inhabitants as Well White as Black: As Also an Accurate Statement of the Food, Clothing, Labor, and Punishment, of Slaves; In Letters to a Friend, Written in the Years 1786, 1787, 1788. London: T. Cadell, 1789.

McKinnen, Daniel. A Tour through the British West Indies, in the Years 1802 and 1803, Giving a Particular Account of the Bahama Islands. London: J. White, 1804.

Moister, William. Missionary Anecdotes: Sketches, Facts, and Incidents Relating to the Heathen and the Effects of the Gospel in Various Parts of the World. London: Wesleyan Conference Office, 1875.

Oliver, Vere L. The History of the Island of Antigua, One of the Leeward Caribbees in the West Indies, from the First Settlement in 1635 to the Present Time. 2 vols. London: Mitchell and Hughes, 1894.

Periodical Accounts Relating to the Missions of the Church for the United Brethren Established among the Heathen. Vol. 20. London: W. J. M'Dowall for the Brethren's Society for the Furtherance of the Gospel among the Heathen, 1851.

Prince, Mary. The History of Mary Prince, a West Indian Slave. London: F. Westley and A. H. Davis, 1831. Reprinted as Mary Price, The History of Mary Prince: A West Indian Slave. Edited by Sara Salih. New York: Penguin Classics, 2000.

Schaw, Janet. Journal of a Lady of Quality, Being the Narrative of a Journey from Scotland to the West Indies, North Carolina, and Portugal, in the Years 1774–1776. Edited by Evangeline W. Andrews. New Haven, CT: Yale University Press, 1921.

Sewell, William. The Ordeal of Free Labour in the British West Indies. London: Sampson Low & Co., 1862. Reprint, London: Frank Cass & Co., 1968.

Smith, Keithlyn B., and Fernando C. Smith. To Shoot Hard Labour: The Life and Times of Samuel Smith, an Antiguan Workingman, 1877–1982. Scarborough, ON: Edan's Publishers, 1986.

Sturge, Joseph, and Thomas Harvey. The West Indies in 1837; Being the Journal of a Visit to Antigua, Montserrat, Dominica, St. Lucia, Barbados and Jamaica; Undertaken for the Purpose of Ascertaining the Actual Condition of the Negro Population of Those Islands. London: Hamilton, Adams & Co., 1838.

Thome, James A., and Joseph Horace Kimball. Emancipation in the West Indies: A Six Month's Tour in Antigua, Barbados and Jamaica in the Year 1837. New York: American Anti-slavery Society, 1838.

Wesleyan Methodist Missionary Society. Rules and Regulations of the Wesleyan Methodist Sunday School Institution of Saint John's, Antigua. London: D. Marples and Co., 1836.

Secondary Sources

Abu-Lughod, Lila. "The Romance of Resistance: Tracing Transformations of Power through Bedouin Women." American Ethnologist 17, no. 1 (February 1990): 41–55.

Adamson, Alan H. *Sugar without Slaves: The Political Economy of British Guiana, 1838–1904*. New Haven, CT: Yale University Press, 1972.

Adderley, Rosanne. *"New Negroes from Africa": Slave Trade Abolition and Free African Settlement in the Nineteenth-Century Caribbean*. Bloomington: Indiana University Press, 2006.

Alleyne, Mervyn C. *The Construction and Representation of Race and Ethnicity in the Caribbean and the World*. Kingston, Jamaica: University of the West Indies Press, 2002.

Altink, Henrice. "Slavery by Another Name: Apprenticed Women in Jamaican Workhouses in the Period, 1834–1838." *Social History* 26, no. 1 (2001): 40–59.

———. " 'To Wed or Not to Wed?' The Struggle to Define Afro-Jamaican Relationships, 1834–1838." *Journal of Social History* 38, no. 1 (2004): 81–111.

Amussen, Susan Dwyer. *Caribbean Exchanges: Slavery and the Transformation of English Society, 1640–1700*. Chapel Hill: University of North Carolina Press, 2007.

Anderson, John. *Between Slavery and Freedom: Special Magistrate John Anderson's Journal of St. Vincent during the Apprenticeship*. Edited by Roderick McDonald. Philadelphia: University of Pennsylvania Press, 2001.

Andrews, George Reid. *Afro-Latin America, 1800–2000*. Oxford, UK: Oxford University Press, 2004.

Austin-Broos, Diane. *Jamaica Genesis: Religion and the Politics of Moral Orders*. Chicago: University of Chicago Press, 1997.

Bardaglio, Peter W. *Reconstructing the Household: Families, Sex, and the Law in the Nineteenth-Century South*. Chapel Hill: University of North Carolina Press, 1995.

Barickman, B. J. " 'A Bit of Land, Which They Call Roca': Slave Provision Grounds in the Bahian Reconcavo, 1780–1860." *Hispanic American Historical Review* 74, no. 4 (November 1994): 649–87.

Beckles, Hilary McD. *Centering Woman: Gender Discourses in Caribbean Slave Society*. Kingston, Jamaica: Ian Randle Publishers; Princeton, NJ: Markus Wiener Publishers, 1998.

———. "An Economic Life of Their Own: Slaves as Commodity Producers and Distributors in Barbados." In *The Slaves' Economy: Independent Production by Slaves in the Americas*, edited by Ira Berlin and Philip Morgan, 31–47. London: Frank Cass, 1991.

———. *Great House Rules: Landless Emancipation and Workers' Protest in Barbados, 1838–1938*. Kingston, Jamaica: Ian Randle Publishers, 2004.

———. "Historicizing Slavery in West Indian Feminisms." *Feminist Review* 59 (1998): 34–56.

———. *Natural Rebels: A Social History of Enslaved Black Women in Barbados*. New Brunswick, NJ: Rutgers University Press, 1990.

———. "Property Rights in Pleasure: The Marketing of Enslaved Women's Sexuality." In *Caribbean Slavery in the Atlantic World: A Student Reader*, edited by Verene Shepherd and Hilary Beckles, 692–701. Princeton, NJ: Markus Wiener, 2000.

Beckles, Hilary McD., and Verene Shepherd, eds. *Caribbean Freedom: Economy and Society from Emancipation to the Present*. Kingston, Jamaica: Ian Randle Publishers, 1993.

Beier, A. L. *Masterless Men: The Vagrancy Problem in England, 1560–1640*. London: Methuen, 1985.

Bender, Thomas, ed. *The Antislavery Debate: Capitalism and Abolitionism as a Problem in Historical Interpretation*. Berkeley: University of California Press, 1992.

Benitez-Rojo, Antonio. *The Repeating Island: The Caribbean and the Postmodern Perspective*. Durham, NC: Duke University Press, 1992.

Bennett, Herman. *Africans in Colonial Mexico: Absolutism, Christianity, and Afro-Creole Consciousness, 1570–1640*. Bloomington: Indiana University Press, 2004.

Bennett, J. Harry. *Bondsmen and Bishops: Slavery and Apprenticeship on the Codrington Plantations of Barbados, 1710–1838*. Berkeley: University of California Press, 1958.

Berleant, Riva. "The Failure of Agricultural Development in Post-emancipation Barbuda: A Study of Social and Economic Continuity in a West Indian Community." *Boletín de estudios Latino-americanos y del Caribe* 25 (1978): 21–36.

Berlin, Ira. *Many Thousands Gone: The First Two Centuries of Slavery in North America*. Cambridge, MA: Belknap Press of Harvard University Press, 1998.

Berlin, Ira, and Philip Morgan, eds. *Cultivation and Culture: Labor and the Shaping of Black Life in the Americas*. Charlottesville: University of Virginia Press, 1993.

———, eds. *The Slaves' Economy: Independent Production by Slaves in the Americas*. London: Frank Cass, 1991.

Berry, Daina Raimey. *"Swing the Sickle for the Harvest Is Ripe": Gender and Slavery in Antebellum Georgia*. Urbana: University of Illinois Press, 2007.

Besson, Jean. "Freedom and Community: The British West Indies." In *The Meaning of Freedom: Economics, Politics and Culture after Slavery*, edited by Frank McGlynn and Seymour Drescher, 183–200. Pittsburgh, PA: University of Pittsburgh Press, 1992.

———. "Reputation and Respectability Reconsidered: A New Perspective on Afro-Caribbean Peasant Women." In *Women and Change in the Caribbean: A Pan-Caribbean Perspective*, edited by Janet Momsen, 15–37. Kingston, Jamaica: Ian Randle Publishers, 1993.

Besson, Jean, and Janet Momsen, eds. *Land and Development in the Caribbean*. Warwick University Caribbean Studies Series. London: Macmillan, 1987.

Bethell, Leslie. *The Abolition of the Brazilian Slave Trade: Britain, Brazil, and the Slave Trade Question*. Reprint ed. Cambridge, UK: Cambridge University Press, 2009.

Bhabha, Homi. "Of Mimicry and Man: The Ambivalence of Colonial Discourse." In *The Location of Culture*, 121–31. Oxford, UK: Routledge, 1994.

Blackburn, Robin. *The Overthrow of Colonial Slavery, 1776–1848*. London: Verso, 1988.

Blassingame, John. *The Slave Community: Plantation Life in the Antebellum South*. New York: Oxford University Press, 1972.

Boa, Sheena. "Experiences of Women Estate Workers during the Apprenticeship Period in St. Vincent, 1834–38: The Transition from Slavery to Freedom." *Women's History Review* 10, no. 3 (October 2001): 381–408.

———. "Young Ladies and Dissolute Women: Conflicting Views of Culture and Gender in Public Entertainment, Kingstown, St. Vincent, 1838–1888." In *Gender and Slave Emancipation in the Atlantic World*, edited by Pamela Scully and Diana Paton, 247–66. Durham, NC: Duke University Press, 2005.

Bolland, O. Nigel. *The Politics of Labour in the British Caribbean: The Social Origins of Authoritarianism and Democracy in the Labour Movement.* Kingston, Jamaica: Ian Randle Publishers, 2001.

———. "Systems of Domination after Slavery: The Control of Land and Labor in the British West Indies after 1838." *Comparative Studies in Society and History* 23, no. 4 (1981): 591–619.

Brereton, Bridget. "Family Strategies, Gender, and the Shift to Wage Labor in the British Caribbean." In *Gender and Slave Emancipation in the Atlantic World*, edited by Pamela Scully and Diana Paton, 143–61. Durham, NC: Duke University Press, 2005.

———. "Post-emancipation Protest in the Caribbean: The 'Belmanna Riots' in Tobago, 1876." *Caribbean Quarterly* 30, no. 4 (1984): 110–23.

———. *Race Relations in Colonial Trinidad, 1870–1900.* Cambridge, UK: Cambridge University Press, 1979.

Brereton, Bridget, and Kevin Yelvington, eds. *The Colonial Caribbean in Transition: Essays on Postemancipation Social and Cultural History.* Gainesville: University Press of Florida, 1999.

Brown, Christopher Leslie. *Moral Capital: Foundations of British Abolitionism.* Chapel Hill: Published for the Omohundro Institute of Early American History and Culture by the University of North Carolina Press, 2006.

Brown, Christopher Leslie, and Philip D. Morgan, eds., *Arming Slaves: From Classical Times to the Modern Age.* New Haven, CT: Yale University Press, 2006.

Brown, Laurence, and Tara Inniss. "Family Strategies and the Transition to Freedom in Barbados." In *Women and Slavery: The Modern Atlantic*, vol. 2, edited by Gwyn Campbell, Suzanne Miers, and Joseph C. Miller, 172–85. Athens: Ohio University Press, 2008.

Bryan, Patrick. *The Jamaican People, 1880–1902: Race, Class and Social Control.* London: Macmillan, 1991.

Buckridge, Steve O. *The Language of Dress: Resistance and Accommodation in Jamaica, 1760–1890.* Kingston, Jamaica: University of the West Indies Press, 1998.

Burton, Richard. *Afro-Creole: Power, Opposition, and Play in the Caribbean.* Ithaca, NY: Cornell University Press, 1997.

Bush, Barbara. *Slave Women in Caribbean Society: 1650–1838.* London: James Currey, 1990.

———. "White 'Ladies,' Coloured 'Favourites' and Black 'Wenches': Some Considerations on Sex, Race and Class Factors in Social Relations in White Creole Society in the British Caribbean." *Slavery & Abolition* 2, no. 3 (1981): 245–62.

Butler, Kathleen. *The Economics of Emancipation: Jamaica and Barbados, 1823–1843.* Chapel Hill: University of North Carolina Press, 1995.

Butler, Kim D. *Freedoms Given, Freedoms Won: Afro-Brazilians in Post-abolition Sao Paulo and Salvador.* New Brunswick, NJ: Rutgers University Press, 1998.

Byrd, Alexander X. *Captives and Voyagers: Black Migrants across the Eighteenth-Century British Atlantic World.* Baton Rouge: Louisiana State University Press, 2008.

Camp, Stephanie M. H. *Closer to Freedom: Enslaved Women and Everyday Resistance in the Plantation South.* Chapel Hill: University of North Carolina Press, 2004.

Campbell, Carl C. *The Young Colonials: A Social History of Education in Trinidad and To-bago, 1834–1939.* Kingston, Jamaica: University of the West Indies, 1996.

Campbell, John. "As 'A Kind of Freeman'? Slaves' Market-Related Activities in the South Carolina Up Country, 1800–1860." In *Cultivation and Culture: Labor and the Shaping of Black Life in the Americas*, edited by Ira Berlin and Philip Morgan, 243–74. Charlottesville: University of Virginia Press, 1993.

Campbell, Mavis. *The Dynamics of Change in Slave Society: A Socio-political History of the Free Coloreds of Jamaica, 1800–1865.* London: Associated University Presses, 1976.

———. *The Maroons of Jamaica, 1655–1796: A History of Resistance, Collaboration and Betrayal.* South Hadley, MA: Mergin and Garvey, 1988.

Carmody, Caroline M. "First among Equals: Antiguan Patterns of Local Level Leadership." PhD diss., New York University, 1978.

Cervantes-Rodríguez, Ana Margarita. *International Migration in Cuba: Accumulation, Imperial Designs, and Transnational Social Fields.* University Park: Pennsylvania State University Press, 2010.

Childs, Matt. *The 1812 Aponte Rebellion in Cuba and the Struggle against Atlantic Slavery.* Chapel Hill: University of North Carolina Press, 2006.

Clegg, Claude A. *The Price of Liberty: African Americans and the Making of Liberia.* Chapel Hill: University of North Carolina Press, 2004.

Clinton, Catherine, and Michele Gillespie, eds. *The Devil's Lane: Sex and Race in the Early South.* Oxford, UK: Oxford University Press, 1997.

Cooper, Frederick, Thomas Holt, and Rebecca Scott. *Beyond Slavery: Explorations of Race, Labor, and Citizenship in Postemancipation Societies.* Chapel Hill: University of North Carolina Press, 2000.

Cooper, Frederick, and Ann Laura Stoler. *Tensions of Empire: Colonial Cultures in a Bourgeois World.* Berkeley: University of California Press, 1997.

Cox, Edward L. *Free Coloreds in the Slave Societies of St. Kitts and Grenada, 1763–1833.* Knoxville: University of Tennessee Press, 1984.

Cox, Oliver Cromwell. *Caste, Class, and Race: A Study in Social Dynamics.* Garden City, NY: Doubleday, 1948.

Craton, Michael. *Empire, Enslavement and Freedom in the Caribbean.* Kingston, Jamaica: Ian Randle Publishers, 1997.

Craven, Paul, and Douglas Hay. "The Criminalization of 'Free' Labour: Master and Servant in Comparative Perspective." In *Unfree Labour in the Development of the Atlantic World*, edited by Paul E. Lovejoy and Nicholas Rogers, 71–101. Ilford, UK: Frank Cass, 1994.

Cross, Malcolm, and Gad Heuman, eds. *Labour in the Caribbean: From Emancipation to Independence.* London: Macmillan, 1988.

Cumming, Mark, ed. *The Carlyle Encyclopedia.* Madison, NJ: Farleigh Dickinson University Press, 2004.

Dadzie, Stella. "Searching for the Invisible Woman: Slavery and Resistance in Jamaica." *Race and Class* 32, no. 2 (1990): 21–38.

De Barros, Juanita. *Order and Place in a Colonial City: Patterns of Struggle and Resistance* in *Georgetown, British Guiana, 1889–1924*. Montreal: McGill-Queen's University Press, 2003.

———. *Reproducing the British Caribbean: Sex, Gender, and Population Politics after Slavery*. Chapel Hill: University of North Carolina Press, 2014.

de la Fuente, Alejandro. "Slave Law and Claims-Making in Cuba: The Tannenbaum Debate Revisited." *Law and History Review* 22, no. 2 (2004): 339–70.

Dubois, Laurent. *Avengers of the New World: The Story of the Haitian Revolution*. Cambridge, MA: Belknap Press of Harvard University Press, 2004.

———. *A Colony of Citizens: Revolution and Slave Emancipation in the French Caribbean, 1787–1804*. Chapel Hill: Published for the Omohundro Institute of Early American History and Culture by the University of North Carolina Press, 2004.

Dunaway, Wilma. *The African-American Family in Slavery and Emancipation*. Cambridge, UK: Cambridge University Press, 2003.

Dyde, Brian. *A History of Antigua: The Unsuspected Isle*. London: Macmillan Publishers, 2000.

Eltis, David, and Paul Lachance. "The Demographic Decline of Caribbean Slave Populations: New Evidence from the Transatlantic and Intra-American Slave Trades." In *Extending the Frontiers: Essays on the New Transatlantic Slave Trade Database*, edited by David Eltis and David Richardson, 335–64. New Haven, CT: Yale University Press, 2008.

Eltis, David, and David Richardson. "A New Assessment of the Transatlantic Slave Trade." In *Extending the Frontiers: Essays on the New Transatlantic Slave Trade Database*, edited by David Eltis and Richardson, 1–62. New Haven, CT: Yale University Press, 2008.

Emmer, Pieter. "Between Slavery and Freedom: The Period of Apprenticeship in Suriname (Dutch Guiana), 1863–1873." *Slavery & Abolition* 14, no. 1 (1993): 87–105.

English, Barbara. "The Kanpur Massacres in India in the Revolt of 1857." *Past and Present* 142 (February 1994): 169–78.

Eudell, Demetrius L. *The Political Languages of Emancipation in the British Caribbean and the U.S. South*. Chapel Hill: University of North Carolina Press, 2002.

Farquhar, David. *Missions and Society in the Leeward Islands, 1810–1850: An Ecclesiastical and Social Analysis*. Boston: Mount Prospect Press, 1999.

Fergus, Howard. *A History of Education in the British Leeward Islands, 1835–1945*. Kingston, Jamaica: University of the West Indies Press, 2003.

Fernandez Olmos, Margarite, and Lizabeth Paravisini-Gebert. *Sacred Possessions: Vodou, Santeria, Obeah, and the Caribbean*. New Brunswick, NJ: Rutgers University Press, 1997.

Ferrer, Ada. *Insurgent Cuba: Race, Nation, and Revolution, 1868–1898*. Chapel Hill: University of North Carolina Press, 1999.

———. "Talk about Haiti: The Archive and the Atlantic's Haitian Revolution." In *Tree of Liberty: Cultural Legacies of the Haitian Revolution*, edited by Doris Garraway, 21–40. Charlottesville: University of Virginia Press, 2008.

Fick, Carolyn. *The Making of Haiti: The Saint Domingue Revolution from Below.* Knoxville: University of Tennessee Press, 1990.

Fields, Barbara J. *Slavery and Freedom on the Middle Ground: Maryland during the Nineteenth Century.* New Haven, CT: Yale University Press, 1985.

———. "Slavery, Race, and Ideology in the United States of America." *New Left Review* 181 (1990): 95–118.

Figes, Orlando. *The Crimean War: A History.* London: Macmillan, 2010.

Figueroa, Luis A. *Sugar, Slavery, and Freedom in Nineteenth-Century Puerto Rico.* Chapel Hill: University of North Carolina Press, 2005.

Foner, Eric. *Free Soil, Free Labor, Free Men: The Ideology of the Republican Party before the Civil War.* Reprint ed. New York: Oxford University Press, 1995.

———. *Nothing but Freedom: Emancipation and Its Legacy.* Baton Rouge: Louisiana State University Press, 1983.

———. *Reconstruction: America's Unfinished Revolution, 1863–1877.* New York: Harper and Row, 1988.

Fox-Genovese, Elizabeth. *Within the Plantation Household: Black and White Women of the Old South.* Chapel Hill: University of North Carolina Press, 1988.

Frankel, Noralee. *Freedom's Women: Black Women and Families in Civil War Era Mississippi.* Bloomington: Indiana University Press, 1999.

Frucht, Richard. "Emancipation and Revolt in the West Indies: St. Kitts, 1834." *Science and Society* 39 (1975): 199–214.

Fuentes, Marisa. "Power and Historical Figuring: Rachael Pringle Polgreen's Troubled Archive." *Gender and History* 22 (2010): 564–84.

Gaspar, David Barry. *Bondmen and Rebels: A Study of Master-Slave Relations in Antigua.* Baltimore, MD: Johns Hopkins University Press, 1985.

———. "Slavery, Amelioration, and Sunday Markets in Antigua, 1823–1831." *Slavery & Abolition* 9, no. 1 (1988): 1–28.

Gaspar, David Barry, and Darlene Clark Hine. *Beyond Bondage: Free Women of Color in the Americas.* Urbana: University of Illinois Press, 2004.

———, eds. *More Than Chattel: Black Women and Slavery in the Americas.* Bloomington: Indiana University Press, 1996.

Gikandi, Simon. *Slavery and the Culture of Taste.* Princeton, NJ: Princeton University Press, 2011.

Gilroy, Paul. *The Black Atlantic: Modernity and Double Consciousness.* Cambridge, MA: Harvard University Press, 1993.

Glymph, Thavolia. *Out of the House of Bondage: The Transformation of the Plantation Household.* Cambridge, UK: Cambridge University Press, 2008.

Goldberg, David Theo, ed. *Anatomy of Racism.* Minneapolis: University of Minnesota Press, 1990.

Gomez, Michael. *Exchanging Our Country Marks: The Transformation of African Identities in the Colonial and Antebellum South.* Chapel Hill: University of North Carolina Press, 1998.

Gott, Richard. *Britain's Empire: Resistance, Repression and Revolt.* London: Verso, 2011.

Goveia, Elsa V. *Slave Society in the British Leeward Islands at the End of the Eighteenth Century.* New Haven, CT: Yale University Press, 1965.

Gray White, Deborah. *Ar'n't I a Woman? Female Slaves in the Plantation South.* New York: Norton, 1985.

Green, Cecilia A. " 'The Abandoned Lower Class of Females': Class, Gender, and Penal Discipline in Barbados, 1875–1929." *Comparative Studies in Society and History* 53, no. 1 (2011): 144–79.

Green, William. *British Slave Emancipation: The Sugar Colonies and the Great Experiment, 1830–1865.* Oxford, UK: Clarendon Press, 1976.

Gregory, Desmond. *The Beneficent Usurpers: A History of the British in Madeira.* Cranbury, NJ: Associated University Presses, 1988.

Guha, Ranajit. *Elementary Aspects of Peasant Insurgency in Colonial India.* New Delhi: Oxford University Press, 1983; reprint ed., Durham, NC: Duke University Press, 1999.

Gutman, Herbert. *The Black Family in Slavery and Freedom, 1750–1925.* New York: Pantheon Books, 1976.

Hahn, Steven. *A Nation under Our Feet: Black Political Struggles in the Rural South from Slavery to the Great Migration.* Cambridge, MA: Harvard University Press, 2003.

Hall, Catherine. *Civilising Subjects: Colony and Metropole in the English Imagination, 1830–1867.* Chicago: University of Chicago Press, 2002.

Hall, Douglas. *Five of the Leewards, 1834–1870: The Major Problems of the Postemancipation Period in Antigua, Barbuda, Montserrat, Nevis and St. Kitts.* St. Laurence, Barbados: Caribbean Universities Press, 1971.

———. "The Flight from the Estates Reconsidered: The British West Indies, 1838–42." *Journal of Caribbean History* 10–11 (1978): 7–24.

———. *Free Jamaica, 1838–1865: An Economic History.* New Haven, CT: Yale University Press, 1959.

Hall, Neville A. T. "Maritime Maroons: 'Grand Marronage' from the Danish West Indies." *William and Mary Quarterly* 42, no. 4 (October 1985): 476–98.

———. "The Victor Vanquished: Emancipation in St. Croix: Its Antecedents and Immediate Aftermath." *New West Indian Guide* 58 (1984): 3–36.

Hall, Stuart. "Race, Articulation and Societies Structured in Dominance." In *Sociological Theories: Race and Colonialism,* edited by Marion O'Callaghan, 305–45. Paris: UNESCO, 1980.

Hamilton, Keith, and Patrick Salmon, eds. *Slavery, Diplomacy, and Empire: Britain and the Suppression of the Slave Trade, 1807–1975.* Eastbourne, UK: Sussex Academic Press, 2009.

Handler, Jerome S. "Slave Medicine and Obeah in Barbados, ca. 1650 to 1834." *New West Indian Guide* 74 (2000): 57–90.

Hannaford, Ivan. *Race: The History of an Idea in the West.* Baltimore, MD: Johns Hopkins University Press, 1996.

Hartman, Saidiya V. *Lose Your Mother: A Journey along the Atlantic Slave Route.* New York: Farrar, Straus and Giroux, 2007.

————. *Scenes of Subjection: Terror, Slavery, and Self-Making in Nineteenth-Century America.* Oxford, UK: Oxford University Press, 1997.

————. "Venus in Two Acts." *Small Axe* 26 (June 2008): 1–14.

Helg, Aline. *Our Rightful Share: The Afro-Cuban Struggle for Equality, 1886–1912.* Chapel Hill: University of North Carolina Press, 1995.

Henry, Paget. *Caliban's Reason: Introducing Afro-Caribbean Philosophy.* New York: Routledge, 2000.

————. *Peripheral Capitalism and Underdevelopment in Antigua.* New Brunswick, NJ: Transaction Books, 1985.

————. *Shouldering Antigua and Barbuda: The Life of V. C. Bird.* Hertfordshire, UK: Hansib Publications, 2010.

Herskovits, Melville. *The Myth of the Negro Past.* New York: Harper & Bros., 1941.

Hertzman, Marc. *Making Samba: A New History of Race and Music in Brazil.* Durham, NC: Duke University Press, 2013.

Heuman, Gad J. *Between Black and White: Race, Politics, and the Free Coloreds in Jamaica, 1792–1865.* Westport, CT: Greenwood Press, 1981.

————. *The Killing Time: The Morant Bay Rebellion in Jamaica.* Knoxville: University of Tennessee Press, 1994.

————. "Post-emancipation Resistance in the Caribbean: An Overview." In *Small Islands, Large Questions: Society, Culture and Resistance in the Post-emancipation Caribbean*, edited by Karen Fog Olwig, 123–34. London: Frank Cass, 1994.

————. "Riots and Resistance in the Caribbean at the Moment of Freedom." In *After Slavery: Emancipation and Its Discontents*, edited by Howard Temperley, 135–49. London: Frank Cass, 2000.

Heuman, Gad, and David Trotman, eds. *Contesting Freedom: Control and Resistance in the Post-emancipation Caribbean.* Oxford, UK: Macmillan Caribbean, 2005.

Highmore, Ben. *Everyday Life and Cultural Theory: An Introduction.* London: Routledge, 2002.

Higman, Barry W. "Remembering Slavery: The Rise, Decline and Revival of Emancipation Day in the English-Speaking Caribbean." *Slavery & Abolition* 19, no. 1 (1998): 90–105.

————. *Slave Populations of the British Caribbean, 1807–1834.* Baltimore, MD: Johns Hopkins University Press, 1984.

Hine, Darlene Clark. "Lifting the Veil, Shattering the Silence: Black Women's History in Slavery and Freedom." In *The State of Afro-American History: Past, Present and Future*, edited by Darlene Clark Hine, 223–49. Baton Rouge: Louisiana State University Press, 1986.

Hine, Darlene Clark, and Jacqueline McLeod, eds. *Crossing Boundaries: Comparative History of Black People in Diaspora.* Bloomington: Indiana University Press, 1999.

Hobsbawm, Eric. *Primitive Rebels: Studies in Archaic Forms of Social Movement in the 19th and 20th Centuries.* New York: W. W. Norton and Co., 1965.

Holt, Sharon Ann. "Making Freedom Pay: Freedpeople Working for Themselves, North Carolina, 1865–1900." *Journal of Southern History* 60, no. 2 (1994): 228–62.

Holt, Thomas. "Marking: Race, Race-Making, and the Writing of History." *American Historical Review* 100 (1995): 1–20.

——. *The Problem of Freedom: Race, Labor, and Politics in Jamaica and Britain, 1832–1938.* Baltimore, MD: Johns Hopkins University Press, 1992.

House-Midamba, Bessie, and Felix K. Ekechi, eds. *African Market Women and Economic Power: The Role of Women in African Economic Development.* Westport, CT: Greenwood Press, 1995.

Hunefeldt, Christine. *Paying the Price of Freedom: Family and Labor among Lima's Slaves, 1800–1854.* Berkeley: University of California Press, 1995.

Hunter, Tera W. *To 'Joy My Freedom: Southern Black Women's Lives and Labors after the Civil War.* Cambridge, MA: Harvard University Press, 1997.

James, C. L. R. *The Black Jacobins: Toussaint L'Ouverture and the San Domingo Revolution,* 2nd rev. ed. New York: Vintage Books, 1963.

James, Winston. *Holding Aloft the Banner of Ethiopia: Caribbean Radicalism in Early Twentieth-Century America.* New York: Verso, 1998.

Johnson, Howard. *The Bahamas from Slavery to Servitude, 1783–1933.* Gainesville: University of Florida Press, 1996.

——. "Patterns of Policing in the Post-emancipation British Caribbean." In *Policing the Empire: Government, Authority and Control, 1830–1940,* edited by David Anderson and David Killingray, 71–91. Manchester, UK: Manchester University Press, 1991.

Johnson, Walter. *Soul by Soul: Life inside the Antebellum Slave Market.* Cambridge, MA: Harvard University Press, 1999.

——. "Time and Revolution in African America." In *Rethinking American History in a Global Age,* edited by Thomas Bender, 148–67. Berkeley: University of California Press, 2002.

Jones, Cecily. "Contesting the Boundaries of Gender, Race, and Sexuality in Barbados Plantation Society." *Women's History Review* 12, no. 2 (2003): 195–231.

Joseph, Gilbert. "On the Trail of Latin American Bandits: A Reexamination of Peasant Resistance." *Latin American Research Review* 25, no. 3 (1990): 7–53.

Joseph, Gilbert, and Daniel Nugent. "Popular Culture and State Formation in Revolutionary Mexico." In *Everyday Forms of State Formation: Revolution and the Negotiation of Rule in Modern Mexico,* edited by Gilbert Joseph and Daniel Nugent, 3–23. Durham, NC: Duke University Press, 1994.

Jung, Moon-Ho. *Coolies and Cane: Race, Labor, and Sugar in the Age of Emancipation.* Baltimore, MD: Johns Hopkins University Press, 2006.

Kars, Marjoleine. *Breaking Loose Together: The Regulator Rebellion in Pre-revolutionary North Carolina.* Chapel Hill: University of North Carolina Press, 2002.

Kelley, Robin D. G. *Freedom Dreams: The Black Radical Imagination.* Boston: Beacon Press, 2002.

——. *Race Rebels: Culture, Politics, and the Black Working Class.* New York: The Free Press, 1994.

Kenny, Gale. *Contentious Liberties: American Abolitionists in Post-emancipation Jamaica, 1834–1866.* Athens: University of Georgia Press, 2010.

Kerr, Paulette A. "Victims or Strategists? Female Lodging-House Keepers in Jamaica." In *Engendering History: Caribbean Women in Historical Perspective*, edited by Verene A. Shepherd, Bridget Brereton, and Barbara Bailey, 197–212. Kingston, Jamaica: Ian Randle Publishers, 1995.

Kincaid, Jamaica. *A Small Place*. New York: Farrar, Straus, Giroux, 1988.

King, Peter. *Crime and Law in England, 1750–1840: Remaking Justice from the Margins*. Cambridge, UK: Cambridge University Press, 2006.

Knight, Franklin. *Race, Ethnicity, and Class: Forging the Plural Society in Latin America and the Caribbean*. Waco, TX: Baylor University Press, 1998.

Knight, Franklin, and Colin Palmer, eds. *The Modern Caribbean*. Chapel Hill: University of North Carolina Press, 1989.

Konadu, Kwasi. *The Akan Diaspora in the Americas*. New York: Oxford University Press, 2010.

Lake, Edgar. "Antigua and the Antiguans: The Question of Its Authorship." *The Antigua and Barbuda Review of Books* 6, no. 1 (Summer 2013): 112–46.

Lambert, David. *White Creole Culture, Politics and Identity during the Age of Abolition*. Cambridge, UK: Cambridge University Press, 2005.

Lazarus-Black, Mindie. *Legitimate Acts and Illegal Encounters: Law and Society in Barbuda and Antigua*. Washington, DC: Smithsonian Institution Press, 1994.

Lefebvre, Henri. *Critique of Everyday Life*. Vol. 1, *Introduction*. Reprint ed. London: Verso, 1991.

Lewis, Gordon. *The Growth of the Modern West Indies*, reprint ed., with an introduction by Franklin Knight. Kingston, Jamaica: Ian Randle Publishers, 2004.

———. *Main Currents in Caribbean Thought: The Historical Evolution of Caribbean Society in Its Ideological Aspects, 1492–1900*, reprint ed., with an introduction by Anthony Maingot. Lincoln: University of Nebraska Press, 2004.

Levy, Claude. *Emancipation, Sugar and Federalism: Barbados and the West Indies, 1833–1876*. Gainesville: University of Florida Press, 1980.

———. "Slavery and the Emancipation Movement in Barbados 1650–1833." *Journal of Negro History* 55, no. 1 (January 1970): 1–14.

Lightfoot, Natasha. "The Hart Sisters of Antigua: Evangelical Activism and 'Respectable' Public Politics in the Era of Black Atlantic Slavery." In *Toward an Intellectual History of Black Women*, edited by Mia Bay, Farah J. Griffin, Martha S. Jones, and Barbara D. Savage, 53–72. Chapel Hill: University of North Carolina Press, 2015.

———. " 'Their Coats Were Tied Up Like Men': Women Rebels in Antigua's 1858 Uprising." *Slavery & Abolition* 31, no. 4 (2010): 527–45.

Linebaugh, Peter. *The London Hanged: Crime and Civil Society in the Eighteenth Century*. New York: Penguin, 1992.

Lobdell, Richard. "Women in the Jamaican Labour Force, 1881–1921." *Social and Economic Studies* 37, nos. 1–2 (1988): 203–40.

Louis, Michael. " 'An Equal Right to the Soil': The Rise of a Peasantry in St. Lucia." PhD diss., Johns Hopkins University, 1982.

Lovejoy, Paul. "The African Diaspora: Revisionist Interpretations of Ethnicity, Culture and Religion under Slavery." *Studies in the World History of Slavery, Abolition and Emancipation* 2 (1997): 1–23.

Lowenthal, David, and Colin G. Clarke. "Slave-Breeding in Barbuda: The Past of a Negro Myth." *Annals of the New York Academy of Sciences* 292 (1977): 510–33.

Lowes, Susan. "The Peculiar Class: The Formation, Collapse, and Reformation of the Middle Class in Antigua, West Indies, 1834–1940." PhD diss., Columbia University, 1994.

———. "'They Couldn't Mash Ants': The Decline of the White and Non-white Elites in Antigua, 1834–1900." In *Small Islands, Large Questions: Society, Culture and Resistance in the Post-emancipation Caribbean*, edited by Karen Fog Olwig, 31–52. London: Frank Cass, 1994.

Maingot, Anthony P. "Race, Color, and Class in the Caribbean." In *Americas: New Interpretive Essays*, edited by Alfred Stepan, 220–47. New York: Oxford University Press, 1992.

Mair, Lucille. *The Rebel Woman in the British West Indies*. Kingston: Institute of Jamaica, 1975.

Markovits, Stephanie. *The Crimean War in the British Imagination*. Cambridge, UK: Cambridge University Press, 2009.

Marshall, Woodville. "Apprenticeship and Labour Relations in Four Windward Islands." In *Abolition and Its Aftermath: The Historical Context, 1790–1916*, edited by David Richardson, 203–24. London: Frank Cass, 1985.

———. "The Post-slavery Labour Problem Revisited." In *Slavery, Freedom, and Gender: The Dynamics of Caribbean Society*, edited by Brian Moore, 115–32. Kingston, Jamaica: University of the West Indies Press, 2001.

———. "'Vox Populi': The St. Vincent Riots and Disturbances of 1862." In *Trade, Government and Society in Caribbean History: Essays Presented to Douglas Hall*, edited by Barry Higman, 83–115. Kingston, Jamaica: Caribbean Universities Press, 1983.

———. "'We Be Wise to Many More Tings': Blacks' Hopes and Expectations of Emancipation." In *Caribbean Freedom: Economy and Society from Emancipation to the Present*, edited by Hilary Beckles and Verene Shepherd, 12–20. Kingston, Jamaica: Ian Randle Publishers, 1993.

Martínez-Vergne, Teresita. "The Liberation of Women in the Caribbean: Research Perspectives for the Study of Gender Relations in the Post-emancipation Period." *Caribbean Studies* 27, nos. 1–2 (1994): 5–36.

———. *Shaping the Discourse on Space: Charity and Its Wards in Nineteenth-Century San Juan, Puerto Rico*. Austin: University of Texas Press, 1999.

Mason, J. C. S. *The Moravian Church and the Missionary Awakening in England, 1760–1800*. Suffolk, UK: Boydell & Brewer, 2001.

Matos-Rodríguez, Félix V. "Street Vendors, Peddlers, Shop-Owners and Domestics: Some Aspects of Women's Economic Roles in Nineteenth-Century San Juan, Puerto Rico, 1820–1870." In *Engendering History: Caribbean Women in Historical Perspective*, edited by Verene Shepherd, Bridget Brereton, and Barbara Bailey, 176–96. Kingston: Ian Randle; London: James Currey, 1995.

Matthews, Gelien. *Caribbean Slave Revolts and the British Abolitionist Movement*. Baton Rouge: Louisiana State University Press, 2006.

McClintock, Anne. *Imperial Leather: Race, Gender and Sexuality in the Colonial Contest*. New York: Routledge, 1995.

McDonald, Roderick. *The Economy and Material Culture of Slaves: Goods and Chattels on the Sugar Plantations of Jamaica and Louisiana*. Baton Rouge: Louisiana State University Press, 1993.

McGlynn, Frank, and Seymour Drescher, eds. *The Meaning of Freedom: Economics, Politics, and Culture after Slavery*. Pittsburgh, PA: University of Pittsburgh Press, 1992.

Mehta, Uday. "Liberal Strategies of Exclusion." *Politics and Society* 18 (December 1990): 427–54.

Menezes, Mary Noel. "The Madeiran Portuguese Woman in Guyanese Society, 1830–1930." In *The Colonial Caribbean in Transition: Essays on Post-Emancipation Social and Cultural History*, edited by Bridget Brereton and Kevin Yelvington, 159–73. Gainesville: University of Florida Press, 1999.

Midgley, Clare. *Women against Slavery: The British Campaigns, 1780–1870*. New York: Routledge, 1992.

Miers Suzanne, and Richard Roberts, eds. *The End of Slavery in Africa*. Madison: University of Wisconsin Press, 1988.

Mintz, Sidney. *Caribbean Transformations*. Chicago: Aldine Publishing, 1974.

———. "From Plantations to Peasantries in the Caribbean." In *Caribbean Contours*, edited by Sidney Mintz and Sally Price, 127–53. Baltimore, MD: Johns Hopkins University Press, 1985.

———. *Sweetness and Power: The Place of Sugar in Modern History*. New York: Viking. 1985.

Mintz, Sidney, and Douglas Hall. "The Origins of the Jamaican Internal Marketing System." *Yale University Publications in Anthropology* 57 (1960): 1–26.

Mintz, Sidney, and Richard Price. *The Birth of African-American Culture: An Anthropological Perspective*. Philadelphia: Institute for the Study of Human Issues, 1976.

Mitchell, Dayo. "The Ambiguous Distinctions of Descent: Free People of Color and the Construction of Citizenship in Trinidad and Dominica, 1800–1838." PhD diss., University of Virginia, 2004.

Moitt, Bernard. *Slave Women in the French Antilles, 1635–1848*. Bloomington: Indiana University Press, 2001.

Moore, Brian. *Cultural Power, Resistance, and Pluralism: Colonial Guyana, 1838–1900*. Montreal: McGill-Queen's University Press, 1995.

———. *Race, Power, and Social Segmentation in Colonial Society: Guyana after Slavery, 1838–1891*. New York: Gordon and Breach Science Publishers, 1987.

Moore, Brian, Barry Higman, and Patrick Bryan, eds. *Slavery, Freedom, and Gender: The Dynamics of Caribbean Society*. Kingston, Jamaica: University of the West Indies Press, 2001.

Morgan, Jennifer. *Laboring Women: Reproduction and Gender in New World Slavery*. Philadelphia: University of Pennsylvania Press, 2004.

———. " 'Some Could Suckle over Their Shoulder': Male Travelers, Female Bodies, and the Gendering of Racial Ideology, 1500–1770." *William and Mary Quarterly* 54, no. 1 (1997): 167–92.

Morgan, Kenneth. *Slavery and the British Empire: From Africa to America.* Oxford, UK: Oxford University Press, 2007.

Morrissey, Marietta. *Slave Women in the New World: Gender Stratification in the Caribbean.* Lawrence: University of Kansas Press, 1989.

Morton, Patricia, ed. *Discovering the Women in Slavery: Emancipating Perspectives on the American Past.* Athens: University of Georgia Press, 1996.

Mullin, Michael. *Africa in America: Slave Acculturation and Resistance in the American South and the British Caribbean, 1736–1831.* Urbana: University of Illinois Press, 1992.

Murphy, Joseph. *Working the Spirit: Ceremonies of the African Diaspora.* New York: Beacon Press, 1994.

Murray, David. *Odious Commerce: Britain, Spain, and the Abolition of the Cuban Slave Trade.* Cambridge, UK: Cambridge University Press, 2002.

Neptune, Harvey. *Caliban and the Yankees: Trinidad and the United States Occupation.* Chapel Hill: University of North Carolina Press, 2007.

Netzloff, Mark. *England's Internal Colonies: Class, Capital, and the Literature of Early Modern English Colonialism.* London: Palgrave Macmillan, 2003.

Newton, Melanie. *The Children of Africa in the Colonies: Free People of Color in Barbados in the Age of Emancipation.* Baton Rouge: Louisiana State University Press, 2008.

———. "The King v. Robert James, a Slave, for Rape: Inequality, Gender and British Slave Emancipation, 1823–1833." *Comparative Studies in Society and History* 47, no. 3 (2005): 583–610.

———. " 'New Ideas of Correctness': Gender, Amelioration, and Emancipation in Barbados, 1810s–50s." *Slavery & Abolition* 21, no. 3 (2000): 94–124.

Nicholson, Desmond V. *Antigua, Barbuda and Redonda: A Historical Sketch.* St. John's: Museum of Antigua and Barbuda, 1991.

Northrup, David. *Indentured Labor in the Age of Imperialism, 1834–1922.* Cambridge, UK: Cambridge University Press, 1995.

O'Hanlon, Rosalind. "Recovering the Subject: Subaltern Studies and Histories of Resistance in Colonial South Asia." *Modern Asian Studies* 22, no. 1 (1988): 189–224.

Okihiro, Gary Y., ed. *In Resistance: Studies in African, Caribbean and Afro-American History.* Amherst: University of Massachusetts Press, 1986.

Olsen, Kristin. *Daily Life in 18th-Century England.* Westport, CT: Greenwood Publishing, 1999.

Olwig, Karen Fog, ed. *Small Islands, Large Questions: Society, Culture and Resistance in the Post-emancipation Caribbean.* London: Frank Cass, 1994.

O'Neal, Eugenia. *From the Field to the Legislature: A History of Women in the Virgin Islands.* Westport, CT: Greenwood Press, 2001.

Ortner, Sherry. "Resistance and the Problem of Ethnographic Refusal." *Comparative Studies in Society and History* 37, no. 1 (1995): 163–93.

Paton, Diana. "Decency, Dependence and the Lash: Gender and the British Debate over Slave Emancipation, 1830–34." *Slavery & Abolition* 17, no. 3 (1996): 163–84.

————. "The Flight from the Fields Reconsidered: Gender Ideologies and Women's Labor after Slavery in Jamaica." In *Reclaiming the Political in Latin American History: Essays from the North*, edited by Gilbert M. Joseph, 175–204. Durham, NC: Duke University Press, 1999.

————. *No Bond but the Law: Punishment, Race, and Gender in Jamaican State Formation, 1780–1870*. Durham, NC: Duke University Press, 2004.

Paton, Diana, and Maarit Forde, eds. *Obeah and Other Powers: The Politics of Caribbean Religion and Healing*. Durham, NC: Duke University Press, 2012.

Patterson, Orlando. "Persistence, Continuity, and Change in the Jamaican Working-Class Family." *Journal of Family History* 7, no. 2 (1982): 135–61.

————. *Slavery and Social Death: A Comparative Study*. Cambridge, MA: Harvard University Press, 1982.

————. *The Sociology of Slavery: An Analysis of the Origins, Development and Structure of Negro Slavery in Jamaica*. London: MacGibbon and Kee, 1967.

Peabody, Sue. "*Negresse, Mulatresse, Citoyenne*: Gender and Emancipation in the French Caribbean, 1650–1848." In *Gender and Slave Emancipation*, edited by Pamela Scully and Diana Paton, 56–78. Durham, NC: Duke University Press, 2005.

Piccato, Pablo. *City of Suspects: Crime in Mexico City, 1900–1931*. Durham, NC: Duke University Press, 2001.

Polanyi, Karl. *The Great Transformation*. Boston: Beacon Press, 1957.

Proctor, Robert. "Early Developments in Barbadian Education." *Journal of Negro Education* 49, no. 2 (1980): 184–95.

Reddock, Rhoda E. "Women and Slavery in the Caribbean: A Feminist Perspective." *Latin American Perspectives* 12, no. 1 (1985): 63–80.

————. *Women, Labour, and Politics in Trinidad and Tobago: A History*. Kingston: Ian Randle Publishers, 1994.

Rediker, Marcus, and Peter Linebaugh. *The Many-Headed Hydra: Sailors, Slaves, Commoners, and the Hidden History of the Revolutionary Atlantic*. Boston: Beacon Press, 2001.

Regosin, Elizabeth. *Freedom's Promise: Ex-Slave Families and Citizenship in the Age of Emancipation*. Charlottesville: University of Virginia Press, 2002.

Reid, Douglas. "The Decline of Saint Monday, 1766–1866." *Past and Present* 71 (1976): 76–101.

Reis, Joao Jose. *Slave Rebellion in Brazil: The Muslim Uprising of Bahia in 1835*. Baltimore, MD: Johns Hopkins University Press, 1993.

Richards, Novelle. *The Struggle and the Conquest*. London: Eyre and Spottiswoode, 1967.

Richardson, Bonham. *Caribbean Migrants: Environment and Human Survival on St. Kitts-Nevis*. Knoxville: University of Tennessee Press, 1983.

————. *Igniting the Caribbean's Past: Fire in British West Indian History*. Chapel Hill: University of North Carolina Press, 2004.

Robertson, Claire, and Martin Klein, eds. *Women and Slavery in Africa*. Madison: University of Wisconsin Press, 1983.

Rodney, Walter. *A History of the Guyanese Working People, 1881–1905.* Baltimore, MD: Johns Hopkins University Press, 1981.

Rodriguez-Silva, Ileana. "A Conspiracy of Silence: Blackness, Class, and National Identities in Post-Emancipation Puerto Rico, 1850–1930." PhD diss., University of Wisconsin, Madison, 2004.

Rosen, Hannah. *Terror in the Heart of Freedom: Citizenship, Sexual Violence, and the Meaning of Race in the Postemancipation South.* Chapel Hill: University of North Carolina Press, 2009.

Rugemer, Edward. *The Problem of Emancipation: The Caribbean Roots of the American Civil War.* Baton Rouge: Louisiana State University Press, 2008.

Safa, Helen I. "Economic Autonomy and Sexual Equality in Caribbean Society." *Social and Economic Studies* 35, no. 3 (1986): 1–21.

San Miguel, Pedro L. "Economic Activities Other Than Sugar." In *General History of the Caribbean*, vol. 4, *The Long Nineteenth Century: Nineteenth-Century Transformations*, edited by K. O. Laurence, 104–48. London: Macmillan Education/ UNESCO, 2011.

Schmidt-Nowara, Christopher. *Empire and Antislavery: Spain, Cuba, and Puerto Rico, 1833–1874.* Pittsburgh, PA: University of Pittsburgh Press, 1999.

Schuler, Monica. *"Alas, Alas, Kongo": A Social History of Indentured African Immigration into Jamaica, 1841–1865.* Baltimore, MD: Johns Hopkins University Press, 1980.

———. "Liberated Africans in Nineteenth-Century Guyana." In *Slavery, Freedom and Gender: The Dynamics of Caribbean Society*, edited by Brian Moore, Barry Higman, and Patrick Bryan, 133–60. Kingston, Jamaica: The University of the West Indies Press, 2001.

Schwalm, Leslie. *A Hard Fight for We: Women's Transition from Slavery to Freedom in South Carolina.* Urbana: University of Illinois Press, 1997.

Schweninger, Loren. "Property Owning Free African-American Women in the South, 1800–1870." *Journal of Women's History* 1, no. 3 (1990): 13–44.

Scott, David. *Conscripts of Modernity: The Tragedy of Colonial Enlightenment.* Durham, NC: Duke University Press, 2004.

———. *Refashioning Futures: Criticism after Postcoloniality.* Princeton, NJ: Princeton University Press, 1999.

Scott, James. *Domination and the Arts of Resistance: Hidden Transcripts.* New Haven, CT: Yale University Press, 1990.

———. *The Moral Economy of the Peasant: Rebellion and Subsistence in Southeast Asia.* New Haven, CT: Yale University Press, 1976.

Scott, Julius S. "The Common Wind: Currents of Afro-American Communication in the Age of the Haitian Revolution." PhD diss., Duke University, 1986.

Scott, Rebecca J. *Degrees of Freedom: Louisiana and Cuba after Slavery.* Cambridge, MA: Belknap Press of Harvard University Press, 2005.

———. *Slave Emancipation in Cuba: The Transition to Free Labor, 1860–1899.* Princeton, NJ: Princeton University Press, 1985.

Scott, Rebecca J., Seymour Drescher, Hebe Maria Mattos de Castro, George Reid

Andrews, and Robert Levine. *The Abolition of Slavery and the Aftermath of Emancipation in Brazil*. Durham, NC: Duke University Press, 1988.

Scully, Pamela. *Liberating the Family? Gender and British Slave Emancipation in the Rural Western Cape, South Africa, 1823–1853*. Portsmouth, NH: Heinemann, 1997.

Scully, Pamela, and Diana Paton, eds. *Gender and Slave Emancipation in the Atlantic World*. Durham, NC: Duke University Press, 2005.

Sensbach, Jon. *A Separate Canaan: The Making of an Afro-Moravian World in North Carolina, 1763–1840*. Chapel Hill, NC: Omohundro Institute of Early American History and Culture, 1998.

———. "Slavery, Race, and the Global Fellowship: Religious Radicals Confront the Modern Age." In *Pious Pursuits: German Moravians in the Atlantic World*, edited by Michele Gillespie and Robert Beachey, 223–38. Oxford, UK: Berghahn Books, 2007.

Shanley, Mary Lyndon. *Feminism, Marriage, and the Law in Victorian England, 1850–1895*. Princeton, NJ: Princeton University Press, 1993.

Sheller, Mimi. "Acting as Free Men: Subaltern Masculinities and Citizenship in Postslavery Jamaica." In *Gender and Slave Emancipation in the Atlantic World*, edited by Pamela Scully and Diana Paton, 79–98. Durham, NC: Duke University Press, 2005.

———. *Citizenship from Below: Erotic Agency and Caribbean Freedom*. Durham, NC: Duke University Press, 2012.

———. *Consuming the Caribbean: From Arawaks to Zombies*. New York: Routledge, 2003.

———. *Democracy after Slavery: Black Publics and Peasant Radicalism in Haiti and Jamaica*. Gainesville: University Press of Florida, 2000.

———. "Quasheba, Mother, Queen: Black Women's Public Leadership and Political Protest in Postemancipation Jamaica." *Slavery & Abolition* 19, no. 3 (1998): 90–117.

Shepherd, Verene, ed. *Working Slavery, Pricing Freedom: Perspectives from the Caribbean, Africa, and the African Diaspora*. New York: Palgrave MacMillan, 2002.

Shepherd, Verene, Bridget Brereton, and Barbara Bailey, eds. *Engendering History: Caribbean Women in Historical Perspective*. Kingston, Jamaica: Ian Randle Publishers; London: James Currey, 1995.

Sheridan, Richard B. "The Rise of a Colonial Gentry: A Case Study of Antigua, 1730–1775." *Economic History Review* 13, no. 3 (1961): 342–57.

———. *Sugar and Slavery: An Economic History of the British West Indies, 1623–1775*. Kingston, Jamaica: Caribbean Universities Press, 1974.

Slatta, Richard, ed. *Bandidos: The Varieties of Latin American Banditry*. New York: Greenwood Press, 1987.

Smallwood, Stephanie. "Commodified Freedom: Interrogating the Limits of Antislavery Ideology in the Early Republic." *Journal of the Early Republic* 24, no. 2 (2004): 289–98.

———. *Saltwater Slavery: A Middle Passage from Africa to American Diaspora*. Cambridge, MA: Harvard University Press, 2007.

Smith, Keithlyn B. *No Easy Pushover: A History of the Working People of Antigua and Barbuda, 1836–1994*. Scarborough, ON: Edan's Publishers, 1994.

Smith, Keithlyn B., and Fernando C. Smith. *To Shoot Hard Labour: The Life and Times* of *Samuel Smith, an Antiguan Workingman, 1877–1982*. Scarborough, ON: Edan's Publishers, 1986.

Smith, M. G. *The Plural Society in the British West Indies*. Berkeley: University of California Press, 1965.

Smith, Raymond T. "Race, Class, and Gender in the Transition to Freedom." In *The Meaning of Freedom: Economics, Politics and Culture after Slavery*, edited by Frank McGlynn and Seymour Drescher, 257–90. Pittsburgh, PA: University of Pittsburgh Press, 1992.

———. "Social Stratification, Cultural Pluralism and Integration in West Indian Societies." In *Caribbean Integration: Papers on Social, Political and Economic Integration*, edited by S. Lewis and T. Mathews, 226–58. Río Piedras, Puerto Rico: Institute of Caribbean Studies, 1967.

Stanley, Amy Dru. *From Bondage to Contract: Wage Labor, Marriage, and the Market in the Age of Emancipation*. Cambridge, UK: Cambridge University Press, 1998.

———. " 'We Did Not Separate Man and Wife, but All Had to Work': Freedom and Dependence in the Aftermath of Slave Emancipation." In *Terms of Labor: Slavery, Serfdom, and Free Labor*, edited by Stanley L. Engerman, 188–212. Stanford, CA: Stanford University Press, 1999.

Steinfeld, Robert J. *The Invention of Free Labor: The Employment Relation in English and American Law and Culture, 1350–1870*. Chapel Hill: University of North Carolina Press, 1991.

Stewart, Robert J. *Religion and Society in Post-emancipation Jamaica*. Knoxville: University of Tennessee Press, 1992.

Stinchcombe, Arthur L. *Sugar Island Slavery in the Age of Enlightenment: The Political Economy of the Caribbean World*. Princeton, NJ: Princeton University Press, 1995.

Stoler, Ann Laura. *Race and the Education of Desire: Foucault's History of Sexuality and the Colonial Order of Things*. Durham, NC: Duke University Press, 1995.

———. "Rethinking Colonial Categories: European Communities and the Boundaries of Rule." *Comparative Studies in Society and History* 31, no. 1 (1989): 134–61.

Suarez-Findlay, Eileen. *Imposing Decency: The Politics of Sexuality and Race in Puerto Rico, 1870–1920*. Durham, NC: Duke University Press, 1999.

Sutton, Constance R., and O. Nigel Bolland. *Revisiting Caribbean Labour*. Kingston, Jamaica: Ian Randle Publishers, 2005.

Sweet, James. *Recreating Africa: Culture, Kinship, and Religion in the African-Portuguese World, 1441–1770*. Chapel Hill: University of North Carolina Press, 2003.

Tannenbaum, Frank. *Slave and Citizen: The Negro in the Americas*. New York: Vintage Books, 1946.

Terborg-Penn, Rosalyn. "Black Women in Resistance: A Cross-Cultural Perspective." In *In Resistance: Studies in African, Caribbean and Afro-American History*, edited by Gary Y. Okihiro, 188–209. Amherst: University of Massachusetts Press, 1986.

———. "Women and Slavery in the African Diaspora: A Cross-Cultural Approach to Historical Analysis." *Sage: A Scholarly Journal on Black Women* 3, no. 2 (1986): 11–15.

Thompson, Edward P. *The Making of the English Working Class*. New York: Vintage Books, 1963.

———. "The Moral Economy of the English Crowd in the Eighteenth Century." *Past and Present* 50 (February 1971): 76–136.

Thompson, Robert Farris. *Flash of the Spirit: African and Afro-American Art and Philosophy*. New York: Vintage Books, 1984.

Thomson, Sinclair. *We Alone Will Rule: Native Andean Politics in the Age of Insurgency*. Madison: University of Wisconsin Press, 2002.

Thornton, John. *Africa and Africans in the Making of the Atlantic World, 1400–1650*. Cambridge, UK: Cambridge University Press, 1992.

Titus, Noel. *The Amelioration and Abolition of Slavery in Trinidad, 1812–1834*. Bloomington, IN: Authorhouse, 2009.

Tolstoy, Leo. *The Sebastopol Sketches*, trans. Frank D. Millet. New York: Harper and Bros., 1887.

Tomich, Dale. *Slavery in the Circuit of Sugar: Martinique and the World Economy, 1830–1848*. Baltimore, MD: Johns Hopkins University Press, 1990.

Trotman, David. *Crime in Trinidad: Conflict and Control in a Plantation Society, 1838–1900*. Knoxville: University of Tennessee Press, 1986.

Trotz, D. Alissa, and Linda Peake. "Work, Family, and Organizing: An Overview of the Emergence of the Economic, Social, and Political Roles of Women in British Guiana." *Social and Economic Studies* 49, no. 4 (2000): 189–222.

Trouillot, Michel-Rolph. "Labour and Emancipation in Dominica: Contribution to a Debate." *Caribbean Quarterly* 30, nos. 3–4 (1984): 73–84.

———. *Peasants and Capital: Dominica in the World Economy*. Johns Hopkins Studies in Atlantic History and Culture. Baltimore, MD: Johns Hopkins University Press, 1988.

———. *Silencing the Past: Power and the Production of History*. Boston: Beacon Press, 1995.

Turner, Mary. "The 11 O'clock Flog: Women, Work and Labour Law in the British Caribbean." *Slavery & Abolition* 20, no. 1 (1999): 38–58.

———. *From Chattel Slaves to Wage Slaves: The Dynamics of Labour Bargaining in the Americas*. Bloomington: Indiana University Press, 1995.

Viotti da Costa, Emilia. *Crowns of Glory, Tears of Blood: The Demerara Slave Rebellion of 1823*. New York: Oxford University Press, 1994.

Wade, Richard C. *Slavery in the Cities: The South, 1820–1860*. New York: Oxford University Press, 1964.

Ward, J. R. *British West Indian Slavery, 1750–1834: The Process of Amelioration*. Oxford, UK: Clarendon Press, 1988.

Ward, W. R. "The Tithe Question in England in the Early Nineteenth Century." *Journal of Ecclesiastical History* 14, no. 1 (1965): 67–81.

Watkins-Owens, Irma. *Blood Relations: Caribbean Immigrants and the Harlem Community, 1900–1930*. Bloomington: Indiana University Press, 1996.

Wertz, Dorothy C. "Women and Slavery: A Cross-Cultural Perspective." *International Journal of Women's Studies* 7, no. 4 (1984): 372–84.

White, Deborah Gray. *Ar'n't I a Woman?: Female Slaves in the Plantation South*. New York: W. W. Norton, 1985.

White, Shane, and Graham White. *Stylin': African-American Expressive Culture from Its Beginnings to the Zoot Suit*. Ithaca, NY: Cornell University Press, 1997.

Williams, Christolyn A. "Labor Organization, Political Leadership, and Gender Exclusion in Antigua and Barbuda, 1917–70." PhD diss., Graduate Center, City University of New York, 2007.

———. *No Women Jump Out! Gender Exclusion, Labour Organization and Political Leadership in Antigua 1917–1970*. Bern: Peter Lang, 2013.

Williams, Eric. *Capitalism and Slavery*, reprint ed., with an introduction by Colin Palmer. Chapel Hill: University of North Carolina Press, 1994.

Wilmot, Swithin. " 'Females of Abandoned Character'? Women and Protest in Jamaica, 1838–65." In *Engendering History: Caribbean Women in Historical Perspective*, edited by Verene Shepherd, Bridget Brereton, and Barbara Bailey, 279–95. Kingston, Jamaica: Ian Randle Publishers; London: James Currey, 1995.

———. " 'Not Full Free': The Ex-Slaves and the Apprenticeship System in Jamaica, 1834–38." *Jamaica Journal* 17 (1984): 2–10.

———. "Politics at the 'Grassroots' in Free Jamaica, St. James 1838–1865." In *Working Slavery, Pricing Freedom: Perspectives from the Caribbean, Africa, and the African Diaspora*, edited by Verene Shepherd, 449–66. New York: Palgrave MacMillan, 2002.

Wood, Donald. *Trinidad in Transition: The Years after Slavery*. Oxford, UK: Oxford University Press, 1968.

Zipf, Karin L. "Reconstructing 'Free Woman': African-American Women, Apprenticeship, and Custody Rights during Reconstruction." *Journal of Women's History* 12, no. 1 (2000): 8–31.

INDEX

Note: Page numbers in italics indicate figures.

Carlyle, Thomas, 168, 177

Carty, Daniel, 108–9

Carty, Margaret, 211

Catholic church, 172

Cawnpore. See Kanpur

Cayman Islands, 8, 88

Cecelia (freedwoman), 160

Charles (freedman), 155

Charles, Jane, 128

children: and adults' access to friendly society benefits, 151–2, 155; care of after emancipation, 102, 104, 174, 211; care of during slavery, 1–2, 253n6; education of, 104–5, 126–7, 150, 173; in free villages, 124, 126–7; and infant mortality rates, 25, 212, 242n38; occupations of after emancipation, 101, 104, 150, 174; occupations of during slavery, 45–46; parents keep out of labor force, 101, 104–5, 124, 127; planters require mothers to work extra days to cover cost of providing for, 252n6; presence at markets, 48, 52, 54; punishment for neglecting, 97; and women's decisions about who to marry, 155, 172

citizenship: and economic status, 132, 230; freedpeople actively seek, 115, 175, 237n24; freedpeople's concepts of, 213, 230, 279n37; incompleteness of for freedpeople, 4, 9, 12–13; whites as obstacles to, 8, 15, 91–92, 168, 176

Clark, William, 39

Coconut Hall Estate, 29

Codrington College, 31

Codrington family, 31, 108, 190, 204

Codrington, Christopher, 25, 33–34, 77, 94, 242n33, 242n35, 253n19, 255n38, 266n38

Colbrook's Estate, 73–74

Cole, Charity, 210

Cole, Jane, 210

Colebrooke, Governor William, 114, 122–24

Colonial Office: annexes Barbuda to Antigua, 204; creates stipendiary magistrates, 98; denies Christopher Codrington's request for more funds for slave purchase, 34; freedmen petition to protest vestry taxation, 179–79; and labor migration, 113; lack of interest of in Antiguan slaves' welfare, 38; rejects Contract Act, 97; mentioned, 38, 113, 173, 255n51, 259n104; response of to Morant Bay Rebellion, 225

compensation for loss of slaves after abolition, 34, 64–65, 253n16, 253n19, 255n38

Contract Act (1834): amendments to, 98–99, 107; freedpeople's strategies for challenging, 87, 99–107, 129; harsh terms of labor contracts under, 97–98; and housing, 86, 91, 98, 122; legal provisions of, 98–99; limits freedpeople's ability to negotiate for wages, 96–97; impact on wages and hours, 130; as model for region, 256n62; planters use as legal weapon, 109, 111, 122; restrictions of, 97, 109, 252n2; whites' justification for, 91, 97. See also stipendiary magistrates; free villages

contract disputes, 98–101, 103

Cook's Estate, 103–5, 109

Cornelius (freedman), 155

Coromantee, 29

corporal punishment: after 1831 uprising, 69, 75; and Antigua's rejection of apprenticeship plan, 89; antislavery women influence amelioration code provisions of vis-à-vis women, 250n40; of children of slaves, 1; fails to motivate enslaved workers,

corporal punishment (*continued*)
84; male slaves forced to administer, 144; for marketing on Sunday, 23; Mary Prince describes, 41; for practicing obeah, 185–86; tools of financed by legislature, 41; techniques of described, 44
Count, William, 113
Court (enslaved man), 29
Court of King's Bench and Grand Sessions, 99, 256n59
courthouse in St. John's, 38–39, 40
courts-martial, 70–76
Cox, James, 151, 167, 169–70
Crabb's Estate, 184, 257n88
Crimean War, 227–28, 284n12
Crump, Nathaniel, 29
Cuba, 12, 130, 169–70, 263n41
Cuff, Hezekiah, 205
Cunningham, Governor, 172

Daily Meal Asylum, 125
Daily Meal Society, 188
Daniel, Lidia, 210
Darby's Estate, 218
Davey, Darius, 100–101, 206
David (enslaved man), 73–74
Davis, Anthony, 203
Day, Charles, 33, 137–39, 183, 186
de Freitas, Antonio, 205
Demerara, 16, 62–64, 205, 249n28, 252n71. *See also* Guyana
Denbow, Charles, 155
Denbow, George, 155
Dianna (freedwoman), 155
Dolly (freedwoman), 165
domestic violence, 144–45, 157–59. *See also* freedmen's use of violence
Dominica, 172, 196, 210, 224–25, 230, 240n7, 240n10
Donowa, Frances, 202
droughts, 45, 105, 111, 123, 184, 255n39, 258n100

Earl Grey, 179–81
earthquakes, 37, 131, 152
education: of adult freedpeople, 105; black families prioritize, 150; of children of freedpeople, 104–5; decline in funding for after 1845, 174; funding for by British government, 173–74; missionaries and, 105; poverty precludes for many freedpeople in late 1840s, 174; white authorities recommend industrial training for freedpeople, 173
Edward, Henry, 137
86th Regiment, 68, 70, 72, 78. *See also* Antiguan militia
Elizabeth (freedwoman, The River), 128
Elizabeth (freedwoman), 158
Ellis, C. B., 141
Emancipation Act, 69, 150. *See also* Abolition Act
Emancipation Day, 93, 103, 106, 109, 181
Emancipation Day Strike (1835), 106–9, 181, 257n85
Emanuel (freedman), 121–22
English Harbour, Antigua, x, 36, 51, 101, 261n14
English laborers, 171, 173
enslaved men: occupations of, 33, 40, 44–46, 72–74, 244n64
enslaved women: and pregnancy, 49–50; marketing activities of, 50–51, 61; occupations of, 39–40, 46, 48–49, 244n64; sexual abuse of, 41, 244n65
Ephraim, Richard, 213
estate managers: charge freedpeople with trespass, 126, 212; complain about price of labor, 131; describe recruiting agents, 258n101; fear rebellion, 195; monitoring of freedpeople under Contract Act, 98; monitoring

of slaves, 77; report theft, 129; severity of, 277n1. *See also* Jarritt, Robert; Martin, W. H.

Estridge, E., 220

Falmouth, Antigua, x, 36, 51
Federation Riot (Barbados, 1876), 225
Finch, Susannah, 128
Fisher, John McKenzie, 215
Floyd, Anthony, 164
Floyd, Patience, 164
Foote, Thomas, 191
Foreman, Mr., 219
Frances (freedwoman), 156–59
Francis, Nathaniel, 215
Frank, Sarah, 202, 206
Frederick, Letitia, 216
Free Soil Party (United States), 177
free people of color: and Antiguan militia, 281n57; legal rights of, 78; missionaries and, 60–61, 148; poverty of during slavery, 104; as property owners, 178; as sellers at public markets, 51; and slave society revolts, 247n98; social position of during slavery, 27; trade with slaves at public markets, 48, 54–55; and voting, 78. *See also* Loving, Henry
free villages, 118, 121–29, 131
freedmen's occupations, 99, 101–2, 124, 137–38, 140, 147, 155. *See also* black entrepreneurs.
freedmen's petitions: to Antiguan governor after 1858 uprising, 218–19; to Earl Grey about vestry taxes (1848), 180–81; to Parliament about Sugar Duties Act (1847), 176–78
freedmen's use of violence: against freedwomen, 144, 157–159, 163–64; during 1858 uprising, 196, 202–8, 214–22, 277n3, 278n11; at public dances, 138; against whites, 190.

See also uprisings in British colonial holdings
freedpeople as consumers, 118, 132–36
freedpeople's rental of land, 127–28. *See also* free villages
freedwomen's occupations, 102–3, 124, 127–28, 130, 157–58, 160. *See also* black entrepreneurs; marketing; Prince, Mary
freedwomen's use of violence: against other women, 202–3; in domestic disputes, 157, 160; during 1858 uprising, 196, 208–9, 212, 215, 277n3, 278n11
Freeman, Caroline, 128
French's Estate, 76, 251n54
Friars Hill Estate, 76, 251n54
friendly societies, 151–52. *See also* Moravian societies; mutual benefit associations

Gable's Estate, 73
Galley Bay Estate, 155, 160, 163
Gamble's Estate, 42, 156, 165
Gardiner, Mary, 216, 281n66
George (enslaved man), 73–75
George, Grace, 202, 208
Gilbert, Anne Hart, 146
Gilbert's Estate, 184
Gilchrist, Mr., 77, 251n55
Gilliard, Frances, 209–10
Goderich, Viscount. *See* Viscount Goderich
Gordon, James, 217–18
Gordon, Rebecca, 205
Grace Hill, 123, 137
Graeme, L., 134
Green Castle Estate, 28
Grenadines, xi, 33
grievance process for contract laborers, 98–99
Guadeloupe, 29, 197
Guerre Negre (Dominica, 1844), 224

63–64, 245n70; attempts to regulate Sunday market, 47–48, 245n70; composition of, 38, 71; and Contract Act, 97–99; and Emancipation Day, 103; expresses alarm about Sugar Duties Act, 170; fails to appropriate funds for education of freedpeople's children, 150; freedpeople petition, 176–81; mandates slave holidays, 244n67; mentioned, 52, 95; passes act making migration more difficult for freedpeople, 111; passes first slavery amelioration act, 60–61; passes law penalizing obeah practitioners, 146; passes laws about selling liquor on Sundays, 63; passes New Consolidated Slave Bill, 63; proposes emancipation plan that Colonial Office rejects, 90; refuses to designate a market day, 79; rejects Parliament's apprenticeship plan, 88–89; requires militia at markets, 53; requires slaves to carry passes, 67; petitions King William IV for compensation for loss of slaves, 64–65; petitions Parliament regarding sugar economy, 170; raises prices of consumer goods to fund importation of laborers, 171–72; structure of, 240n10; surveys plantations, 182. See also House of Assembly

Joseph, John, 227
Joseph, Rebecca, 216
Joseph, Susanna, 155
Joshua, Eliza, 205
Jost Van Dyke, 230
Juncho (enslaved woman), 1–2
Junior, Israel, 203

Kanpur, 229, 285n14
Kimball, Joseph Horace, 84–85, 105, 150
Kirwan, John, 70–75, 77–78
Knight, William, 214–15

labor contracts: freedpeople break, 100–101, 130–31; freedpeople petition British authorities about terms of, 107; linked to housing, 98, 107–10, 12; and migration, 111–12; and natural disasters, 175; secretary of state for colonies attempts to make more fair, 97; and strikes, 106; terms of, 97–98, 252n2; and white workers, 171–73, 272n22. See also Contract Act (1834); free villages; independent gang labor
labor recruiters, 110, 112–13, 258n101
Ladies Negro Education Society, 150
Lafovey, Samuel, 214
Lanaghan, Mrs.: comments on freedpeople's naming practices, 134–35, comments on freedpeople's weddings, 135; comments on grogshops, 137; comments on obeah, 147–47; describes freedpeople's consumption patterns, 132; describes freedpeople's entertainment, 134; describes freedwomen, 133, 135, 208–9; describes Sunday markets, 52; identity of, 120, 260n9; racializes descriptions of freedmen's character, 193
Leah (freedwoman), 160
Ledeatt, William, 189, 191
Leeward Islands: and amelioration of slavery, 60–61; Codringtons' power in, 31; described, 240n10; geology of, 45; low wages in, 110; map of, 32; Parliament restructures, 229; and regulation of slave markets, 47; and sugar trade, 25. See also joint legislature of the Leeward Islands
Lewis, Henry, 202
Liberta, ix, 123, 218
leisure time: of freedpeople, 3–4, 18, 87, 116, 118–19, 131–38, 188, 193, 209, 231; of slaves, 67, 82, 244n67. See also barter economy of slaves; marketing; Otto's Pasture

literacy: and bias in sources, 4, 13, 17, 238n25; of blacks, 27, 105, 126, 177, 201, 260n9

London (freedman), 121–22

London Missionary Society, 63

Long, Edward, 53

Lord Carnarvon, 220

Lord Glenelg, 101

Lord Stanley, 90, 174

Loving, Henry: assaulted by Robert Jarritt, 78–79; background of, 78; and Contract Act, 97, 99–100, 109; criticizes black youth, 104; and Emancipation Day Strike, 106; mentioned, 251n57, 254n30; as newspaper editor, 77–78; as police chief, 93–95, 281n57; proposes that freedpeople be given access to unused land, 122; tells governor of plans of freedpeople to strike, 106–7

Lowry, John, 215

Lucy (freedwoman), 158–59, 269n52

Luffman, John, 27–28, 53–54

Lyon, James, 69

MacGregor, Governor Evan, 93, 99, 122, 183

MacKinnon's Estate, 1

Mackintosh, Lieutenant Governor, 183

Madeira, 171, 173, 272n22

Madeirans (Portuguese Madeirans): British government and, 272n22, 272n25; migration patterns of, 171–73; religion of, 172; targeted during uprisings, 213–14, 225; upward mobility of in Antigua, 173

manumission, 11, 26, 78, 104, 247n2

marketing: after 1831 uprising, 76–77, 80; as an established slave custom, 58; legislature attempts to regulate, 47–48; outlawed in 1831, 57, 63–64, 245n70; in Saint-Domingue, 239n3; women and, 50–51; whites feel

threatened by, 248n21. See also black entrepreneurs; Otto's Pasture; uprising of 1831

maroon communities, 28

Marques, Joaquim, 213

marriage: British Parliament and Leeward Islands legislature encourage among slaves, 60–61; after emancipation, 105; in free villages, 126–27, and Moravian church polices, 154; across plantations, 121–22

martial law, 73, 197, 217

Martin, Samuel, 28, 241n24

Martin, W. H., 129, 131

Mary Magdalen (freedwoman), 163

McChand, Elizabeth, 211

Methodist church in St. John's, described, 37; fails to attract large numbers of slaves, 60; and freedpeople, 148–49; missionaries of observe buildup to 1831 uprising, 65–67; and schools for black children, 150

Mico charity schools, 150, 174, 267n5, 273n41

missionaries: concerns of about failure to observe the Sabbath, 60–61; disapprove of freedpeople's consumption choices, 136–37; impact of decline of British sugar trade on, 12; influence on joint legislature, 59–60, 64–65; observe slaves' dissatisfaction in aftermath of market closure, 79; provide schools for black children, 150–51; push white authorities to make land accessible to freedpeople, 122–23; size of congregations during slavery, 248n8. See also Moravian helpers; Moravian church in St. John's

mobility: attempts to restrict after emancipation, 18, 99, 110–11; as a response to Contract Act, 105, 193, 258n99; during slavery, 9, 22–23, 29,

40, 42, 47–48, 58, 65, 87; of women, 102. *See also* An Act for Preventing a Clandestine Departure of Labourers, Artificers, Handicraftsmen, and Domestic Servants (1836); migration; pass laws; free villages; trespass charges

Montserrat: freedpeople migrate from, 110; migration to, 111–13; and streamlining of government in British Caribbean holdings, 230; uprisings in, 224

moral economy of freedpeople: defined, 86; and use of employers' resources, 128–29, 134, 190; as a survival strategy, 193

Morant Bay Rebellion (Jamaica, 1865), 16, 225–27, 229, 239n33, 283n3. *See also* Jamaica.

Moravian church in St. John's: attracts more freedpeople than other denominations, 148–49; described, 37; excludes freedpeople from congregations, 137, 142–43, 154–55, 158–61, 163–66; fails to attract large numbers of slaves, 60; insists on monogamy among church members, 144–45; offers land to freedpeople, 123; and schools for black children, 150; strict rules of, 152. *See also* Moravian helpers; "sinful conexions"

Moravian helpers, 155–58, 160, 164–66, 269n49

Morris, Polly, 127

Moses, Mary, 216

multiple partnerships, 145, 154, 156–62, 165

mutual benefit associations, 151. *See also* friendly societies

Nanton, Alexander, 228

Nanton, Martin, 124

Nanton, Richard, 106

Nanton, William, 214

Ned, Edward, 207

Ned, Richard, 207

Nevis, 110, 230, 240n10, 258n99

New Consolidated Slave Bill (1827), 63

New Division Estate, 100

Newton, Richard, 107, 123, 147

Nicholas, John, 155–56

Nicholson, Adam, 195

Nugent, George, 121–22

Nugent, Nicholas, 70–73, 91

obeah, 29, 145–48, 185–87, 216, 242n27

"Oedipus Jr.," 187

Old Cotton Work Estate, 108–9

Old Road Plantation, 105

open-air markets, 47–48, 63–67

Ord, Captain John, 112–13, 259n108

Orr, John Sayers, 206

Otto's Estate, 156, 158, 163

Otto's Pasture, 51–52, 53–55, 253n11. *See also* marketing; uprising of 1831

"our side," 203–4, 214

Parham, Antigua, x, 36, 51, 101

parish taxation, 178–79

pass laws, 51–52, 67, 246n89

Paul (freedman), 165

petitions from freedmen: 174–76, 180–81, 192, 274n48

Phebe (freedwoman), 155–56

Phipps, Quashy, 210–11

Point, the, 196, 198, 200–204, 206, 209, 213–14, 216–17, 219, 227, 278n11, 278n12

police force on Antigua: assaults on members of, 78–79; and Belmanna Riots in Tobago, 225; described, 281n57; describes labor force to governor, 124–25; development of, 197; freedmen's employment as, 187; inadequacy of during slavery, 246n95; intervenes in domestic disputes, 157;

police force on Antigua (*continued*)
reports on labor practices of freedpeople, 94, 100, 106; searches for
missing workers, 111; standing force
established in Antigua, 93, 265n29;
and uprising of 1858, 196–97, 203,
205, 207, 209, 211, 214–20, 225–28,
277n4, 278n11, 282n66
Poor Law guardians, 188–89
poor relief, 178, 188, 276n901. *See also*
Daily Meal Asylum; Daily Meal
Society
Popeshead Division, 106, 258n89
Portuguese Madeirans. *See* Madeirans
(Portuguese Madeirans)
Price, Thomas, 189
Prince, Mary, 41, 51, 57, 161–62,
269n58
Pringle, Thomas, 161
prostitution, 41, 163, 165, 270n66
provision grounds, 48–49, 87, 94, 124,
127, 157, 182, 270n61
Punter, Mary Ann, 202

"Quashee" stereotype, 168, 271n5

Rachael (freedwoman), 105
Richards, Charles, 215
Richards, Rachael, 211, 216
Richmond Estate, 76–77
Riot Act, 215
Road Town Riots (Tortola, 1853), 224,
227–29
Roberts, Thomas, 203
Rodin, Mr., 219
Rodrigue, Antonio, 213
Rooms Estate, 43
Roses, Elizabeth, 160–61
Ross, Patrick, 65, 68, 75, 79
Ryan, Father J., 172

Saint-Domingue, 23, 239n3, 239n4
Sandersons Plantation, 105

Sarah (freedwoman), 128
Schaw, Janet, 133
Scotland, James, 122
seasoning, 6, 25, 235n13
Shorediche, Edward, 215, 217
Siege of Sevastopol, 227, 229
"sinful conexions," 154–56
Skerrett's Estate, 72–75
slave codes, 28–29
slave registry bill (1816), 30, 62
slaves' conceptions of their rights: and
abolitionist movement in Britain,
69–60; and British law, 66, 81–82;
and marketing, 58–59
slaves' use of free time, 51–53
slave trade: Antiguan legislature asks
British Parliament to suppress
in Cuba and Brazil, 170; British
Parliament discusses ending, 15, 60;
clandestine, 30; and demography
of Antigua, 25–26; end of, 14, 30;
impact of end of on freedpeople, 3;
liberation of illegally obtained Africans, 187, 238n28; and replacement
of indentured servants, 25
Smith, Patience, 127–28
Smith, Samuel, 121, 261n12
Smith's Estate, 257n85
Solomon, Harriet, 208
South Carolina, 29
Spring-Rice, Thomas, 97–98
St. John (Danish colony), 29
St. John Parish, Antigua: Codringtons own plantations in, 31; desire
of rural slaves in to market goods
on Sunday, 76–77; free villages
in, 124–25, 131; free villagers from
protest parish taxes, 179; location of
Otto's Pasture, 51; mentioned, 1, 100,
155–56, 158, 163, 258n89, 269n58;
petitions from, 176, 274n48
St. John's Anglican Cathedral.
See Anglican Church

St. John's, Antigua, attempts of
freedpeople to migrate from, 112;
Catholic church in, 172; Daily Meal
Society of, 188; described, 23, 36–39;
economic decline in after Sugar
Duties Act, 18; and Emancipation
Day Strike, 106–7; free villages in,
124–25, 131; grogshops in, 137, 188;
Guy Fawkes Day celebrations in,
137; obeah practitioners in, 187;
and open-air markets, 47, 50–51, 53,
61; location where new slaves were
received, 41; location where slaves
were punished, 41; Madeiran traders in, 173; map of, 36; mentioned,
160–61, 165; off-plantation occupations of freedmen in, 101–2; slaves in
angered by closure of Sunday markets, 65; uprising in (1831), 67–70;
uprising in (1858), 195–223
St. Kitts: English colonists from settle
Antigua, 24; freedpeople migrate
from, 110; riots in, 16; and streamlining of government in British Caribbean holdings, 230; sugar industry
of, 25; uprisings in, 224
St. Lucia, 224
St. Mary Parish, Antigua: free villagers
in, 128–29, 180; mentioned, 84, 100,
106, 186, 206, 219, 257n85
St. Paul Parish, Antigua: free villages
in, 123; freedpeople's dances in,
137–38; independent work gangs
in, 129; on map, x; mentioned,
77, 258n89; "ten-acre" settlement
program and, 261n14; unoccupied
land in, 122
St. Peter Parish, Antigua: arson in,
176; freedmen's petitions from,
176; freedpeople demand higher
compensation for labor in, 106;
freedpeople withdraw labor in,
108; on map, x; mentioned, 31, 105,

257n88, 261n12; slave unrest in, 29;
and uprising of 1858, 218
St. Philip Parish, Antigua: arson in,
73–75; images of, x, 43; mentioned,
72, 251n54
St. Vincent, 69, 225
Stephens, Charles, 202
stipendiary magistrates: appointed,
90, 99; Colonial Office creates, 98;
and comment on consumer behavior
of freedpeople, 134; Contract Act,
99, 107, 130, 175, 188; describe obeah
practices, 148; and Emancipation
Day Strike, 107–8; Henry Loving
serves as, 78; and importation of
European laborers, 171; planters
oppose idea of, 89–90; recommend
industrial training in schools, 173;
surveyed about condition of freedpeople, 123
Sturge, Joseph, 112, 147, 178
Sugar Duties Act (1846): freedmen
protest, 176, 192; impact on Anglican Church revenue, 177; impact on
Antiguan sugar industry, 19, 175–77;
impact on planters' policies toward
freedpeople, 167–70; white elites
protest, 169–70
sugar economy in Antigua: decline in
during nineteenth century, 12, 15,
27, 31, 38, 142, 183, 225; and demand
for slaves, 41; dominance of island's
economy, 25, 27, 36, 42–43, 49, 189,
276n91; freedpeople seek ways to
withdraw labor from, 94–95, 99,
103, 113–14, 121, 126, 142, 182–83,
231; impact of American Revolution
on, 30; impact of emancipation on,
90, 98; impact of natural disasters
on, 123, 131, 175, 183; impact of
Sugar Duties Act on, 19–20, 169–70,
175–77; planters' attempts to prevent freedpeople from finding other

sugar economy in Antigua (*continued*)
employment, 17–18, 92, 99–100, 115,
173; and planters' policies toward
slaves, 23, 28; impact on freedpeople's search for land, 17; tight margins in, 115; whites' need for cheap
labor and, 10–11, 191; and women's
labor, 8, 47, 102–3, 127; work routine
of, 44–47, 275n72. *See also* arson;
Contract Act; free villages; independent work gangs; migration; Sugar
Duties Act (1846)

terminology used in book, 16–17
The River, Antigua, 128
Thomas (freedman), 137
Thomas, Reese, 203
Thome, James, 84–85, 105, 150
Thwaites, Charles, 151
Tobago, xi, 225
Tortola, 224, 228, 230
trespass charges, 95, 121–23, 126
Trinidad: development of peasantry
in, 121; escaped slaves shape culture
of, 238n28; food production in, 49;
mass strikes in, 16; migration to,
110–11, 114; Portuguese Madeiran
laborers migrate to, 171; uprisings
in, 224

uprising of 1831 (Antigua), 68–75,
80–83, 247n1. *See also* Kirwan, John
uprising of 1858 (Antigua), 195–223,
277n3, 278n11
uprisings in British colonial holdings,
224–29

Vagrancy Act (1834), 99, 185, 187–88
Vernon Estate, 183–84
vestries, 178
violence. *See* corporal punishment;
domestic violence; freedmen's use

of violence; freedwomen's use of
violence
Virgin Gorda, 230
Viscount Goderich, 69

wages: Contract Act limits ability of
freedpeople to negotiate, 96–98; decrease in Antigua, 111, 121, 169–70,
173, 176; denied to Barbudan freedpeople, 95–96; differences by gender
after emancipation, 46, 143; differences by race in Antigua, 171–73, 177;
freedpeople search for better, 85,
99–100, 115, 193; and freedpeople's
expectation of bargaining power,
94, 130; and freedpeople's standard
of living, 162, 170, 174, 178, 191;
increase in Antigua after earthquake,
131–32, 142; as a percentage of
plantation costs, 272n12; planters attempt to standardize, 130; source of
panic for planters immediately after
emancipation, 77; in Trinidad and
Guyana, 110–11, 113, 258n96; in the
West Indies, 101. *See also* Emancipa-
tion Day Strike (1835); independent
gang labor
Walker, William, 130, 138
Warner, Henry C., 126
Wickham, Robert, 94
Wilcox, David, 217
Williams, Edward, 206
Williams, Mary Ann, 161
Willis, Catharine, 210, 215
Willock Frye's Estate, 112
Willock's Folly Estate, 165
Wills, William, 201, 206
Windward Islands, 171, 225, 252n6
Winter, John, 95–96
Winter, Maria, 185–86

Zecharias (freedman), 155